Okinawa Island

SHU

132° E

30' N

28° N

26° N

tō Islands
大東諸島

Iheya Island

Noho I.

Gushikawa I.

Izena Island

Yanaha I.

Cape Misaki

Hedo

Oku

Uka

Sosu

Yona

58

Okuma

Ada

Ukuma Beach

Hiji Falls

Aha Falls

Ie Island

Ie

Higashiemae

Gushiken Beach

Uppama Beach

Koyri I.

Ogimi

Mt Yonaha
503 m

Aha

Emerald Beach

Okinawa
Churaumi
Aquarium

Ocean Expo Park

Nakijin
Castle

Unten

58

Minna I.

Toguchi

505

Yagaji I.

Tsuha

Taiho

Arakawa

Sesoko I.

Motobu

Ojima I.

Higashi

Shiokawa Beach

Mt Yae
453 m

449

Nakaoshi

Miyagi

Yabu

Nago

Arume

Tara Bay

Nago Bay

Oura Bay

Arume Bay

Sedake

331

Segaraki Beach

Kyoda

Kayo

58

329

Onna

Kushi

Moon
Beach

Mt Onna

Ginoza

Tancha

Sokei Beach

Nakadomari

Kin

Ryukyu-mura

Yamada

Ishikawa

Kin Bay

Zakimi
Castle

Higashionna

Kei I.

Yomitan

Uruma

Tonahan
Beach

Kadena

Gushikawa

Miyagi I.

Uku-no-Hama Beach

Kadena Airbase

329

Katsuren
Castle

Henza I.

58

Okinawa

Yonagusuku

Hamahiga I.

Katsuren

Futenma

Kitanakagusuku

Ukibaru I.

PACIFIC OCEAN

Futenma Airbase

Nakagusuku Castle

Ginowan

Nakagusuku

Cape Canna

i-dori
Street

Naha

Urasoe

Nakagusuku
Bay

Nishihara

Tsuken I.

Shuri
Castle

setsu Ichiba

Yonabaru

N

ha
ort

Haebaru

Azama Sun Sun Beach

igusuku

Underground Naval
Headquarters

Chinen

Okinawa World & Snake Park

Kudaka I.

331

Kechinda

Nanjo

Hyakuna
Beach

toman

507

Ojima I.

Himeyuri-no-to

331

Yaese

Mabuni

10 km

iro
ch

5 miles

Kiyan

Komesu

Okinawa Peace
Memorial Museum

Cape Kyan

Cape Zampa

Published by Tuttle Publishing, an imprint of Periplus Editions (HK) Ltd

www.tuttlepublishing.com

Text and photos © 2014 Robert Walker, except for the following:
Pages 1: © Sean Pavone/Dreamstime.com; 2 top left: © leungchopan/istockphoto.com;
2 top right: © Club4traveler/Shutterstock.com; 3 top left: © Runinex/Dreamstime.com;
3 top right: © Leung Cho Pan/Dreamstime.com; 15: © bonchan/Shutterstock.com;
23 top left: courtesy of JAXA (Japan Aerospace); 27 middle: © Yasufumi Nishi/© JNTO;
30 top: courtesy of Japan Meteorogical Agency; 45 above: courtesy of Prof. Yukio Hayakawa; 51 top
right: courtesy of Leanne and Rik Brezina; 58 top: photo by Hiromitsu Katsu, courtesy of Prof. Fumio
Hamada; 68 bottom: courtesy of www.japanupdate.com; 73: Jean-Marie Hullot, Wikipedia Commons;
117 top: courtesy of Reef Encounters; 150 bottom: courtesy of Mikimoto; 158 top left: courtesy of Reef
Encounters; 243 below: courtesy of Japan-guide.com

ISBN 978-4-8053-1233-9

Distributed by

North America, Latin America & Europe
Tuttle Publishing
364 Innovation Drive
North Clarendon, VT 05759-9436 USA
Tel: 1 (802) 773-8930; Fax: 1 (802) 773-6993
info@tuttlepublishing.com; www.tuttlepublishing.com

Japan
Tuttle Publishing
Yaekari Building, 3rd Floor
5-4-12 Osaki, Shinagawa-ku
Tokyo 141 0032
Tel: (81) 3 5437-0171; Fax: (81) 3 5437-0755
sales@tuttle.co.jp; www.tuttle.co.jp

Asia Pacific
Berkeley Books Pte Ltd
61 Tai Seng Avenue #02-12
Singapore 534167
Tel: (65) 6280-1330; Fax: (65) 6280-6290
inquiries@periplus.com.sg; www.periplus.com

18 17 16 15 14   5 4 3 2

Printed in Singapore   1411CP

TUTTLE PUBLISHING® is a registered trademark of Tuttle Publishing,
a division of Periplus Editions (HK) Ltd.

Okinawa
and the Ryukyu Islands

The First Comprehensive Guide
to the Entire Ryukyu Island Chain

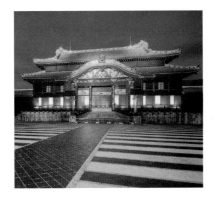

ROBERT WALKER

TUTTLE Publishing

Tokyo | Rutland, Vermont | Singapore

CONTENTS

Welcome to Okinawa and the Ryukyus

Although it is said that Japan (日本; Nihon or Nippon, literally "sun's origin" but usually translated as "land of the rising sun") is an island nation, it's perhaps more accurate to describe it as a nation of islands for, depending on who's counting, there are anywhere from 3,000 to 6,852 of them. The first figure, although an approximation, is widely agreed upon by most encyclopedias and reference manuals. It includes islands that are at least 0.039 square miles (0.1 square kilometer) in size. The larger number of 6,852 is published by the Japan Maritime Public Relations Center and includes all islands that have at least 330 feet (100 meters) of shoreline. Obviously, that latter figure would include virtually every rock, isle and islet in the Japanese Archipelago. More useful perhaps is the often-cited number of inhabited islands. That number is 426.

From north to south, Japan's four main islands are Hokkaido (北海道; Hokkaidō, lit. "North Sea Circuit," circuit being a mostly archaic political subdivision); Honshu (本州; Honshū, meaning "Main State"), where the capital Tokyo is located; Shikoku (四国; Shikoku, meaning "Four Provinces") and Kyushu (九州; Kyūshū; "Nine Provinces").

Honshu is the largest of Japan's islands, Hokkaido the second largest, then Kyushu, then Shikoku. In total, Japan has about 18,645 miles (30,000 kilometers) of shoreline. Since, ultimately, it is an archipelago of islands, it has no land boundaries with any other country. Its northern shores on Hokkaido face the Russian Sea of Okhotsk and its eastern shores front the Pacific Ocean. Most of the country's west faces the Sea of Japan and its southwest looks to the East China Sea.

Ranked by size, Japan is the 61st largest country on earth. Its area is 145,920 square miles (377,930 square kilometers), a bit larger than Germany and somewhat similar in overall shape and size (a little smaller) than the US state of California. Together, the four main islands, often called the Japanese "homeland" or "mainland," account for 97 percent of Japan's total land area.

Thus, thousands of small, very small and really, really small islands constitute the remaining 3 percent of Japan's territory. These islands are located at all points of the compass surrounding Japan, but one group in particular runs along a more or less north–south line from the southern end of the Japanese mainland to Taiwan. There are several hundreds of these islands and they are known as the Ryukyus—the subject of this book.

We use several names in English to describe these islands, and our use of some of the terms differs from the meaning the Japanese ascribe to them. Most commonly we call the group of islands between Kyushu, the southernmost of Japan's big four islands, and the Republic of China, otherwise known as Taiwan and historically as Formosa, the Ryukyus (琉球; Ryūkyū). We also refer to the entire chain as the Ryukyu Islands (琉球諸島; Ryūkyū-shotō) and sometimes we say the Ryukyu Archipelago (琉球列島; Ryūkyū-Rettō).

However, the Japanese do not use these terms in the same sense as we do. They collectively refer to the island chain as the Nansei Shoto (南西諸島; Nansei-shotō), literally "Southwest Islands." Or sometimes they'll say Amami-Okinawa Chiho (奄美-沖縄地方; Amami-Okinawa Chihō), which means Amami-Okinawa Region and has the same meaning as Southwest Islands. A term almost never used in the sense that we use it is Ryukyu (琉球; Ryūkyū). Rather, they say Okinawa (沖縄; Okinawa), which is considered a synonym, whereas we use that word just for the one main island. Whichever term the Japanese may use, they in turn divide the geographic term Ryukyu into two political subdivisions: Kagoshima Prefecture

(鹿児島県; Kagoshima-ken) for the northern half of this island chain and Okinawa Prefecture (沖縄県; Okinawa-ken) for the southern half.

In other words, in the West when we use the term Ryukyu, it's in a geographic sense for the whole chain of islands. The Japanese equivalent of our sense of that term is Nansei Shoto. When the Japanese say the Ryukyus, they mean only the southern half of the islands, the modern political subdivision of Okinawa Prefecture. Occasionally, if they use the now historical term Ryukyu Retto, they are referring to what was once the territory of the former Okinawan kingdom, which includes most, but not all, of the archipelago—the Amami Islands, Okinawa Islands, Miyako Islands and Yaeyama Islands.

On the following pages, we use the terms Ryukyu Retto, Ryukyu Shoto, Ryukyu Islands, Ryukyu Group, Ryukyu Archipelago, Nansei Shoto, Nansei Islands, Southwest Islands and Southwest Group interchangeably. We'll start at the top, in the north, and work our way down to the southernmost islands next to Taiwan. We'll visit the entire archipelago, going from one group of islands to the next, exploring each island, one by one, as we go.

The Ryukyu chain starts just below Kyushu, the southernmost large island of mainland Japan. Kyushu holds, among others, the cities of Fukuoka (福岡市; Fukuoka-shi), Nagasaki (長崎市; Nagasaki-shi) and Kagoshima (鹿児島市; Kagoshima-shi).

Kagoshima City is the capital of Kagoshima Prefecture, which is close to where Kyushu Island terminates. It's an important place because it is the Japanese mainland's hub of ferry traffic to all the islands to the south. From here, one takes ferries to the relatively close islands of the Ōsumi and Tokara chains, plus it's the departure and arrival points of ferries to the more distant Amami Islands and Okinawa. It's a city of about 600,000 people and famous for its multitude of hot springs resorts.

Starting at Kagoshima, near Kyushu's southern end, the land cleaves most dramatically into two long pincer arms. The western fork is the Satsuma Peninsula (薩摩半島; Satsuma-hantō). The longer eastern arm is the Ōsumi Peninsula (大隅半島; Ōsumi-hantō). The Ōsumi Peninsula's extreme final tip is Cape Sata (佐多岬; Sata-misaki), the southernmost point of mainland Japan. Within the fork is an extraordinary deep water inlet and natural harbor, Kagoshima Bay (鹿児島湾; Kagoshima-wan), which is also widely known as Kinkō Bay (錦江湾; Kinkō-wan), where Kagoshima City is located. The city is known as the "Naples of the East" and is, in fact, a sister city to Naples. Like its Italian counterpart, a gorgeous bay overlooked by volcanic Mt Vesuvius, Kagoshima also enjoys a spectacular vista. Upon the clear, blue waters of its bay floats a great volcano, Sakurajima (桜島; Sakura-jima).

One of the most active volcanoes in Japan, if not the world, Sakurajima has had a number of violent and destructive eruptions in its history. Its 1914 eruption was the most powerful in 20th-century Japan. Its activity commenced again in 1955 and it has more or less been erupting ever since. Thousands of small explosions occur every year and not a day goes by that residents and visitors do not experience a minor earthquake or witness a rising smoke plume, volcanic ash or some other pyroclastic display. In fact, the continual emission of volcanic ash is a real annoyance to the people who live there. Cars must

Kagoshima Harbor, mainland Japan's jumping-off point for the Ryukyus.

be continually washed, windows cannot be left open and hanging laundry must be rushed into the house. Most people carry an umbrella not for rain but for ash.

Forming an island (but now connected by a land bridge) and rising 3,665 feet (1,117 meters) above sea level, Sakurajima is one of Japan's major tourist attractions. It forms one part of Kirishima-Yaku National Park (霧島屋久国立公園; Kirishima-Yaku Kokuritsu Kōen), Japan's first national park. The other sections of this disconnected park are the ancient Sugi forests on the island of Yaku-shima; the land's end at Cape Sata, and the 23 volcanic peaks of Kirishima (霧島市; Kirishima-shi) about 19 miles (30 kilometers) and less than an hour to the north. The two tallest peaks in the Kirishima Mountain range, 5,577-feet (1,700-meter) Mt Karakuni (韓国岳; Karakuni-daké) and 5,164-feet (1,574-meter) Mt Takachiho (高千穂岳; Takachiho-daké), are the mythological origin of the Japanese sun goddess Amaterasu (天照; Amaterasu) and the birthplace of Japan. You may have already seen the Kirishima Mountains. They were filmed as the volcano lair of Ernst Stavro Blofeld, the evil head of SPECTRE, in the 1967 James Bond movie *You Only Live Twice.*

Part of Kagoshima-ken is on the mainland and part of it spreads across the Satsunan Islands (薩南諸島; Satsunan-shotō), which constitute the northern half of the Ryukyus. The Satsunans include about 25 inhabited islands and extend southwards across the Ōsumi, Tokara and Amami chains for about 312 miles (500 kilometers), all the way to Okinawa. The southernmost Satsunan Island, and the southernmost island of Kagoshima Prefecture, is Yoron, which lies a mere 14 miles (22 kilometers) above Okinawa's north-ernmost tip at Cape Hedo.

Where Kagoshima Prefecture ends, Japan's southernmost prefecture of Okinawa begins. Okinawa Island, which is located just about in the middle of the Ryukyu chain, serves as the dividing line between the two prefectures. Okinawa-ken consists of the group of islands collectively called Ryukyu-shotō by the Japa-nese and includes more than 50 inhabited islands. Starting at the north and heading south, the prefecture begins just below Yoron Island at Okinawa main island (沖縄本島; Okinawa-hontō), the largest island landmass in the Ryukyu Archipelago. Okinawa is, in turn, surrounded by many lesser islands, including one lesser group of islands, the mini-archipelago of the Keramas.

Formerly an island in Kagoshima Bay, Sakurajima volcano attached itself to the mainland of Kyūshū in 1914 by a narrow isthmus when its lava flows connected it to the Ōsumi Peninsula. There's a causeway on it now.

Cape Sata (Sata-misaki), mainland Japan's southernmost point.

Every several minutes, ferries shuttle across Kagoshima Bay to Sakurajima volcano.

The southern Ryukyu chain is subdivided into several groups, including the Okinawa, Miyako and Yaeyama Islands. These island groups extend southwest from the main island of Okinawa more than 312 miles (500 kilometers) to the small island of Yonaguni, only 68 miles (110 kilometers) east of northern Taiwan. In addition, Okinawa Prefecture includes the geologically and geographically unrelated small archipelagos of the Daitō Islands, 219 miles (350 kilometers) to the east of Okinawa Island in the Pacific Ocean, and the Senkakus, a disputed, uninhabited group close to mainland China and above Taiwan.

Altogether, the Satsunan Islands of the northern half of the Ryukyus constitute about 966 square miles (2,503 square kilometers). The southern half of the Ryukyus, Okinawa-ken, is 879 square miles (2,276 square kilometers). It's a bit difficult to make suitable comparisons when they're this little, but the smallest state in the US is Rhode Island (not an island incidentally). Its total land area is 1,045 square miles (2,706 square kilometers). So we really are talking about a large number of very small islands in a small space.

We'll first outline the islands in the Ryukyu Archipelago, including all the inhabited ones, from north to south, then discuss them in more depth in the chapters that follow.

THE RYUKYU ARCHIPELAGO

The Ryukyu Archipelago is a 684-mile (1,100-kilometer)-long chain of approximately 150 islands divided in two halves: the Satsunan-shotō and the Ryukyu-shotō. The Satsunans are further divided into three lesser chains, the Ōsumi, Tokara and Amami Islands, while the Ryukyus are divided into five minor archipelagos, the Okinawa, Miyako, Yaeyama, Daito and Senkaku Island groups.

Satsunan Shoto

The northern half of the Ryukyus is part of Kagoshima Prefecture. The Satsunans include the three island groups of Ōsumi, Tokara and Amami.

Ryukyu Shoto

The southern half of the Ryukyu Island Archipelago, which constitutes Okinawa Prefecture, is usually divided into the three major north–south groups of Okinawa Shotō, the Miyakos and the Yaeyama Islands, plus the more distant Daitō and Senkaku Island groups.

Getting around

Many of the inhabited Ryukyus have airports, or at least an airstrip. For the northern group, the Satsunans, most air services originate from Kagoshima, although there are also some flights to and from Fukuoka. There is also occasional service to some islands from Osaka and Tokyo, but not much and not often. In the south, in the Ryukyu group, almost all air services start or end at Okinawa. Most local flights in the islands are handled by Japan Transocean Air (JTA) and its subsidiary Ryukyu Air Commuter (RAC), both owned by Japan Air Lines (JAL). All Nippon Airlines (ANA) also has several subsidiary carriers, including Air Next (AN) and Air Nippon (ANK), which offer flights from Naha out to a number of islands.

Other than from the hubs of Kagoshima and Naha, however, there is very limited (or no) air service from one island to another. In other words, if you wish to fly, for example, from Yoron-tō to Amami, you might have to fly first to Naha, then to Amami; or first to Naha, then to Kagoshima and then to Amami, or maybe even from Yoron to Naha, from there to Tokyo, then to Amami, direct

The "A" Line's Akebono

Both the "A" and "Marix" Lines sail daily from Okinawa's Naha and Motobu ports to the Amami Islands and on to Kagoshima on the Japanese mainland. As it takes twelve hours from Naha to reach Amami-Ōshima and then another twelve to reach Kagoshima, a total of four ships alternate on the route so that all islands are served twice daily, one from the north and one from the south. The service is 24/7/365 and only interrupted in the event of typhoons or other severe inclement weather.

Why Some Islands Are Uninhabited

Although many of the inhabited Ryukyu are very small, sometimes only 2–3 miles (4–5 kilometers) or less in diameter, they are for the most part arable and suitable for cultivation and habitation, although adequate fresh water supplies are always a challenge. In general, uninhabited islands are uninhabited for a reason: they are either too small, too low-lying, too rocky or possess no fresh water—or all of the above.

Traditional Okinawan Houses

A classic Okinawan house is usually encircled by a coral stone wall or *fukugi* trees for protection against winds and typhoon damage. It has a ceramic tiled roof often sporting a *shīsā* dog and is raised off the ground on stones to guard against dampness and insects. It is surrounded by an overhanging roof supported by wooden pillars for shade protection from the sun and for air circulation. It's a structure that's been completely adapted over the centuries to perfectly fit into its environment.

The Shīsā Lion Dog (シーサー)

Symbol of Okinawa, good luck charm of the Ryukyu kingdom and defender of the home from evil spirits, *shīsā* originated in the early blend of Chinese and Ryukyuan cultures. They're placed at the entrance of homes, shrines and graves and on rooftops. Often set in pairs, the one with the open mouth summons good fortune, the one with the closed mouth prevents its escape. Together they keep evil from coming into the house.

or through Kagoshima. Similarly, flying from Tokyo to Ishigaki would usually mean flying from Tokyo to Naha, then taking a local flight to Ishigaki. In fact, because Ishigaki happens to be a particularly popular place, there are some direct flights to there from Tokyo but that's not usually the case with most islands.

One thing that's definitely not possible by air, unless you pilot or charter your own plane, is island hopping in a straight line from one island to another. For that, you're going to have to get your feet wet, figuratively, not literally. In other words, to island hop, you'll have to take an ocean cruise or, more precisely, one of the many sea ferry voyages that run throughout the Ryukyus.

Don't worry, for this is no hardship and is indeed a great way to meet the people of the Ryukyus and discover their wonderful way of life. Although any sailing will take longer than an air flight, the opportunity to live life as the people who live here do will be unsurpassed and worth every minute of your time. One final consideration: in many cases, you've got no choice but to sail. There are no airports and thus no flights to many of the Ryukyu Islands. So, for example, if you wish to navigate and explore the Amazon of Japan, the Urauchi-gawa, the longest river in Okinawa, on Iriomotejima Island, then you'll have to take a local ferry from Ishigaki. There's simply no other way to get there.

Every day throughout the year in the Ryukyus there are scores of ships shuttling around from one island to another. Carrying passengers and hauling vehicles and freight, the Japanese ferry service is the lifeline of the Nansei-shotō. Short distances, under an hour or two, are handled by local ferries. Generally, these are small ships, under 50–60 feet (15–20 meters) in length. For islands further than two, three or four hours sailing time from Kagoshima or Okinawa, larger ships of 330 feet (100 meters) and more, are used. As for the expense, naturally the longer the sailing distance, the more remote the island, the less frequent and more expensive the ferry service will be. Ferries are not inexpensive but they can sometimes be a good deal less than airfares to the same destinations.

As a very rough approximation of fares, a journey of an hour will cost around $10–$15. A longer trip of two hours will run to $25. A four–six hour sailing will set you back about $50–$75, and an overnight journey will cost around $100–$125. Halve those numbers

Cafeteria on the ferry "Akebono."

Welcome aboard an "A" Line ferry!

for your bicycle, if you bring one. Figure about the same amount as the passenger fare for a motorcycle, and double those numbers for your car

Larger ships used for longer sailings always have a cafeteria on board. By and large, the food is good and not unreasonably priced. For trips over twelve hours, more comfortable overnight accommodations are available—at a price. All the ships on the longer routes offer a variety of cabins: for two, for four and for eight. Private cabins generally have their own TV sitting area and more comfortable berths than the tatami mats, but of course the mats are free.

On all large ferries, you can always bring along your car or bike. That's one good reason to take the ferry. However, because Japanese ferries are expensive, especially for vehicles, on longer trips it's worth considering sailing without your vehicle (or flying) and then renting a car, scooter or bicycle once there. On all of Okinawa's larger islands, you'll find car rentals and usually bicycle rentals. Scooters are more problematic. Sometimes they're available, sometimes not. And if available, the dealer may or may not want a motorcycle license from you.

Roads are often small but they're usually well maintained and safe. Island traffic is

Passengers board an ANA Air Next flight at Ishigaki Airport.

always light. Driving in the Ryukyus, except for Okinawa main island, never poses the same challenges as it does in Tokyo. Finally, on larger islands, taxicabs are usually available and can always be hired by the hour or the day. But they're never cheap. Count on 10,000 Yen (US $125) for a half day. And don't forget to negotiate your fare before climbing in!

The Ryukyus In Depth

We'll start again in the north and work our way south, this time taking our time to discuss in more detail each island's general characteristics, any special or unusual features and how to reach them. As the Ryukyu's axis is generally north–south, the eastern shores of the islands greet the sun each morning, rising up out of the Pacific Ocean (太平洋; Taiheiyō), while their western shores see the sun set each evening into the East China Sea (東シナ海 or 東支那海; Higashi Shina Kai).

Recall that the Ryukyu Archipelago (琉球列島; Ryūkyū-rettō) or Southwest Islands (南西諸島; Nansei-shotō) is a 684-mile (1,100-kilometer)-long north to southwest arc of roughly 150 islands, approximately 75 of which are inhabited, divided in two halves: the Satsunan group (Satsunan-shotō) and the Ryukyu group (Ryukyu-shotō). Let's get going!

Island Nomenclature

In English, a chain or cluster of islands is properly called an archipelago. It comes to us from the Greek *arkhi* (ἀρχι), meaning "chief," and *pélagos* (πέλαγος) which means "the sea." The term describes a group of islands. In Japanese, there are several words with the meaning of archipelago. Quite commonly used is *shoto* (諸島; shotō), which describes any group of islands. Also widely used is *retto* (列島; rettō), which again means a group of islands but has the added sense of a line or an arc of islands. Finally, a third term, *gunto* (群島; guntō), is used to describe a mixed or round cluster of islands.

As a practical matter, all three terms are used more or less interchangeably and, in fact, any discrete group or chain of islands may be collectively referred to as a *shoto, retto* or *gunto*. Notice that all three terms incorporate 島 as their second character. This Kanji character means "island" and is pronounced *jima, shima* or *tō* depending on usage and context.

Depending on how you count them, there are at least a half dozen minor archipelagos comprising the main great archipelago of the Ryukyus. Each minor group consists of three to five or ten or more inhabited islands, plus many more uninhabited isles and islets. The words *jima, shima* or *tō* are used to describe one individual island and are appended as a suffix to the island's name. You'll also see the characters 離島 from time to time. This means isolated or outlying island and is pronounced *ritō*. There's also *kotō*, which means solitary island. Its characters are 孤島. Finally, on occasion, you'll see 岩 at the end of an island's name. This character is *iwa* and can be translated as "islet" but is more usually "rock."

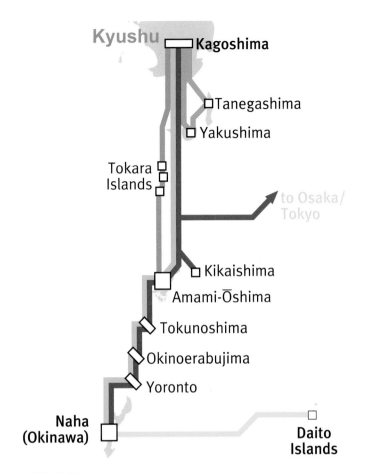

Marix Line
Kagoshima – Amami~Oshima – Naha

A Line
Kagoshima – Amami~Oshima – Naha
Kagoshima – Kikaishima – Amami~Oshima – Okinoerabujima
Osaka – Amami~Oshima – Naha
Tokyo – Shibushu – Amami~Oshima – Naha

Tokara
Kagoshima – Tokara Islands – Amami~Oshima

Daito Kaiun
Naha – Daito Islands

Various Companies
Kagoshima – Yakushima
Kagoshima – Tanegashima
Tanegashima – Yakushima

AWAMORI (泡盛)

Unique to the islands of Okinawa, Awamori is distilled, high-proof liquor similar to vodkas, rums and whiskeys, and is therefore much more powerful than fermented or brewed beverages such as beer, wine or saké. Made with long-grained Indica rice from Thailand, fermented with black *koji* yeast, then subject to a single-distillation process, Awamori is typically found in the 60–80 proof range (30–40 percent alcohol), although some are distilled as high as 120 (60 percent alcohol). High-quality Awamoris are aged in cool underground caves in clay pots. When aged for at least three years, Awamoris may be called

kūsu (古酒; old liquor). Premium Awamoris can run into the hundreds of dollars for one container. Perhaps for this reason, the traditional Awamori drinking vessel is a tiny, thimble-sized cup called a *saka-jiki*. When properly served, Awamori is accompanied by a carafe of mineral water and some ice. It may be taken neat, on the rocks or diluted with a little water. A special version of Awamori is made by the addition of herbs, spices, honey and . . . a whole poisonous Habu pit viper! Thought to have medicinal, restorative or even some aphrodisiac properties, this version is called Habushu (ハブ酒) after the deadly Habu snake.

USEFUL JAPANESE ISLAND TERMS

north **kita** 北
south **minami** 南
east **higashi** 東
west **nishi** 西
great/large/big **dai, ōkii** 大
small **ko, shō, chiisai** 小
prefecture **ken** 県
park **kōen** 公園
garden **teien** 庭園
hot spring **onsen** 温泉
archipelago (many islands) **shotō** 諸島
archipelago (mixed/round) **guntō** 群島
archipelago (arc/straight line) **rettō** 列島
island **shima, jima, tō** 島
rock/islet **iwa** 岩
isolated (outlying) island **ritō** 離島
solitary island **kotō** 孤島
main island **hontō** 本島
mainland **hondo** 本土

offshore **oki** 沖
port/harbor **minato, kō** 港
cape **misaki** 岬
promontory/point **zaki** 崎
lighthouse **tōdai** 灯台
sea/ocean **umi, kai** 海
coast/shore **kaigan** 海岸
bay **wan** 湾
strait/channel **kaikyō** 海峡
beach **hama** 浜
river **gawa, kawa** 川
lake **ko** 湖
peninsula **hantō** 半島
hill **oka** 丘
mountain **yama, zan, san** 山
peak **daké, také** 岳
cave **do** 洞
valley **dani, tani** 谷
waterfall **taki** 滝

SAFETY AND COMFORT ON BOARD

Since there are thousands of islands in Japan every day, from Wakkanai, Hokkaido to Yonaguni-jima, there are hundreds of ships with tens of thousands of passengers at sea. How safe, and how comfortable, are the ferries?

First consideration: Safety. Japan's passenger shipping industry is second to none in its safety record. It is subject to one of the world's most rigorous inspection regimens and the fleet is regarded as one of the best maintained in the world. Nevertheless, there have been catastrophes. The last major disaster was in 1963. Then, the *Midori Maru* bound for Kumejima hit sudden squalls and unusually high seas and foundered on a sand island, an uninhabited outcropping in the Keramas. She went down and 112 lives were lost. Since that time, there have been no such disasters in the Ryukyus.

Second consideration: Comfort. Broadly speaking, there are three sizes of ships used for passenger ferry traffic: small, medium and large. Small ships, for trips under an hour, usually offer hard plastic seats both in the cabin and outdoors. It's not very comfortable but at least the trip is short. Medium-sized ships, used for journeys that take 2–4 hours, generally have reclining airline-style seating, air-conditioning, restrooms and a snack bar. In addition, there is always outdoor space on top for better viewing or fresh air. On longer journeys of 5–20 hours or more, large ships will always have comfortable in-board seating, *tatami*-style resting accommodations, dining facilities and, at additional

The Queen Coral getting underway for Yoron-to.

Typical passenger seating on board.

expense, private cabins, the most comfortable of all. But don't worry. Most passengers sleep quite well in the tatami rooms. One important safety and comfort note: passengers are not allowed to sleep in their vehicles. There is the danger of poisoning from carbon monoxide gas or other fumes.

Clean and comfortable tatami-style sleeping/ resting accommodations are available on longer voyages.

Long-distance ferries are big. Parking your car is like driving in a great covered parking lot or on an aircraft carrier.

Okinawa's Bitter Melon

I t's been claimed to be a cure-all for just about everything that ails you: cancer, diabetes, high blood pressure. In fact, the bitter melon or bitter gourd has a remarkable combination of nutritional value and vitamins. In Okinawa, where they are favored, they are called *goya* (ゴーヤー). The Japanese word is *nigauri* (苦瓜) but in Japan everyone calls them *goya* too. Technically, the plant is *Momordica charantia*, a tropical and subtropical vine in the gourd family. Their nearest relations are squash, pumpkins, zucchini, watermelons, cucumbers, luffa plants and various melons. What makes *goya* stand out is that they are really, really bitter, almost inedible.

But that doesn't stop the Okinawans from eating them. Known as the longest-lived people on earth, Okinawans claim that their longevity comes from their easygoing island lifestyle, happiness in family life and diet, which mostly comprises fish and vegetables. The *goya* is credited with all kinds of superlatives and believed to be about the most healthful food one can eat. Given its bitterness, the plant is prepared and eaten when it is young and freshly light green, even yellowish. As it gets older and darker, it is increasingly inedible.

The most popular Okinawan dish featuring the *goya* melon is called *goya chanpuru* (ゴーヤーチャンプルー). *Chanpuru* is Okinawan for "something mixed" and refers to the combination of ingredients stir fried in the dish as well as Okinawan culture as a whole. It's not Japanese and it's not Chinese. Rather, it's a rich combination mixed up and only found in the Ryukyu Islands. Here's a simple, favorite recipe for stir-fried *goya*.

A bitter gourd hanging from a vine.

A plate of stir-fried goya chanpuru.

Goya Chanpuru (Stir-fried Bitter Gourd)

Serves 2

1 bitter melon
pinch of sea salt
5 oz (150 gm) pork back ribs or thinly sliced
   pork (Okinawans often use spam)
1 pack tofu
sesame oil
cooking liquor such as Okinawa awamori
1 cup (50 g) soybean sprouts (other vegetables can be added as well, such as small
   slices of onions, carrots, green peppers,
   and mushrooms)
soy sauce
instant bouillon (or dried bonito powder)
2 eggs, beaten

1. Slice the bitter gourd in half lengthwise
   and remove the seeds and pulp with a
   spoon. Then dice the halves about ½ inch
   (1.25 cm) thick. You'll get many crescent-
   shaped pieces.
2. Mix the bitter gourd with a pinch of salt
   in a bowl and leave to stand for about 10
   minutes. This removes much of the
   bitterness.
3. Cut the pork into bite-sized pieces.
4. Break the tofu with your fingers into
   bite-sized pieces and fry them in a pan
   with the sesame oil until they become
   brown. Then transfer them to a dish.
5. Fry the pork in the pan with the sesame
   oil and cooking liquor at low heat until it's
   brown and crispy.
6. Put the bitter gourd back in the pan and
   fry with the pork at high heat.
7. When the bitter gourd wilts, add the tofu
   and soybean sprouts and more cooking
   liquor. Fry and mix well.
8. Season with soy sauce and bouillon (or
   dried bonito powder).
9. Add the beaten egg to the pan. Mix and
   cook all at low heat until the egg is half
   cooked.

PART 1
THE SATSUNAN ISLANDS
薩南諸島

The Satsunans (薩南諸島; Satsunan-shotō) are the island portion of Kagoshima-ken. The balance of the prefecture lies on the mainland. Unlike the more southerly Okinawan Islands, the Satsunan Islands, especially the northerly ones, have a more temperate climate, only vaguely subtropical. Although it rarely ever freezes, it can be cool, even cold, in the winter. The islands are best visited in the summer, but of course at that time it can be very hot and humid. Spring is best as fall can mean typhoons. Overall, the vegetation of southern Kyushu Island, the Kagoshima area, the Satsuma and Ōsumi Peninsulas and the Satsunan Islands is blessed with more than abundant rainfall. Thus it is lush, with cycads, tree ferns and some of the more hardy species of various palm trees found in great profusion.

The Satsunan group consists of about 25 inhabited islands and more than another dozen uninhabited islands spread out over three major groups: the Ōsumi, Tokara and Amami. The Satsunans occupy a total of 966 square miles (2,503 square kilometers). The tiny, uninhabited chains of the Kusagaki (草垣群島; Kusagaki-guntō) and Uji Islands (宇治群島; Uji-guntō), found approximately 31 miles (50 kilometers) further west and 37 miles (60 kilometers) northwest, respectively, of Kuroshima in the East China Sea are not included in this definition.

Cape Sata (Sata misaki), the final tip of mainland Japan at the end of the Ōsumi Peninsula on Kyushu Island.

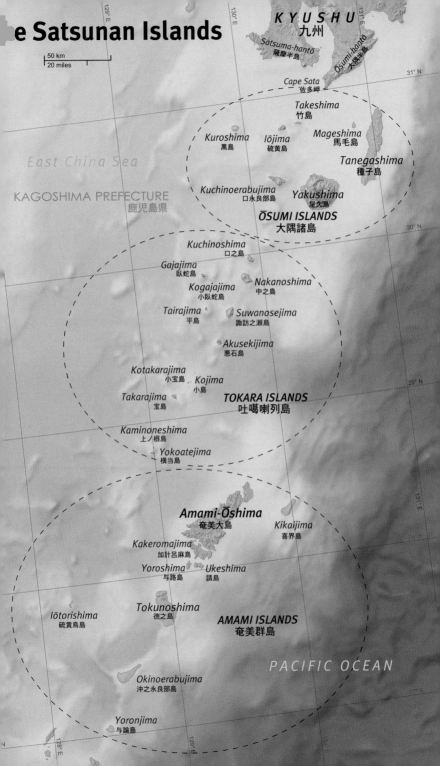

Chapter 1

THE ŌSUMI ISLANDS 大隈諸島
Ancient outcrops, modern spaceport

1 **Tanegashima** 種子島
2 **Mageshima** 馬毛島
3 **Yakushima** 屋久島
4 **Kuchinoerabujima** 口永良部島
5 **Takeshima** 竹島
6 **Iōjima** 硫黄島
7 **Kuroshima** 黒島

The northernmost group of the Satsunan Archipelago, the Ōsumi Islands (大隈諸島; Ōsumi-shotō), lies about 37 miles (60 kilometers) south of Kyushu Island's southern tip, the Ōsumi Peninsula. The islands are volcanic in origin and have a combined area of 400 square miles (1,035 square kilometers). Altogether there are seven inhabited islands and several tiny named uninhabited ones. The island chain's total population is around 52,000, with about 18,000 living in Nishinoomote on Tanegashima.

There are two airports on the Ōsumi Islands, one each on the two largest islands of Tanegashima and Yakushima, and an airstrip and unmanned control tower on the island of Iōjima. The latter is kept in good working order and used by air charter services. Almost all the islands (and this is true throughout the Ryukyus) also sport a helicopter landing pad, but these are generally only used for emergency medical evacuations or other government purposes, not for commercial services.

More usually, both Tanegashima and Yakushima are reached by regular and frequent ferry service from the north out of Kagoshima City. Ferries, which carry passengers, vehicles and cargo, take about four hours. High-speed jetfoils, which don't carry vehicles or cargo, take about two. There are also passenger and vehicle ferries but not high-speed hydrofoils from Kagoshima to Takeshima, Iōjima and Kuroshima. Service to these three islands takes place only three times a week.

There are multiple ferry terminals in Kagoshima with several competing lines. Moreover, sailing schedules change all the time. It is most important to verify your ferry

A high-speed hydrofoil service from Kagoshima runs to several of the Ōsumi Islands.

Mt Kirishima ▲
韓国岳

KYUSHU ISLAND
九州島

Kirishima City
霧島市

Kagoshima ●
鹿児島 ▲ Sakurajima
Volcano
桜島

Satsuma-hantō
薩摩半島

Ōsumi-hantō
大隅半島

Kagoshima Bay
鹿児島湾

*East China
Sea*

Mt Kaimon ▲
開聞岳

MISHIMA GROUP
三島列島

Cape Sata
佐多岬

Mageshima
馬毛島

Shōwa-Iōjima
昭和硫黄島

Takeshima
竹島

● Nishinoomote
西之表市

Kuroshima
黒島

Iōjima
硫黄島
Mt Iō ▲
硫黄岳

Tanegashima
種子島

Kuchinoerabujima
口永良部島

Miyanoura Port
宮浦港 ⚓

Shimama ●
島間

JAXA
Japanese Aerospace
Exploration Agency
種子島 宇宙センター

Mt Shin ▲ ▲ Mt Furu
新岳　　古岳

Cape Nagata
永田岬

Mt Miyanoura ▲
宮之浦岳

⚓ Anbo Port
安房港

Cape Kadokura
門倉岬

*PACIFIC
OCEAN*

Yakushima
屋久島

Kuchinoshima
口之島

20 km
10 miles

The Ōsumi Islands

Nakanoshima
中之島

Tanegashima marina and ferry dock.

Otatsu Metatsu Rock, a black basalt formation.

and its current timetable. In the case of several islands, you will have several choices but for others service is much more limited.

As a matter of convenience, the Ōsumi Islands are sometimes divided into two subgroups: the northeast and northwest.

The Northeastern Group

This group contains the Ōsumi's two largest islands, plus two very small islands. All four are inhabited.

1 TANEGASHIMA 種子島

A long, narrow and mostly flat island, Tanegashima (種子島; Tanéga-shima) is almost 37 miles (60 kilometers) in length from north to south and ranges from 3–7 miles (5–12 kilometers) east to west. Its area is 172 square miles (445 square kilometers), making it the second largest of the Ōsumi Islands. The island was supposedly named Tané (meaning "seed") because that's what its shape resembles. Tanegashima has a coastline of 103 miles (165 kilometers) and a population of 36,000.

Although there are a half dozen villages sprinkled around the island, most are quite small and the majority of the island's people live in and around the island's biggest city and port, Nishinoomote (西之表市; Nishi no Omoté-shi), on Tanegashima's northwest side. This is where most of the ferries to and from Kagoshima dock and where you'll find a couple of very nice, small hotels and *minshuku* (民宿; lit. "small inn" or "pension"). There are also several good restaurants, but otherwise there is not too much going on in Nishinoomote. The town's greatest attraction is an excellent Gun Museum that we'll mention in more detail below.

Overall, the island is sparsely populated. Indeed, much of it seems wild and uninhabited. Although sugar cane is grown, it's not densely cultivated as it is on so many islands in the Ryukyus. Here, it seems more like an afterthought, just the occasional cane field here and there.

Although it may be technically correct to characterize Tanegashima as "flat," that term really doesn't fully describe the topography, for in many places it is moderately to quite hilly, with most scenic ups and downs in all directions. In fact, the island's highest point is a not too shabby 925 feet (282 meters) at Mt Tennyogakura (天女ケ倉山; Ten-nyo gakura-yama). It's on the island's northeast side, about a 5-mile (8-kilometer) drive from Nishinoomote. Tanegashima is a very pretty island to drive around. Moreover, it has a beautiful coastline—and a lot of it. Its shores vary considerably, from great black basalt rock formations, as at Otatsu Metatsu Rock (雄龍雌龍の岩; Otatsu Metatsu no iwa; lit. "Male Dragon–Female Dragon Rock") along the central west coast to extremely fine white sand beaches found in several places, but most famously along the full length of the island's southern coast. Along the southeast shore, you'll find Chikura Caverns (千座の岩屋; Chikura no iwa ya), a group of water-eroded caves on a white sand beach. The caves can be entered at low tide. There are picnic tables and some foods stands here as well.

Most visitors will arrive by sea or by air, for there is an airport. By sea, and depending on the season, there are 3–5 high-speed "Rocket" or "Toppy" jet hydrofoils per day. The less than two-hour sailing originates in Kagoshima, but one or two per day continue over to nearby Yakushima. Less expensive,

The Toppy hydrofoil in Tanegashima Port.

but of course slower, the Cosmo Line runs the vehicle, freight and passenger ferry "Princess Wakasa." It's a beautiful ship and a comfortable sail, a little less than four hours. Most of the year, service is daily except Sundays. In the busy summer season, it runs every day.

Alternatively, there is a ferry service, though less frequent, to Yakushima from a second city on Tanegashima, the southwestern port of Shimama (島間; Shimama). If you are planning on using that port, be sure to double check your ferry schedule.

For those in more of a hurry, Tanegashima has a small, modern airport more or less located in the center of the island, about 9.5 miles (15 kilometers) and 20 minutes south of Nishinoomote. There are usually about five flights a day to Kagoshima, which take 30 minutes, and occasional service to Osaka and Fukuoka. All flights are on Japan Air Commuter turboprop planes.

Tanegashima is well known for at least two things. First, on August 25, 1543, its southernmost point, Cape Kadokura (門倉岬; Kadokura-misaki) was the landing site of the first Europeans to enter Japan. The ship, which had been blown off course in the waters between China and Okinawa, carried several Portuguese sailor/explorer/adventurers, among them, so he claimed, Fernão Mendes Pinto (ca. 1509–83). According to his memoirs, he was the first European to set foot in Japan and to introduce the matchlock arquebus, a type of firearm.

Although Pinto's claims are subject to dispute (other accounts place him in India or Burma at the same time he supposedly landed in Japan), there's no doubt that firearms were introduced by the Portuguese into Japan at this time. Indeed, for the next several hundred years, the Japanese name for a gun was Tanégashima Téppō (種子島鉄砲). Whether it was Pinto who introduced firearms is the subject of the controversy. Somewhat like Marco Polo's *Travels*, Pinto's tales are so extraordinary, so fantastical and so imaginative, it's impossible to accurately assess them. On the other hand, his accounts of events and life in many far-flung places of 16th-century Asia are detailed so perfectly, no one doubts he was witness to them. His great autobiographical work is entitled *Peregrinação* (The Pilgrimage). It was published posthumously in 1614.

Because of this Portuguese–Japanese historical connection, Tanegashima's island's largest city, Nishinoomote, has a "sister" city in Vila do Bispo, Portugal. Nishinoomote's

Cosmo Line's Princess Wakasa provides a comfortable sail to Tanegashima from Kagoshima.

The Tanegashima Gun Museum.

Gun Museum is built in the shape of the early visiting ship, a Chinese junk, and there are several historical plaques and commemorative markers celebrating Portuguese–Japanese friendship around the island.

The Gun Museum, which is formally known as the Tanegashima Center for Research and Development (種子島 開発 総合センター; Tanégashima kaihatsu sōgō sentā) but usually referred to as Teppō Hall (鉄砲館; Teppō-kan; lit. "iron-tube" (gun) hall), is for most visitors the highlight of Nishinoomote. There are over 100 priceless original early firearms. On display are weapons from all phases of their early development. In addition, the museum displays examples of Japanese metalworking skills used in the 16th century to produce scissors, samurai swords and metal armor.

Tanega Island's second big claim to fame is that it's the headquarters of the Japan Aerospace Exploration Agency (JAXA) and the Tanegashima Space Center (種子島 宇宙 センター; Tanégashima uchū sentā). Located at the southeastern end of the island, JAXA and the Space Center lie at the heart of Japan's research and development of rockets, missiles and satellites. The Space Center develops, tests, launches, tracks and retrieves rocket engines and satellites.

The launch complexes are open daily to the public except Mondays unless there is an actual space launch. In that case, only press and media people are allowed on the complex for viewing. The general public may view space launches from a number of designated points on the southern end of the island. The Space Exhibition Hall in the Space Center allows visitors to study everything from space development to planet exploration. The Space Center also includes a Space Information Center, a Rocket Launch Theatre and a Museum Gift Shop. The center includes exhibits on such things as the mechanisms

The Tanégashima Téppō Arquebus, Forerunner of the Modern Rifle

The Portuguese (European) Arquebus was a muzzle-loaded firearm with a matchlock firing device. Used between the 15th and 17th centuries, its successor was the flintlock musket. Immediately after their introduction in Japan, the weapons were widely reproduced and had a major impact on civil wars of that era. Japanese craftsmen and metallurgists were able to faithfully copy the designs and reproduce them in quantity due to their skills at manufacturing high-quality steel for traditional weapons, notably the Japanese blades known as *katana* (刀), otherwise known as the Japanese backsword and commonly referred to as samurai swords. The history of Japan's use of Western firearms was brilliantly detailed in Noel Perrin's essay "Giving Up the Gun: Japan's Reversion to the Sword, 1543–1879," published in 1979.

A rocket launch at the Tanegashima Space Center.

Cape Kadokura looking northeast.

and functions of satellites, the launching, tracking and controlling of rockets and the International Space Station project.

Essentially, visitors are permitted to roam about most of the complex on their own self-guided tours. There is no admission charge. Guided tours in English or Japanese may be reserved but those arrangments must be made in advance.

But if you're not all that interested in rockets and outer space, and maybe would rather just hit the beach, wander over to Takezaki Beach (竹崎海岸; Také-zaki kaigan; lit. "Bamboo Point Coast") which is more than 5 miles (8 kilometers) of pure white sand, in fact the whole southern end of the island. It's not for nothing that JAXA claims on its website that "It is known as the most beautiful rocket-launch complex in the world."

In addition to its fine beach, the southern end of Tanegashima holds three prominent capes: one famous historically, the other two occupied by the Aerospace Exploration Agency (JAXA). The two controlled by JAXA hold a number of islets/rocks just offshore. We'll describe them below. The southernmost (and southwesternmost) point of the island is occupied by Cape Kadokura, previously mentioned as the first European landing place in the empire of Japan. There

are several small monuments, memorial stones and a Shintō shrine in commemoration of this event at the cape.

Approximately 5 miles (8 kilometers) to the northeast is a second cape, Ōtakézaki (大竹崎; Ōtaké-zaki), which holds two sets of islets. A bit more than a mile (3 kilometers) to the north and east is the final cape, Yoshinobuzaki (吉信崎; Yoshino-bu zaki), which has a double set of islets offshore. Of these twin capes, it could be said that Cape Ōtaké occupies Tanegashima's southernmost eastern point and Cape Yoshinobu occupies its easternmost southern point. Both capes are fully developed and covered with numerous administrative and service buildings, a launch pad and other high-tech equipment of JAXA. Offshore, each cape peters out to a series of large rocks. Coincidentally, in each case there are two separate collections of rocks off each of the capes. We'll describe these four islet groups in our usual north to south sequence.

YOSHINOBUZAKIIWA (吉信崎岩; Yoshino bu zaki-iwa. The more northerly of the twin capes is Yoshinobu-zaki (Ōtaké-zaki is about a mile (1.5 kilometers) to the south). Directly off Cape Yoshinobu there are approximately 20 rocks in all.

A rocket on display at the Tanegashima Space Center.

Cape Yoshinobu and its offshore rocks.

There is one batch of about a half dozen large rocks (see photo page 24) to the southeast of the cape and around 15 more smaller ones (not visible in the photo above), some 1,000 feet (300 meters) to the northeast.

The large rock islets start only 100 feet (30 meters) offshore and extend about 1,640 feet (500 meters) to the south and east. They vary in shape and size from ovals 490 by 575 feet (75 by 175 meters) in size to more or less round islets about 500 feet (150 meters) in diameter. The smallest ones in this batch measure close to 165 feet (50 meters) across.

The second batch of Yoshinobu rocks is several hundred meters north above the first set. They start approximately 490 feet (75 meters) offshore and extend 1,310–1,640 feet (400–500 meters) north and east. The islets in this group vary in size from 33 by 50 feet (10 by 15 meters) in diameter to the largest, which is about 330 feet (100 meters) long. Almost all the islets in this double set of rocks are covered in vegetation and several of them have nice beaches. Given their proximity to shore, at low tide you can walk or swim out to a number of them.

ŌTAKEZAKIIWA (大竹崎岩; Ōtaké zaki-iwa).

The most extreme southeastern point of Tanegashima is called Ōtakézaki, which means "Big Bamboo Point." The cape is about 2,620 feet (800 meters) across, 660 feet (200 meters) wide and entirely covered in clean, smooth white sand. It's a beautiful beach and there's a small fishing port and marina there as well. There are two sets of rocks just offshore at the point. Those to east are the Ōtakézaki rocks and those to the west are the Kawasoenohana rocks.

Rock outcrops at Cape Ōtakezakiiwa.

The Big Bamboo Point rocks start about 660 feet (200 meters) east offshore and continue about another 1,970–2,300 feet (600–700 meters) further east and southeast. Altogether, there are more than dozen of them. They range in size from as small as 80 feet (25 meters) in diameter to as large as 525 feet (160 meters) across. Almost all are half-covered in vegetation and none of them have any good beaches.

KAWASOENOHANAIWA (カワソエノ鼻岩

Kawa so éno hana-iwa). At the western end of Ōtaké cape, a little more than a kilometer west of the Big Bamboo Point rocks, are the Kawasoenohana rocks. They begin a mere 410 feet (125 meters) due south of the marina and continue south another 1,640 feet (500 meters). Most of them are quite large, ranging in size from the smallest at about 165 feet (50 meters) in diameter to the largest, which is 1,310 feet (400 meters) long. There are about a half dozen of these rocks. Together with a number of strategically placed giant tsunami jacks, they effectively and completely shelter the marina.

As mentioned earlier, from the cape at Big Bamboo Point (Ōtakézaki, the island's south-

Kawasoenohanaiwa boasts a fine beach along its southern coast.

eastern end) to Cape Kadokura (Kadokura-misaki, the island's southwestern end), it's about 5 miles (8 kilometers). This entire stretch of coast is a fine beach. There's a designated campground along the shore and it has freshwater showers and toilet facilities.

2 MAGESHIMA 馬毛島

Magé Island is a tiny, almost uninhabited islet about 7 miles (12 kilometers) due west of Nishinoomote Port on Tanegashima but there's no ferry service from that port, or any other port, to Mageshima (馬毛島; Magé-shima; lit. "Horsehair Island"). Although Mageshima has a port and a good-sized concrete dock for landing watercraft, you'll have to pilot or charter your own to get there. The island is privately owned and there is no commercial service to it. A couple of families live on the island and raise some sugarcane, but it's marginal. The island is no longer productively farmed and most of it is covered in scrub vegetation. Mageshima is triangularly shaped, about 3 miles (5 kilometers) long from north to south and about a mile (1.5 kilometers) wide from its east–west base to its middle section. From there, it tapers down to its pointy northern end.

At one time there was a working airstrip on the island but it was abandoned a long time ago and is no longer operable. Recent press reports have stated that the Japanese government is negotiating with the US Forces Japan to convert the island into an airbase in replacement for the present, widely disputed, Marine Corps Air Station (MCAS) Futenma on the island of Okinawa. If that were to occur, presumably the airstrip would be reconditioned and upgraded. The island is completely flat and could easily be converted to a good airbase. Whether several thousands of young and single Marines would wish to live on this remote, isolated and almost uninhabited islet is another matter. But, for the moment, the talk of US base relocation is in a real paralysis. and the former agreement to move the Futenma Air Station to Okinawa's northern Marine Camp Schwab seems to have been put aside and forgotten.

3 YAKUSHIMA 屋久島

Bring your raincoat because the locals boast that in Yakushima (屋久島; Yaku-shima) "It rains 35 days a month." In fact, it is Japan's wettest place—and one of the wettest in the world with annual precipitation ranging from

Mageshima, a small, low-lying islet to the northwest of Tanegashima.

Yakushima Iwasaki Hotel.

Yakushima Airport.

5,000 to 10,000 millimeters (16–30 feet or 5–10 meters). For comparison, Mt Waialeale on Hawaii's Kauai Island, often cited as earth's wettest place, receives 39 feet (12,000 millimeters) per year. Rain or shine, Yakushima is considered one of Japan's most beautiful islands and it is a true nature-lover's destination. Over 90 percent of Yakushima is forested and a good percentage of the island has either been designated a UNESCO World Heritage Site or is a protected zone under Japanese law.

Geographically speaking, Yakushima is an almost perfectly round disc of an island, 16 miles (26 kilometers) in diameter and 195 square miles (505 square kilometers) in area. Its 82-mile (132-kilometer) circumference is entirely ringed by a road—and that's about the only road on the island for the interior is steeply mountainous and covered in forest. Count on at least three hours to encircle it by car and easily a whole day if you make a lot of stops along the way. As you drive, you will undoubtedly come across some Yaku monkeys (屋久猿 or ヤクザル; *Yaku-shima-zaru* or *Yaku-zaru;* Latin: *Macaca*

fuscata yakui), a type of macaque; and Yaku deer (屋久鹿; *Yaku-shika;* Latin: *Cervus nippon yakushimae*). There's an estimated 7,000 of each of them. Both are small and not afraid of people. In fact, the monkeys can be downright aggressive, so take care not to approach them too closely as they can viciously bite.

The population of the island is approximately 13,500. Administratively, Yakushima Town (屋久島町; Yaku-shima-chō) encompasses the entire island, but the largest settlement, which houses a good percentage of the population, revolves around Miyanoura Port (宮浦港; Miyanoura-kō). Miyanoura is on the island's northeast side.

There is frequent, daily, year-round ferry and hydrofoil services to both Kagoshima and Tanegashima. Kagoshima's about 80 miles (130 kilometers) due north and jetfoils take a little more than two hours if they don't stop at Tanegashima on the way. Ferries take twice as long, four hours, but are less expensive. For an additional cost, they can also transport your car, motorcycle or bike, which the hydrofoils cannot.

Arrival at Miyanoura Port by the Yakushima Ferry

Round-trip ferry services are available daily from Kagoshima. Travel time is four hours one way. In addition, there are a half dozen daily round trips on high-speed jetfoils. They only take two hours but cost about twice as much.

Tanegashima's southern end is only 12 miles (20 kilometers) across the Vincennes Strait (種子島海峡; Tanégashima-kaikyō) from Yakushima and ferries from Miyanoura Port go to both Nishinoomote, on Tanega's northern end, and Shimama in the south. Travel time is around two hours and one hour, respectively. Ferry services to Kuchinoerabujima, the last island in the Ōsumi's northeast group (which is the next island we'll discuss), located west of Yakushima Island, are also found at Miyanoura Port. These ferries take a little less than two hours. There are no jetfoils on this route. Service is not that frequent to Kuchinoerabu, only twice a week.

The Yakusugi Forest and Yakushima are visited by over 300,000 people a year and thus the local tourist infrastructure is well-developed. There are plenty of good small hotels, *minshuku* inns and restaurants in all price ranges. There are also several top deluxe luxury resorts on the island, but none are in Miyanoura. The largest resort hotel with golf facilities is the Yakushima Iwasaki Hotel (屋久島 いわさきホテル; Yakushima Iwasaki Hoteru) located on the southwest end of the island.

There are almost 40 *minshuku* inns in Miyanoura and there's a friendly tourist information desk right at the harbor when you arrive. If you don't already have an advance booking (probably not a good idea), someone at the desk can call and make a reservation for you. Although almost all *minshuku* always serve meals, there are also a number of restaurants in town as well as a couple of museums, environmental and cultural centers and other points of interest. Miyanoura is easily the best place to stay if you are looking for something to do in addition to hiking.

Yakushima's second largest village is located at Anbo (安房; Anbo), which surrounds Anbo Port (安房港; Anbo-kō) on the island's central eastern side. A few daily ferries and jetfoils also use this port to go to both Kagoshima and Tanegashima. There are approximately 25 *minshuku* in Anbo. If the over 60 *minshuku* in Miyanoura and Anbo are not enough for you, note that there are almost 80 more scattered about more or less equally in all of the many villages that ring Yakushima Island.

Lastly, if the 2–4 hour cruise to Yakushima seems too long, be aware that Yakushima has an airport (屋久島空港; Yaku-shima-kūkō).

Yakushika Deer (屋久鹿). Dark brown with a white tail, Yaku deer are most prevalent on the island's wild western side, especially along the Seibu Rindō (西部林道), the dramatic serpentine Western Forestry Road. The Yakushika is one of the world's smallest deer. A full-grown male only stands about 1–1.5 meters (3–4 feet) and weighs 30–45 kilograms (60–100 pounds).

Miyanoura-daké (宮之浦岳). Mt Miyanoura, Yakushima's tallest peak, is the southernmost point in Japan where snow falls.

Hirauchi Kaichuu Onsen (平内海中温泉). One of the nicest outdoor hot springs (*onsen*) on Yakushima, all that's required is a small 100 Yen contribution.

Depending on the time of year, there are between five and ten round-trip flights a day. Most are from Kagoshima, but there are also flights from Fukuoka and Ōsaka. Flying time to or from Kagoshima is 30 minutes. The airport lies midway between Miyanoura and Anbo, about 6 miles (10 kilometers) from either of them.

There are not too many places in Japan that have been designated as UNESCO World Heritage Sites, but Yakushima's warm temperate Yakusugi Forest is one of them and, in fact, was Japan's first. Yaku Island's dense, verdant green forests contain some of the largest and oldest species of Cryptomeria (屋久杉; *Yaku-sugi*; Latin: *Cryptomeria japonica*) in the world. The term Yakusugi generally refers to large Japanese cedars that are more than 1,000 years old and grow in the mountains usually 1,640 feet (500 meters) or more above sea level. Though called cedar trees both in English and Japanese, sugi are taxonomically unrelated to that group. One giant specimen, the Jōmon-sugi (縄文杉) is tree-ring dated at over 2,000 years. Former reports of it being over 7,000 years old, and thus making it earth's oldest living thing, have now been discounted.

The Jōmon-sugi is 83 feet (25 meters) tall and has a circumference of 53 feet (16 meters), making it the largest conifer in Japan. The sugi is Japan's national tree. Perfectly straight, giant Cryptomeria beams are the favored wood for *torii* gates. If properly protected, the wood never rots. Two of the most spectacular specimens from this island and forming a great *torii* are at the entrance to the Buddhist temple and Shinto shrine at Asakusa (浅草) in Tokyo (東京; Tōkyō).

In addition to the sugi trees, another plant found in abundance and in giant proportions is the rhododendron. For fans of the king of all evergreen shrubs, the magnificent spring bloom-viewing is unparalleled. In Yakushima's climate, rhododendrons are not merely shrubs, they are trees, many with trunks over a foot thick and heights of 33 feet (10 meters).

For the most part, viewing the trees will require some hiking. The island's interior is extensively marked with trails and this is the number one outdoor activity for most visitors. Some will also camp. Worth remembering is that Yakushima's climate is one of the wettest in the world. There are signs posted everywhere warning hikers to make sure that

Senpiro-no-taki (千尋の滝). With a vertical drop of 100 feet (30 meters), this magnificent waterfall flows from the Tainoko River in the southeast part of Yakushima. On the left side of the falls is a great slab of solid granite.

Okawa-no-taki (大川の滝). Also spelled Ohko-no-taki, Great River Falls has a height of some 80 meters, making it one of the tallest falls in Japan. It is located on the southwest side of the island, above Kurio village.

Yakushima Todai (屋久島灯台). Perched on the island's westernmost point of Cape Nagata (永田岬), the Yakushima Lighthouse is one of the most picturesque images of Yakushima.

hey have adequate foul weather gear and
a plan for their hike. Only designated trail
shelters may be used for overnights in the
mountains. These are free. A round-trip day
hike to the Jōmon-sugi, for example, requires
about ten hours, and that's through and over
mountains.

The island's tallest mountains, many of
which are over 5,900 feet (1,800 meters), are
mostly located at its center. The three highest
are appropriately known as San-daké (三岳;
lit. "Three Peaks"). These are Miyanoura-
daké (宮之浦岳) at 1,935 meters (6,350 feet),
Nagata-daké (永田岳) at 6,188 feet (1,886
meters), and Kurio-daké (栗生岳) 6,125 feet
at (1,867 meters).

If all this hiking has worn you out,
Yakushima has several ways to relax. There
are beaches and there are hot springs baths
(*onsen*) (温泉). One of the best *onsen* is right
on the ocean near Hirauchi, the Kaichuu
Onsen. That's on the southern coast. Very
close by is the Yudomari Onsen, also on the
ocean, and just a bit further to the east is the
Onoaida Hot Springs. On the island's northern shore, near Isso, you'll find the Ohura
Hot Springs, and between Miyanoura and
the airport you'll see signs for the Kusugawa
Onsen. In addition, the resort hotels all have
their own hot springs on their properties.

As for beaches, although Yakushima is not
known as a beach destination, and indeed
most of its coast is much too rocky and steep
for beach-goers, there are a few here and
there. Closest to Miyanoura is the beach at
Isso, not far from the Isso Lighthouse near
Cape Yahazu. Another relatively decent beach
is Kuriohama, near the village of Kurio in the
southwest of the island. It, along with nearby
Nakama and Sagoshino-hama beaches, however, could be closed if you're visiting during
the sea turtle egg-laying season. Yakushima's
most famous beach area—and it's most
famous sea turtle sites—are the beaches at
Nagata: the Inakahama and Maehama
Beaches. If there are warning signs posted,
you won't be able to walk on the beach due
to the sea turtles.

From Yakushima we have a choice of several different destinations for it is possible to
catch ferries outbound east to Tanegashima,
return north to Kagoshima, or continue west
to Kuchinoerabujima. Let's catch one of the
twice-weekly ferries to Kuchierabu (the same
island as Kuchinoerabujima, simply another
pronunciation and spelling of its name).

"Friendly" Yaku monkeys.

④ KUCHINOERABUJIMA 口永良部島

At its closest point, Kuchinoerabu (口永良部
島; Kuchi-no-érabu-jima, also commonly
referred to as Kuchi-érabu-jima) is only 7
miles (12 kilometers) northwest of Yakushima, but the ride on the ferry *Taiyo* from
Miyanoura Port takes about an hour and 45
minutes.

Kuchinoerabu's port is at Kanagatake
(金岳; Kanaga-také), which is adjacent to
the largest island village of Honmura (本村;
Honmura), where there are three *minshuku*.
In each of the island's other three tiny villages
there are one or two more *minshuku*. The
total population of all the villages is about
140 and it's said that the local junior high
school has two students. It's a very small
island with twin volcanoes side by side, fairly
centrally located on the island's main section.
The volcanoes are the reason most people
come to Kuchinoerabu.

The island is oddly shaped and a little hard
to describe, but it's almost two islands in one.
One is small, about 1 by 3 miles (1.5 by 5
kilometers) and the other larger, about 3
by 12 miles (5 by 7 kilometers). They are
connected by a half mile-wide isthmus. The
island's circumference is 30 miles (48 kilometers). Much of the surface of the island is
covered in lava beds and volcanic debris.
It's a rugged place. Where it's not buried by
lava fields, it is sometimes referred to as the
"Green" volcanic island as its other sections
are lushly covered with vegetation. A decent
road encircles and connects all the island's
several villages, so it's easy to get around. In
fact, to climb to the volcanoes, it's less than a
half mile from the main circle-island road.

As for that climb, take an experienced
guide. One of the last victims not to do so was
University of Wyoming professor and poet

Aerial View of Kuchinoerabujima
The twin craters/peaks of Furu-daké and Shin-daké are at the center, the road is just below, while the harbor is visible at top left.

Craig Arnold. A well-known author and experienced in volcanoes, he was visiting the island in April 2009, doing research for an upcoming book. He disappeared and has never been seen since. It's assumed that he had a fatal fall into one of the craters. Kuchierabu is completely dominated by the twin peaks of 2,130-foot (649-meter) tall Mt Furu (古岳; furu-daké, meaning "old peak") and 2,155-foot (657-meter) Mt Shin (新岳; shin-daké or "new peak").

If you like *onsen* (and who doesn't), the entire island is really an underground bubbling cauldron of volcanic activity, and there are a number of *onsen* sprinkled around the island. Several nice ones are the Yumugi Hot

What Exactly is a Volcano?

The Japanese word for volcano is *kazan* (火山). Our word comes from the Latin *vulcanus*, the mythological Roman god of fire and the use of fire. He is the patron of blacksmiths, the arts of metallurgy (including the manufacture of arms and jewelry) and trades related to ovens (cooks, bakers and confectioners). His forge was underneath Sicily's Mt Etna. For a wife, Jupiter gave him Venus, the goddess of love, beauty, sexuality and fertility, but not faithfulness. Every time Venus was fooling around, usually with Mars, Vulcan became enraged and beat the red hot metalworks in his forge with such force that fire, smoke and ash rose up and caused a volcanic eruption. Now, if that explanation's not good enough for you, how about volcanoes are ruptures in the earth's surface that allow gas, ash, lava, pumice, magma—all sorts of pyroclastic debris—to escape, often with extraordinary force. Volcanoes are usually, though not always, found where the earth's tectonic plates are diverging or converging. Technically, there are many types of volcanoes but the most well known and the most dangerous, are "stratovolcanoes." Japan's Mt Fuji and Sakurajima and Italy's Mt Vesuvius and Etna are classic examples. To volcanologists, the distinctions among active, dormant and extinct volcanoes are virtually meaningless. All volcanoes, given enough time, can potentially explode. What scientists watch for are the warning signals a volcano may give: its activity, smoke, earthquakes, lava flows, etc. Pictured below is 3,776-meter (12,388-feet)-tall Mt Fuji or Fuji-san (富士山), Japan's greatest volcano.

Springs near Yumugi Port, Nemachi Onsen near Nemachi Village and the Nishino Hot Springs, which are the closest to Kuchierabu Port. Relaxing in hot volcanic springs is the other reason that people come to the island.

The Northwestern Group

The three islands of Takeshima, Iōjima and Kuroshima are often called by their collective geographic name, the Mishima Islands (三島列島; Mishima-rettō), which appropriately means "three islands." A fourth islet, Shōwa Iōjima, is a relative newcomer. Literally an upstart, it popped up out of the ocean in 1934 as a result of an undersea volcanic explosion. It is uninhabitable. Mishima, the political entity, is the Japanese administrative district encompassing the three populated islands. It more formally is called Mishima Mura (三島村 Mishima-mura; *mura* means "village"). The total population of the village is about 400, spread out over a three-island area of a little more than 12 square miles (31 square kilometers) in total.

There's not a lot of traffic to these islands and there is no commercial air service, though there is an airstrip on Iōjima which can be used by charter aircraft and emergency evacuation flights. The usual mode of transport is the ferry *Mishima* (みしま), also known as the "M" Line, which makes the trip from Kagoshima three times a week. The regular departure time is 9:30AM although on certain days it is 8:30AM, so you must double check.

The sailing distance to the first destination of Takeshima is 60 miles (94 kilometers) and travel time from Kagoshima is not quite three hours. There's a 20 minute discharge and reboard time at Takeshima and then it's only 9 miles (14 kilometers) and a quick 25 minutes to Iōjima, arriving around 1:00PM. After a 20-minute stop, from Iōjima it's another 22 miles (35 kilometers) and one hour to the island of Kuroshima and its first eastside port, Ōsato. After the usual 20-minute unload/reload, the ship departs for the brief 5-mile (8-kilometer) 20-minute sail to Kuroshima's second port, Katadomari, on the island's west side. It usually arrives about 3:00PM.

Thus, the sequence is Kagoshima → Takeshima → Iōjima → Kuroshima (two ports), where the ship overnights. In general, two times a week, the next day, she reverses the journey, starting from Katadomari →

then Ōsato → Iōjima → Takeshima → and finally Kagoshima. Sailing times are roughly similar except that on the return journeys the M Line starts the day around 8:00AM and arrives back in Kagoshima around 1:30PM. In general, on one out of the three weekly sailings, the ship waits two days before making the return journey. Therefore, pay attention to the ferry schedule on your days of travel. It's easy to confuse it and find yourself stuck an extra day.

Note that with this ferry schedule, unless you've got your own watercraft, or you hire a local fisherman (which is not difficult to do, but very expensive) or are a real good swimmer, visiting each island means staying there at least one overnight, if not a couple of days. That's not generally a big problem as there are a couple of *minshuku* on each island and after all, it's why you came out here.

There's really no other way off these islands once you've landed. And there are no other public services on any of the Mishima Islands: no taxis or buses, no rental cars, no scooters or bikes, and no banks or ATMs, so bring adequate cash. You'll probably eat at your *minshuku* as almost all include meals in their daily rates. Most visitors come to snorkel or dive, soak in *onsen* or just hike and peacefully relax. There are some rather obscure ties to very ancient Japanese history but these will be of interest mostly to Japanese nationals and historians.

⑤ TAKESHIMA 竹島

Takeshima (竹島; Také-shima), whose name translates as "Bamboo," is quite a small island and is infrequently visited. Its most recent census listed the population at 83 residents. It is said that there is a larger number of cows. The island's overall shape is that of a well-formed rectangle, not quite 2.5 miles (4 kilometers) long and less than a mile (about 1 kilometer) wide, but with an extension running out of the island's southwest point to Cape Ombozaki (オンボ崎; Ombo-zaki). Altogether, this gives the island an area of 1.6 square miles (4.20 square kilometers). Its circumference is 8 miles (13 kilometers). Takeshima's relatively long, narrow neck plus an approximate 1,640 feet (500 meters) triangular protuberance in the middle of its northern shore, combine to give it a rather unusual shape, somewhat resembling that of a hummingbird or maybe a mosquito.

The approach to the triangular-shaped, cliff-ringed Takeshima or Bamboo Island.

The port is on the north shore, sandwiched into a natural bay partially formed by the northern triangular cape. It's a small port, more a dock than anything else, with a few buildings and a cement factory. The port is used by the thrice weekly *Mishima* ferry out of Kagoshima. That schedule is described above. Just up the hill from the port is a very small village, the only habitation on the island. There are two *minshuku* in Takeshima village. As is almost always the case on these small islands, their owners will meet you at the harbor on arrival and they include all your meals in their nightly rates.

Although there are no great mountains on Takeshima, it's not accurate to say that it is flat, Rather, is it elevated, with an overall height ranging from 165 to 720 feet (50 to 220 meters) above sea level at its highest point. For the most part, it is ringed by cliffs. There are no beaches.

There is one main road and it pretty well covers the island, running from end to end, east to west, with just a couple of short side branches. Takeshima is almost entirely covered in bamboo and there is no agriculture to speak of, only some cattle grazing in the north and east. Although there is not too much happening on Takeshima, the island does have its own natural beauty.

6 IŌJIMA 硫黄島

The name Iōjima means "Sulphur Island" but it should not be confused with the island of the same name where the heroic battle of World War II took place. That Iwōjima is about 870 miles (1,400 kilometers) to the east of Okinawa in the Pacific Ocean, approximately 745 miles (1,200 kilometers) due south of Tokyo, roughly midway between Tokyo and the US Mariana Islands and Guam.

There are a number of small islands in Japan that bear the name Iōjima, Iwōjima, Iwōtō or Iōtō. They are simply alternative spellings of the same Kanji characters (硫黄島) and all are named for the same reason: they are all "sulphur" (that is, volcanic) islands. They are merely spelled differently in English depending on the transliteration of the Kanji which, of course, is always the same. Thus, for example, Iōjima,

Bamboo forms a picturesque backdrop to Takeshima's cement plant and dock.

Iwojima and Ioujima are all correct. In point of fact, the name of "Iwo Jima" of epic World War II fame was officially changed by Japan in 2007 to the English language spelling and pronunciation of Iōtō, *tō* simply being yet another variant of "island" (島), along with *jima* and *shima*.

Like its more famous namesake, this Iōjima (硫黄島; Iwō-jima), which is also called Mishima Iōjima, Satsuma Iōjima and Tokara Iōjima to help distinguish it from the other Iōjima, is a tiny place. It's about 2 by 4 miles (3 by 6 kilometers) in width and length, which translates to a total land area of a little under 5 square miles (12 square kilometers) and a circumference of a tiny bit over 12 miles (20 kilometers). A recent report put the island's population at 142.

Iōjima is served by the thrice weekly "M" Line ferry from Kagoshima. Usually, for each day that there is a drop of passengers and cargo on the westbound sailing, the following day the ship returns sailing eastbound back to Kagoshima. However, on one sailing per week, there is a two-day delay between the drop and the return. The ferry schedule is more fully described at the beginning of this section on the northwestern group of Mishima Islands.

Essentially, Iōjima is one highly active 2,310-foot (704-meter)-high volcano, Mount Iō (硫黄岳; Iō-daké; lit. "Sulphur Peak"), which is centered on the island's larger east

The sulphur-colored waters of Iōjima's port.

side, and a little village and port (硫黄島港; Iōjima-kō), which is about as far away on the other side of the island as possible. When visiting Iōjima, you almost can't miss witnessing some kind of volcanic activity out of Mount Iō for Sulphur Peak is always erupting, spewing clouds of sulphur dioxide into the air and iron and sulphur into the ocean through various underwater vents. The sea around the island is permanently colored in striking shades of ochre, from yellow-orange to red-brown. This is particularly noticeable in the harbor because the waters there are partially contained by the tsunami barriers. At the port's entrance, you'll see the end of marine-blue ocean waters and the abrupt transition to the island's sulphur-colored waters. It's quite dramatic.

Iōjima is a particularly beautiful small island with a fair amount of things to do or see. It is mountainous, covered with lush vegetation, surrounded by sulphur waters

The "M" Line serves the three Mishima.

The entrance to Iōjima harbor.

The Shintō Shrine in Iōjima village.

and sports a fabulous open-air *onsen*. The port village, which is the only settlement on the island, is neat, clean and quaint. There are five *minshuku*. All serve meals with their accommodations as there are no restaurants or other services on the island. If you bring your vehicle (car or motorcycle), bring it with a full tank of gas because there is no filling station on Iōjima. There is one small shop that carries some basic essentials like laundry soap and instant ramen noodles.

The main sight in town is a small and peaceful Shintō Shrine (硫黄神社). It's set off a bit, surrounded by trees and separated from the rest of the world, as is customary, by a *torii* gate. Its calm and contemplative atmosphere is only occasionally interrupted by the screeches of magnificent wild peacocks (クジャク; *kujaku*), which roam wild everywhere on Iōjima. Let loose some years ago, they have thrived. Remarkably, a large percentage of

these extraordinary birds are pure white. There are so many that Iōjima could just as accurately be called Peacock Island instead of Sulphur Island.

Because Iōjima's massive volcano Mt Iō occupies so much of its land area, and because the volcano blocks passage to Iōjima's eastern end, there is no road that encircles the island. All roads essentially begin and end or revolve around the port town. The lack of a circle-island route, however, in no way subtracts from an otherwise excellent little network of roads going to almost every corner of the island. For instance, the road leading from town to the island's northeasternmost tip first passes through a deliciously scented stretch of citrus grove, then a bamboo forest sheltering a hidden Shintō Shrine (a short hike off the road), then a now forbidden wild road (too dangerous) that twists and turns almost to the top of Iō peak, then to

Mount Iō at left and its little sister and new neighbor, Shōwa Iōjima, at right.

Higashi Onsen and Higashi-no Tatigami-iwa.

The natural "emergency" port of Ōura.

the Sakamoto Onsen (坂本温泉; Sakamoto-onsen) and finally ends at the Heike Castle Ruins site (平家城跡; Heike-jō ato). All this in the space of 3 miles (5 kilometers)! Incidentally and unfortunately, the Sakamoto outdoor hot springs are no longer operative. Their underground source stopped or became diverted and they've been abandoned for now. It's perfectly conceivable that Mt Iō's boiling waters could return to Sakamoto again some day.

Fortunately, there's another free outdoor hot springs on Iōjima, and this one is even more beautiful. Here, you follow the road out of town, at first through the same orange tree groves but then southeast past an observation platform where you can see Kuchinoerabu, Yakushima and Tanegashima Islands, then a little further following the signs to the Higashi Onsen (東温泉; Higashi-onsen; lit. "Eastern Hot Springs"). It's a total

of 5 miles (3 kilometers) from the port to the *onsen*, not including the little side branch off to the Observation Platform.

Higashi is an open-air boiling spring located at the foot of Mount Iō volcano and right on the seashore. Try soaking here. Most likely you'll have the pools completely to yourself as there's usually no one else around. The air, sea and sky are crystal clear. A sunset or a star-filled night sky, melting in a bubbling hot pool on the ocean, is about as a romantic and soothing experience as one can ever have. In other words, it just doesn't get any better than this.

The large upright rock just offshore is Higashi-no Tatigami-iwa or "Eastern Standing God Rock." We'll describe it below.

There are two more interesting scenic, though shorter, drives or hikes on Iōjima. They are west of town. Both start on the road that leads due north from the port straight up the hill behind town. Once you've crested the hill, continue west past the lighthouse. You'll be on top of the island's plateau, surrounded by pasture land full of black cattle, horses and peacocks. Quickly enough, less than a mile (2 kilometers) from town, you'll come to the airstrip. It was possible to build an airstrip on Iōjima as this natural plateau is just large enough to handle small aircraft landings and take-offs. As mentioned earlier, even though it looks pretty lonely, it's not been abandoned. The strip and control tower are maintained and are used by charter aircraft and for emergency air evacuations.

If you backtrack just a bit and then continue west a little less than a mile (1 kilometer) beyond the airstrip, you'll reach the western end of the island. It's a high bluff, and on a clear day you can see almost exactly 19 miles (30 kilometers) to the last of the Mishima, the "black" island or Kuroshima.

Where the road ends, a long descent on a set of at least 100 steps begins. This takes you down to Oura Port (大浦港; Ōura-kō), a small natural port used as a typhoon emergency harbor. Interestingly enough, the clear waters of this extremely well-sheltered port are home to a multitude of tropical fish. Species like angels, box, puffer, batfish, clowns, butterflyfish, lionfish, moorish idols, tangs and triggerfish can be seen from the dock. Although there's no beach, it's an excellent place for a swim, even better perhaps for snorkeling. Speaking of beaches, other than the black sand beach at Iōjima's port, there are no beaches on this island. Its shoreline is completely rock or inaccessible.

The presence of these exotic, colorful tropical fish so far north—almost 375 miles (600 kilometers) from Naha, Okinawa—demonstrates just how powerful and far-reaching is the Kuroshio Current (黒潮; Kuro-shio; lit. "Black Tide" but often translated as "Japanese Current"). Starting from the tropical waters of the Philippines and Taiwan, then traveling north thousands of miles/kilometers on its way to the northern Pacific, it is comparable to the Atlantic Ocean's Gulf Stream. Its warm waters sustain tropical fish species and coral reefs further north than anywhere else in the world.

Our last drive or hike also begins in town, climbs the same hill as in the previous route, but after a mile (1.5 kilometers), shortly after the lighthouse and just before the turn to the airstrip, we'll take the road that veers to the left and follow it for another mile (1.5 kilometers) until its end. This 2-mile (3-kilometer excursion) takes us over the high bridge visible west from down at the port. It's so high and narrow it's a little scary but it takes us to an Observation Lookout at the very end of Cape Erabu (永良部崎; Erabu-zaki). We're on that long, narrow spit of land jutting out due south from Iōjima's harbor. The view is breathtaking. Below is the town and the sulphur waters of the port, while across to the east are the smoking slopes of Mount Iō.

We'll end our visit of Iōjima here by having a quick look at its two satellite islets, then we'll ferry onwards to Kuroshima.

SHŌWA IŌJIMA (昭和硫黄島; Shōwa-Iwō-jima). This tiny islet is Iōjima's little sister and "new" neighbor. Shōwa Iōjima is an uninhabited volcanic rock about a mile (2 kilometers) offshore from Iōjima's northeast coast. It was formed in the fall of 1934 as a result of an undersea eruption from Iōjima's volcano. The islet is an irregularly shaped oval, about 410 x 575 feet (125 x 175 meters)

Iōjima's Peacocks (硫黄島孔雀)

In nature, peafowl (male: peacock; female: peahen; juveniles: peachicks) are birds of the forest. They roost in trees but make their nests on the ground. They are foragers and omnivores, feeding on virtually all plants, seeds, insects, worms and small reptiles or amphibians. They generally travel in packs. Worldwide there are two species: the Indian Blue (*Pavo cristatus*), which is relatively common and breeds well, and the Burmese Green (*Pavo muticus*), which is rare and endangered. They are both members of the pheasant family. The white peafowl comes from a genetic mutation called Leucism. They are not albinos and do not have red eyes. Leucism is characterized by reduced pigmentation in the hair and skin of animals and humans. Unlike albinism, it is caused by a reduction in all types of skin pigment, not just melanin. It is rare in peacocks and other animals, but on Iōjima at least a quarter of the peafowl have it and are white.

Shōwa Iōjima, a new piece of terra firma that emerged in 1934.

wide from north to south and about 1,310 feet (400 meters) long from east to west. There is no public transportation service to the island. If you wish to visit, you'll have to hire a local fisherman to take you there.

HIGASHI-NO TATIGAMIIWA (東ノ立神岩; Higashi-no Tatigami-iwa). Here is yet another monolith of stone called "Standing God Rock" or, in this case, "Eastern" Standing God Rock. It is located 490 feet (75 meters) offshore from the nearby Higashi Onsen on Iōjima's southern shore. It is visible in the photograph of Higashi Onsen shown on page 35.

⑦ KUROSHIMA 黒島

The most distant of the Mishima mini archipelago, "Black Island" is sometimes said to be a "mini Yakushima" for it also an almost perfectly round, mountainous though not super tall lush and green island, only it is smaller than Yakushima. Kuroshima (黒島; Kuro-shima) ranges between 2.5–3.5 miles (4–5.5 kilometers) in diameter. Its area has been measured at 6 square miles (15.5 square kilometers) and its circumference 8 square miles (20 square kilometers).

There are two villages on the island, Ōsato (大里; Ō-sato) and Katadomari (片泊; Katado mari). Between them they have a total population of about 175. The thrice weekly ferry from Kagoshima stops at both villages. There are four *minshuku* in Ōsato and three in Katadomari.

It takes about five hours to reach Kuroshima as the ferry *Mishima* (the "M" Line) stops at Takeshima and Iōjima along the way. Westbound, coming from Iōjima, it first stops on Kuroshima's northeast side, at Ōsato. On most days the arrival time is scheduled for 2:25PM, although one day a week it is one hour earlier than that. After a 20-minute unloading and reloading of freight and passengers, the ferry continues for 20 minutes (5 mile/8 kilometers) to the

island's central west side, arriving just after 3:00PM at Katadomari, docking for the night.

The next morning (once a week, two days later), the "M" Line ferry departs Katadomari at 8:00AM and 20 minutes later makes its first 20-minute stop back at Ōsato. Departing there at 8:40AM, it continues on its eastbound journey for one hour (23 miles/37 kilometers) to Iōjima, arriving at 9:40AM. At 10:00AM, it departs and sails 25 minutes (9 miles/14 kilometers) to Takeshima. A 10:45AM departure and an almost three-hour sail north (58 miles/93 kilometers) brings the *Mishima* back to Kagoshima at 1:35PM, altogether taking about five and a half hours.

Kuroshima Island's name "black" refers to the black volcanic soil, and black sand and black basalt rock beaches, found here. As for "beaches," they're really nonexistent. Almost entirely, the island's 12-mile (20-kilometer) circumference is ringed by steep cliffs and a narrow rocky coastline. Although it must be said that the island's strong suit is not beaches, it can be said that it is good for hikers. Because the mountains are not exceptionally tall, Kuroshima is criss-crossed and encircled by a number of good roads and paths. The island's central highlands section has a half dozen peaks ranging in height from 1,837-feet (560-meter) Mt Eboshi (鳥帽子山; Eboshi-yama) to 1,936-feet (590-meter) Mt Yokodake (横岳山; Yoko-daké yama) to 2,041-feet (622-meter) Yagura Peak (櫓岳; Yagura-daké).

Virtually every section of Kuroshoma is accessible to hikers, bikers, motorcyclists or drivers. It's a very pleasant and scenic island on which to get around, all 6 square miles (15 square kilometers) of it.

That wraps up our coverage of the Mishima Group and of the Ōsumi chain. From here, we'll return to Kagoshima and wait for the next Monday or Friday night departure of the *Tokara*, the ship that will take us to the Toshima group of islands, otherwise known as the Tokara Archipelago.

Chapter 2

THE TOKARA ISLANDS 吐噶喇列島
Remote isles, volcanic peaks

1 **Kuchinoshima** 口之島
2 **Kogajajima** 小臥蛇島
3 **Gajajima** 臥蛇島
4 **Nakanoshima** 中之島
5 **Tairajima** 平島
6 **Suwanosejima** 諏訪之瀬島
7 **Akusekijima** 悪石島
8 **Kojima** 小島
9 **Kotakarajima** 小宝島
10 **Takarajima** 宝島
11 **Kaminoneshima** 上ノ根島
12 **Yokoatejima** 横当島

The Tokara Islands (吐噶喇列島 or トカラ列島; Tokara-rettō, also called Shichi-tō (七島), which means "Seven Islands," consists of 12 very small islands scattered across 100 miles (160 kilometers) of Japanese waters between the northeastern group of the Ōsumi's and the Amami's northernmost and largest island, Amami-Ōshima. Seven islands are inhabited, five are not. The group is also commonly called the Toshima Islands (十島; Toshima-mura) although that name is more properly applied to the Japanese administrative district, which is the village of Toshima.

Toshima means "ten islands," a reference to the former administrative union of the present seven inhabited islands plus the Mishima, the three inhabited islands of the Ōsumi's northwestern group. Although the political boundaries were realigned some years ago, the name Toshima has stuck. The total area of all 12 islands of the present Tokara group is 39 square miles (100 square kilometers). The population of all the Tokara Islands combined is about 650, which averages some 30–170 people on each inhabited island. The largest island in the group is Nakanoshima. It has an area of 13 square

miles (34 square kilometers) and a population of about 170.

By and large, the islands of the Tokara group are infrequently visited. Inter-island traffic primarily consists of residents on shopping trips to Kagoshima, "mainland" fishermen pursuing a few days of new waters, and adventurous travelers seeking uncrowded hot springs (*onsen*). What little settlement there is consists of fishing villages and some limited sugar cane farming and cattle raising. There are no commercial flights to any of the Tokaras, although there is an abandoned airstrip on Suwanosejima. In general, the islands can only be reached on the twice weekly service of the Tokara-Toshima ferry (フェリーとしま; Ferie To-shima).

Here's how it works. The Tokaras are roughly aligned in an arc from the northeast to the southwest and are clustered into several lesser groups. Year round, at 10 minutes before midnight every Monday and Friday, except during bad weather, the ferry departs Kagoshima on its 125-mile (204-kilometer) overnight journey to Kuchinoshima, the most northerly of the Tokara Island group, about 40 miles (60 kilometers) southwest of Yakushima and Kuchinoerabujima. Kuchinoshima is at the top of the first and largest Tokara cluster of seven islands. The ferry arrives there a little more than six hours later, at 6:05AM. Fifteen minutes afterwards, at 6:20AM, the ship is underway on its 11-mile (18-kilometer) journey southwest to the next island, Nakanoshima, arriving at 7:10AM. There's no reason to stop at either Kogajajima or Gajajima, the pair of uninhabited islets 14 and 19 miles (22 and 30 kilometers) due west, but you'll see them off in the distance if the sky is clear.

After passengers and cargo have been unloaded and reloaded at Nakanoshima, the ferry departs at 7:30AM for Tairajima, about

The Tokara Islands

20 km
10 miles

East China Sea

Kuchinoerabujima
口永良部島

ŌSUMI ISLANDS
大隅諸島

Yakushima
屋久島

204 km · North to Kagoshima

30° N

130° E

Kuchinoshima
口之島

Mt Mae
前岳 ▲ ▲ Mt Yoko
横岳

18 km

Gajajima
臥蛇島 ▲

Mt Ontake
御嶽山

Mt Mitake
御岳山 ▲

Nakanoshima
中之島

Kogajajima
小臥蛇島

35 km

Mt Ontake
御嶽山

Tairajima
平島 ▲

Mt Ontake
御嶽山

18 km ▲

Suwanosejima
諏訪之瀬島

20 km

Mt Ontake
御嶽山

Akusekijima
悪石島 ▲

Mt Naka
中岳

37 km

Kotakarajima
小宝島

Kojima
小島

KAGOSHIMA PREFECTURE
鹿児島県

14 km

Takarajima
宝島 ▲

Mt Imakira
イマキラ岳

29° N

PACIFIC OCEAN

Kaminoneshima
上ノ根島

90 km

Yokoatejima
横当島

AMAMI ISLANDS
奄美群島

Naze Port

Kikaijima
喜界島

Amami-Ōshima
奄美大島

129° E

130° E

The western approach to Kuchinoshima on the ferry.

The *Tokara*, lifeline of the Tokara Island group.

There's no extra charge for the common area tatami-style sleeping rooms on the *Tokara* but it is possible to upgrade to private cabins with either two or four berths.

Treasure Island (1911 Edition)
This classic edition was published by New York's C. Scribner's Sons. The cover and its illustrations were by Newell Convers Wyeth (1882–1945), one of America's greatest illustrators and the father of Andrew Newell Wyeth (1917–2009) and grandfather of Jamie Wyeth (1946–). It would be quite a treasure to own this edition.

Tamoto Lily (*Lilium nobilissimum*)
Of the more than 200 genera called *Lilium* found within the Liliaceae family, and the more than 2,000 species of lily, a good number originate in the Ryūkyū Islands where they are called *yuri* (百合). One, in particular, comes from the volcano island of Kuchinoshima, an indigenous white lily known as Tamoto Yuri. It has very fragrant pure white, funnel-shaped flowers with bright yellow pollen on the inside and green shading on the outside.

19 miles (30 kilometers) southwest, arriving at 8:50AM. After a ten-minute stop, at 9:00AM, it's 9 miles (15 kilometers) southeast to Suwanosejima, arriving about 9:50AM. Passengers and cargo are again discharged and boarded. Departing at 10:00AM, it takes a little less than an hour to sail the 12 miles (20 kilometers) due south to Akusekijima, with the arrival time usually about 10:50AM. Akusekijima is the last island in this little Tokara subgroup.

Quickly enough, at 11:00AM, the ship is underway again, now a long 22 miles (35 kilometers) southwest to the next little cluster of three islands, starting with Kotakarajima, where arrival is scheduled for 12:20PM. The ship bypasses tiny uninhabited Kojima just over a mile (2 kilometers) before reaching Kotakara Island. At 12:30PM, from Kotakara-jima it's 9 miles (14 kilometers) southwest to the last island in this subgroup, Takarajima, arriving at 1:05PM. The trip takes altogether about 13 hours from departure at Kagoshima the previous evening.

If the ship departs from Kagoshima on the Friday sailing, it will dock at Takara on Saturday afternoon, stay there the remainder of the day and over night until 7:15AM Sunday morning. Then it will depart north-bound, make all the same Tokara Island stops in reverse and arrive back in Kagoshima at 8:30PM the same day. If, however, the ship departs Kagoshima southbound on the Monday sailing, it will first make all the same ports of call described above and likewise arrive at Takarajima at 1:05PM the next day, which in this case is Tuesday. But rather than docking and spending the night, after a 15-minute stop, at 1:20PM, the ship will depart and continue due south another 56 miles (90 kilometers) to Nazé, the principal city of Amami-Ōshima, the northernmost and largest island of the Amami-shotō. About midway along the way, and approximately 25 miles (40 kilometers) to the west, lies the final cluster of Tokara Islands— the two uninhabited volcano isles of Kaminoneshima and Yokoatejima. They are too far away to be seen from the ferry.

This last leg of the cruise is three hours and arrives in Nazé at 4:20PM, Tuesday. Here the ship moors and stays until 4:00AM Wednesday morning. Then it will depart northbound, sailing three hours to arrive back at Takarajima at 7:00AM. From there, starting at 7:15AM, the ship will make all the

same Tokara Island stops in reverse, arriving back in Kagoshima at 8:30PM Wednesday evening. Late Friday night, two days later, the cycle begins all over again. Note that the only day the ship is at rest is Thursday. This day is a catch-up for weather and any other delays that have interfered with the normal weekly schedule. By the way, this schedule has not changed in over ten years. As the saying goes, if it ain't broke, don't fix it.

As for these dozen islands, although to the casual observer it may seem as though one is more or less the same as another, that's not true. Every island is a little different and each has its own special attraction. Some, like Suwanosejima, have active volcanoes. Others, like Nakanoshima, have good *onsen*. Yet another will have a good beach or a coral reef for diving or snorkeling. And some, like Tairajima, will have some historical ties to ancient Japan. Akusekijima is the island of the mask god Bozé and each summer a festi-val is held there.

Each and every island is an individual and, like people, each is unique and special. Kotakarajima may be unusual merely because it is so small and yet inhabited. All the islands have sago palms and hibiscus flowers and stars and ocean. All have beauty. Finally, for dreamers, some believe that the coral island Takarajima, literally, "Treasure Island," is the spot on which Robert Louis Stevenson based his eponymously named novel.

☐1 KUCHINOSHIMA 口之島

The northernmost island of the Tokara group and the first stop on the semi-weekly ferry when sailing south out of Kagoshima is Kuchinoshima (口之島; Kuchi-no-shima). It's an irregularly shaped island, more or less a 2 by 3-mile (3 by 5-kilometer) rectangle but with an extra extension on its northern end. The port is located in the northwest in a natural bay formed at the junction of the island's main body and its northern exten-sion. Other than a cement plant, there's almost nothing to see at the port itself.

Just over the hill, beyond the port, there are two small villages, Nishinohama and Kuchinoshima, although it's difficult to tell where one ends and another begins. The total population is only about 160. There are three *minshuku* inns in town and a nice public bath. At the other end of the island, at its southeasternmost point, there's another *onsen*. It's outdoors and free.

Uninhabited Kogaja (left) and Gaja (right), the two "Lying Down Snake Islands."

Altogether, Kuchinoshima's area is a little over 5 square miles (13 square kilometers), with a circumference of a bit over 12 miles (20 kilometers). The Kanji character 口 (*kuchi*) means "mouth," a reference to the craters of several good-sized volcanoes on this island: Mt Mae (前岳; Maé-daké), with an elevation of 2,062 feet (628 meters), and Mt Yoko (横岳; Yoko-daké) at 1,647 feet (502 meters). Both are located near the center of the main body of the island. There's a good circle-island road that goes right around them and there are trails almost to the very top of both.

2 KOGAJAJIMA 小臥蛇島

This micro-sized uninhabited islet lies about 14 miles (22 kilometers) west of Nakanoshima. It is egg-shaped, about 1,640 feet (500 meters) wide from east to west and almost a mile (1.6 kilometers) long from north to south. Its name literally translates as "Little Lying Down Snake Island," which doesn't make it sound all that attractive. Maybe that's why it's not inhabited. Maybe JNTO (the Japan National Tourism Organization) should get to work on this and rename it, something like "Happy Island" or "Isle of Beauty and Peace." Why not? Years ago, the Bahamas renamed "Hog Island" as "Paradise Island" and look what it

did for that place. Neither Kogajajima (小臥蛇島; Ko-gaja-jima) nor Gajajima (臥蛇島; Gaja-jima) is inhabited or inhabitable.

3 GAJAJIMA 臥蛇島

Four miles (6 kilometers) further west from Kogajajima (19 miles/30 kilometers west of Nakanoshima) is Gajajima (臥蛇島; Gaja-jima) or "Lying Down Snake Island." It's Little Lying Down Snake Island's larger brother and is also uninhabited. It's roughly triangular in shape, less than a mile (1 kilometer) wide and 1.5 miles (2.5 kilometers) long from top to bottom. Ditto the renaming idea. There's a volcano on the island, Mt Ontake (御岳; On-také).

4 NAKANOSHIMA 中之島

As the ferry approaches, Nakanoshima (中之島; Naka-no-shima) looms, a green mountain floating on a blue sea. Popular with divers, it is ringed by coral reefs. The island, whose name translates as "Middle or "Central Island," is the largest in the Tokara group. It's about a 3 by 5-mile (5 by 8-kilometer)-shaped oval, except for a short protuberance on its southeastern side. It has a coastline circumference of 20 miles (32 kilometers) and an overall area of not quite 13 square miles (35 square kilometers). Around 170 people live on the island. Nakanoshima town and the port are located on the island's central west side. There are three *minshuku* in town but almost nothing at the port.

Only a mile (2 kilometers) or so to the north as the crow flies is the island's dominating feature—3,212-foot (979-meter)-tall Mt Mi (御岳; Mi-také), which is the highest peak in the Tokaras. There is a road that encircles the volcano, plus a small, extremely twisty road that goes almost to the caldera at the top. There are an additional two roads

Nakanoshima dock on the largest Tokara Island.

Dawn arrival at the symmetrical cone-shaped Nakanoshima.

hat start in town. One goes to the island's southeast corner, the other to the southwest nd. There's an unpaved road that connects hose two along the southern coast. It's pretty rugged but drivable.

Incidentally, there are many volcanoes and mountains in Japan that use 御 as their first character, including Nagoya's Mt Ontake (御嶽山; On-také-san), Japan's second highest volcano and eighth highest mountain at 10,062 feet (3,067 meters). It's located in Japan's northern "Alps" on Honshu main island. Another well-known volcano is Tokyo's Mt Mitake (御岳山; Mi-také-san) at 3,048 feet (929 meters). The Kanji character for the Mi-, O- and On- peaks is the same, 御, and carries the meaning "imperial" or "royal." It's only the pronunciation of the mountain's name that may be different. And speaking of that, the Kanji character that means peak, 岳, also has several pronunciations: *také* and *daké* are both used.

For hundreds of years, sulphur deposits were mined on Mt Mi but that ceased after World War II. What hasn't ceased are the hot springs flowing from the volcano. There are two hot springs near the port. The sulfurous, mineral-rich waters of Onsen Nishiku (西区) and Onsen Higashiku (東区) are open 24/7 and are clean and free.

There's also a free astronomical observatory, the Nakanoshima-tenmondai (中之島 天文台). It has the largest telescope in Kyushu, a 24-inch (60-centimeter) mirror. All that's required are reservations made with the telescope's keeper. Nakanoshima also has the Tokara Museum (歴史民俗資料館; Rekishi-minzoku-shiryokan), the only historical museum in the islands. It contains some interesting exhibits but the captioning is only in Japanese.

The island has an elementary and junior level school, with seven students at last count. Other than the school, *minshuku* inns, the baths and private homes, that's about all

you'll find. On Nakano Island, and on all the Tokara Islands, there are virtually no shops, no Family-Marts or 7-11s, no gas stations, no restaurants, bakeries, book stores or anything else—nothing! You usually won't even find vending machines because there is no one to restock them. Because it's so isolated, most people order and buy everything, including their groceries, from the stores in Kagoshima. Goods are delivered by the ferry service. Residents who own cars must purchase fuel in 200-liter drums which are likewise delivered to the islands. Throughout the Tokaras, the ferry is an indispensible lifeline to Japan and the outside world.

There are not too many places where you'll find the air cleaner and the skies clearer than at Nakanoshima Observatory.

Tokara horses roam wild at Cape Seri.

The port at Tairajima, the third inhabited island, is visible lower left. Dese rock is on the far right.

But, having said all that, perhaps this lack of "civilization" is the reason why you have come. For if you wanted to be on the Tokyo Ginza (東京銀座; Tōkyō-ginza), you'd be there. Rather, you're here, and here is a quiet, calm and peaceful natural beauty. In the southeast of the island, cultivated pastures spread out before you. You'll find Okinawan black cows, famous for their fine beef, and you'll see Tokara horses, a smaller breed than most. There are also goats. At the southeast land's end, you'll come to the Yaruse Lighthouse (ヤルセ灯台; Yarusé tōdai) at the end of Cape Seri (セリ岬; Seri-misaki) and there you'll look out over the vast and endless Pacific and perhaps think about the tiny space we each occupy, like the tiny space each of these islands occupies. And although tiny and seemingly insignificant, each of us on this great, large planet is significant.

HIRASE (平瀬; Hirasé). There are not many named "satellite" islets in the Tokaras as most islands are small enough on their own. But here's one. It's really tiny, a little oval about 490 by 275 feet (150 by 250 meters) planted right at the bottom of Nakanoshima, a little less than a mile (1 kilometer) southwest of Cape Seri. Hirase's name literally means "flat stretch of shallow water ending at a sandbank" or, more figuratively, the "flat utmost tip of a cape."

A sign at the dock welcomes visitors to Tairajima.

5 TAIRAJIMA 平島

This is the third inhabited island in the middle of Tokara's first group of islands. It's quite small, only about 0.75 by 1.25 miles (1 by 2 kilometers), with an area of 0.08 square miles (2.08 square kilometers) and a circumference of 4.5 miles (7 kilometers).

At the most recent count, 84 persons were said to live on Tairajima (平島; Taira-jima; lit. "Flat Island"). They live in the only village which is located towards the center of the island. It's less than a mile (1 kilometer) north of the port where there is not much more than the dock. There are three *min-shuku* in town and there is a public bath at the village community center, Akahigé Onsen (あかひげ温泉). It's named after a popular local bird, the "red beard."

The island's high point is Mt On (御岳; On-také), which rises to 797 feet (243 meters). It is claimed that Tairajima has a rich historical background and that a number of monuments and historic places exist. But for most Western tourists, these are extremely obscure, lost in translation and the mists of time. There are several massive *gajyumaru* (banyan) trees on the island claimed to be over 1,000 years old.

DESE (出瀬; Desé). As small as Taira is, it's got a little sidekick. It's that large rock on the right-hand side of the photo of Tairajima on

page 44. Its dimensions are approximately 410 by 740 feet (125 by 225 meters) and it's separated from the bottom of Tairajima by only 80 feet (25 meters) of water. The rock's name translates as "out of a sandbank in a stretch of water that is visible at low tide." That's quite a mouthful from two little Kanji characters, but they can do that. Its context also has the meaning of something at the end of a cape.

6 SUWANOSEJIMA 諏訪之瀬島

The second largest island in the Tokara group by area, but one of the least populated, Suwanose Island is roughly an oval with dimensions a little larger than 3 by 5 miles (5 by 8 kilometers). It's not quite 10.7 square miles (28 square kilometers) in area and has a circumference of a bit more than 17 miles (27 kilometers). The population is 67. The island's high point is Mt Mitake (御岳; Mi-také; also pronounced On-také) at 2,621 feet (799 meters) above sea level.

The only inhabitable portion of the island is the extreme southern tip. Altogether it covers about a third of a square mile (1 square kilometer). It's the only section that's level enough for habitation. The rest of Suwanosejima (諏訪之瀬島; Suwanosé-jima) is too steep. On the east side of this small tip

The crater of Suwanosejima's Mt Mitaké.

Suwanosejima's volcano erupted a moment before this photo was taken.

is the modest port. It has no facilites and is merely a dock.

From the dock, a road leads up a slight hill and crosses over a plateau about three-quarters of a mile (1 kilometer) to the west side of the island, where the village lies. There are three *minshuku* here. About 1,640 feet (500 meters) to the south of the town is an airstrip. Suwanose is the only Tokara Island to have an airstrip although there are no flights! It was built some years ago when Yamaha Resorts was contemplating building a luxury resort on the island. Presumably, it might be used to airlift the residents in the event of a major eruption by Mitake. To the north of the village, a road runs about three-quarters of a mile towards the center of the island and the volcano. There are no other roads on the island. From the end of the road, a paved path leads another three-quarters of a mile towards the summit. Given Mitake's almost constant activity, great consideration should be given to the thought of climbing this volcano.

Mitake is one of the most active volcanoes in Japan—and the world. Essentially, apart from the settlement at the southernmost tip of Suwanosejima, the entire island is a volcano, one that's erupting in one manner or another every single day. Several of Suwanosejima's more recent dramatic seismic activities were in November 2008, when multiple explosions created ash plumes that rose 1.25 miles (2.4 kilometers) into the sky; and in October 2009, when a magnitude 6.9 earthquake occurred 34 miles (55 kilometers) southeast of the island. The island's largest recorded historical eruption took place in 1813–14, when it had to be completely evacuated. It remained unpopulated for the next 70 years.

7 AKUSEKIJIMA 悪石島

Akusekijima (悪石島; Akuséki-jima; lit. "Evil Stone Island") is the fifth and final inhabited island in this northern cluster of the Tokara-rettō. If you let your imagination run a bit wild, you might say that the shape of this small island is that of a headless, armless and legless torso. It's a little over 1 mile (2 kilometers) across from east to west, and about 2 miles (3 kilometers) from north to south. Altogether, it has an area of 3 square miles (7 square kilometers) and a circumference a bit more than 8 miles (13 kilometers). You'd have to run around the island's perimeter

The port at Akuseki forms a small bay.

Akuseki is surrounded by steep cliffs.

more than three times to complete a marathon. And that would be dangerous as Akuseki Island is encircled by steep cliffs. As is the case with most of the Tokara Islands, there are no beaches on Akusekijima.

The island's port is built into a natural inside elbow on the center west side of the island, which, with the addition of tons of sturdy Japanese concrete, forms a small bay. There's no village there, however. To reach town you travel up the hillside a little less than a mile (1 kilometer). Because Akuseki is fairly popular with adventurous Japanese travelers, it gets more visitors than most other Tokara Islands. Thus, there's a grand total of five *minshuku* on this island! The village is set on a plateau in the southwest corner of Akusekijima.

Akuseki has two fairly good-sized peaks: 1,916-feet (584-meter)-tall Mt Ontake (御岳; On-také) and 1,453-feet (443-meter) Mt Nakadake (中岳; Naka-daké), But as the whole island is relatively elevated, they don't particularly stand out. The population is about 75 and, like many of Japan's remote islands, has been gradually declining for years. Most young people today are simply not content with a sugar cane farmer's life or a fisherman's. Once they leave, they essentially never return. That's why on almost all the smaller Ryukyus, you'll see lots of old people, a few youngsters and not so many middle-aged. It's a real conundrum and is nowhere close to being solved.

It's difficult to say why the early peoples who named Akuseki decided that it was a "bad" or an "evil" stone island, but they did, and that's its name. Perhaps from an agriculturalist's point of view, it was just a rock and thus infertile. With its dramatic cliffs, it was also tough to approach. That sounds like a good reason to name it "bad," but "evil"?

In more recent times however, there was a terribly tragic event nearby Akuseki. Just offshore, on the night of August 22, 1944, the *Tsushima-maru* (対馬丸), an unmarked, unlit passenger and cargo ship, fully loaded with 1,484 evacuee civilians, including 826 schoolchildren, on their way to Kagoshima from Okinawa, was torpedoed by the USS *Bowfin*, an American navy submarine. Only 59 children survived. Everyone else perished. It's one of the uglier incidents in a terrible war and something that's not usually mentioned in US schoolchildren's history books. Not until 20 years after the sinking did the crew of the *Bowfin* learn of the victims. In Japan, the survivors were forbidden to speak of the incident. The *Bowfin* was decommissioned in 1954 and presently serves as a memorial and submarine museum in Pearl Harbor, Hawaii. The wreck of the *Tsushima-maru* was located and identified in December 1997. There is a small museum dedicated to the *Tsushima-maru* story in Naha, Okinawa.

Akusekijima has a couple of hot springs less than a mile (1 kilometer) north of the port, but the island is best known for its unusual Mask God Festival, held every year. The Bozé Matsuri (ボゼ祭) is dedicated to the island's mask god Bozé. It's a local variant of Japan's Bon festival, held each year on the 16th day of the 7th month on the traditional lunar calendar, which translates to sometime between August and September on today's Western calendar. The festival is a unique

Akusekijima Bozé mask gods.

Kojima's Most Common Residents
Typical on all the Tokara Islands are wild hibiscus bushes (*Hibiscus rosa-sinensis*) and the Red Helen butterfly (*Papilio helenus*), a type of black swallowtail.

and special event: the island's men dress up in bizarre costumes made of palm leaves, representing the masked god Bozé. Their dance is supposed to scare away the devils and bring in the New Year.

8 KOJIMA 小島

Kojima (小島; Ko-jima) is an uninhabited islet about three-quarters of a mile (1 kilometer) to the east of Kotakarajima, its big brother. The ferry does not stop, it just passes by on its way to Kotakara Island. Kojima's name, which most appropriately means "Little Island," is a fairly well-formed circle about 1,890 feet (575 meters) across when the tide's out. When the tide's in, that is during a high tide, only its central, vegetated core is above water. At those times, it would be an isle with a diameter of approximately 660 feet (200 meters). Kojima and its two "treasure island" neighbors to the west and southwest form a little subgroup of three 30 miles (50 kilometers) to the southwest of the first seven islands and an equal distance to the northeast of the final, tiny group of two uninhabited islets.

KOTAKARAJIMA 小宝島

As the ferry makes its way south, island to island, perhaps you might have mused that the previous inhabited island, Akusekijima, was indeed small, about 1.25 by 2 miles (2 by 3.5 kilometers) and, after all, how can anyone live there? Well, contemplate this: Kotakarajima (小宝島; Ko-takara-jima) is smaller. In fact, this island, whose name means "Little Treasure Island," is the smallest inhabited island in the Tokara Archipelago, measured both by population and area. As for people, the most recent population count was 37 inhabitants. As for size, the island is a little round circle just about exactly three-quarters of a mile (1 kilometer) in diameter.

Since one is such a nice easy number, let's figure out just how big (or small) this island really is. If you remember your high school geometry, the area of a circle is its radius squared times pi. For our purposes, *pi* (π) can be approximately 3.1416. The mathematical formula is: $A = r^2 \times \pi$. Therefore, since the diameter of Kotakara is three-quarters of a mile (1 kilometer), its radius is ½ or .50 of three-quarters of a mile (1 kilometer). One-half times one-half equals one-quarter

The southern port side of Kotakarajima, the smallest inhabited island in the Tokara Archipelago.

(½ x ½ = ¼ or .50 x .50 = .25). One-quarter times π equals 0.7854 kilometers (.25 x 3.1416 = 0.7854). Thus, Kotakarajima's area is a bit more than ¾ of a square kilometer. Euclid move over!

Expressed another way, 0.7854 square kilometers equals 0.3033 square miles or less than ¹/₃ of a square mile. By any means of reckoning, that's pretty small.

Here's one more calculation. The circumference of a circle is its diameter times *pi*, or expressed mathematically, C = d x π. It can also be expressed as C = (2 x radius) x π. Therefore, the circumference of Kotakara is three-quarters of a mile (1 kilometer) times π (1 x 3.1416 = 3.1416) or 3.1416 kilometers. In fact, the circumference of the island is a little bigger as it's not a perfect circle. Walking its slightly irregular shoreline measures 3 miles (4.5 kilometers); and similarly, its area is a bit closer to one full square kilometer. Like tiny uninhabited Kojima next door, Kotakarajima loses about one-quarter to one-third of its surface area twice a day during high tides. Therefore, the homes and other structures on the island are built on the higher ground, which is otherwise covered in year-round vegetation.

Kotakarajima is not particularly flat or low. Its high point reaches 338 feet (103 meters) above sea level, and most of the island is elevated. It's the island's 650-foot (200-meter)-wide outer rim that is bare, barren coral rock. That's the section that's washed over by the sea in very high tides.

Kotakara Island has a complete circle island road. Taking it from the port, which is on the island's southwest side, either clockwise or counter-clockwise, to the only village, which is on the island's northeast side, is also almost exactly three-quarters of a mile (1 kilometer). You just can't go too far on Kotakara. There are three *minshuku* in the village and a free hot spring natural bath. There's another small port on the island's northern side as well, but it's for small fishing craft, not the commercial ferry service. So, if you were looking for a getaway to a place that's not too big and not too busy, you might have found your type of place here.

⑩ TAKARAJIMA 宝島

On a southbound sailing out of Kagoshima, this coral, not volcanic, island is the last stop in the Tokaras. There are two more Tokara Islands to the southwest, but they are unin-

habited and no stops are made by the ferry. Takarajima (宝島; Takara-jima) is the seventh inhabited island and the ferry's final port of call in the archipelago. Again, depending on the sailing, the ship alternates its twice-weekly journeys with once a week overnight stops at Takara, reversing and returning to Kagoshima the next day, or once a week continuing to Nazé City on Amami Ōshima before reversing and sailing back to Kagoshima the next day. There is no airport on the island.

Along with Akusekijima, Takarajima is the most popular island of all the Tokaras for visitors. It has a few minor sights, some good hiking opportunities, a bit of historical lore and, unlike many Tokaras, a few beaches.

Unlike the circular-, rectangular-, egg- or torso-shaped islands previously visited in the Tokara group, Takara is a nicely formed triangle. Its Pacific (eastern) shoreline is just about 2 miles (3.2 kilometers) long and its northern top coastline is also approximately 2 miles (3.2 kilometers) across. The island's western to southwestern side, which faces the East China Sea, is 3 miles (5 kilometers) in length. All told, this gives the island an area of 2.75 square miles (7.14 square kilometers) and a circumference of 8.5 miles (13.77 kilometers). Takara Island's highest spot is Mt Imakira (イマキラ岳; Imakira-daké) at 958 feet (292 meters) above sea level. Takarajima also has several other peaks over 660 feet (200 meters), among them Mt Hiru (蛭岳; Hiru-daké), Mt Gonata (ごんた山; Gonata-yama), and "Goddess" Mountain, Mt Megami (女神山; Mégami-yama).

Exactly in the center of the northern shoreline is a good-sized natural harbor where the ferry lands, and only a few hundred feet up the road from the port is the island's only village. There are approximately

Approach to Takarajima.

The name Takarajima literally translates as "Treasure Island" and the few travel brochures one finds on the Tokaras usually make the claim that Takara was the inspiration, if not the actual burial place, of pirate's gold, believed to be at the center of Robert Louis Stevenson's work *Treasure Island*. The tourist information map displayed at the harbor where the ferry arrives states: "As the name Takarajima (Treasure Island) implies, there is a legendary story that says Captain Kidd once hid his treasures on this island. There is a limestone cave which is believed to be the place where treasures were hidden. This island has been visited by many explorers and bounty hunters from all over Japan and the world."

Great limestone cave and Kannon-dō shrine.

120 residents on Takara. The islanders are dependent mainly on fishing and seasonal tourism. There are four *minshuku* inns available for tourists. The town also has a free public *onsen* with separate facilities for men and women. The island is ringed and crisscrossed by a series of roads and virtually no place is inaccessible. You can even drive to the top of Imakira. There's a great observation platform and viewpoint up there.

The legend has it that Kidd and his men attacked Takarajima seeking food and cattle from the island's inhabitants. They were refused and as a result 23 of the pirates landed and burned the inhabitants alive in a lime cave. Afterwards, it is said that Kidd hid his treasure in the cave and never came back for it due to his execution in England. In real

"Treasure Island"—Takarajima?

Robert Louis Balfour Stevenson's (1850–94) *Treasure Island* was first published in 1883. It quickly became one of the most popular books for young people ever written. Its depictions of pirates and adventure, tales of buried gold, treasure maps marked with an X, and peg-legged, bloodthirsty seamen with parrots on their shoulders soon became archetypes of what it means to be a pirate. Stevenson was 30 years old when he started writing the book in the summer of 1881 while in the Scottish Highlands. Starting at an early age, and although sickly (he was believed to have suffered from tuberculosis), he traveled widely, including journeys to Europe, North America, Hawaii and many islands of the South Pacific. At the age of 44 he died and was buried in Samoa. There is no evidence to suggest that he ever visited, or indeed ever heard of, Takarajima. Rather, the most widely speculated upon contenders for his Treasure Island are Unst in Scotland's Shetland Islands, Norman Island or Dead-Man's Chest Island in the British Virgin Islands of the Caribbean, or Osborn, a small islet in Brielle, New Jersey's Manasquan River, where Stevenson once spent a month. Most scholars agree that it's probably Unst. The drawing of Treasure Island at right resembles that island and is thought to have been penned by Stevenson's own hand. It was published in an early edition of the book.

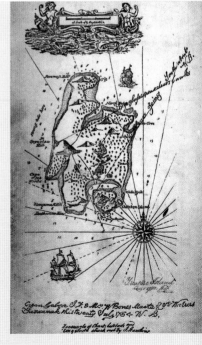

life, Captain William Kidd (ca. 1654–1701), a Scottish seaman and privateer, sailed the waters of Britain, the Bay of Fundy, New England, New York, the Caribbean, the Red Sea, the Indian Ocean and Madagascar. He was eventually tried in London for piracy on the high seas, convicted and hanged. His body was gibbeted—left to hang and decompose in an iron cage—over the River Thames for three years as a warning to other pirates and ne'er-do-wells.

So far as is known, William Kidd never sailed the waters of Japan—or anywhere in Asia for that matter. Therefore, it is doubtful that there is any truth to Takarajima's legend of Captain Kidd and his buried treasure. And although it is true that Robert Louis Stevenson spent a good part of his short life in the Pacific—he traveled in the South Pacific and died and is buried on the island of Samoa—he had no known association with any of the islands of the North Pacific or Japan. It is highly improbable, therefore, that he knew of this particular Treasure Island, Takarajima.

Whether the treasure stories were inspired by the limestone cave or whether the cave inspired the legends, or whether the mere coincidence of the name "Treasure Island" is behind the legends, it's hard to know, but in any case, Takarajima's Kannon-dō Cave (観音堂; Kannon-dō) is an interesting little spot and worth a visit. It's located a little over a mile (2 kilometers) from the village on the island's west side. There are several small shrines within the cave, including a Kannon-dō shrine. Note that the cave is also called "Dai shoun yuu-dō" (大鐘乳洞).

If the limestone cave doesn't impress you, you can walk about 985 feet (300 meters) down to one of Takara's beaches, this one over a mile (2 kilometers) long and encompassing virtually the entire mid-section of Takara's west coast. There are also a couple of small beaches on Takara's southeast and northeast shore, plus the island's best beach, the Ōkago bathing beach (大籠海水浴場; Ōkago-kaisui-yoku-jō), which is adjacent to the port. None of Takara's beaches are great, but they're modestly sandy and accessible, something that's not true on most of the other Tokara Islands.

For many visitors, Takara's big "sight" is the fanciful mural at the port. For one, you can't miss it when you arrive. It's a giant, wildly imaginative drawing that covers most of the cemented hillside. Whatever your take on the aesthetics, it has to be said that it's different.

The last sightseeing spot we'll mention is the island's final spot: the southernmost extremity, Cape Araki (荒木崎; Araki-zaki). Here, the triangular-shaped Tarakajima narrows down to its most acute angle. The road goes right to the end and then it's a short 300-feet (100-meter) walk to the Cape Araki Lighthouse (荒木崎灯台; Araki-zaki tōdai). From here, there's nothing but ocean on all three sides. And from there, it's open waters until our next archipelago—the Amami-shotō.

MUUTACHIIWA (舞立; Muu-tachi iwa). If you do go to the beach on Takarajima's west coast, near the Kannon-do cave and shrine, you'll see this little rock. It's only some 660

The mural on a cemented hillside at Takarajima's Maégomori-kō Port (前籠漁港).

The only way to visit Kaminoneshima and Yokoatejima is to sail, swim or paddle a kayak there. These isolated rocks are well off the regular shipping channels.

Yokoatejima's eastern half is a perfectly formed strato volcano, while its other side, connected by an isthmus, is a lava flow. Barely visible at the far right of the photo is Kaminoneshima.

feet (200 meters) offshore, about exactly midway along the west coast measuring from north to south. It's a little more than three-quarters of a mile (1 kilometer) south from the cave. Muutachi Rock is no big deal, only a green-covered rectangular islet about 330 feet (100 meters) long from east to west and approximately 100–130 feet (30–40 meters) wide from north to south.

FUCHI-NO HANARE (ふちのはなれ; Fuchi-no hanare). To get a little technical, Cape Araki, mentioned above, is not quite the very end of Tarakajima. These rocks are. Just offshore, just off the very end of the cape, lies this little collection of stones. From the Cape Araki Lighthouse you'll have to scramble over rock about 820 feet (250 meters) to the very end of the island. From there it's about 165 feet (50 meters) over water, south and a bit west, to this last piece of Treasure Island. It's not exactly one large rock. Rather, it's a fused collection of several. They're so tightly bound together, however, that it almost appears as one. The tiny islet is more or less an oval in shape, approximately 165 feet (50 meters) long and 80 feet (25 meters) wide.

11 KAMINONESHIMA 上ノ根島

Once a week the *Tokara* ferry sets sail from Takarajima and travels south 55 miles (90 kilometers) to Nazé, Amami-Ōshima's port and main city. The trip takes three hours. About halfway there, if you could change the ship's course and travel due west about 25 miles (40 kilometers), you would arrive at Kaminoneshima (上ノ根島; Kaminoné-shima) and its larger neighbor Yokoatejima.

Both are tiny volcanic islands and both are uninhabited. That's why the ferry doesn't go there. Since they're so far away, you won't, in fact, see them. Kaminone Island is the smaller and more northerly of the two. It's an oddly shaped rectangle with a number of little protrusions. The islet is about 1,640 feet (500 meters) across from east to west and almost three-quarters of a mile (1 kilometer) in length from north to south.

12 YOKOATEJIMA 横当島

Only 1.5 miles (2.4 kilometers) south of Kaminone Island is Yokoatejima (横当島; Yokoaté-jima), the most southerly of the islands in the Tokara chain. This uninhabited rock may also be the most unusually shaped islet in the Tokara-rettō. It resembles a sideways figure eight, with its eastern side about twice as large as its western. Forming two halves of an island, they are connected by a narrow 490-foot (150-meter)-wide isthmus. The larger half of the island is circular and about a mile (1.5 kilometers) in diameter. It is nothing more or less than a perfectly shaped volcano, with a crater dead center at the top. The western side of the island is somewhat of a squished box in shape, perhaps 2,620 feet (800 meters) at its longest in any direction.

Unless you have paddled out to these remote little isles, you more than likely have safely arrived in Nazé (Amami City) on the *Tokara* ferry. That's the starting place for our next group of Ryukyu Islands: the Amamis or the Amami-shotō. It's a particularly beautiful set of islands and, after coming from the Tokaras, will seem like Robinson Crusoe is indeed rejoining civilization.

Chapter 3

THE AMAMI ISLANDS 吐噶喇列島
Splendid vistas, rugged coasts

1. **Amami-Ōshima** 奄美大島
2. **Kakeromajima** 加計呂麻島
3. **Kikaijima or Kikaigashima** 喜界島
4. **Tokunoshima** 徳之島
5. **Iōtorishima** 硫黄鳥島
6. **Okinoerabujima** 沖之永良部島
7. **Yoronjima** 与論島

Compared to the previous Tokara Islands, most of the Amami Islands (奄美諸島; Amami-shotō) seem almost gigantic, though of course this is only relative. There are eight inhabited islands and several semi-inhabited or uninhabited ones worth mentioning. Starting from the north, the chain begins with Amami-Ōshima, the largest island in

Gangplank on to an "A" Line ferry.

the group, located 235 miles (375 kilometers) south of Kagoshima City, which is situated on mainland Japan's southernmost Kyushu Island. From there, the Amami chain stretches some 125 miles (200 kilometers) south to Yoron-tō, which lies just above the northern tip of Okinawa at Cape Hedo. Although geographically and geologically a part of the Ryukyu Archipelago, politically the Amamis are located in Kagoshima Prefecture, along with the Tokara and Ōsumi groups. Thus, on a map of Okinawa or, more specifically, of Okinawa Prefecture, you won't find them.

Culturally, the islands are quite distinct, being neither tropical Okinawan nor exactly the same as mainland Japan. Gravesites and tombs, for example, are in the style of the mainland and not the "turtleback" style of Okinawa. Yet, the Amami dialect of Japanese language is within the group of Ryukyuan languages, not mutually intelligible with Japanese nor, for that matter, with other Ryukyuan dialects. The "separateness" of the Amamis, as with most of the Ryukyu Islands, goes back hundreds, if not several thousands, of years and includes an eight-year occupation by the United States after World War II. The US returned control of the neighboring Tokara Islands in February of 1952 and the Amamis on December 25, 1953. It held Okinawa and the southern islands until 1972. Upon the Amamis' return to Japan, they became part of Kagoshima Prefecture.

The largest island in the Amami-shotō is Amami-Ōshima (奄美大島; Ō-shima literally means "Big Island"), and at approximately 38 miles (60 kilometers) in length is one of the largest islands in the Ryukyus. Its main city, formerly and still sometimes called Nazé (名瀬; Nazé) but now properly known as Amami City (奄美市; Amami-shi), is the transportation hub where most ferries and airline services are found.

The Amami Islands

The Amami Islands form a green and mountainous chain.

Amami-Ōshima's airport (奄美空港; Amami-kūkō) is located 14 miles (22 kilometers) northeast of Amami City. It takes 30–40 minutes to drive there from downtown. Amami is about a two-hour flight from Tokyo. From Osaka it's around one and a half hours and from Kagoshima a bit less than an hour. Flights from Okinawa also take less than an hour. By ship from Tokyo it's approximately 37 hours, from Osaka close to 30 hours and from Kagoshima about 12 hours. From Okinawa it's around 13 hours sailing time, including the several stops along the way. The Amami chain is especially well served by ferry service. Two shipping companies, the Marix and "A" Lines, serve the route. Alternating daily departures with a fleet of four great ships ensure that each

island on the route is visited twice daily (one northbound, one southbound), every day of the year, barring severe inclement weather. Here's how the service operates (both lines' scheduled departure/arrival times are within minutes of one another, so give or take 5–10 minutes from all the times stated as follows). Each day a ship departs at 7:00 AM from Okinawa's Naha Port (那覇港; Naha-kō) and heads two hours north along Okinawa's west coast, 35 miles (56 kilometers) to Motobu Port (本部港; Motobu-kō), near the end of the Motobu Peninsula, arriving at 9:00 AM. At about 9:15 AM, the ship departs and sails 50 miles (80 kilometers) north, about two and a half hours, to Yoron Island (与論島; Yoron-jima, almost always called Yoron-tō). Arriving around 10 minutes before noon, it departs about 12:10 after a 20-minute stop. The next port is Wadomari, 30 miles (48 kilometers) and about two hours later, at 2:00PM on the island of Okinoerabu (沖之永良部島; Oki-no-érabu-jima), where the ship loads and unloads for half an hour.

Departing Okinoerabu about 2:30PM, the ship continues 35 miles (56 kilometers) north, approximately two hours, to Tokuno (徳之島; Toku-no-shima), where it arrives at 4:30PM. The ferry discharges and reloads passengers and freight, taking about 30 minutes, then leaves at 5:00PM. The next leg is 68 miles (109 kilometers), about three and a half hours north, to Amami City, arriving at 8:30PM. Here, there's about a 45-minute stop for restocking. At 9:20PM the ship departs Nazé Port and sails 240 miles (384 kilometers) through the night, with no further stops, arriving at Kagoshima City at 8:30AM the next morning.

Sailing the route from north to south, each day a ship leaves Kagoshima Port at 6:00PM, arriving non-stop on Amami at 5:00AM the next morning. At 5:50AM, the ship departs Nazé for Tokuno and arrives at 9:10AM. Half an hour later, at 9:40AM, it departs for Okinoerabu, arriving at 11:30AM. The ship stops there for 30 minutes, then departs at 12:00 noon. An hour and forty minutes later, it arrives at Yoron-tō. Some 20–30 minutes later, at around 2:00PM, the ship sails approximately two and a half hours south to Okinawa's Motobu Port, arriving near 4:30PM. Loading and reloading there for half an hour, the ship departs about

There are over 250 miles (400 kilometers) of picture postcard vistas along the convoluted coastline of Amami-Ōshima.

5:00PM for its last leg to Naha Port, arriving two hours later, at 7:00PM. The ship docks for the night, then departs at 7:00AM the next morning, starting the cycle all over again.

Let's look at the Amami Archipelago in detail, for it is very beautiful. Although the islands are not tropical for the most part, they receive more than adequate rainfall and thus are lush and green. Their climates vary from mild temperate to subtropical. Here's a run-down of the islands traveling from north to south.

① AMAMI-ŌSHIMA 奄美大島

Commonly called Ōshima ("Big Island"), this is the northernmost island in the Amami group. It has an area of 275 square miles (713 square kilometers) and is the largest island in the Amami Archipelago and second largest

Marix Line's "Queen Coral 8" on its way around the Amami Island chain.

(after Okinawa) in all the Ryukyus. At its greatest length, it is approximately 38 miles (60 kilometers) long. Its width varies from almost 19 miles (30 kilometers) to as little as 10 (16 kilometers), and at one place in the north it narrows to a less than 1-mile (1-kilometer)-wide isthmus. A trianglular-shaped island, Ōshima's irregular coastline gives it an expansive circumference of 265 miles (426 kilometers). The island's highest point is Mt Yūwan (湯湾岳; Yūwan-daké), which rises to a height of 2,277 feet (694 meters).

In addition to being the largest Amami Island by area, Ōshima is by far the largest Amami in terms of population. Ōshima has approximately 66,000 residents, a number that dwarfs the populations of all the other Amamis combined. A large majority of the inhabitants (47,000) live in the main city of Amami (奄美市; Amami-shi), which is located on the island's northwest side. Prior to 2006 the city was known as Nazé (名瀬; Nazé), but it was renamed after its merger with two surrounding towns, Kasari (笠利町; Kasari-chō) and Sumiyō (住用村; Sumiyō-son). Many people still refer to Amami City as Nazé and that's what the port is almost always called.

The city has plenty of good hotels and restaurants and is especially lively after dark. There is a host of bars and clubs downtown, all located within easy walking distance of one another, where anyone can pleasantly spend a few evenings. The people are friendly and don't see many Western tourists. In virtually every pub and club, you'll be asked where you are from and what you are doing in Nazé.

Amost all of Amami-Ōshima (奄美大島; Amami-Ō-shima) is mountainous. In fact, over 90 percent of the island is covered in dense vegetation and only a small percentage is level enough to support sugar cane growing or other agriculture. Luckily for golfers, there's one nicely created carve-out of the jungle just for them. Only a few miles north of Nazé, there's a beautifully sited club, the Amami-Ōshima Country Club, high in the hills overlooking the East China Sea. Day passes are available, but of course it's easier to ask on weekdays. On weekends the club is extremely popular with Ōshima's "in-crowd" and tee times are limited. There's an excellent restaurant in the clubhouse and a nice 19th hole bar as well.

The ocean approach to Ōshima's Nazé harbor passes by tiny Yagi Island, which hosts a small resort hotel.

Golf at the Amami-Ōshima Country Club.

Due to its pristine condition, Ōshima is well known in Japan as a nature lover's destination. There are several large reserves. One is the Kinsakubaru Virgin Forest (金作原原生林; Kinsakubaru gensei-rin), which features several hundred hectacres of jungle with well-marked paths for hiking. It's just south of Nazé. The forest contains many semi-tropical plant species, including vast growths of dinosaur-era giant tree ferns. For vast quantities of dinosaur-era sago palms, there's a great hillside in Tatsugō Town (龍郷町; Tatsugō-chō) that's covered in them. Primaeval, although perhaps not as primordial as the preceding two dinosaur forests, another very interesting preserve is the mangrove forest at the estuary of Sumiyō River (住用村川; Sumiyō-gawa) at the town of Sumiyō. It's a popular place to rent kayaks and explore the river/swamp/ocean outlet.

Moving from brackish waters to salty ones, Ō Island is ringed by coral reefs and is also popular with divers, although its more northern location means that most divers,

On account of its unique topography, the northern Ayamaru-zaki cape is almost always windy and is a top spot for paragliders.

snorkelers, beach-goers and swimmers will visit in the summertime. If you are a beach lover, you'll most likely be exploring Ōshima's northern end, where you will find innumerable coves, bays, points and capes. It's probably the most twisted and hairpin-turned section of the island. Virtually around every bend of the road there's another beach and another scenic vista. Two of the finest

views of endless ocean and uncrowded beaches may be found just north of the airport, from Cape Ayamaru (あやまる岬; Ayamaru-misaki) to Cape Kasari (笠利崎 or 用岬); Kasari-zaki or Yō-misaki), at the northernmost tip of the island.

It almost does not matter where you may stop and explore the coast on this isolated end of the island for you will find a good beach at every turn. In fact, just below the airport, where you can watch the planes come and go, you'll find as beautiful and untrammeled a beach as any you might see anywhere on Ōshima.

Amami-Ōshima truly has something for just about everyone. Although for those not accustomed to the Ryukyu Islands it may seem small, it's not. Driving the northern one-third end of the island above Nazé and stopping along the way for a dip, a hike or to take a photo will take a whole day. A grand circle of the north, usually following the coast, will easily run 80 miles (128 kilometers) or more. If you take even a few of the side roads, you'll put 95 or 110 miles (152 or 176 kilometers) on your car's odometer.

Casually exploring by car the southern two-thirds of the island will take longer. Following the coast and primarily driving a circle route will easily occupy two days and cover some 125–155 miles (200–248 kilometers). Again, if you branch out on to just a few of the interior roads, you'll drive over 188 miles (300 kilometers). Although there

Sago Palms (*Cycas revoluta*)

Indigenous to southern Japan and the Ryukyus and now employed as attractive landscape and garden specimens throughout the tropical and subtropical regions of the world, so-called sago "palms" are only very distantly related to the palm family, nor are they ferns. They are cycads, a millions of years old family of plants unchanged since the time of dinosaurs and more closely related to ginkos and conifers. There are several hundred species spread over a dozen genera. Very slow growing but long-lived, they can reach heights of 20 feet (6 meters) in 50–100 years. They are dioecious, that is, they are male and female plants, with the males bearing large cones and the females bearing great groups of furled new leaf-type organs called *megasporophylls*. Although generally quite poisonous, the plant's starch may be consumed after proper preparation. In Japan, sago palms are known as *sotétsu* (蘇鉄 or ソテツ). The cluster at right is one of some 100,000 sagos covering a hillside in Tatsugō on Amami-Ōshima.

Edatekujima, an uninhabited islet off Ōshima's western shore.

are no major highways and the roads can be relatively narrow in places, they are well maintained and safe. All that's required is some moderation in speed, especially if it's been raining, for then they are slick.

As mentioned, the island's interior is mountainous. Some of the older roads twist and turn up the mountains and can be slow-going. However, in many sections, newer roads pass straight through the mountains via tunnels, some of which are quite long. Towards Ōshima's southeastern end, just outside of Uken Village (宇検村; Uken-son), you'll find Mt Yūwan, the island's highest peak and a good place for hiking. It's in a protected forest park zone. The further south you travel, the wider the island becomes. It terminates at the southwesternmost point of Cape Sotsuko (曾津高崎; Sotsuko-zaki). From this long, narrow and scenic cape you'll see to the north to little, uninhabited Edateku Island, and to the south across the Ōshima Strait (大島海峡; Ōshima-kaikyō), the fairly large island of Kakeroma. There is a ferry service to the latter, but if you wish to go to Edateku, you'll need a boat—or you can swim. It's not too far.

As the crow flies, it's 18 miles (29 kilometers) from Sotsuko Point to Ōshima's opposite point, its southeasternmost tip at Cape Kaitsu (皆津崎; Kaitsu-zaki). By the contorted roads that for the most part track right alongside Ōshima's southern shore, it's 35 miles (56 kilometers), and that does not include a final 1.5-mile (2-kilometer) hike at either end, for the road does not go all the way to the very end of each promontory. This southern end island drive is particularly scenic as it follows closely along the Ōshima Strait, where the view is always looking south to Kakeromajima.

YAGIJIMA (山羊島; Yagi-jima). This tiny islet, whose name means "Goat Island," is located at the ocean approach to Nazé and forms part of the tsunami barrier which protects the harbor. It's connected to the "mainland" by an 80-foot (25-meter) bridge. The islet is roughly circular in dimension and measures about 575 feet (175 meters) in diameter. It would be uninhabited but for a small resort hotel on its southern (protected) side. It's called the Amami Seaside Hotel (奄美 シーサイド ホテル; Amami shī-saido hoteru) and it's a nice choice for those who like to be on the water but not far from downtown.

EDATEKUJIMA (枝手久島; Edatéku-jima). This little uninhabited isle is just off Ōshima's western shore, north of Sotsuko Point. It's oval-shaped, about 2.5 miles (4 kilometers) long and not quite 1.25 miles (2 kilometers) wide. The road heading west out of Uken runs right past it, a bit north of its closest point to shore. You could easily swim to it, but watch the tides for there can be swift currents.

2 KAKEROMAJIMA 加計呂麻島

The largest town on Ōshima's southern shore is Setouchi (瀬戸内町; Sétouchi-chō). It's on the eastern side. From the harbor at Koniya (古仁屋; Koniya) there is a daily ferry service available on the Kakeroma Ferry (フェリー かけろま; Ferie-Kakéroma) to two ports on Kakeroma Island. One route crosses the Ōshima Strait in 5 miles (8 kilometers) and lands at the northwestern port of Seso (瀬相; Séso), the other route sails just 3 miles (5 kilometers) to the southeastern port of Ikenma (生間; Ikenma). Either sailing takes about 15 minutes. The two ports

Amami Black Rabbit (*Pentalagus furnessi*)

One of the world's truly unique creatures is the *Amami no Kuro-Usagi* (奄美の黒兎), also known as the Ryūkyū rabbit, a living fossil found only on Amami-Ōshima and Tokunoshima. It's a single species of a single genus, a survivor of an extinct line of ancient rabbits that once lived on the Asian mainland. The Amami rabbit has short legs, a rotund body, smaller ears than other rabbits and large, curved, non-retractable claws, which it uses to dig out its nest. You might not see one because it is mostly nocturnal. It is considered endangered, not only because of man and *habu* snakes but because of the mongoose, released years ago to control the *habu*.

The Ōshima-Kakeromajima ferry goes daily to two ports on Kakeroma Island.

The north shore of Kakeroma looking towards the Ōshima Strait.

are located on Kakeroma's northern shore and are 9 miles (14 kilometers) apart by road.

Describing Kakeromajima's (加計呂麻島; Kakéroma-jima) shape presents a great challenge but wonderfully illustrates the supposed Chinese proverb that "One picture is worth 1,000 words" for the shape of this island is almost beyond words. Its size, however, can be more easily measured and described. At its longest, and as the crow flies, it's about 12 miles (20 kilometers) from end to end. Its width varies from as much as 5–6 miles (8–10 kilometers) to as few as one or two in its most narrow places. Kakeromajima has been calculated to have an area of approximately 30 square miles (77 square kilometers) and due to its very irregular shape a rather long coastline of 92 miles (148 kilometers).

There is one main road and it more or less follows along the northern shoreline. From the eastern end of the island near Doren (渡連; Doren) to the westernmost end at Saneku (実久; Sanéku), it's a grand total of 22 miles

(35 kilometers). You could drive it in less than an hour without making any stops. But it's a lovely drive and you may wish to stop. You can do this virtually anywhere along the route and take a swim.

In addition to the main northern road, there are several minor roads covering the island's southern end where there are tiny settlements sprinkled throughout. In fact, there are enough roads generally tracking along the southern coastline that it's possible to drive a complete circuit of Kakeromajima, although some of the southern roads are very small indeed. If another car approaches, someone must find a spot and pull over. If you circle the island's circumference, you'll put about 44 miles (70 kilometers) on your odometer. It will take the better part of a day. If you find the mini-mountain roads too stressful, bear in mind that these back roads are connected to the main northern road at several points along the way and you can always bail out and reconnect. Finally, you would have to be equipped with a pretty

You'll be passing through Koniya Ferry Terminal if you're visiting the neighboring islands below Amami-Ōshima.

Kakeromajima, with its convoluted coastline, is an island full of twists and turns. Here, ferry routes are shown in red, main roads in black.

clueless GPS to get lost on this small an island. You could, however, take some turns that would lead to a dead end.

There is no question about it, Kakeromajima is a perfect island on which to get away from it all. And most fortunately, some enterprising and artistic Japanese has built a lovely pension on the island where you may stay while you're here. It's called the Pension "Marine Blue" and it's about as laid back and funky a place as you could find. It has have about a dozen rooms and bungalows, a full-service restaurant and all the equipment necessary for water sports. It's right on the beach on the northeast end of the island, just past Ikenma.

Before leaving Kakeroma, let's point out a few of its neighbors, for there are a number of lesser islands to its west and south. From Kakeromajima's far northwesternmost point, just off Saneku, you'll see Eniyabanarejima. It's not much but we'll describe it below. A bit to its south, and off the southwestern coast of Kakeroma, you'll see two tiny islets, Yubanareshima and its larger neighbor Sukomobanarejima. And, finally, due south and visible from almost anywhere along Kakeroma's southern shore, you'll see two rather large islets, Ukeshima and Yoroshima. They, in turn, have several neighbors, which we'll also describe.

Altogether, not including the few isolated rocks sprinkled about this mix, we're looking at eight small islands, the two largest of which are inhabited. Although all of these islets are only a few miles offshore, there's

no ferry service from Kakeroma. We'll have to drive back to either Ikenma or Seso Port and return to Koniya on the Amami-Ōshima mainland.

From there, ferries run to the two inhabited islands, Ukeshima and Yoroshima. If you wish to visit the others, you'll have to arrange your own boat. There are plenty of fishermen around, so, in fact, this is not so difficult as long as your Japanese is good or you can make yourself understood. Or wave money around. I've found this sometimes helps.

Kakeromajima's Pension "Marine Blue."

A view from Kakeromajima's far northwestern coast of Saneku Beach (left) and the uninhabited Eniyabanarejima (right).

ENIYABANAREJIMA (江仁屋離島; Eniya-banaré-jima). You'll find this uninhabited islet, approximately 2,300 feet (700 meters) northwest off the northwestern-most point of Kakeroma Island, just beyond Saneku Beach. It's a small island. No matter which way you measure it, Eniyabanare never gets larger than about 2,300 feet (700 meters) across in any one direction. It's generally square-shaped with white sandy beaches on three of its four sides. As is the case with most of the Amami Islands, it's hilly and covered in dense vegetation.

SUKOMOBANAREJIMA (須古茂離島; Sukomo-banaré-jima). About 4 miles (6.4 kilometers) due south of Eniyabanare, and around 3.5miles (5.6 kilometers) southwest of the village of Sukomo (須古茂; Sukomo), on western Kakeroma, lie the twin uninhabited islets of Sukomobanare and Yubanare. Sukomobanare Isle is the larger of the two. It's more or less rectangular in shape, a little over a mile (2 kilometers) long and anywhere from 1,315 to 2,300 feet (400 to 700 meters) wide.

YUBANARESHIMA (夕離島; Yū-banaré-shima). A little more than three-quarters of a mile (1 kilometer) to the northwest of Sukomobanare is its little twin brother, Yubanare. This tiny islet is generally oval-shaped except for a minor protrusion at its northeastern end. The island is about 1,150 feet (350 meters) wide by 1,725 feet (525 meters long). Its little protruding extension adds another 500 feet (150 meters) to its northeast coast.

UKESHIMA (請島; Uké-shima). Ferry service is not frequent to Ukeshima (or its next door neighbor, Yoro), but when the ship sails, it's the Setonami Ferry (フェリーせとなみ; Ferie-Sétonami). It begins at Koniya, the port of Setouchi town at the southern end of Amami-Ōshima. From there, it exits the Ōshima Strait east, sails around the eastern end of Kakeroma, then south and west to Ukeamuro (請阿室; Uké-amuro), some 14 miles (22 kilometers) sailing distance, and the first stop on Ukeshima. If you could fly a straight path from Koniya to Ukcamuro over Kakeroma, it would be 9 miles (15 kilometers), about due south. In any case, it takes less than an hour by ship. The ferry's stop here is brief. Ten or fifteen

minutes later, the ship sails approximately 2.5 miles (4 kilometers) in 10 minutes around a small cape to Uke Island's second port, Ikeji (池地; Iké-ji).

Once again, the ship briefly docks, then sails a bit less than 6 miles (10 kilometers) in about 20 minutes to its final destination, Yoro Port (与路港; Yoro-kō) on Yoro Island (与路島; Yoro-shima) After a brief pause, the ferry reverses its course, returning to Uke's twin ports, then home to Koniya port, all in one day.

It would appear that almost none of the Amami Islands are very regular in shape. All seem to have the most convoluted profiles. Very loosely, it might be said that Ukeshima has a semi-rectangular shape, although arguably it's also a sideways figure eight, except that its bottom half (eastern side) has a couple of extra bumps. It's probably easier, and more accurate, to look at a map. At its longest extremity, east–west, it's almost 4 miles (6 kilometers). Measuring from north to south, it's about 2 miles (3.5 kilometers) at its widest, and three-quarters of a mile (1 kilometer) at its more narrow sections. However you measure it, it's a small island.

Ukeshima is quite mountainous and almost all of it is uninhabited. Except for one 2.25-mile (3.6-kilometer)-long, very winding road between the two villages, there are no other main roads on the island. There are several minor roads from both villages south through the valleys behind them, where there is some agriculture, but both sets of these local routes are cul-de-sacs. There are some jeep paths to other sections of the island and there are completely isolated beaches all around the island, but

A headland cape on Ukeshima.

Offloading the Koniya ferry.

you'll have to find someone to take you, or let you use their car, because there are no auto rental agencies.

Ikeji is the larger of the two towns. It has around 100 inhabitants, a post office and an elementary and junior high school. After that, children have to go to Koniya on Ōshima for high school. They usually board there, going home on weekends. Ukeamuro is smaller. It has maybe 50 or 60 residents and no school. There are no tourist services on the island.

KIYAMASHIMA (木山島; Ki-yama-shima). Less than 985 feet (300 meters) immediately to Uke's east is this uninhabited islet whose name means "Wood Mountain." A postage stamp-sized islet, it can be reached by a several mile long jeep track from Ukeamuro town on Uke Island. Once you reach the beach, you can swim if you wish. The islet is about 2,950 feet (900 meters) long by 1,475 feet (450 meters) wide.

JANARESHIMA (シヤナレ島; Janaré-shima). Only about 660 feet (200 meters) offshore from the southeasternmost end of Ukeshima lies this tiny rugged islet. It's a triangle in shape, about 900 feet (275 meters) north to south and 1,475 feet (450 meters) east to west across the longest points of its southern base. A jeep can get you to Uke's southeast end, but from there it's a swim or a boat, if you have one.

YOROSHIMA (与路島; Yoro-shima). At their closest points, it's only about 2 miles (3 kilometers) due west from Ukeshima to Yoro Island, although sailing from Uke's Ikeji Port to Yoro Port (与路港; Yoro-kō) it's closer to 6 miles (10 kilometers). In any case,

it's not far. Somewhat like Uke, Yoro is also somewhat of a rectangle although a better formed one. It's a little island, about 4 miles (6.4 kilometers) from end to end, north to south, and in most places about 1.25 miles (2 kilometers) wide from east to west. Also like Uke Island, it's mountainous and virtually uninhabited. The only settlement is Yoro town, which has a population of about 150. There's a post office, an elementary and a junior high school. No other services are available.

Interestingly, like Ukeshima, the island is criss-crossed with unpaved jeep tracks, so getting around, at least with the right type of vehicle, is possible. The whole island is ringed by beautiful but very remote beaches. This is particularly so on Yoro's western side. Less than 1.25 miles (2 kilometers) east of Yoro town and only 2,460 feet/750 meters) from Yoro's closest point is the tiny islet of Hanmyashima. We'll look at it next.

HANMYASHIMA (ハンミヤ島; Hanmya-shima). Another miniscule, uninhabited, islet, this one is just off the east coast of Yoroshima. Alternatively, it could be reached in less than 1.25 miles (2 kilometers) from the western shore of Ukeshima. Of course, if you did go there, from either island, what's there? Not much. Hanmya Islet is mostly rock and a bit of sand, with just a touch of vegetation. It's oblong in shape, about 2,300 feet (700 meters) in length and 660 feet (200 meters) in width.

③ KIKAIJIMA OR KIKAIGASHIMA 喜界島
For the Ryukyus, where size is always relative, Kikaijima (喜界島; Kikai-jima or Kikaiga-shima) is a moderately large island. Its shape is something like that of an elongated pear or perhaps a triangle. Better yet, how about the shape of an arrowhead or an eggplant? You get the idea. It's wider at the bottom than at the top. It's about 9 miles (15 kilometers) long and its width varies from around 2–2.5 miles (3.2–4 kilometers) through its northern two-thirds to approximately 6 miles (10 kilometers) at its lower southern one-third. Kikai's area is 22 square miles (57 square kilometers) and its population a little more than 8,000.

That's actually quite a few people for an essentially small place. The reason for the relatively high population is that unlike so many of the Amamis, Kikaijima is not

The "A" Line's Amami, one of twin ships, the other being the Kikai, that serve Kikaijima.

mountainous. It's mostly level, with the exception of one good-sized high ridge which occupies about one-third of the central east side of the island. The escarpment is crowned along its length with a scenic road connecting a couple of parks. But for this exception, most of the rest of Kikai is fully settled, with close to two dozen villages, and highly developed, with almost its entire land surface devoted to agricultural production. Although the primary farming crop is sugar cane, many other crops and fruits are grown, including melons, mangoes and dragon fruit. For this reason, Kikai is sometimes referred to as the "fruity" island.

Because Kikai is a little off the beaten path, few persons visit it. This is a shame, for it is a very pretty island. On the other hand, if you like uncrowded places, Kikai might be just right for you. However, because there is not much tourism, there are not many accommodations. One of the larger hotels in town

(maybe 20 rooms) is the Business Hotel Hayashi (ビジネスホテル林; Bisnesu hoteru Hayashi-0997-65-3838). In addition, there are several *minshuku* inns (民宿).

Basically, everything in Kikai Town is within walking distance from the port, even the airport, which is a little less than a mile (1 kilometer) away. The town is primarily composed of the villages of Nakazato (中里; Naka-zato) and Akaren (赤連; Akaren) which surround Wan Port (湾港; Wan-kō).

Kikai is only 15 miles (24 kilometers) east of Amami-Ōshima at the two islands' closest points, and by coincidence those points are Ōshima's Airport (奄美空港; Amami-kūkō), which is located on the northeasternmost corner of that island, and the Kikai Airport (喜界空港; Kikai-kūkō), which is on the southwest side of Kikai. It follows therefore, that it's a short flight between the two islands, about 15 minutes, three times a day. Flying time to Kagoshima on the Japanese "main-

Kikai is so compact you can walk into town from Kikaijima Airport.

"Mattress" (tatami) class aboard the "A" Line's Kikai.

and," is a little further, about one hour. There are one or two flights a day there.

As the crow flies, it's 27 miles (43 kilometers) east–west between Nazé, Amami and Kikai Town, both of which are located next to their respective seaports. However, ships don't fly like crows. By ferry, over the ocean route, around the top northern end of Ōshima and then back down to Kikai, it's closer to 45 miles (72 kilometers) and takes about two hours in good weather. There are five sailings a week in both directions on the "A" Line Ferry (マルエー; Maru-A) service. The twin ships, the *Amami* and the *Kikai*, make the run.

As with all things ferry-related, things change. So it always pays to double and triple check, but here's how the service has been operating for the last several years. Five days a week, Monday through Friday, either the *Amami* or the *Kikai* departs Kagoshima North Sea Terminal at 5:30PM. It's about a 238-mile (380-kilometer) cruise, so it takes all night. The ships arrive non-stop at Kikai's Wan Port the next morning at either 4:30 or 5:30AM.

Half an hour later, at 5:00 or 6:00AM, Tuesday through Saturday, the "A" Line departs and cruises approximately two hours over the northern end of Amami-Ōshima to Nazé Port (名瀬港; Nazé-kō). A half hour later, at approximately 7:30 or 8:30AM, the ships depart Nazé and head southwest along Amami's west coast, then turn east through the Ōshima Strait that divides Amami from Kakeromajima, and arrive in the southern Amami port of Koniya (古仁屋; Koniya). Altogether, it's about 45 miles (72 kilometers) and takes two and a quarter hours. The ships arrive at approximately 9:45 or 10:45AM, respectively.

Fifteen minutes later, at about 10:00 or 11:00AM, the *Amami* or *Kikai* departs and heads south to Hetono (平土野; Hétono), the west side port on the island of Tokuno. That sailing is also 45 miles (72 kilometers) and takes two hours and fifteen minutes, arriving at 12:15 or 1:30PM, respectively.

Note that on some days (about half the departures), one of the ships continues from Tokunoshima to the port of China (知名; Chee-na) on the next island south, Okino-Erabujima. Those sailings depart between 12:30 and 2:00PM and arrive at China at 2:45 and 4:15PM. These less frequent sailings recommence their return journeys north

between 3:00 and 4:30PM and start the cycle all over again.

For most ships terminating at Hetono, the return journey north begins at 12:45PM for the *Amami* and 1:55PM for the *Kikai*. Service is five days a week, Tuesdays through Saturdays, with occasional differences. Arrival time at Koniya is 3:10 and 4:20PM, respectively. Twenty minutes later, at 3:30 and 4:40PM, the ships depart and cruise north to Nazé, arriving at 5:40 and 7:00PM.

If you are traveling from Amami-Ōshima to Kikai, here's when you'll board. Tuesdays through Saturdays, one of the "A" Lines, the *Amami* departs Nazé at 6:10PM. The other, the *Kikai*, leaves at 7:20PM. Sailing time is about two hours, so you'll arrive at Kikai's Wan Port at 8:20 or 9:30PM.

To return to Kagoshima from Kikai, on Tuesdays through Saturdays you'll board the *Amami* at 8:50PM and the *Kikai* at 9:50PM and cruise overnight, arriving Wednesdays through Sundays at Kagoshima at 8:00AM and 9:50AM, respectively. Note, and this is very important, on the days one of the ships makes the round-trip extension to China Port, the preceding times are extended by

Four-person berths aboard the Kikai.

Sugira Beach is popular for snorkeling and diving.

The Kikai Garden Golf Course.

The "Esplanado" path along Kikai's western shore.

several hours. It's best to verify your actual shipping time prior to your date of departure.

Kikai is popular for its good snorkeling and diving in safe, sheltered lagoons. Nakazato (中里; Naka-zato) is one of the most popular, with its long stretch of white sand. There are two tiny coral islands in the middle of the cove that are perfect for exploring. But Sugira Beach (スギラビーチ; Sugira bīchi) is the most convenient as it is close to town. The beach is part of the Airport Seaside Park (空港臨海公園; Kūkō rinkai kōen) and you can walk there from town. It's located just behind the airport. There are changing facilities, toilets and showers at the beach.

As is the case with all the northern Ryukyus, swimming is best from late April through November since December to March is cool and often rainy. If you enjoy snorkeling, the waters of Kikai are perfect natural aquariums full of colorful fish and coral.

If you're interested, next door to Sugira Beach and its children's playground is Kikai's only golf course. It's a nine-hole set-up and guest privileges are available. It's called the

Kikai Garden Golf Course (喜界ガーデンゴルフ; Kikai gāden gorufu) and it's located in between the airport and the beach. An errant wild shot has an equal chance of landing on the runway or in the ocean.

Before leaving this southwest section of the island, there's one more thing worth mentioning. Just a little to the west of the end of the airport runway and Sugira Beach begins what is called the "Esplanado" (遊歩道; Esplanado). It's a 1.5-mile-(2.4-kilometer)-long path running north to south along the island's far western shore. It ends at Araki (荒木; Araki) village. It's mostly coral and rock, but sections of the trail also go through dense banyan tree groves, and at one point there's an observatory with splendid views of the sea. It's a beautiful walk, one of the nicest you'll find anywhere. It's also Kikai's best place to watch the sun set into the ocean. Incidentally, some signs refer to it by a rather longer name: the Arakinakasato Promenade (荒木中里遊歩道; Arakinakasato Esplanado).

There's one more sightseeing attraction not far from this end of the island. A little less than a mile (2 kilometers) southeast of Araki, you'll see signs for the Gajyumaru Big Banyan Tree (ガジュマル巨木; Gaju maru kyo boku). There's no question about it, it's big. And if you really like giant banyan trees, there's a whole grove of them about halfway up the escarpment on the way to Nakanishi Park. It's called the Couple Banyan Tree (夫婦ガジュマル; Fūfu gaju maru) and there are well over a dozen of them—all giants. The road goes right through it. We'll drive there next.

At this point we've been more or less following Kikai's circle-island road, Route 619, counter-clockwise. From the Giant Banyan to the Couple Banyans, it's about 4 miles (6 kilometers). The road goes around the southernmost end of Kikai, then heads north along the east coast. Watch for the signs for the Couple Banyan and Nakanishi Park just after the village of Keraji (花良治; Keraji). The left-hand turn is less than half a mile (0.7 kilometer) north just after exiting the village. From the turn-off at Route 619, it's a bit more than 1.5 miles (2.4 kilometers) up a twisting, winding road past the Couple Banyans to the Nakanishi Park.

You will crest the mountain and find yourself on the top of Kikai's escarpmen. This spot is crowned by a little observation

Gajyumaru Big Banyan Tree.

Nakanishi Park, the highest point on Kikai.

platform on the island's highest point at 695 feet (212 meters) at Nakanishi Park (中西公園; Nakan-ishi kōen). On a clear day, you'll get some splendid views looking down over the cultivated fields, the small villages and the unending expanse of the Pacific Ocean. Incidentally, if you look behind you to the west, you'll see a fairly large barracks and an enormous circular something. It's a Japanese military installation and the big circle is a "listening" post.

From Nakanishi Park, perhaps the scenic highlight of the island begins. There is a road, or you can hike along the trail, that follows the crest of the Kikai escarpment 3 miles (5 kilometers) north, all along the heights of the east coast of the island. This especially lovely drive terminates at the almost equally tall 666-feet (203-meter) Hyakunodai Park Observation Platform (百之台公園 展望台; Hyaku no-dai kōen Tenbō-dai). From this vantage point there are great views towards the north of island. It truly is beautiful and you'll wonder why more people don't know about this island. But they don't, so we'll leave it at that.

From the northern end of the escarpment, there are several alternative routes that may be taken. There are many roads that criss-cross over and through Kikai Island. Most of this part of Kikai's mid-section is a fairly level but elevated plateau, and there are

View of Kikai Island from the Hyakunodai Park Observation Platform.

The Tonbizaki Lighthouse near Cape Tonbi.

attractive villages scattered around even up here. For the most part, it's all cultivated with sugar cane.

Let's, however, stay on Route 619 and continue north to the top end of the island. As we do, we'll gradually descend. The topmost third of Kikai is for the most part uniformly flat and not elevated. The end of the island is marked by the Tonbizaki Lighthouse (トンビ崎灯台; Tonbi-zaki tōdai) near Cape Tonbi (トンビ崎; Tonbi-zaki). Essentially, we're rounding the northern tip of Kikai on a small road that parallels just above Route 619. You'll see signs here and there for a couple of miles/kilometers along this section of shoreline for Tonbizaki "Beach" (トンビ崎海岸;

Karimata Spring, a sacred fresh water spring.

Tonbi-zaki kaigan). Despite the signs, there is no beach. The better translation of the Kanji characters would be coast, not beach. It may have some interest to visitors, but it's more a long stretch of rather desolate coral stone and tidal basins on the northwest coast of Kikai.

Now driving southwest, you'll soon come to the village of Onotsu (小野津; Onotsu). There is one minor attraction here and one nearby.

It so happens that the 130th East Longitude Meridian Line (東経130度線 - 子午線モニュメント; Tōkei 130 (sha ku tan jie) do-sen-Shigosen Monyumento) runs through Kikai's northern end. To celebrate this invisible meridian, there's a small marker and a couple of yellow lines in the road. It's right on the shore of town, perhaps 330 feet (100 meters) to the west of the fishing port and overlooking the ocean. Naturally, the line would continue across the island and indeed continue around the world from the North to the South Pole. It exits Kikai someplace near the east coast village of Sōmachi (早町; Sōmachi) but there's nothing special over there to mark it although it is indicated where it passes through Hyakunodai Park.

Let's admit it, there are longitude and latitude lines all over the face of the earth, at least on maps. We don't normally pay too much attention to them unless they are, for example, the Greenwich Prime Meridian, International Date Line, Equator, Arctic Circle or something like that. But this is Kikai and things are on a slightly smaller scale here. Embrace it.

From Onotsu it's just a bit up the hill leaving town and you'll see a sign for the Karimata Spring (雁股の泉; Karimata-no izumi). Again, it's nothing too, too special, but one can easily imagine that it was something special a few hundred years ago. Miraculously flowing fresh water supplies on small islands surrounded by the undrinkable ocean are always special, usually revered. The Japanese town website reports that there is a wealth of legend surrounding this particular fountain and thus it is a sacred place. If fresh water springs interest you, there is another one, which includes a small waterfall, in the village of Ōasato (大朝戸; Ōasato), which is approximately in the center of the island, on the east side. Its waters are brilliantly clear.

Not far from the Ōasato Spring, perhaps less than three-quarters of a mile (1 kilome-

Pachinko (パチンコ)

Okinawa and the Ryukyus may be another world, and they are, but they are still Japan, and that means Pachinko. Like Sumo wrestling and Kabuki theater, Pachinko is wholly unique to this country and found nowhere else. Superficially, a Pachinko machine resembles pinball, but it's vertical and there are no levers (flippers) for the player. Also, the steel balls are much smaller than those used in pinball. The player initiates the ball's speed, but then has no further control over it. The ball travels downwards through a maze of pins, in most cases, to be lost at the bottom. But some, by chance, are diverted to side pockets, which then generate more balls for the player. As gambling is illegal in Japan, that's essentially the payout: more balls and thus more playing time. Patrons may while away countless hours in brightly lit, smoke-filled Pachinko Parlors, where the sound levels are always a deafening cacophony of machine noise. Not so surprisingly perhaps, you'll find fairly large Pachinko Parlors on even some of the smallest islands in the Ryukyus. It may be a little difficult for a *gaijin* (外人) (foreigner) to understand, but after all, what's a sugar cane farmer to do in the off season?

ter), you'll come to the last place we'll visit on Kikai, the Ufuyaguchi Limestone Caverns (ウフヤグチ鍾乳洞; Ufu yaguchi shōn yūdō). It's a little difficult to find. There are only a couple of small signs and they are only in Japanese. Watch for the last Kanji character "洞" as it means cave or cavern. There's a small parking area on the side of the road and then a short walk up a hill leads you there. The caverns are not commercialized and therefore entry is free.

The Ufuyaguchi site is a good example of the difference between a cave and a cavern. Rather than a tunnel or some narrow, confined space, this opening into the earth is large—"cavernous." There are several chambers and they may be reached from several entrances. You'll need a flashlight, so bring one. There's usually no one around and it's a

A chamber in the Ufuyaguchi Limestone Caverns.

little spooky. Watch your step. In a couple of places there are vents in the ceilings allowing some light to stream in. There are few stalactites or stalagmites but there are some limestone formations. Altogether the caverns are fairly large. It's no Kentucky Mammoth Cave, but it is impressive enough.

From either the Ōasato Spring or the Ufuyaguchi Limestone Caverns, you're only about 2.4 miles (4 kilometers) east of Kikai Town. You can either head back over the local roads or turn north, back on to the coast, and take the last section of Route 619, completing this big circle we've made around the island.

Kikai is a surprising place, a lovely, peaceful island that seems to have fallen off the radar screen. No doubt the town fathers would like to promote tourism. The widely available free island map and directory (only in Japanese) is nicely put together and comprehensive. Yet, few people seem to have heard of the place. Most travelers, if they get to the northern Ryukyus at all, never leave Amami-Ōshima. That's understandable for it takes an extra flight or ferry ride to reach Kikaijima.

Nonetheless, it's worth the effort. Finally, it's also worth mentioning that Kikai is one of the few Ryukyu Islands that does not have *habu* snakes. For whatever reason, they're not part of the island's indigenous wildlife. Among the Ryukyus, only Kikai, Okinoerabu and Yoron share this distinction.

Tokunoshima's air terminal and control tower.

The marine terminal at Kametoku Port.

4 TOKUNOSHIMA 徳之島

For the Ryukyus, Tokunoshima (徳之島; Tokuno-shima) is a fairly large island (the second largest of the Amamis) as it has an area of 96 square miles (248 square kilometers) and a circumference of 52 miles (84 kilometers). Depending on your point of view, it's a rectangle or an oval. It spans almost exactly 15 miles (24 kilometers) from north to south and anywhere from 5–8 miles (8–13 kilometers) east to west. Tokuno also has a large population of about 26,750. The island is divided administratively into three "towns": Tokunoshima (徳之島町; Tokuno-shima-chō), Amagi (天城町; Amagi-chō), and Isen (伊仙町; Isen-chō). The largest is Tokunoshima Town whose village is called Kametsu (亀津; Kamétsu). This is where the main port is located and where most of the island's hotels, restaurants and other services are found. It's on Tokuno's Pacific Ocean side.

Tokuno Island has a small airport, (徳之島空港; Tokuno-shima-kūkō), which is located on the island's northwest side, approximately 15 miles (24 kilometers) driving distance from Kametsu. There are two flights a day to Amami-Ōshima (25 minutes) and two daily flights to Kagoshima (one hour). There is occasional service to Naha, Okinawa through Okinoerabu.

The island is well served by the alternating "A" Line and Marix Ferries, which run daily from Okinawa to Kagoshima and vice versa. Sailing time south from Nazé Port is about three hours and 30 minutes. Sailing north from Naha, Okinawa, it takes the best part of a day, almost 10 hours, as the ferry stops at Motobu Port, Yoron and Okinoerabu along the way.

The ferry usually docks at the marine terminal at Kametsu's Kametoku Port (亀徳港; Kamétoku-kō), but when the Pacific Ocean is stormy, the ferries often dock at Hetono Port (平土野港; Hétono-kō) on the island's East China Sea side. Hetono lies just below the airport.

Ryukyu Bullfighting

Known as Tōgyū or Ushi-zumō (闘牛大会; "bull sumo"), it's tough, potentially dangerous and probably politically incorrect but it's popular on Okinawa and especially so on Tokunoshima. It's a match between bull and bull. Thus, it really has nothing to do with Spanish, Portuguese or Mexican bullfighting where the contest is between man and bull and which, in many cases, ends in the bull's death. Okinawan bullfighting, as it's often

called, is more like Sumo wrestling for bulls. The animals are guided by their coaches. Bulls will lock horns, push and shove one another, each attempting to force the other to yield. The match is over when either bull relents or tires, then withdraws. Great care is taken so that bulls are not harmed. Should a bull be gored, the contest is immediately stopped and the bull is given medical aid.

The Mushiroze volcanic rock formations.

A view of the East China Sea from Cape Inutabu.

Much easier to find and see because they never move and don't hide themselves at night are the great rock formations at the island's northwesternmost tip: Mushiroze (むしろ瀬; Mushi-rozé). They are volcanic, thus giving a clue to Tokuno's origins. It's not a coral island. At Tokuno's opposite northern cape, the northeasternmost Promontory Kanami (金見崎; Kanami-zaki), you'll find the Kanami Sotetsu (Sago Palm) Tree Tunnel (金見ソテツトンネル; Kanami Sotésu), a 400-year-old oceanside collection of these great ancient cycads. There's one more seaside natural attraction, the "Glasses' Rocks" (メガネ岩; Mégama-iwa) of Innojofuta (犬門蓋; Innojo-futa) near Hetono. It's a twin set of natural arches carved by the sea bearing a resemblance to a pair of eyeglasses.

Another good view, this one from the island's most prominent southwest cape, is from the Observatory at Inutabu (犬田布岬; Inutabu-misaki). The vista from the cliffs here is as long as the eye can see. It's an impressive great stretch of headlands fronting the East China Sea. Close by on this same cape is an enigmatic monument for a non-Japanese, for there is nothing on or around the monument in English to describe it. If there were a plaque in English, its significance would still be virtually unknown except perhaps to naval historians.

The memorial is to the Battleship *Yamato* (大和) and the men who perished on her. She was, at the time of her construction, the largest ship ever built. Commissioned and launched at the beginning of the 1940s, the Yamato class of warships was intended to counter the numerical superiority of the

The Glasses' rocks, a twin set of natural arches.

In many ways, Tokuno is a perfect model of a typical Ryukyu Island. It's small but not too small. It has beautiful waters, a couple of good beaches, friendly people and several nice hotels and *minshuku* in its small main town. All in all, Tokuno has at least a couple of days of interesting sightseeing.

First worth seeing are two rather unusual items. Along with Okinawa's main island, Tokuno is one of the centers of "Tōgyū," otherwise known as "Okinawan" or "Ryukyu" Bullfighting. It's a unique form of the sport and has nothing to do with the bullfighting found in Spain or other places. In Tōgyū, the bulls fight each other, not a matador, and nobody dies.

The second, in this case rare, item is the presence of the prehistoric Amami Black Rabbit (奄美の黒兎; Amami no Kuro-Usagi). Along with Amami-Ōshima, Tokuno is the only other island, indeed the only other place in the world, where this nocturnal and secretive creature may be found. Unfortunately, since they truly are an animal of the jungle—and a nighttime one at that—most casual visitors will not get to see one.

United States' fleet. The flagship *Yamato* and her sister ship *Musashi* (武蔵) were the heaviest and most powerfully armed battleships ever constructed, displacing over 70,000 tons fully loaded and armed with the largest caliber of naval artillery ever placed on a warship. The *Yamato* had an extraordinary length of 863 feet (263 meters), a beam of 128 feet (39 meters) and a draft of 36 feet (11 meters). Originally intended to be a group of five such ships, these two were the only ones to be built. Neither survived World War II.

Although the *Yamato* saw action in 1944 at the Battle of the Philippine Sea and was damaged in the Japanese naval disaster of Leyte Gulf, by this stage of World War II the Empire of Japan was all but vanquished and near desperation. In April of 1945, in what was planned to be a final "special attack" (特攻; tokkō; lit. "suicide"), a euphemism for a suicide mission, the *Yamato*, along with nine other battleships, was ordered to sail to Okinawa and once there to beach itself and thereby implant its armory to defend the island. The mission was code-named Operation "Ten-go"

(天號作戰 or 天号作戦; Kyūjitai or Shinjitai) and is usually referred to as "Ten-gō Sakusen." Once the ship had exhausted its munitions, or was destroyed, the crew was to join the island's defenders.

It never happened. Exiting Japan's inland sea, the ship and its escorts were spotted by American submarines. On April 7th, attacking in three waves, US dive bombers pounded the *Yamato* with bombs and rockets while torpedoes pummeled the port side. Broken, battered and listing badly, the crew was ordered to abandon ship. As the great battleship capsized, it created a suction that drew hundreds of swimming crewmen back towards it to drown. As the ship began its final death roll, an enormous explosion ripped through it as fires had reached the ammunitions magazines. The resulting mushroom cloud was over 4 miles (6.4 kilometers) high and witnessed hundreds of miles/kilometers away on Kyūshū. Of the *Yamato*'s crew of 2,778, only 269 survived. The US Navy lost 10 aircraft and 12 airmen. Five of the other warships were also destroyed and several thousands of men on those ships perished as well.

The Yamato Memorial (大和慰霊塔) is a lonely memorial, but sacred and moving, for out at sea from this place thousands of men lost their lives in service to their country.

This photo was taken from a carrier plane from the USS Yorktown shortly after the Yamato was destroyed by bombs and torpedoes and just before it sank.

The highlight of the Kure Yamato Museum is this 1:10 scale model of the battleship Yamato. It is 86 feet (26.3 meters) long. In Tokyo, at the Odaiba Maritime Museum (船の科学館; Fune no kagakukan), there is a 13-foot (4-meter) 1:20 scale model of the ship.

From the start of the attack, about 30 minutes after noon on April 7th, 1944, to the *Yamato*'s drop beneath the waves, about 2:30PM, it is estimated that the ship was hit by at least eleven torpedoes and eight bombs. The wreckage of the battleship was located in 1985 and explored more extensively in 1999. The remains of the *Yamato* lie under 1,115 feet (340 meters) of water in two main pieces. Undersea dive photographs show the bow portion, severed from the rest of the ship, in an upright position, the 7-foot (2-meter)-wide golden chrysanthemum crest still glowing in a faint hue. The midships and stern section are upside-down nearby, with two great holes in the bottom, the result of powerful internal explosions.

For the West, the message was clear. The battle convincingly demonstrated Japan's willingness to sacrifice large numbers of its own citizens—as well as its remaining war machine—in increasingly impossible attempts, such as the Kamikazé (神風; lit. "Divine Wind") missions, to stop the Allied advance on the Japanese home islands at any cost. Operation Ten-Go, had it been successful, would have resulted in thousands of soldiers dying in hand-to-hand combat.

There was simply no stopping the Japanese war machine. It is widely agreed by most historians that President Harry S. Truman's decision to employ the atomic bomb against Japan was a direct result of the apparent willingness of Japan to sacrifice countless numbers of its citizens using suicidal tactics such as Operation Ten-Go and their resistance in the Battle of Okinawa. Although to this day there is no clear consensus among scholars and historians of the moral correctness of the decision to use the atomic bombs, the fact remains that Japan did not surrender until after the twin bombings of Hiroshima and Nagasaki on August 6th and 9th, respectively.

After the war, the Battleship *Yamato* became an object of intense interest and, in some quarters, veneration in Japan. It remains a very sensitive and controversial topic. One of the reasons the sinking of the *Yamato* is such an emotionally charged issue, and one that has such special significance in Japanese culture, is that the very word "Yamato" is used as a poetic name for Japan. The ship's destruction and the disaster of Operation Ten-Go is eulogized, to one degree or another, in modern Japan and in

The nicest hotel in Tokunoshima Town is the Hotel Grand Ocean Resort. And the people running the place? They couldn't be nicer either. It's a pleasure to stay here.

Pot of Gold in Tokuno? A sugar cane field, the ocean in the background and a rainbow after a drench—it's all anyone might ask for—except perhaps for that pot of gold.

popular Japanese culture, as a heroic, selfless but ultimately futile effort by the Japanese to defend their homeland. Thus, the *Yamato* is a symbolic emblem of great national pride and its fate has come to represent the end of the once invincible Imperial Japanese Navy, Japanese militarism and the Empire of Japan.

The Cape Inutabu Memorial Tower was dedicated in April 1968 to the *Yamato* crew and all the seamen who died in Operation Ten-go on their way to defend Okinawa. In addition to many films and books published on the *Yamato*, there is a second memorial in mainland Japan. Opened in 2005 and built near the site of the former Kure shipyards in Hiroshima where the *Yamato* was built, the Kure Maritime Museum, commonly known as the Yamato Museum (大和ミュージアム; Yamato myuujiamu) is dedicated to the battleship and its engineering.

5 IŌTORISHIMA 硫黄鳥島

By all accounts this little islet, geographically located in the Amami group, should be included in Kagoshima Prefecture as it's only 40 miles (65 kilometers) due west of Tokuno-shima and thus way north of Okinawa. As the crow flies, it's located 70 miles (112 kilometers) due north of Okinawa's Cape Hedo and that's much further north than either Yoron-tō or Okinoerabujima, both of which are in Kagoshima.

Yet, despite this geography, whenever one finds a reference to Iōtorishima (硫黄鳥島; Iwō-tori-shima) it's invariably described as being 135 miles (216 kilometers) northeast of Kume Island, which is almost 60 miles (96

kilometers) west of Okinawa and nowhere near Iōtori. So what's the connection? Well none, geographically, but politically the reason is grounded in history. Long ago it was included in the Ryukyu Kingdom and another name for it was "Okinawa Torishima," or in English "Okinawa Bird Island." An island of birds? Perhaps, but there's a reason for this as well. It's common in the Ryukyus to call any minor, offshore, unnamed islet "Bird Island" (鳥島; Tori-shima). And historically this Bird Island, which is an active volcano, was mined for its sulphur by Okinawans, not people from Amami. Sulphur was an important source of tribute in the Ryukyu Kingdom.

As is the case with so many active volcanic islands in Japan, it also became known as "Iōjima," Japanese for "Sulphur Island," (硫黄島; Iwō-jima), the most famous example of which is the battle-scarred island of this same name far to the east in the Pacific. For one reason or another, over time this little islet earned itself a combination of the two names: "Iō" (硫黄 = sulphur) plus "tori" (鳥 = bird) equals "Iōtori" plus naturally then "shima" (島 = island). Therefore, literally "Iōtorishima" (硫黄鳥島) is "Sulphur Bird Island."

To make matters just a bit more confusing, there is another "Iōjima" or "Iwōjima" (硫黄島) in the Ōsumi Islands' Northwestern Group (the Mishimas), discussed earlier, on page 32, and another "Torishima" (鳥島) some 15 miles (24 kilometers) north of Kume Island, discussed later, on page 189. The latter islet is uninhabitable and used for a bombing range. Even among Japanese people and Okinawans, these tiny obscure places get mixed up. For this reason, the Torishima near Kume is often referred to as "Kume-Torishima" to help distinguish it from this Iōtorishima near Tokuno, which, incidentally, is sometimes called "Okinawa Torishima" or "Okinawa Iōtorishima" even though it's really nowhere near Okinawa.

That's a big story for a little place, especially an uninhabited volcanic isle. You can't get there, unless perhaps you have your own boat, and even then it's prohibited because it's too dangerous. It should go without saying that since it's forbidden to go there, there is no commercial service to there. Rising to a height of 696 feet (212 meters), most of Iōtori Island is just a bit less than three-quarters of a mile (1 kilometer) wide east to west and about 2 miles (3 kilometers) long from north to south. Its shape is that of an elongated oval. It has an area of 0.98 square miles (2.55 square kilometers), a circumference of 4.5 miles (7.3 kilometers) and about 330 feet (100 meters) of beach. It's quite isolated and is the only active volcano in this section of the East China Sea.

Amazingly, until the beginning of the 20th century, the island was inhabited. Its residents were sulphur gatherers and their families. There's not much left of this occupation today. After a violent volcanic eruption and explosion in 1903, the island's entire population of 600 people was relocated to Kume. After World War II, some of its former residents returned, to again mine sulphur, but another volcanic eruption forced their evacuation in 1967. The island has remained uninhabited since then.

Iōtorishima consists of two overlapping volcanoes: Sulphur Peak (硫黄岳; Iō-daké), on the island's northwest side, and Maé-daké (前岳), which lies at the southeast tip of the island. A lava dome occupies the center of the island. Technically, Iōtorishima is the northernmost island of Okinawa Prefecture.

⑥ OKINOERABUJIMA 沖之永良部島

Sailing south out of Nazé Port on Amami-Ōshima, the ferry takes a little less than six hours to reach Okinoerabujima (沖之永良部島; Oki-no-érabu-jima), which its residents often call Okiérabu (沖永良部). Both ferry lines, on alternating days, depart at 5:50AM and are scheduled to arrive at 11:30AM. The journey includes a half-hour stop at Tokunoshima along the way. Northbound out of Okinawa, the sailing takes about seven hours. The ferries leave Naha at 7:00AM and arrive on Okinoerabu right around 2:00PM. The northbound sailings include a couple of brief stops. The sailing time is two hours less if starting from Okinawa's northern port at Motobu. From there, the ferries depart about 9:00AM.

Alternatively, there are multiple daily flights to Okinoerabu Airport (沖之永良部空港; Oki-no-érabu-kūkō) from Kagoshima, Amami-Ōshima, and Naha. From Kagoshima it's over 312 miles (500 kilometers) by air and flights to or from there take about 90 minutes. It's almost 94 miles (150 kilometers) as the crow flies to or from Nazé and flights there are about 40 minutes. To or from Naha, it's almost 110 "air" miles (176 kilometers). Flights there take a little longer, just a bit under an hour.

Commercial Uses of Sulphur

One of the by-products of volcanoes is sulphur, a bright yellow, crystalline, solid, non-metallic chemical element. It has been mined or gathered by man for millennia. Also known as "brimstone," when burned it melts to a blood-red liquid and emits an intense blue flame. Depending on other chemicals, with which it may be associated, it can give off a strong smell, usually compared to that of rotten eggs. Sulphur has important commercial uses, primarily as a component in fertilizers, black gunpowder, insecticides, fungicides and, of course, matches. It is also has important medicinal and antibacterial properties and is used in ointments and creams for the treatment of a number of skin conditions such as scabies, ringworm, psoriasis, eczema and acne.

Okinoerabu Island

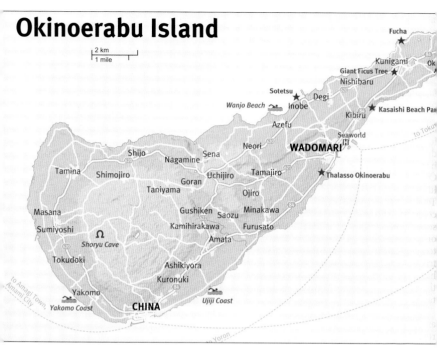

Geographically, Okinoerabu Island has an area of not quite 36 square miles (94 square kilometers) and a coastline circumference of 35 miles (57 kilometers). The island is shaped as a nicely rounded long triangle. Its maximum length is a little more than 12 miles (20 kilometers) and its maximum width is about 6 miles (10 kilometers). That width gradually decreases as the island tapers to the northeast. In its middle section, the island is approximately 3 miles (5 kilometers) wide and towards its narrow pointy end it's less than 2 miles (3.2 kilometers). The airport is at the far northeasternmost point.

Okinoerabujima is home to about 16,000 people who are more or less evenly divided into the island's two towns of China (知名町; Chee-na-chō) and Wadomari (和泊町; Wado-mari-chō). Wadomari has the larger of the island's two main ports, (和泊港; Wadomari-kō) and this one is used by the Marix and "A" Line Ferry services. The other port is at China.

Okinoerabu is a coral island and thus almost all its coast is ringed by coral reefs. It's a popular island for snorkelers and divers. As is the case on other good diving islands in the Ryukyus, there are competent dive shops where advice, instruction and equipment rentals may be had. The only problem for some is that English is not often spoken. Never mind, divers are used to communicating in sign language. Both inside and outside the reef you can see all kinds of colorful fish and other sea creatures. It's not uncommon to view sea turtles, sea snakes and stingrays or the ocasional octopus or reef shark.

Several sections of Okinoerabu's interior are quite mountainous and provide good hiking opportunities. Several sections of the shoreline are high cliffs, which also make for interesting walks. If you're one of those people with a great fear of snakes, you need not worry when hiking here as Okinoerabu is one of the three Ryukyus, along with Kikai and Yoron, to be free of them. However, the island is big enough, and hilly enough, that unless you're a mountain biker it might be easier to see it all with a rental car or scooter. You can complete a full circle island jaunt in a couple of hours, about 40 miles (64 kilometers) on the main road around the island.

The island's flat portions are, as would be expected, devoted primarily to agriculture. In addition to the usual sugar cane and sweet potato fields, if you're lucky and are there in ate winter or early spring, you'll see thousands upon thousands, maybe even millions, of 3-foot (1-meter)-high spiky green stalks capped with brilliant white lilies, for Okinoerabu is famous for its "Erabu" variety (永良部鉄砲百合; Erabu-teppō-yuri; Latin: *Lilium longiforum*). This is the "classic" form of the lily, better known in the West as the "Easter" or "trumpet" lily. The Japanese word for any lily is *yuri*. "Teppō" means a matchlock rifle and has its origins on Tanégashima, described on page 22. This lily is believed to have originated on southern Kyushu and the Ōsumi Islands, which includes Tanéga. The lily draws its name from the Tanégashima Teppō rifles that were introduced, then copied, from the Portuguese. For this reason, sometimes you'll see these lilies referred to or translated as "rifle" lilies. On Okinoerabu today, they are grown for the horticulture trade and shipped all over the world. If you happen to be on the island around Easter, the almost-glowing white fields are a spectacular sight.

Some of Okinoerabujima's best-known and year-round sights include the mushroom rock formations along the Ujiji coast (ウジジ海岸; Ujiji-kaigan) near China, as well as at Cape Tamina (田皆岬; Taminamisaki) on the northwesternmost tip of the island, and at the 11,500-foot (3,500-meter)-long Shōryū Caves (昇竜洞; Shōryū-do). The caves were discovered in 1963 and opened to the public later that year.

A bit west of China there is also one of the largest beaches on the island, Yakomo (屋子

Mushroom rock formations along the Ujiji coast near the town of China.

母海岸; Yakomo-kaigan), which is nearly a mile (1 kilometer) in length. Another popular beach, this one northeast of Wadomari, is at the Kasaishi Beach Park (笠石海浜公園; Kasa-ishi-hama kōen). From here it's only a couple of miles to the airport and just north of there is one of Okinoerabu's most well-known sights, the Fucha (フーチャ; Fucha). The Fucha is about a third of a mile (half a kilometer) of coastal needle-like coral formations, indented with a fairly good-sized spray cave formed by erosion from waves crashing against the cliffs. This large "cave" is, in fact, a blowhole.

If you've come this far, you've rounded the island's narrow northeastern tip. From here it's close to the "Gajyumaru" or Giant Ficus Tree (ガジュマル; Gajyumaru), which is located in a public schoolyard in the village of Kunigami (国頭; Kunigami). It's reputed to be the largest banyan tree in Japan. A little

Sailing into Wadomari Port on Okinoerabu Island.

The Fucha blowhole northeast of Wadomari.

Inside the Thalasso Okinoerabu Spa Center.

further down the coast from here, west of Inobe (伊延; Inobé) and near Wanjo Beach (ワンジョ海岸; Wanjo-kaigan), you'll find the Sotetsu (Sago Palm) Tree Park (ソテツジャングル; Sotétsu ji yanguru). It's a nice collection of sago palms alongside the ocean.

Lastly, if you're exhausted from all this sightseeing and need to wind down, stop by

at the seaside therapeutic center Thalasso Okinoerabu (タラソ おきのえらぶ; Taraso Okino-érabu). It's a brand-new, deluxe and beautiful full-service public spa. It's not expensive and you can while away hours with steam and heated pools. It's a little south outside of Wadomari Town. You'll spot it just below the large electric-generating windmill, which is used to power the spa.

7 YORONJIMA 与論島

Universally called Yoron-tō, this beautiful little island is a beach holiday destination for tens of thousands of sun-starved Japanese every year. Perhaps because it is the southernmost island of Kagoshima Prefecture, it has the "feel" of Okinawa. The southern end of Yoron-tō is only a little more than 14 miles (22 kilometers) from the northernmost tip of Okinawa at Cape Hedo. The islands are visible to one another on a clear day. Thus, it's the first island where you'll see *shīsā* lion dogs on the roofs of houses and it's the first island where some of those roofs will be red- or white-tiled in the Okinawan style. It's also the first island where you'll find a few "turtleback" tombs, although the majority of graves are in the Japanese style, not the traditional Okinawan style found in the southern Ryukyus.

Like a number of the Amami Islands, Yoronjima (与論島; Yoron-jima) is served twice daily (one going south, one north) by ferries from the "A" and Marix Lines. Northbound from Naha Port, via Motobu, it's 90 sea miles (141 kilometers) with travel time a little more than five hours. From Motobu Port, it's 50 miles (80 kilometers) and takes

The Gajyumaru Banyan Tree (榕樹) (*Ficus microcarpa*)

Found in tropical and sub-tropical regions throughout the world, banyan trees, a type of fig, can in time reach enormous proportions, their aerial prop roots spreading

out laterally, covering hundreds of square meters. Their seeds are spread by fruit-eating birds and bats. They are also known as "Chinese banyan" or "Indian laurel" trees for they are common in both of those countries. Okinawan legends say that *jijimunā* (キジムナー; lit. wood spirit) live in the Gajyumaru (ガジュマル) and can only be seen by children because they are still pure of heart. The banyan pictured above is located in a schoolyard at Kunigami on Okinoerabujima.

three hours. Going to or coming from Yoron's next northern neighbor, it's 30 miles (48 kilometers) by ferry to Wadomari Port on Okinoerabujima and travel time is a bit less than two hours. To or from Amami-Ōshima, it's about eight hours. Kagoshima is a long 20 hours away. There's only one main port on the island, Yoron Port (与論 港; Yoron-kō).

Yoron also has a convenient little airport (与論空港; Yoron-kūkō) and there are daily flights to and from Naha and Kagoshima. There are also flights, though less frequent, to Okinoerabu and Amami-Ōshima. Yoron's airport and harbor are practically next to one another and both are close to the island's best resort hotel, the Pricia. All are just a couple of minutes away from the island's "capital" city, Chabana (茶花; Chabana; lit. "Tea Flowers").

At its widest, east to west, Yoron is almost 4 miles (6.4 kilometers) across. From north to south, it's about 3 miles (5 kilometers). Its circumference is 14.6 miles (23.5 kilometers) and its area is 8 square miles (20.5 square kilometers). Yoron is mostly flat and devoted to agriculture, primarily sugar cane. Its highest point is a none too breathtaking 322 feet (98 meters) above sea level. A 2010 census listed the island's population at 5,373.

Because of the island's proximity to Okinawa, Yoron became a place of refuge just before the end of World War II. In the weeks leading up to the invasion, hundreds of Okinawans escaped their island by swimming or floating on anything available to reach Yoron-tō. Their boats had been confiscated by the Japanese Army. Yoron was

You'll spot the Okinoerabujima Seaworld Hotel as you come into Wadomari Port. It's as cozy and friendly a place as you can ask for. The staff are super and the food is good.

spared during the war and was not invaded during the Battle of Okinawa.

But, just as it was forgotten during the war, the island was forgotten after the war. Yoron did not have electricity until the late 1960s. Fortunately, at about the same time, inexpensive flights were introduced and tourism began to develop. Because the US military still entirely controlled Okinawa Prefecture until 1972, there were travel restrictions on Japanese visitors to Okinawa. Thus Yoron, as part of Kagoshima Prefecture, became the most southerly island in Japan that could be freely visited by Japanese sun-seeking tourists. An industry was born and Yoron became, and still remains, a popular beach getaway.

Yoron is a coral island and coral reefs surround more than 80 percent of its coast. The island has a large number of beautiful white sand beaches. Its most western beach

Blowfish, Pufferfish, Porcupinefish

These and other common names are used for over 100 different species commonly known in Japan as *fugu* (河豚 or 鰒フグ; lit. "river pig") Our little spikey friend, after proper preparation, will find himself on someone's dinner plate. He's an expensive delicacy and, if not correctly cooked, deadly poisonous. An average blowfish contains enough tetradotoxin to kill 30 people, making it one of the world's most toxic substances, 1,200 times more lethal than cyanide. To be licensed, Japanese chefs must be specially trained to remove the poison portions of the fish, then it's said to be delicious. Nevertheless, each year, about a dozen people in Japan die from eating *fugu*.

Ō-Ganéku-kaigan is Yoron's most popular beach and is also its longest, offering over a mile (2 kilometers) of powder sand and acqua water.

The Pricia Resort Hotel on Yoron-tō is a first-class resort less than five minutes from the airport or the harbor. Sunset Beach is visible at upper right.

starts at the Pricia Resort Hotel and wraps itself around the little cape where the airport runway begins. In fact, but for a security fence you could walk from the hotel to the air terminal. Since this beach is the last to see the sun go down, it's popularly known as Sunset Beach (兼母海岸; Kenébo-kaigan). Much longer, almost the entire length of the island's east coast is one great beach, or rather more precisely, one beach after another. Starting from the north and traveling south, you'll see Minata bīchi (ミナタビーチ), then Crystal (クリスタルビーチ; Kurisutaru-bīchi), then "Funagura" (船倉海岸; Funagura-kaigan), then Yoron's most popular and longest beach, the 1.25-mile (2-kilometer) Ō-Ganéku-kaigan (大金久海岸).

But it's not over, for it is from "Big-Ganéku Beach" that you catch the glass-bottom boats 1 mile (1.6 kilometers) out to Yoron's most unusual beach, the disappearing Yuri-ga-hama (百合ケ浜; lit. "100 Lily Beach"). It's a pure white sandbar that appears twice every 24 hours at high tide. Yuriga Beach is most famous for its "star sand."

Yoron's several other sights include the popular caves Akasaki (赤崎) and the 3,280-foot (1,000-meter) Yago-Gokuraku-do (屋川一極楽洞), the Hida cultural folk village (飛騨民族村; Hida Minzoku-mura) and the Southern Cross Center (サザンクロスセンター); Sazankurosu Sentā, a small museum which features the history and culture of Yoron and the Amami Islands. The museum is so-named because Yoron Island is the northernmost place in Japan where the Southern Cross constellation may be seen.

For tropical garden fans, there is the Yunnu-Rakuen (ユンヌ楽園) Botanical Gardens. Colorful flowers bloom all over Yoron. The botanical gardens feature as many flowers as possible that bloom all the year

Star Sand or Hoshizuna (星砂)

Several of the southern Ryukyus, including Taketomi, Iriomote and Yoron, are famous for their beautiful "star sand." These tiny grains—most species are less than 1 mm in size—are the shells of microscopic, single-celled organisms called foraminiferans (lit. "hole bearers") or forams. There are about 275,000 species recognized, both living and fossil. Forams commonly produce a calcium carbonate "test" or shell which can have one or multiple chambers, some quite complex. Live forams are primarily marine creatures, though some live in brackish waters. They feed on small organisms such as diatoms or bacteria.

"Seikai Sou" Blue Sea Village Hotel.

Cape Hedo, on the northern tip of Okinawa, provides a first look at our next stop, Okinawa-hontō, as seen on a very clear day. From this vantage point at the southern end of Yoron, it's 14 miles (22 kilometers) due south to Hedo Point.

round, including over 40 species of hibiscus and 150 other kinds of tropical and semi-tropical plants.

By the way, if you find the Pricia Resort

Hotel too pricey, don't worry as there are many *minshuku* on the island plus several nice hotels. My favorite is right in downtown Chabana. Run by a charming lady and her daughter, a more friendly place you will not find. It's the "Seikai Sou" (青海荘; lit. "Blue Sea Village") Hotel, and its reasonable rates are a real bargain. They serve an excellent breakfast too.

MINATABANAREJIMA (皆田離島; Minata-banaré jima). More than almost any other island in the Ryukyus, Yoron-tō is ringed by coral reefs. However, it is reefs, not true land masses, that surround it. For the most part, the bits of land circling around Yoron are low coral outcroppings and sandbars, not true land.

This little islet is an exception. Although tiny, it's a true island. It lies less than 660 feet (200 meters) offshore from Minata Beach (皆田海岸; Minata-kaigan) on the northeastern side of Yoron-tō. There's a small fishing port here as well. Running parallel to the shore, the "island" is actually a set of about five or six mini-islands from south to north, each one smaller than the next. All told, their length is almost 1,650 feet (500 meters). The southernmost islet accounts for about 580 feet (175 meters); the next is 410 feet (125 meters) long; the next about 200 feet (60 meters); then 130 feet (40 meters); then 50 feet (15 meters). Each is separated from the other by 15 or 30 feet (5 or 10 meters). They are all narrow. The first is about 200 feet (60 meters) wide and the rest are less and less wide as they go north. The set of them is covered in wild tropical vegetation.

Minatabanarejima, a series of green rock mini-islands "floating" in crystal waters.

PART 2
THE RYUKYUS
琉球列島

The southern half of the Ryukyu Archipelago (琉球列島; Ryūkyū-rettō), which constitutes today's Okinawa Prefecture (沖縄県; Okinawa-ken), may be divided into the three major north–south groups of Okinawa-shotō, the Miyakos and the Yaeyama Islands, plus two more, the distant Daitō and Senkaku Island groups. Note, however, that the Japanese often refer to the prefecture another way. They customarily divide the Ryūkyū-rettō (which for them is only the southern half) into two subdivisions: Okinawa-shotō, which consists of Okinawa main island and all the near islands, including

the Keramas, surrounding it, and the Sakishima Islands (先島諸島; Saki-shima-shotō), which constitute all the islands further south. Sakishima means "Further Islands." For the Japanese, these are the Miyako and Yaeyama Island groups plus the disputed Senkaku Islands.

The combined area of all the islands in Okinawa Prefecture is 879 square miles (2,276 square kilometers), that's about 115 square miles (300 square kilometers) less than the tiny European state of Luxembourg. Half a million people live in Luxembourg. By contrast, the population of Okinawa-ken is approximately 1,385,000 spread out over more than 50 inhabited islands.

A shīsā lion dog.

Okinoerabujima
沖永良部島

Yuronjima
与論島

Okinawa-hontō
沖縄本島

● Naha
那覇

Kita Daitōjima
北大東島

26° N

Minami Daitōjima
南大東島

... A N D S

DAITŌ ISLANDS
大東諸島

...INAWA PREFECTURE
沖縄県

25° N

Oki Daitōjima
沖大東島

PACIFIC OCEAN

24° N

100 km
50 miles

The Ryukyu Islands

Chapter 4

THE OKINAWA ISLANDS 沖縄諸島
Subtropical getaway, cultural hub

Not only is the main island of Okinawa (沖縄本島; Okinawa-hontō) the largest single island in the Ryukyu chain, the Okinawa Island group (沖縄諸島; Okinawa-shotō) is the largest in the Ryukyu Archipelago. Since there are so many islands in the Okinawa group, for convenience we'll start with Okinawa Island, dividing it into south, central and north, then go on to explore all the related islands. Again, merely for convenience, we'll divide the surrounding islands in half. After discussing Okinawa-hontō, we'll discuss Okinawa-shotō, beginning with the islands on the east side of Okinawa in the Pacific Ocean, going from north to south, then round Okinawa's southern tip at Cape Kyan and move on to the islands on the western side of Okinawa main island, that is those in the East China Sea, from south to north.

In other words, we'll first cover Okinawa Main Island by starting in the south, move up through the central part of the island and finish in the north. From there, starting at Cape Hedo at the top of Okinawa-hontō, we'll cover the Okinawa-shotō by going all the way around the island in a clockwise fashion.

Okinawa-shotō refers to the group of islands closely related or adjacent to or within a short distance of the main island of Okinawa. A number of these islands are so close that you can drive or walk to them, for more than a dozen are connected to Okinawa by bridges or causeways. For those who are a bit more adventurous or those wanting a short ocean voyage, there are a number of islands reachable by public ferry. Some of these ferries run back and forth several times a day. Therefore, a few islands are close

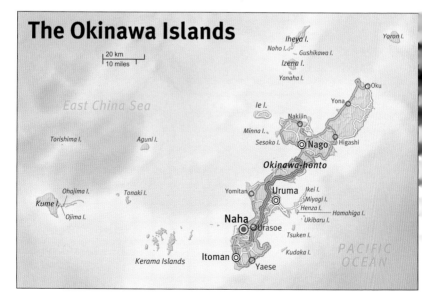

enough to visit and return to Okinawa the same day if you wish, although many also offer relaxing and comfortable accommodations if you'd like to spend a few nights or a weekend. There's no shortage of beautiful islands in the Ryukyu Archipelago. Generally, the further and more remote the island is from Okinawa main island, the more removed from the present time and the stresses of everyday life you'll be. Although some of the further islands are popular with Japanese "mainland" tourists for cultural reasons or as beach and holiday resorts, others, it seems, are seldom visited, except by occasional supply and postal ships.

In the pages that follow, we'll give the approximate sailing times and departure ports (Okinawa has eight ports with commercial ferry services) for each island, but be careful as ferry transportation schedules change all the time due to demand, season and weather. You must always call and confirm your passage, especially if you're bringing a car. Bikes and motorcycles never need reservations as there's always room for them.

A traditional "old Okinawa" exists. It's simply a question of looking for it. For many of the more remote islands, however, there may not be a daily ferry, but there is usually service at least several times a week. Obviously, you will need to visit these for several days. If that's too long, it's worth mentioning that some have airports and regularly scheduled passenger plane service. For example, there are daily flights to Aguni (25 minutes), Kume (35 minutes), Yoron (45 minutes), Okinoerabu (50 minutes), Miyako (60 minutes) and Ishigaki (70 minutes).

The principal island of the Okinawa group of islands (沖縄諸島; Okinawa-shotō) and indeed of the Ryukyu Archipelago (琉球列島; Ryūkyū-Rettō), Okinawa (沖縄本島; Okinawa-hontō) is by far the largest island in the chain. Comprising about half of the archipelago's total landmass, Okinawa's area is 466 square miles (1,208 square kilometers), spread over a most irregularly shaped island, giving it an extended circumference of 296 miles (476 kilometers). Located at the center of the 680-mile (1,100-kilometer)-long Ryukyu chain, Okinawa is approximately 70 miles (112 kilometers) long from its northern tip at Hedo Point to its southern point at Cape Kyan. Its width varies from as narrow as 1.75 miles (3 kilometers) between Moon Beach and Kinbu Bay to a little more

Clean, modern and efficient, Naha Airport is the central transportation hub of flights throughout the Ryukyu Islands.

than 19 miles (30 kilometers) across the Motobu Peninsula.

The population of Okinawa Main Island is approximately 1,250,000, of whom about 315,000 live in the capital city, Naha (那覇市; Naha-shi). The million plus population of Okinawa includes more than 100,000 Americans of whom about 35,000 are active-duty military personnel. The rest are mostly spouses and dependents, contractors affiliated with the US forces and their spouses and dependents, and retirees and their family members. There's a fairly substantial community of former military members who have intermarried with Okinawan women, raised families and made Okinawa their home.

There are several versions of the meaning of the word "Okinawa" (沖縄), but the most common and literal translation is "offshore rope." It's usually more figuratively translated as "rope over" or "rope across" the sea. It was reputedly named by its early inhabitants who believed this long and narrow island, when seen from afar, resembled a piece of rope floating in the ocean.

Okinawa's capital, Naha, is located approximately 400 miles (650 kilometers) southwest of Kagoshima city on mainland Japan's southernmost Kyushu Island. Japan's capital, Tokyo, is located 960 miles (1,540 kilometers) to the northeast. Okinawa's nearest foreign neighbors are the Peoples' Republic of China (Mainland China) and the Republic of China (Taiwan), about 435 and 390 miles (700 and 625 kilometers) to the west and southwest, respectively. Flying time from Naha Airport

(那覇空港; Naha-kūkō) to Tokyo or Seoul, Korea, is about two and a half hours. Taipei and Shanghai are close; flights there take about two hours. Hong Kong and Manila are a little further and can be reached by air in about three hours.

There are more than a dozen Japanese domestic destinations that may be reached on direct flights to and from Naha. To Tokyo, there are more than 20 flights a day. Similarly, cities such as Osaka, Kagoshima and Fukuoka, may be reached at least several times a day. A number of the Ryukyu Islands, such as Ishigaki, Yonaguni, Miyako, Yoron-tō, Okinoerabu, Amami Ōshima, the Keramas and the Daitōs, may also be reached daily. There are daily flights to Taipei and Hong Kong as well, and flights several times a week to Shanghai, Seoul and Manila. Domestic flights use the relatively new (10-year-old) large passenger terminal, which is connected to the Naha monorail service. For the moment, international flights (because of customs and immigration) use what used to be the old and only airline terminal. A brand new international terminal is sched-uled to open, which should considerably

alleviate the pressure on the old terminal, which will then be demolished.

Naha is also the transportation hub for passenger ferries although there is less and less of this service every year. More often, it's cheaper to fly and, of course, it's much faster. If you are taking a ferry to or from Okinawa, note that Naha has three ports, all downtown and within several kilometers of one another.

Naha New Port (那覇新港; Naha shin-kō), which is also commonly called Aja Port (安謝港; Aja-kō), is the terminus for the long-distance ferries to Tokyo, Osaka and, on occasion, other northern Japanese cities. There are six to seven departures every month to Tokyo and Osaka. Operated by the "A" Line, the full run to Tokyo takes approxi-mately 48 hours. It's 40 hours to Osaka. A one-way ticket to Tokyo in second class costs about $250, double that amount for first class. To Osaka, it's less, about $200. An aver-age sized car costs approximately $1,400 to Tokyo and $1,200 to Osaka. There are several stops along the way on each of these routes.

Naha Port (那覇港; Naha-kō) is the depar-ture and arrival place for both the "A" and

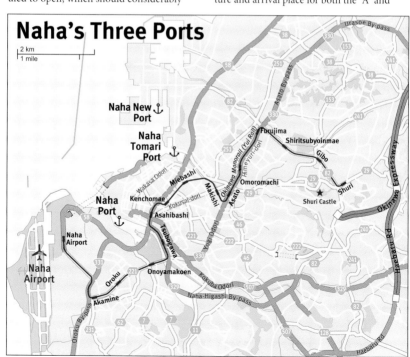

Naha's Tomari Port, the transport hub for ferries to the nearby islands off Okinawa's west coast.

Marix Line alternating daily ferries to the Amami Islands and Kagoshima. It is also Okinawa's main commercial freighter port and used by the military and the Japanese Coast Guard. But if you're going north to the Amami Islands, you don't necessarily have to depart from there. Worth considering is that two hours north (sailing time), the ferries stop at Motobu Port (本部港; Motobu-kō), located near the end of the Motobu Peninsula. The drive from Naha to Motobu using the tolled expressway is 50 miles (80 kilometers) and takes about an hour. The savings on the ship's fare is about $15 per person, plus more for your vehicle if you're bringing one along. So it can make sense to drive to Motobu and catch the ferry from there. Also, if you're leaving your car, parking at Motobu is free. At Naha Port, there is no free parking.

Ferry fares to the Amamis naturally vary on how far you're going. Yoron is the first island northbound and it's about $50 one way for second class from Naha. It's about $35 from Motobu. It's approximately $120 to Amami-Ōshima and $170 all the way to Kagoshima. Deduct about $15 from either of these fares if leaving from Motobu. Private cabins and vehicles cost considerably more.

Naha's third harbor is Tomari Port (泊港; Tomari-kō), also called "Tomarin." It's the transport hub for ferries to the near islands off the west coast of Okinawa-hontō. There is daily service to three of the Kerama Islands, Tokashiki, Aka and Zamami, and daily service to Kume (stopping at Tonaki along the way) and Aguni. Fares to these islands also vary, from around $25 one way to the Keramas and $30 to $35 for Kume and Aguni.

Tomari Port is also the terminal for the once a week ferry to the Daitō Islands. That trip takes 15 hours and costs around $60 one way, second class. The shipping company that used to sail between Naha and the Miyako and Yaeyama Islands went bankrupt several years ago, a victim of low airfares, so there is no longer any public ferry service south of Okinawa. Transport of a vehicle to the Ryukyu southern islands now entails use of a cargo shipping line.

Starting clockwise from Naha, the other five ferry ports on Okinawa are Motobu Port (本部港; Motobu-kō), serving Iejima and just around the next bend of the road from there, Toguchi Port (渡久地港; Toguchi-kō), which serves Minnajima. On the top northern side of the Motobu Peninsula you'll find Unten Port (運天港; Unten-kō), in Nakijin Village (今帰仁村; Nakijin-son), which is the sea terminal for Iheya and Izena Islands. Crossing over to Okinawa's east coast, Katsuren Town's Heshikiya Port (平敷屋港; Heshikiya-kō), is the place to get to Tsuken Island. In southern Okinawa, Chinen Village's Azama Port (安座真港; Azama-kō), is where you'll find the ferries to reach Kudaka Island.

Okinawa is not a tropical destination. It is subtropical. It lies on the same latitude as Orlando, Florida, and enjoys similar, generally mild subtropical weather. The yearly average temperature is around 72 °F (22 °C). Summers are hot, climbing to the mid-90s Fahrenheit (mid-30s Celsius) (95 °F /35 °C), especially in July and August. But winters are milder than Orlando's where, as all orange growers know, it can freeze. Because the island is surrounded by the Pacific Ocean's warm Kuroshio Current (黒潮; lit. "Black Tide"), in winter it never drops below 50 °F (10 °C). Humidity and precipitation are high throughout the year. It rains almost half the days of the year, although much of this is during the rainy season in May and June. Okinawa lies in the path of the East Asian typhoon system known as "Typhoon Alley," and from July through November is often hit by typhoons and monsoon rains.

With the exception of a few of the cooler winter months, Okinawa offers virtually every type of good weather outdoor activity, from golf and tennis, hiking, biking and rock climbing, fishing and whale watching to swimming, snorkeling and scuba diving. There are over a dozen luxury resorts and many more smaller hotels and *minshuku* inns on the island. All feature a variety of activities for their guests and day visitors, or they can connect you to them. Okinawa also has a number of oriental gardens, parks and *gusuku* ruins (ancient fortresses). Finally, and tragically, this wonderful island was the site of the Pacific's most awesome and terrible battle of World War II. As a result, the lower part of Okinawa is covered with historic war memorials, monuments and museums.

Okinawa is a big enough place to divide our coverage of its major sights and places of interest into several sections: the Southern part (南部; Nan-bu), the Middle section (中部; Chu-bu) and the North (北部; Hoku-bu). There are no markers of any kind indicating these delineations. The divisions are more a matter of custom. So, for example, although the Southern section only encompasses the lower 9–14 miles (15–22 kilometers) of the island, it includes the vast majority of the island's population and many, if not the majority, of its best-known sights.

The South begins, quite logically, at Okinawa's bottom, Cape Kyan (喜屋武埼 or 喜屋武岬; Kyan-zaki or Kyan-misaki). The

Cape Kyan, the southwesternmost tip of Okinawa.

Southern section of the island includes the major World War II memorials like the Peace Memorial Park, as well as Okinawa's largest city, Naha, and the airport. Naha's sights include Shuri Castle, the Japanese Naval Underground Headquarters, the main shopping street, Kokusai-dōri, and several of Okinawa's gardens. The airport is just below Naha City and can be reached by the metro. Naha also holds three sea ports, two for long-distance ferries and one for the Kerama Islands and many of the other closer islands.

The South can more or less be said to end shortly above Naha, around Urasoe and Ginowan, giving way to the island's Central section. This area includes most of the US bases on the island and much of the US-influenced culture, such as fast food places, Starbucks and the "American Village" at Chatan. The Central section includes the *gusuku* (fortresses) at Nakagusuku and Katsuren, the Yomitan area and Cape Zanpa, and the Katsuren Peninsula and its little collection of causeway-connected islands. The Central section runs a total of about 25 miles (40 kilometers) north, to just below the island's second largest city of Nago. The Central part also includes virtually every one of Okinawa's prime beachfront resort hotels. These string along Okinawa's central west "Onna" coast, from Cape Zanpa to just below Nago.

That leaves the island's Northern section. It begins around Nago and continues north to the end of the island at Cape Hedo, a total of about 25 miles (40 kilometers). In addition to Nago and its few sights, the north includes what many consider to be Okinawa's premier attraction, the Churaumi Aquarium, located near the end of the Motobu Peninsula. Offshore from there, both to the west and north, are about a half dozen inhabited islands included in the Okinawa-shotō. The Motobu Peninsula also holds some *gusuku* ruins. Almost the entire top northern end of Okinawa, the uppermost 20 or so miles (32 kilometers), is virtually uninhabited. It's literally a jungle out there and, in fact, contains the very large, and restricted, US Marine Corps Jungle Warfare Training Center at Camp Gonsalves. One of its more famous former commanders (1973–4) was Captain Oliver North (1943–present), perhaps best known for his role in the Iran-Contra affair during the Reagan administration.

Busena Terrace Beach Resort
Okinawa's top luxury hotel hosted the Year 2000 G-8 Summit. US President Bill Clinton, Russia's Vladimir Putin, Great Britain's Tony Blair, France's Jacques Chirac, Canada's Jean Chrétien, Japan's Yoshiro Mori, Italy's Giuliano Amato and Germany's Gerhard Schröder were housed in private villas costing from $2,000 to $5,000 per night. "Regular" rooms run a bit less, from $500 to $1,200 a night, breakfast not included. There was some criticism of the Summit at the time. Despite a world-wide recession and a pledge to help poor countries, it's reported that Japan spent over US $750 million to host the event.

Naha's Loisir Hotel
This in-town luxury hotel features a beautiful butterfly swimming pool designed by Hanae Mori, Japan's most honored female designer. The hotel also has indoor spa facilities and a natural hot spring.

Screwpine Walking Tree (*Pandanus utilis*)
There are over 600 species in the genus, but one of the most widespread is *Pandanus utilis*, commonly called the screwpine or walking tree. "Screw" refers to the arrangement of their spiraling leaves, which are fashioned into all kinds of hats, mats, baskets and thatch material by many Pacific Islanders. The "walking" refers to their apparent desire to get up and go and walk away from wherever they are. They are also called "pineapple" trees for their fruits' resemblance to a pineapple. The fruit is edible but not good. It's called "famine" food in many places. In Japanese, the trees are called *Nioi-takonoki* or *Nioi-adan* (ニオイタコノキ or ニオイ アダン). They are related to the grass, orchid, lily and palm families and have nothing to do with pines or pineapples. Although screwpines are indigenous to Madagascar and the Indian Ocean, they have spread to all the tropical places of the world. They are extremely tough and are drought-tolerant and salt-, pest- and disease-resistant. They have conquered every remote beachfront in the Ryukyus. Their sturdy roots effectively bind the sand dunes along the coast from eroding water and wind.

Chapter 5

OKINAWA MAIN ISLAND: THE SOUTH
沖縄諸島
Memorial museums, cultural sites

The Southern part of Okinawa Main Island (沖縄本島南部; Okinawa-hontō Nanbu) can be defined as that part of the island which begins near the very bottom of the island, at Cape Kyan, and runs up north to a little past Naha, say to around Ginowan (宜野湾市; Ginowan-shi) and Urasoe (浦添市; Urasoé-shi). This portion is about 12 miles (20 kilometers) from north to south and anywhere from 6 to around 9 miles (10 to around 15 kilometers) from east to west. Although it does not occupy an equal one-third of the island's land area, it has more than three quarters of the island's people living here and

it's Okinawa's most densely populated section. It includes many of the most popular sightseeing attractions on the island. Here's a listing, primarily from south to north, of most of the attractions or memorials that a visitor might wish to see.

1. **OKINAWA PEACE PRAYER PARK AND MEMORIAL HALL** 沖縄戦跡国定公園;奄美大島 Although commonly said to be the "southernmost" point on Okinawa, Cape Kyan and its lighthouse and monument are actually located at the center of the southernmost end of Okinawa, and not quite the very end. From this vantage point there are some great views over the Kyan cliffs to the southeasternmost, and most southern, point on the island, Cape Ara (荒崎; Ara-zaki). If you're flying into Naha on a clear day, you'll also get a good perspective of this end of the island from an even higher vantage point. The usual air approach to Okinawa, due to prevailing winds, is from the south and most flights pass right over this final terminus of the island.

About 5.5 miles (9 kilometers) by road to the east of Kyan-misaki, at Okinawa's southeastern end, is the very large Okinawa Peace Prayer Park and Memorial Hall (沖縄戦跡国定公園; Okinawaken heiwakinen kōen shiryōkan). Construction of the Okinawa Prefectural Peace Museum, as it is formally known, began in 1978 in the town of Mabuni (摩文仁; Mabuni), the area of the last fighting of the Battle of Okinawa. The exhibits give an overview of the battle and the island's subsequent reconstruction. The Peace Art Museum displays Okinawa art while the Memorial Hall is a contemplation chapel, within which is a great lacquer image of Buddha.

There's some interesting architecture in the park, including an enormous horseshoe-

Lacquer Buddha at the Peace Park
Inspired by the death of his two sons who were killed in the Battle of Okinawa, local artist Shinzan Yamada (1885–1977) created this statue over an 18-year period. It is the world's largest lacquer representation of Buddha.

Peace Memorial Park
Regardless of their nationality, the over 240,000 persons killed in the Battle of Okinawa are remembered here, their names engraved on black granite slabs. Southern Okinawa also houses the Peace Art Museum; "Heiwa Kinendo," a giant statue of Buddha, the Japanese Underground Naval Headquarters and "Himeyuri-no-To," the site where more than 200 schoolgirls and their teachers chose to die, rather than face (what they were told) certain rape and slaughter at the hands of the American "barbarians."

shaped cenotaph and a fountain with an eternal flame—a "fire and water" theme. Without question, however, the park's most sobering monument is the Cornerstone of Peace (平和の礎; Heiwa-no Ishiji), a vast collection of stone plaques engraved with the names of the fallen. It was completed in 1995 to commemorate the 50th anniversary of the battle. The deaths of some 240,000 soldiers, sailors and civilians, Japanese, Koreans, Taiwanese, Americans and Britons, men, women and children are recorded here. The sheer volume and magnitude of the dead is overwhelming. This truly was a battle to end all battles, yet it did not. The madness that was Bushidō (武士道; "Way of the Warrior") Japan did not end until it was extinguished in a cloud the shape of a mushroom.

② RYUKYU GLASS VILLAGE 琉球ガラス村

Within 3–4 miles (5–6 kilometers) north of both Cape Kyan and the Peace Park, whichever way you choose to travel, you'll most likely come across the next two sights: the Ryukyu Glass Village (琉球ガラス村; Ryūkyū garasu mura), north above Cape Kyan, and Himeyuri Park, north above the Peace Park.

The Ryukyu Glass Village is the largest glass blowing and glass crafting factory in Okinawa. Here visitors can observe the production process involved in making glassware, cups, bowls and other decorative items. The brilliant use of red, blue, green, and other colors in the glassware is quite lovely. Other traditional handicrafts of Okinawa, such as ceramics and pottery, are also on display and available for sale at the shop within the factory.

Eternal flame fountain at the Peace Park.

Eisa Drum Dance (エイサー)

Obon (お盆) or simply Bon (盆) is the Japanese ceremony to honor the spirits of deceased ancestors. It is the equivalent of the Chinese Festival of the Hungry Ghosts (盂蘭盆), which is primarily a religious affair. In Japan, this Buddhist custom has evolved into a family reunion holiday during which people return to and clean up ancestral grave sites. It has been celebrated for centuries and traditionally ends with a dance, known as Bon-Odori (盆踊り) or Bon Dance. The style of dance varies regionally throughout Japan. In Okinawa it is known as Eisa. The Obon Festival lasts for three days, but its starting date also varies widely. The traditional lunar calendar places it on the 15th day of the 7th month. It usually falls in July or August. It is danced by a dozen or more young men and women to the accompaniment of singing, chanting and drumming. Music is performed on the *sanshin* (三線), a snakeskin-covered, three-stringed small banjo-type instrument, as well as up to three types of drums: *ōdaiko* (大太鼓), a large barrel drum; *shimedaiko* (締太鼓), a medium-sized drum; and *paaranku* (パーランク), a small hand drum. Depending on how much *awamori* is consumed, festivities can go on all day and all night.

3 **HIMEYURI PEACE MUSEUM AND WAR MEMORIAL** ひめゆり.平和祈念資料館
Roughly 1.75 miles (3 kilometers) east of the Ryukyu Glass Village, and just over a mile (2 kilometers) north of Okinawa Peace Park is the Himeyuri Peace Museum and War Memorial (ひめゆり.平和祈念資料館; Himéyuri heiwakinen shiryōkan). The museum and memorial were built in honor of the schoolgirls and teachers mobilized as nurse assistants on March 23, 1945. Just before the Battle of Okinawa, a group of 222 girls and 18 teachers from the Okinawa Women's Normal School and the First Prefectural Girls High School were ordered

by the Japanese Army to join the Haebaru Field Hospital medical unit as nurses. They were called "Himé-yuri" (Red Lilies). The Japanese soldiers told them that if they were captured, the Americans would rape and murder them. Rather than surrendering, they hid in caves and killed themselves. Only five survived. It's reported that many of the schoolgirls plunged to their deaths by leaping over nearby cliffs rather than face the American invaders, so terrorized were they with propaganda.

The Peace Museum exhibits photographs of the victims, their personal effects, model reconstructions of the appalling conditions

Himeyuri War Memorial.

Caverns in Technicolor at Gyokusendo Cave.

under which they lived and testimonies from survivors in an appeal against the misery of war. Every passing year, as memories of the Battle of Okinawa fade further and further, the Himeyuri Peace Museum and War Memorial serve to remind us of war and its insanity. This memorial is more frequently visited by Japanese mainland tourists than by Westerners.

4 CULTURE KINGDOM GYOKUSENDO 文化王国玉泉洞

Around 3 miles (5 kilometers) northeast of Himeyuri or 4 miles (6.4 kilometers) northeast of the Peace Park is Okinawa World, also known as the Culture Kingdom Gyokusendo (文化王国玉泉洞; Bunka ōkoku gyokusendō). It's a tourist theme park about Okinawan culture. The park's main attractions are Gyokusendo Cave, a crafts village, and a *habu* snake exhibit. The Gyokusendo Cave (玉泉洞; Gyokunsen-do) is the longest of many caves in southern Okinawa and Japan's second longest cave. Its total length is approximately 3 miles (5 kilometers). Although only a little less than a mile (1 kilometer) of the cave is open to the public, that section features some quite spectacular stalactites and stalagmites, all lit up in Technicolor. The cave was discovered in 1967 and used as one of the locations for the 1974 monster movie, *Godzilla vs. Mechagodzilla* (ゴジラ対メカゴジラ; Gojira Tai Mekagojira), which played in the US as *Godzilla vs. the Bionic Monster* or *Godzilla vs. the Cosmic Monster*.

The Okinawa World crafts village is a replica of an olden-time Ryukyu village with workshops displaying various traditional Okinawan crafts, such as weaving, dyeing, paper making, pottery, musical instrument making and glass blowing as well as sugarcane processing and brewing. Visitors can see how these crafts were practiced. There's a thrice daily Eisa, the Okinawan drumbeat dance. There's also a large gift shop where typical items can be purchased, and a restaurant which specializes in Okinawan cuisine. The Habu Park area consists of a snake museum, a small zoo and a *habu* snake versus mongoose show. The snakes are sacrificed six times daily to the predator mongoose. Some people object to these "demonstrations" as unnecessarily cruel, for the snakes really don't have much of a chance against the mongoose and are invariably killed.

5 GUSUKU (FORTRESS) RUINS 御城

The southern section of Okinawa has quite a large number of *gusuku* (fortress) ruins, but they are just that—ruins—not too interesting for most casual visitors. If this does interest you, here's a list of many of them, but again, they are mostly piles of stones. Close by to Point Kyan are the ruins of Gushikawa Castle (具志川城) and Kyan Castle (喜屋武城). Near Okinawa Peace Park is Itomansatsuki Gusuku Ruins (糸満城), and near Gushikama village, just below Okinawa World, are the Ona Castle and Gushikama Ruins. Further along the east coast, north to the Chinen Peninsula (知念半島; Chinen-hantō), are several more ruins, including Minton Castle; Chinen Gusuku (知念城), Azama Castle (安座真城) and Sashiki Gusuku (佐敷城). To the north, at the boundary of what we'll call Central Okinawa, at Urasoe, there are the ruins of Urasoe

Gusuku Fortress (御城)

Gusuku is the Okinawan word for a castle or fortress. In Japanese it is *shiro*. The Kanji characters are the same. There are *gusuku* (or *gusuku* ruins) throughout the Ryukyus, but many of the finest examples are on Okinawa. Many have been declared UNESCO World Heritage Sites. The *gusuku*'s heyday was between the 13th and 18th centuries when feudal lords, called *aji*, ruled the Okinawan kingdom. Each had his own fortress. The best examples on the island today are Naha's Shuri Castle, Nakagusuku in central Okinawa, Zakimi in Yomitan, Katsuren Castle on the Katsuren Peninsula and Nakijin on northern Okinawa's Motobu Peninsula. A section of the Katsuren Castle ramparts is shown above.

Seifa Utaki Shinto Shrine
Meaning "purified place of Utaki," this Shinto shrine dates from time immemorial. Along with a few *gusuku* sites, it is one of only a handful of UNESCO World Heritage Sites on the island of Okinawa, or in the whole of the Ryukyus. The Utaki sacred altars are located at one of the highest points on the eastern end of the Chinen Peninsula. The overlook at these giant stones is of Kudakajima, which itself is a holy place in Okinawan lore.

General Buckner Memorial Plaque
The commanding officer of the 10th Army, Lt.-Gen. Buckner, was killed here on June 18, 1945, three days before the island of Okinawa was declared secured. He was surveying the last skirmishes of the battle when he was struck in the chest by shrapnel from enemy fire.

Castle (浦添城). None of these ruins amount to much, at least to a non-archeologist. The better or more substantial or restored *gusuku* are further north.

6 SEIFA UTAKI 斎場御嶽

If you have come to the Chinen Peninsula you'll find one of the island's very few non-*gusuku* UNESCO Heritage Sites. It's Seifa Utaki (斎場御嶽), the most sacred place in Okinawa. A legend of the origin of the Ryukyus holds that the first of all gods, Tedako (god of the sun), ordered two gods to land on the islands and organize them as nations. The legendary creator, Amamikiyo (アマミキヨ), thereupon established sacred sites, one of which was Seifa Utaki. Two great naturally split stone slabs form an upside-down V and mark the entrance to a prayer site that faces Kudakajima, the island of the gods' origin. Former royal rulers of Okinawa used to visit Seifa Utaki every year to pray for a good harvest.

The site is high up on the Chinen bluffs, with a fine view of Nakagusuku Bay and Kudaka Island. In former times, Seifa Utaki was closed to ordinary citizens; only royalty was permitted to pass through the gates. There are six places of worship along a couple of well-marked pathways. Because of its historical and cultural importance, it was designated a World Heritage Site by UNESCO in December 2000.

7 GENERAL BUCKNER MEMORIAL PLAQUE 中将バクナー記念碑

From the Chinen Peninsula, we'll drive back across this southern end of the island, west to Naha City. We'll stop for a moment, however, at one not very well known memorial along the way. It's a small bronze plaque set on to a stone. It bears the inscription: "Lieutenant General Simon Bolivar Buckner Jr. killed on this spot 18 June 1945 Battle of Okinawa." That's it, just a reminder of the fleeting nature of life, and of heroism. It's a small reminder

The Battle of Okinawa

Island by Island, one stepping stone to the next, across the great expanse of the Pacific Ocean, from Pearl Harbor to the Johnston Atoll, to Alaska's Aleutian Islands, to Samoa and Fiji, to Midway, Wake and the Marshall Islands, to New Caledonia, the Coral Sea and the Solomon Islands, to New Guinea and Guadalcanal, to Saipan, Leyte Gulf, the Northern Marianas, Guam, Bataan, Palawan, the Philippines and Borneo, to the Japanese islands of Iwō Jima and, finally, to Okinawa, the Pacific War was the greatest, most massive theater of operations ever witnessed in human history. And of all the many battles in this gargantuan Pacific conflict, the Battle of Okinawa was to become the largest air–sea–land campaign ever undertaken. It's only meaningful comparison is D Day on the beaches of Normandy one year earlier.

Code-named "Operation Iceberg" and also known as the "Typhoon of Steel" (テツの雨; *tetsu no ame* ("rain of iron") or *tetsu no bōfū* ("violent wind of iron"), over 180,000 Allied troops assembled, landed and defeated a dug-in, entrenched army of 120,000 Japanese. More people died during the Battle of Okinawa than all those killed by the twin atomic bombings of Hiroshima and Nagasaki. Allied casualties totaled more than 60,000, with 12,000 of those killed. Japanese soldiers killed numbered 110,000. Only about 10,000 surrendered or were taken prisoner. It is estimated that as many as 100,000 Okinawan civilians also perished in the battle. By comparison, Allied and German casualties at D Day were approximately 10,000 on each side, with only negligible civilian deaths. More ships were engaged, more aircraft flew, more bombs were dropped, more naval guns were fired and more *kamikaze* (神風) boats and aircraft were employed than in any other operation in the Pacific War or in the history of war.

The battle was launched on Easter Sunday, April 1st, 1945, under the command of Lieutenant-General Simon Bolivar Buckner Jr, who was to die three days before the end of the invasion, thus becoming the highest rank-ing US officer to be killed by enemy fire during World War II. The battle lasted until June 22nd, a total of 82 days. Other commanders in the conflict read like a "who's who" of American military history. Major General Roy Geiger, who replaced Buckner after his death, became the only US Marine to command a numbered army of the US Army in combat. He was relieved five days later by General Joseph Stilwell, best remembered for his service in China and Burma. Naval operations were commanded by Admirals Chester W. Nimitz, Raymond A. Spruance and William F. "Bull" Halsey. The document ending the Battle of Okinawa was signed on what is now Kadena Air Base on September 7, 1945. During the course of the battle, two other major events transpired: the death of President Franklin D. Roosevelt on April 12th and the surrender of Nazi Germany on May 8th.

The Battle of Okinawa was the bloodiest of the Pacific War. Over 30 Allied ships were sunk and over 350 were damaged, mostly by *kami-kaze*. The fleet lost almost 800 aircraft. Nearly 5,000 Navy seamen and 8,000 Marines and Army soldiers were killed. Combat stress caused tremendous numbers of psychiatric battle fatigue. There were more than 26,000 non-battle casualties. The rate of combat losses was so heavy that there were calls in Congress for an investigation into the conduct of the American military commanders. Japanese losses were horrific. Of an estimated 110,000 fatalities, over 20,000 were burned alive by flame throwers or entombed in caves. Thousands committed suicide, mostly by blowing themselves up with their own hand grenades. No one really knows how many innocent civilians were killed. Estimates range from 40,000 to 150,000, anywhere from a quarter to a third of the island's population, many of them pressed into service by the Japanese Army. The Empire of Japan lost almost 8,000 aircraft and 16 combat ships. Unsurprisingly, the tremendous cost of this battle in terms of men, material and time weighed heavily on then President Harry S. Truman and his consequent decision to use the atomic bomb against Japan just six weeks later.

A tunnel in the Former Japanese Naval Underground Headquarters, part of the labyrinth where 4,000 men lived and then ended their lives.

The Shikina-en Royal Garden is a classic Ryukyuan garden arranged around a pond and the setting for several restored royal buildings.

of one man among the many men who died in service to their country. The General Buckner Memorial Plaque (中将バクナー記念碑; Chūjō bakunā kinen-hi) is rather hard to find. It's located in Kuniyoshi (国芳; Kuniyoshi), not far from Itoman (糸満市; Itoman-shi), where much of the fighting took place.

8 FORMER JAPANESE NAVAL UNDERGROUND HEADQUARTERS 旧海軍司令部壕

If you're coming into Naha from the south, one of the first places you'll reach is the Former Japanese Naval Underground Headquarters (旧海軍司令部壕; Kyū kaigun shireibugō), now a museum and memorial. It's about 2.5 miles (4 kilometers) from the central downtown. Follow the road signs for there's really no clue to what lies below except that above the headquarters, located in a small and peaceful park on Oroku Hill, there's a memorial tower, a cenotaph, for the war dead.

In 1944, anticipating the US invasion, the Japanese Navy Okinawa District Command ordered the building of an impregnable lair, an underground headquarters designed so that they could survive any possible bombardment. Carved into the coral stone, the marks made by the pickaxes can still be seen on the walls and ceilings. The Imperial Navy Vice Admiral Minoru Ota and 4,000 of his men lived through the invasion, but as the tide turned against them, they committed suicide during the war's last remaining days. The blood and body parts have been removed but traces of the mass suicide remain. Most chose hand grenades and there is shrapnel from the suicide explosions imbedded in the walls. There is a plaintive message written on a wall by Commander Ota. It's a

farewell message for his chief officer and praises the spirit and devotion of the Okinawans who served in the Imperial Army during the battle. The message even acknowledges that the Okinawan people were not always well treated by his Japanese troops.

After the war, the headquarters was left much as it stands today. The tunnels are about 100 feet (30 meters) underground and run in all directions from the Commander's post and quarters, to officer's quarters, barracks, communications, dining and kitchen facilities, a makeshift hospital, ammunitions magazines and various storerooms.

9 SHIKINA-EN ROYAL GARDEN 識名園

If we stay to the east of downtown and drive only a few miles north and east, we'll come to another of Okinawa's UNESCO World Heritage Sites, Shikina-en Royal Garden (識名園; Shikina-en). Built in 1799 and located on a high point above Naha City, this garden contained the royal family's largest country villa. It is Okinawa's least known yet most classic Ryukyuan gardens. The estate was used for a retreat, not only for the royal family but for envoys visiting from the Empire of China. As it was used as a welcoming place for visiting dignitaries, it is by no coincidence that it is one of the few places on Okinawa where the ocean cannot be seen. There is an observatory platform, Kankō-dai, on the southern side of the park where foreign visitors were brought, to impress them with the great size of the Ryukyu kingdom.

The style of Shikina-en incorporates elements of Chinese, Japanese and Ryukyuan design. For example, Rokkaku-do is a small hexagonal pagoda and place of contemplation. Perfectly shaped, its black-glazed-tile

The Main Hall (Seiden) at Shuri Castle.

Shuri Castle seen from the surrounding park.

roof is pure Chinese. It's sited on its own little islet in the pond and reached by crossing over *ishi-bashi* Chinese arched stone bridges. In contrast, Udun, the palace house, is authentically Japanese. It is modeled between the end of the Meiji and the beginning of the Taisho era.

Shikina-en's garden plantings are carefully arranged around its central pond to take advantage of the seasonal changes in subtropical Okinawa. Cherry and plum trees blossom along the east side of the park in spring. Summer blooms include wisteria, then water lotus, among others. Fall brings the dark violet flowers of *kikyo*, Chinese bell flowers, and the sweet fragrance of osmanthus bushes, found everywhere in the park. A freshwater spring, Ikutoku-sen, bubbles up from within limestone heights and supplies the ponds. Their waters exit at Taki-Guchi or Fall Crest, a carved stone culvert that allows overflow to drop without creating damage below. Shikina-en was completely destroyed in the Battle of Okinawa but has been faithfully restored to its original state.

10 SHURI CASTLE 首里城

A little over a mile (2 kilometers) north of Shikina-en you'll come across one more UNESCO World Heritage Site, which also

was obliterated in 1945. Shuri Castle (首里城; Shuri-jō) was the Royal Palace of the Ryukyu Kingdom from the beginning of the 15th century until its bombing in the Battle of Okinawa. It has been reconstructed on its original site based on photographs and historical records. Completed and opened in 1992, Shuri-jō has become one of Japan's best known sites since its Shureimon Gate was chosen to appear on the 2000 Yen banknote.

For almost 500 years, the castle was the seat of the Ryukyuan Royal Court and administrative center of the kingdom. It was the central point of foreign trade as well as the political, commercial and cultural heart of the Ryukyus. Perhaps due to its great historical and cultural significance, it was selected, along with a half dozen *gusuku* and other places, as a UNESCO World Heritage Site. However, it must be said that this castle, even though fully restored and not a ruin by any means, is in many ways the least impressive of the Okinawan *gusuku*. Although its massive coral stone surrounding walls are spectacular, the castle itself seems more like a red-painted plywood reproduction. There are some mildly interesting interior exhibits, but overall, up close and in person, it simply does not seem to be the same impressive edifice seen in photographs. Having said that, this *faux gusuku* is nevertheless one of Naha's top, if not the top, attractions.

Shureimon (守礼門; Shurei no mon)

Pictured on the then new 2000 Yen note issued in the Year 2000 in honor of the 26th G-8 Summit held in Okinawa, the Shuri Gate is the second of Shuri Castle's main entranceways. It was built in the 16th century and clearly reflects Chinese influence. The four Chinese characters framed on top, 守禮之邦 (Shu rei no kuni), roughly mean "the Ryukyus are a Land of Propriety." The gate was destroyed in World War II but rebuilt to its original design in the 1970s.

11 KOKUSAI-DŌRI 国際通り

From the heights of Shuri Castle we'll drop down and head west for about a mile (2 kilometers) right into the heart of downtown Naha, and its most popular and well-known street, Kokusai-dōri (国際通り; lit. "International Street"). It's the main shopping street for tourists and for Okinawan young people and considered one of the top tourist destinations in Okinawa. Kokusai-dōri is a 1-mile (1.6 kilometer)-long selection of restaurants and bars, coffee shops, souvenir stands, clothing stores, music emporiums and everything else in between. The street gives an overall view of modern Okinawan culture in the heart of Naha. It runs from the Asato area to the prefectural area, which includes Palette Kumoji and Naha City Hall. It's served by a monorail at both its ends and by public bus along its length. Kokusai-dōri was born immediately after the end of World War II and quickly became the symbol of Okinawa's revival.

Kokusai-dōri is especially popular in the evening when the lights are on and street merchants and musicians come out to ply their trades and talents. The street gets its name from the former Kokusai Theater

The Heiwa-dōri arcade is one of several glass-roofed pedestrian arcades running perpendicular from Kokusai-dōri.

which was located nearby. On Sunday afternoons, from noon to 6:00PM, Kokusai-dōri is closed to car and bus traffic and is far more pleasant to stroll.

12 HEIWA-DŌRI 平和通り

About midway along the length of Kokusai-dōri you'll come across Heiwa-dōri (平和通り; lit. "Peace Street") and Ichiba-hon-dōri

Indoor Fish Market

Around the world fish, fruit and vegetable markets are usually pretty colorful places. This is no more so than in Okinawa. In the glass-roofed arcades running off Kokusai-dōri, you'll find markets stocking about every kind of fish, fruit and vegetable imaginable, and some almost unimaginable. How about scarlet octopus? How about turquoise parrot fish? Spend time having a good look around the markets. It's a feast for the eyes.

市場本通り; lit. "Main Market Street").
These are long pedestrian-only indoor
arcades covered by glass roofs all the way.
That's a big plus in the summer when the sun
can be brutal, or during the rainy season, for
equally obvious reasons. You'll find hundreds
of shops under these arcades, including a
fabulous fish market. The undersea creatures
on display rival those at Churaumi Aquarium
but with one big difference: these fish are on
ice. They're for sale and meant to be eaten. At
the end of Heiwa-dōri is the Tsuboya (壺屋;
lit. "Pot Shop") area, which is famous for its
many traditional ceramic shops. If this is of
interest to you, be sure to visit the Tsuboya
Pottery Museum (壺屋陶器会館; Tsuboya
tōki kaikan). It's well worth the small admission price.

Three lovely Okinawan ladies out for a stroll in the Fuzhou Garden.

13 FUKUSHU-EN 福州園

We're not done yet. We have a few more
places to see in Naha before we move north
to the central section of Okinawa. Fortunately, if anyone in your party is getting tired,
these next two places are peaceful and both
are good for taking a breather. One is a tranquil garden, the other a historic and contemplative temple.

Fukushu-en (福州園; Fukushū-en; lit.
"Fuzhou Garden") is a beautiful garden with
a large pond, waterfall and various pagodas
designed and constructed using traditional
Chinese techniques. Chinese people first
came to Naha some 600 years ago from
Fujian Province and established a community
in Naha's Kumé neighborhood. Through
the years, their skills became of great value

Ornamental Goldfish

We've borrowed a Japanese
word to describe the large,
beautiful, domesticated goldfish found in many oriental
garden ponds. In fact, the direct
translation of *koi* (鯉) is "carp"
and taxonomically the species
is *Cyprinus carpio*. When the
Japanese refer to what we call
koi, they use the term *nishiki-goi* (錦鯉), which translates
as "brocade carp," the fancy
ornamental variety. Both *koi*
and goldfish are cousins in the
carp family. The average *koi* can
grow to 24–36 inches (60–90
cm) in its lifetime, which can

span several decades. *Koi* breeding is thought to have begun around the 17th century in Japan's
Niigata Prefecture. Farmers working the rice fields noticed that some carp were more brightly colored
than others and thus they captured and raised them. By the 19th century a number of color patterns
had been established, most notably the red and white *kohaku*. *Koi* breeding is complicated since
most varieties do not breed true and much of the knowledge is a closely guarded secret. Fish are
selected for appearance when viewed from above. An aesthetically attractive fish of a rare variety
may cost hundreds or even thousands of dollars.

Fukushu-en viewing pagoda and waterfall.

to the Ryukyu kingdom, particularly in the early years of the dynasty. This relationship included periodic visits from envoys of the Chinese Emperor. In 1992, in commemoration of this long-standing friendship, an authentic example of a formal Chinese garden was created to celebrate the 10th anniversary of the twin cities of Naha and Fuzhou, the capital of Fujian.

Materials from Fuzhou were brought over and Chinese craftsmen assembled them. The plants, which for the most part are marked with their Latin botanical names as well as their English and Japanese equivalents, surround a series of interconnected ponds filled with hungry *koi*. For 100 Yen, vending machines dispense packets of fish pellets. Visitors will be astonished and delighted at just how many giant goldfish are in these ponds. There are lots of turtles too.

The park contains a number of traditional pagodas, varying in shape and style. There are two multistory pagoda replicas, several resting platforms adjacent to or above the ponds, and at the garden's center a magnificent viewing pagoda high above a waterfall. There is a cave underneath this little man-made mountain of stone and water waiting to be explored. The reward is a view of the park through the waterfall from behind it.

14 NAMINOUE SHRINE 波の上宮

If you're not yet at peace from your garden visit, a spiritual visit might better suit you. About five blocks away, maybe 10 minutes on foot, is the Naminoue Shrine (波の上宮; Naminoué-gū; lit. "Above the Waves Shrine") the primary Shinto shrine in Okinawa Prefecture. It's beautifully sited atop a bluff overlooking the East China Sea and the approach to Naha shin-kō and Tomari Harbor.

The shrine's place in history and lore goes back a long way, maybe 1,000 years. Legend holds that a fisherman found a mysterious stone at the site. He prayed, his catches became greater, the stone glowed, but then the gods took the stone away. But the place itself became holy. As early as 1367 historical records show that a Buddhist temple was founded on the site. It came to be called Naminoué-san Gokoku-ji (波上山護国寺; lit. "Naminoue Mountain Temple for the Protection of the Country").

Naminoue was to become associated with the protection of the many ships coming and going from Naha as Okinawa's trade with China, Japan, Korea and regions to the south expanded. Prayers were offered to the gods of the seas for safe journeys, good navigation and successful trade. At the beginning of each year, the Ryukyu king visited the shrine and prayed for the peace and prosperity of the kingdom and for good harvests and good fishing. Naminoue rose to become the most important shrine of the Ryukyu kingdom.

Interestingly, the shrine was to play host and home to an early and controversial Christian missionary. In 1846 Bernard Jean Bettelheim (1811–70), a Hungarian-Jewish would-be rabbi converted to Protestantism, arrived in Naha with his wife and children

The main prayer hall (Haiden) at Naminoue, Okinawa's primary Shinto shrine.

The 1926 memorial to Bettelheim at Naminoue Shinto Shrine.

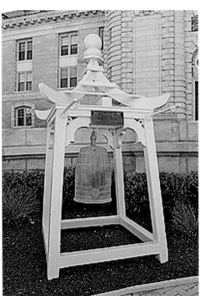

The Naminoue shrine bell at Annapolis Naval Academy in Maryland, US.

by way of Italy, Turkey, England and Hong Kong. Refused permission to disembark, Bettelheim bribed his way ashore, bringing his wife, children and possessions with him. He found refuge at Naminoue and thereupon remained. Difficult as it may be to believe, he was to preach, teach and bully his way on Okinawa without any real reprisal or repercussion for the next seven years. Despite his eccentric and irascible behavior, his frequent run-ins with local officials and his unauthorized occupation of the shrine, he became useful as the unofficial translator for all visiting Western ships and seemingly could not be budged from his new-found residence at the shrine.

When Commodore Matthew C. Perry (1794–1858) came to Japan in 1853, Bettelheim went aboard his ship to meet him. Through his understanding of the language and culture, Bettelheim was uniquely qualified to act as an intermediary between the Ryukyuan authorities and the visiting Americans. His relations with Perry were good and he was able to act as an advisor and agent. Later, in 1854, he left (his wife and children had departed separately a few months earlier) on another of Perry's voyages and resettled in the United States.

Dr Bettelheim and his family eventually were to resettle in Illinois, then Missouri, where he and his wife are buried. In spite of this rather mixed record, it seems somewhat odd that in May, 1926, a memorial to honor Bettelheim was unveiled on the grounds of his former home at the shrine. Nevertheless, the memorial is there today.

But the story is not over. When Perry departed from his final visit to Okinawa more than a year later, having left and returned several times in the interim, he was offered, among other gifts, a temple bell from Shuri Castle. For whatever reason, this was found unsuitable and a bell from the Naminoue Gokoku-ji Shrine was offered instead. It's an historic piece, having been forged in 1456 during the reign of Shō Taikyū. As it was part of the Bettelheim residence, which was considered to have desecrated the shrine and therefore had not been used as a place of worship for eight years, the Ryukyuan authorities were willing to part with it. Bettelheim, who kept meticulous diaries, expressed delight in seeing the "heathen temple" further dismantled.

Intended by Commodore Perry to be mounted atop the Washington Monument which was then under construction, the

Naha's Tsushima-maru Memorial Museum.

The Gallery of lost children at the museum.

committee responsible for the monument rejected the idea and turned down the gift. Later, Perry's widow donated the bell to the US Naval Academy at Annapolis, Maryland, where it was installed just outside Bancroft Hall, the academy's largest building. The bell was kept and rung in celebration of Navy victories in the annual Army–Navy football game for the next hundred years. However, the original bell was considered an important part of Japanese cultural heritage. In the 1980s, negotiations were undertaken by the US Navy to return it to Japan and it was returned to Naminoue Shrine in 1987. An exact replica was cast and it stands at Bancroft Hall today—and it's still rung for football victories.

15 TSUSHIMA-MARU MEMORIAL MUSEUM
対馬丸記念館

There are two more lesser sights in the general area, one in the Kumé neighborhood, in fact, next door to the Naminoe Shrine; the other a few blocks north in the Tomari district.

Around the corner, one block east of the Shinto Shrine, to the right as you are facing it, is a small museum dedicated to a very sad event—the World War II sinking of the *Tsushima-maru*. Mentioned on page 46 in

connection with Akusekijima in the Tokaras, this was the tragic 1944 wartime event that took the lives of some 1,500 civilians, more than half of whom were schoolchildren. All were being evacuated from Naha and Okinawa to the "safety" of Kagoshima on the Japanese mainland when the USS *Bowfin*, a navy submarine, torpedoed the ship.

The Tsushima-maru Memorial Museum (対馬丸記念館; Tsushima-Maru kinen-kan) is dedicated to these young victims as well as the tragedy of war. It's a somber place. One problem, there's nothing in English, everything is in Japanese, but you really don't need a translator. The Gallery of hundreds of photos of the children and babies who perished speaks for itself. It's moving without needing any words. All these little lives, not yet hardly begun, extinguished.

The *Bowfin*, in fact, saw a great deal of action in the Pacific. She sank more than a dozen cargo ships. She served for many years after the war in various capacities until she was decommissioned in 1971. Subsequently, she was taken to Pearl Harbor where she now serves as a memorial museum. Tours are available although some areas of the ship are off-limits. The *Bowfin* was declared a National Historic Landmark in 1986.

The USS Bowfin moored in Pearl Harbor, Honolulu, Hawaii.

The International Cemetery at Tomari.

Contrary to some written reports, Commodore Mathew C. Perry is not buried here. This stone and plaque are only a memorial to him. His remains lie near the place of his birth, in Newport, Rhode Island, US.

16 **INTERNATIONAL CEMETERY AT TOMARI DISTRICT** 那覇沖縄での国際墓

Finally, about a dozen blocks to the north of the Tsushima-maru Museum, just above Tomari Port, is a small cemetery known as the International Cemetery at Tomari District (那覇沖縄での国際墓; Naha Okinawa deno kokusai haka).

American interest in Okinawa Island first developed over 150 years ago when President Millard Fillmore (1800–74) directed Commodore Matthew C. Perry (1794–1858) to "secure one or more ports of refuge of easy access for American shipping and whaling vessels in the Western Pacific." Naha was one of the ports selected by Perry. On July 11, 1854, he signed the "Compact between the United States and the Kingdom of Loo Choo," the old name for the Ryukyu Islands, with representatives of the kingdom. The Compact provided for trading rights and the provisioning of wood and water for American vessels. At that same time, concurrent with the negotiation of the treaty, the International Cemetery was founded. Three members of Commodore Perry's crew had recently died and were buried in the cemetery at that time. It has remained a place of final rest for foreigners who have died in the Ryukyu Islands for the past century.

Although the cemetery was destroyed during the Battle of Okinawa in 1945, it was restored and subsequently re-established in 1955. US Service members and others maintain the cemetery today on an annual volunteer "clean-up" day.

The Kuroshio Current (黒潮)

Okinawa's coral reefs are the northernmost such reefs in the world. They are sustained by the warm Kuroshiro Current (lit. "Black Tide," a reference to its deep dark blue waters), which ranges between 68 and 86 °Fahrenheit (20–30 °Centigrade) throughout the year. Also known as the "Japanese Current" (日本海流; Nihon Kairyū), the flow starts near Taiwan and travels several thousand miles northeast until it meets the cold currents of the North Pacific. It is approximately 60 miles (100 kilometers) wide.

Chapter 6

OKINAWA MAIN ISLAND: THE CENTER
沖縄本島中部
Castle ruins, beachfront resorts

1. **Nakagusuku Castle Ruins** 中城城跡
2. **Nakamura House** 中村家住宅
3. **Shinto Shrine in Futenma** 普天間権現
4. **"American Village" in Chatan** 北谷町
5. **Sunabe District** 砂辺
6. **Awase** 泡瀬
7. **Katsuren Castle Ruins** 勝連城跡
8. **White Beach Naval Facility**
9. **Yomitan Village** 読谷村
10. **Zakimi Castle Ruins Site** 座喜味城跡
11. **Cape Zanpa** 残波岬
12. **Maeda Point** 真栄田岬

The central portion of Okinawa Main Island (沖縄本島中部; Okinawa-hontō Chubu) begins a few miles above Naha, around the towns of Urasoe across to Nishihara. There's no real boundary with the south, and as you drive north from Naha you won't notice any less traffic or congestion. One batch of Okinawan urban sprawl just merges into the next, seemingly without end. About the only visible difference is that Naha's downtown section comprises primarily high-rise office and apartment buildings, whereas as we proceed further north most buildings are only a few stories tall.

For the sake of simplicity, we'll make our boundary point the US Consulate in Urasoe (浦添市; Urasoé-shi), right on the boundary with Nishihara (西原町; Nishihara-chō). And yes, there is an American Consulate on the island of Okinawa. It's at 2-1-1 Toyama, Urasoe City (Tel. 098-876-4211). The consulate is almost exactly in the center of this part of the island, in the little district of Toyama (当山; To-yama) with Urasoe to the west and Nishihara to the east. As the crow flies, it's 2.5 miles (4 kilometers) north of Shuri Castle.

Okinawa Main Island is a little less than 6 miles (10 kilometers) wide at this point and, for our purposes, we'll draw a line across from Urasoe to Nishihara. We'll declare all the places to the south of this line "southern" Okinawa, and all those to the north "central" Okinawa, at least until we reach "northern" Okinawa.

Only a mile or so north of this line, the island starts to narrow down. For example, from east to west, from Nakagusuku on the Pacific Ocean to Ginowan on the East China Sea, it's only 3.75 miles (6 kilometers) wide, and it retains this narrow width until we reach Kitanakagusuku on the east across to Chatan on the west. From there, it starts to expand a bit as we continue north. From the Pacific side, starting north of Kitanakagusuku, then from Awase across to Chatan, then to Kadena, the island widens from about 4 miles (6.4 kilometers) to more than 7 miles (12 kilometers). Okinawa City, the island's second largest city after Naha, is in the middle of this section. North of Kadena,

For the most part, Okinawa's central section is merely a continuation of the southern section, except that there is no high-rise "downtown" as in Naha.

One of the largest citadels on Okinawa, the ruins of Nakagusuku Castle command a sweeping view over Nakagusuku Bay and the Pacific Ocean.

the island widens further west at Yomitan all the way to Cape Zanpa. On the east side, above Awase, it juts out onto a relatively long, southeast running arm, the Katsuren Peninsula.

A little north of Yomitan, Kadena and Okinawa City, the island shrinks to its most narrow. From Ishikawa City and its bay on the east, to Nakadomari and its bay on the west, it's a mere 1.75 miles (3 kilometers) across. This ultra-narrow neck runs north for about 3 miles (5 kilometers), then starts to widen. From Kin town on the east to Onna village on the west, it's about 4.5–5 miles (7–8 kilometers) across. Okinawa Island retains this width for approximately the next 9 miles (15 kilometers). This section has Ginoza village on its eastern and southern shore and most of Okinawa's top luxury resorts on its northern, western side. At the end of the stretch of beachfront hotels, Okinawa's third largest city of Nago begins. And that's where we'll start our discussion of Okinawa's "northern" section in Chapter 7.

☐1 NAKAGUSUKU CASTLE RUINS 中城城跡

Let's first explore the island's central section, starting on the east side. From the US Consulate, it's about 6.5–7.5 miles (11–12 kilometers), depending on the route, northeast between Ginowan and Nakagusuku, to the Nakagusuku Castle Ruins (中城城跡; Naka-gusuku-jōato). For many visitors, this is the most impressive of all the *gusuku* ruins on the island—or in the Ryukyus—for two reasons. As is the case with most citadels, it was sited as a defensive measure high above the surrounding territory. It has a commanding view overlooking Nakagusuku Bay and the Pacific on one side and the East China Sea on the other. The fortress was built atop a precipice of land sited midway between the present-day villages of Nakagusuku and Kitanakagusuku. It's also very large. Built in an age of no mechanization, it's difficult to imagine today how much labor was involved in assembling any great construction project built of stone. As was the case with the great pyramids of Egypt and Mexico, the Gothic

Okinawa Soba (沖縄そば)

A bowl of noodles, a few choice morsels of pork, a little red ginger, all bathed in a steaming broth and you've got a simple and delicious meal. All over Japan, *soba* refers to a dish of buckwheat noodles, but not in Okinawa. Here, *soba* is entirely made from wheat flour. Some popular toppings include a slice of hard-boiled egg, some pink or white fish flakes (*kamaboko* 蒲鉾), stewed, boneless pork spare ribs (*ōki* ソーキ) and a thick slice of stewed pork belly (*san-mai niku* 三枚肉). Two popular garnishes are pickled red ginger (*beni-shōga* 紅生姜) and Korean chili peppers (*kōrēgūsu* 高麗胡椒).

ANCIENT CASTLE OF NA-GA-GUS KO, LEW-CHEW.

Drawing of Nakagusku Castle from Commodore Perry's 1853 Expedition.

cathedrals of Europe and the Great Wall of China, all involved the toil of countless men, so too with these *gusuku*, albeit on a somewhat smaller scale. Nonetheless, it's breathtaking and sobers the mind to think of the amount of back-breaking work required.

The fortress was built starting around 1440 by the legendary Ryukyuan commander Gosamaru. He had it built to defend his kingdom against attacks from the east by Lord Amawari of Katsuren Castle. Although today Nakagusku Castle is a ruin, it is exceptionally well preserved. What remains are the massive surrounding defensive walls and the

castle's interior scheme, which divided it into multiple citadels.

Commodore Matthew Perry and his expedition came to Japan in 1853 to pressure the country to open its borders and trade with the West. Having sailed around Africa, the Indian Ocean and Hong Kong, Perry first landed in Okinawa on his way. At that time it was the Kingdom of the Ryukyus. Over the next two years, while engaged in Japanese "diplomacy," he was to make port at Naha five times. He conducted an inland survey that included Nakagusuku Castle. From this expedition there very fortunately remains a series of remarkable lithographs by the German-American Wilhelm Heine (1827–85), official artist of the journey. The accurate, life-like sketches he drew of the places he visited and the people he encountered were to form the impressions of the Far East for several generations of Europeans and Americans. They remain one of the most important records of Okinawa and Japan as they were before foreigners arrived *en masse*.

In his final years, Perry wrote a three-volume account of his travels in the Orient. Like the lithographs prepared by Heine, Perry's work was very well received and was to form the foundation of the West's early understanding of the East. Titled a *Narrative*

Commodore Matthew C. Perry (1794–1858)

Son of a Navy captain, Perry died in New York City but was born and buried in Newport, Rhode Island. If ever there were a man with saltwater in his veins, it was he. Perry saw action in the Battle of Eire, the War of 1812, the Second Barbary War and the Mexican-American War. He fought pirates and the slave trade in the West Indies and was offered a Tsar's commission in the Russian Navy, which he declined. He was called the Father of the Steam Navy for his work with steamships and he was instrumental in the development of the Naval Academy's curriculum at Annapolis. He is best remembered for his voyages to Japan and his opening of that country to trade with the West. His first visit left Norfolk, Virginia, in 1852. He arrived in Edo (Tokyo) in July of 1853, having stopped in Okinawa along the way. Perry's second visit landed in February of 1854, and on that occasion he concluded the Convention of Kanagawa. The treaty formalized trade relations with the West for the next century. Perry returned to the US in 1855 and spent the last three years of his life writing his memoirs. There is a memorial stone to him at the International Cemetery in Tomari, Naha (page 101).

of the Expedition of an American Squadron to the China Seas and Japan, he states of Nakagusuku Castle: "The material used to build the fortress is limestone and the masonry is an admirable construction. The stones are processed in a very interesting way and are carefully shaped and jointed, even though cement or mortar is not used. I think this work will last for a long time."

Nakagusuku Castle had already been standing for 400 years when Perry and his American sailors visited it. They were suitably impressed with its construction and with the construction of Shuri Castle, which they also visited. Along with several other *gusuku* and a few related sites, Nakagusuku Castle was added to the UNESCO World Heritage Site list in 2000.

2 NAKAMURA HOUSE 中村家住宅

A stone's throw up the road, less than three-quarters of a mile (1 kilometer) north from the Nakagusuku Castle ruins, is Nakamura House (中村家住宅; Nakamura-ka jūtaku). It's an especially well-preserved example of a fine residence owned by a wealthy family. It dates from the mid-18th century. The Nakamura family is said to have been the municipal head of the Nakagusuku region at that time. The museum is a little time capsule into another age and way of life. There are a few similar museums in the Ryukyus like this: one on Kumejima, one in Ishigaki and one in the Keramas. Each presents a real look into an "old" Okinawa that essentially no longer exists.

The overall site measures a little more than 16,145 square feet (1,500 square meters) and includes an eight-room main residence plus several outlying structures for storage and animals. Entering the main stone gate, a large horizontally set stone slab separates the house from the gate. This is the Hinpun (ヒンプン), a protective barrier believed to prevent evil spirits from entering. On top of the house roof, staring down, is the inimitable Okinawan *shīsā* lion dog, another type of talisman said to keep away unwelcome spirits. The property is also protected from more mundane dangers like typhoons by its surrounding stone walls and Fukugi trees. These straight, tall, sturdy trees are over 250 years old. With their tough, evergreen, leathery leaves, they were once commonly planted around Okinawan residences to act as windbreaks during storms.

Nakamura House courtyard and well.

3 SHINTO SHRINE IN FUTENMA 普天間権現

From Nakamura House it's almost 1.75 miles (3 kilometers) west to our next stop, the Shinto Shrine in Futenma (普天間権現; Futenma gongen, usually shortened to Futenma-gū). The village is part of Ginowan City and the shrine is only a few meters off the busy road. Most people drive right past, never noticing that there is a flight of stairs up behind a *torii* gate and several buildings above. There's a set of caves below, but they are not visible. The shrine was commissioned five centuries ago by King Sho Kinpuku during the first Sho Dynasty. For those not familiar with Shinto, the complex has all the traditional elements and is a good introduction to this classic and complex part of traditional Japanese life.

Let's begin at the beginning. Shinto (神道; Shin-tō) is a uniquely Japanese form of spirituality that is, unfortunately, particularly difficult to characterize. The word Shinto literally translates as "way of the gods," but its meaning is more complex than that. The word is a combination of the Kanji character *shin* (神), meaning *kami*, and *tō* (道), meaning a philosophical path or way of study (originally from the Chinese word *tào* or *dào*, as in Tàoism or Dàoism, which means the way or the path). *Kami* is a very complicated word, usually translated as god, but more accurately rendered as deity, essence or spirit. Even these translations don't properly convey the right meaning. It's perhaps more useful to think of *kami* as an abstract concept that ascribes natural forces in the universe to all things. Thus, *kami* exists in human beings and animals. It exists in mountains, rocks and caves, in rivers, seas and ocean waves, in trees, wind and lightning—essentially, in virtually all things, and in this sense it is animistic.

The unpainted torii gate and entrance to Futenma Shinto Shrine.

A hand-washing station is always located near the entrance to a Shinto shrine.

It can be argued, therefore, that Shinto is not really a "religion" at all, at least in the Western sense that one worships a commonly agreed upon god or even a pantheon of deities. Shinto may better be characterized as a way of life, a set of practices and beliefs and a general philosophy that brings together certain unifying principles. Although Shinto teaches that everything contains a *kami* and a *kami* resides in all things, certain places are found to be more conducive for the spirituality of people and the world around them. Thus, a certain stone, an ancient living tree or a body of water may be designated or found to be a particularly attractive meeting place between the common everyday world and the sacred. Shrines are usually built in such places. On Okinawa, the most holy of these places is Seifa Utaki on the Chinen Peninsula.

The approach to any Shinto shrine is the Sandō (参道; lit. "visiting road"), which is the route or pathway to the shrine. In the case of certain, sometimes large, shrines, there may be a "front" passage (表参道; *omoté-sandō*) if it is the main entrance, or a "rear" passage (裏参道; *ura-sandō*) if it is a secondary entrance. In the case of the Futenma shrine, the Sandō is the flight of stairs leading up to the shrine.

Whether it is a primary or a secondary entrance, almost always the Sandō will be crossed or straddled with a *torii* (鳥居; lit. "bird perch") gate or perhaps several *torii* gates. A *torii* is a stylized traditional arch often erected in places of importance to keep bad luck or evil spirits away. The Sandō may also be lined with stone lanterns or other decorations of a spiritual nature. At the base of the stairs at Futenma, there is a *torii*, and this is typical. Shinto shrines can always be

recognized because they employ a *torii* at the entrance. The idea is that all visitors must pass under the *torii* because it symbolically marks one's passing from the secular world to the sacred.

Somewhere along the way, worshippers will come to a hand-washing station called a *chōzuya* or *temizu-sha* (手水舎; figuratively, a ritual ablution). One uses the ladle to pour

A collection of omamori protection amulets.

Folded omikuji fortune papers on a straw rope.

Okinawa's own Meoto Iwa, these "wedded rocks," bound with a shimenawa braided rice straw rope, are near to Cape Manza in Onna village.

resh water over the left hand first, then the right, taking care not to allow the "dirty" water to fall back into the well or basin. Let t fall to the side, usually on rocks below. Serious patrons may rinse out their mouths as well, taking care not to drink the water nor to spit it back into the source. The ladle handle itself may be rinsed with any remaining water in the cup and placed opening down on the rack where it is kept.

Near the entrance to most shrines you'll usually find a small shop or booth selling *omamori, omikuji* and *ema. Omamori* (お守り; lit. "honorable protector") are personal protection amulets. Often in the form of a little trinket or a good luck charm, they are usually purchased with a specific intent in mind, such as to bring good health, successful business or study or, very popular, safe driving. You'll often see them hanging from the rear view mirror inside a car. They're commonly replaced annually to dispose of any bad luck they might have attracted in the previous year. You'll see disposal bins at the shrine for this purpose.

Omikuji (御御籤, 御神籤, or おみくじ; lit. "paper fortune" and "sacred lottery") are little strips of paper upon which a random fortune has been written. One makes a small offering (perhaps a five- or ten-Yen coin into a vending machine) and receives the scrolled or folded piece of paper. If the fortune or advice is good, you might keep it or tie it on to a set of wires or string set up for that purpose. If the fortune is bad, you may wish to tie it on to a nearby pine tree, leaving it there to "wait" for someone else. This custom is a play on the word *matsu*, which means both "pine tree" (松) and the verb "'to wait" (待つ). It is speculated that the *omikuji* paper fortune

custom evolved into the US Chinese restaurant custom of "fortune cookies."

You may also see paper strips tied on to lengths of rope. Thought to ward off evil spirits, *shimenawa* (しめ縄; lit "sacred shrine enclosing rope") are lengths of braided rice straw rope. A space or an object bound by *shimenawa* often indicates something sacred or pure. Perhaps the most famous example of *shimenawa* is the "Wedded Rocks" (夫婦岩; Méoto Iwa) in the sea near Futami, Mie, (三重県二見町) in the south of Japan's main island of Honshu.

One more thing you'll always see at a Shinto shrine is a large collection of *ema* (絵馬; lit. "wooden plaque"), usually affixed or tied on to an *ema* rack. *Ema* are small wooden plaques on which worshippers write their prayers or wishes. The plaques are left hanging at the shrine where the *kami* may (hopefully) receive them. Common *ema* prayers are what one might expect: health, happiness, love, marriage, children, job, school and success.

An ema rack holding wooden prayer plaques.

The Haiden hall of worship at Futenma Shrine.

The underground Honden cave at Futenma.

We finally come to the main buildings of a shrine and often there are two. Remember, the purpose of a shrine is to house and protect some sacred object for worship, something blessed with *kami*. When such objects exist, they are contained within the Honden (本殿; lit. "main building," also called Shinden 神殿; lit. "*kami* building"). It's the most sacred edifice at any shrine and its purpose is solely for the enshrinement of the *kami* objects. Usually, the building is small, at the rear of the shrine complex, and closed to the public. It may be raised or encircled by a fence or a *shimenawa*. Only the Shinto priests may enter the building, although it may be opened on certain holy days. However, if the *kami* object of veneration is a nearby mountain, stone, tree or some other great object, there will be no Honden because it's not needed.

Whether or not there's a Honden, there will always be a Haiden (拝殿; lit. "worship hall," sometimes translated as "offering hall"). And it will always be the largest building at a shrine as it's meant to hold the congregation of worshippers. In it, there will be an altar

Is there *kami* in these *iwa*? Most probably yes. These picturesque unnamed rocks are off northern Okinawa's Pacific Coast, not far from Higashi (東村).

used by the priests to conduct ceremonies. This is the building where the public can come to pray.

At Futenma-gū, there is a fairly large Haiden at the top of the flight of stairs. It's quite attractive, with decorative ornaments trimmed in gold leaf. If you wander around behind the Haiden, you'll find the Honden, raised up high and locked. Interestingly, and unique to Futenma, there's another very ancient Honden. It's underground in a cave. You'll have to ask permission because it is locked. Behind the Haiden is a door that leads down a corridor and a flight of stairs to the cave. This was the original sacred place of worship for the cave contained the *kami*. The original altar still rests at the foot of the stairs. Visitors are asked to pay their respects to the spirits before exploring the path deeper into the cave. Two loud hand claps do the trick. The cave is well lit and overflowing with stalactite and stalagmite formations. In some places there is dripping water seeping down from the ground above. Many of the rock formations are said to symbolize fertility, and young Okinawan women hoping to have children sometimes come to pray here.

4 "AMERICAN VILLAGE" IN CHATAN 北谷町
Having paid our respects, and perhaps having left a small offering, we'll leave the shrine and drive a little less than 3 miles (5 kilometers) northwest to our next stop, the Ferris wheel at the "American Village" in Chatan (北谷町; Chatan-chō). It's probably a safe bet that a thousandfold more people will visit here than at Futenma gongen, the Nakamura House and the Nakagusuku ruins combined. And that's to be expected because the Chatan Town area and the Mihama District (美浜; *Mi-hama*), in particular, are at the heart of

lively fun scene, both day and night. It's especially popular with young people and you'll find them here by the hundreds, both American and Okinawans. The district is full of restaurants, bars, clubs, fast food places, Starbucks, shopping, sightseeing, a beach, and that giant Ferris wheel.

The American Village is somewhat modeled on a California beach town, say Venice Beach or Santa Monica. There are plenty of things to do: shopping and more shopping, and there's a waterfront to stroll along. With enough variety of restaurants and other entertainment, it's an easy place to wander. One side of the Mihama District fronts the East China Sea but the other is virtually surrounded by the Marine Corps Air Station Futenma, Marine Camp Foster, Navy Camp Lester and Kadena Air Base.

It's easy to see why so many Americans come to Chatan. They live nearby and they want something to do. And it's easy to see why so many Okinawans come here too. The American Village is a nice place and it's a safe place. There's not much crime anywhere in Japan and there's little in Okinawa as well. Young people, married couples, families with children, American or Japanese, anybody can enjoy themselves. If you're new to the island and can't find it, just drive along Route 58

Ferris wheel at the "American Village" in Chatan.

until you see the Ferris wheel. The wheel itself is built on top of a large indoor shopping arcade. If you take a ride, you'll get a great bird's eye view of the whole area. In addition to restaurants like Tony Roma's and the A&W, you'll find one of the few "conveyor belt" sushi places on the island. There's a lot here and it's worth checking it out.

5 SUNABE DISTRICT 砂辺

One final note, only a little bit up the road, north on Route 58 less than 1.75 miles (3 kilometers) and due west of Kadena Air Base (嘉手納飛行場; Kadéna Hikōjō) Gate 1, you'll find Chatan's Sunabe District (砂辺; Sunabé). There are plenty of bars and restaurants here, too, so it's also an excellent place for going out, although there is not as much shopping as in Mihama. What makes this place special is the scuba diving and snorkeling. It's one of the most popular spots on the island for divers.

All year long, every week, hundreds of would-be Japanese Jacques Cousteaus fly down from Tokyo and other cold points north to dive the Sunabe Seawall. The area is chock a block full of dive shops with rental gear, qualified instruction and professional guides. Anybody with a couple of days and a couple of hundred dollars (in Yen) can dive. The seawall's undersea coral reef is like swimming in a tropical aquarium. Crystal-clear warm waters full of brightly colored exotic fish—it's gorgeous. Naturally, anyone of any age can dive, but as a practical matter many of the enthusiasts are young people, so the neighborhood is full of *minshuku* inns and small hotels to serve their needs. And aprèsdive? How about a cold Orion? There are plenty of local bars, not high priced, and that's another reason why it's a fun district.

Kadena Air Base (嘉手納飛行場)

Kadena Air Base is headquarters to the US Air Force's largest combat group, the 18th Wing. The base was one of the first targets in the Battle of Okinawa and the US commandeered it early in the campaign. General Joseph ("Vinegar Joe") Stilwell accepted the final surrender of the Japanese forces of the Ryukyu Islands on September 7, 1945. Close to 20,000 Americans and thousands more Japanese and civilian contractors make Kadena their home.

Diving at the Sunabe Seawall coral reef in Chatan's Sunabe District, one of the most popular spots for scuba diving and snorkeling in all of Okinawa.

Okinawa's Own Orion Beer

Fresh, light, delicious and served cold, Okinawa's most popular brew is Orion, pronounced "Or-ee-own," the "ee" sound rhyming with me, he or she and not "O-ri-on," the "i" as in eye. Although the Orion Brewery (オリオンビール株式会社; Orion Bīru Kabushiki Gaisha) only supplies 1 percent of the overall beer market in Japan, in Okinawa its share is 50 percent. It's a true local product. The brewery is in Nago and tours are offered daily. The best part: free mugs of beer at the end of each tour, designated driver excepted.

The American Presence in Okinawa

According to a number of polls, over 70 percent of Japanese citizens appreciate the mutual security and defense treaty with the United States and the presence of the US Forces Japan (在日米軍 Zainichi Beigun). However, a growing percentage of the population has been demanding a reduction in the numbers of US bases and military personnel in the country. Nowhere are these issues more acute than in Okinawa where some 75 percent of all the US military facilities in Japan are located. On Okinawa, US military installations occupy almost 20 percent of the total land area or one-fifth of the island.

The issues may be said to encompass two broad complaints: base location and base personnel. First, many bases, such as Yokota Air Base near Tokyo, the Naval Air Facility at Atsugi, Kadena Air Base on Okinawa and, most strikingly, the Marine Corps Air Station at Futenma, Okinawa, are located in the vicinity of or in the heart of residential districts. They may not have been residential districts when established more than 60 years ago. For example, most of Futenma then was a sugar cane field but the population has grown all around it. Local citizens have been complaining for years about excessive aircraft noise as well as the occasional aircraft accident or flight mishap. By far the most heated discussion has been over MCAS Futenma. In an agreement signed between the US and Japan in October of 2005, the US agreed to the relocation of the base to a remote area further north on the island. In addition, the US agreed to the permanent relocation of some 8,000 Marines to the US Territory of Guam. But what was at the time seen as the beginning of an end has now morphed into an endless beginning, with no end in sight. The ink was barely dry when Japan reneged on the agreement, insisting simply that Futenma be closed and that no alternative air station be built. Naturally, the US insists that the original agreement be kept in accordance with its terms. Japanese Prime Minister Yukio Hatoyama, who had rashly staked his reputation on the base's removal, was forced to resign his office when it became clear that he could not deliver on his bold promises. Although local Okinawan officials keep beating the Futenma anti-base drum, no senior Japanese politicians dare touch the controversy. No new air station is being built, no one is packing up at Futenma, no Marines are moving to Guam and no negotiations are taking place, at least for now. At the moment, it is a stalemate.

Also at issue is the behavior of some US Service members. From 1952 to 2004, it's been reported that there were over 200,000 accidents and crimes involving US personnel in which 1,076 Japanese civilians were killed. Although over 90 percent of the incidents were vehicle or traffic related, the few cases of violent crime, especially rape and murder, have severely strained relations between the two countries. Between 1972 and 2003, there were 5,157 crimes committed by Americans against civilians in Okinawa. Of these, 533 were deemed by the Okinawa authorities to be "heinous crimes such as murder, robbery and sexual assault." Twelve murders have been committed by US service-men in Okinawa.

According to the US–Japan Status of Forces Agreement (SOFA), US personnel have partial "extraterritorial rights" (meaning the right of a foreigner charged with a crime to be turned over for trial in accordance with his own national laws). The US has argued that the status granted to its military members is necessary to afford them the same rights that exist under the US criminal justice system. Since the SOFA also exempts most US military members from Japanese visa and passport laws, past incidents

occurred in which US military members charged with crimes by Japanese authorities were trans-ferred back to the US without facing prosecution in Japanese courts. In the opinion of many Okinawans, the US has used the SOFA to shield its citizens who have committed violent crimes against Japanese citizens.

In a case that made headlines around the world, in 1995 two US Marines and one US Navy sailor abducted and gang-raped a 12-year-old schoolgirl. Okinawans were outraged and over 100,000 took to the streets in protest. Then American Ambassador to Japan Walter Mondale apologized for the incident almost immediately after he was notified about it. US Department of Defense Secretary William Perry also publicly apologized on a visit to Tokyo. However, the rape incident led to demands for the removal of all US military bases in Japan, not just those in Okinawa.

In March of 1996, the three service members were tried by a Japanese court, found guilty and sentenced six and seven years in prison. Many Okinawans thought the sentences too lenient as they could have been committed to life in prison. In February of 2008, the reported rape of a 14-year-old Okinawan girl triggered another wave of protest against the American military presence in Okinawa, second only to the 1995 rape case. The incident led to tight restrictions on off-base activities and the designation of a "Day of Reflection" for all US military personnel in Japan. Although in that case the accuser later withdrew her charges (reputedly on payment by the accused of "solace" money, *isha-ryō* (慰謝料; lit. conso-lation money or solatium), the US military authorities court-martialed the suspect and sentenced him to four years in prison. The US military thereupon set up a Sexual Assault Prevention and Response Task Force in an effort to prevent similar incidents. Incidentally, to date, despite a lot of talk, the SOFA has not been changed.

| 20 km |
| 10 miles |

OKU

OKUMA

Camp Gonsalves

NAGO

Camp Schwab

Camp Hansen

KADENA
Camp
Torii Station   Shield   Camp Courtney
                        Camp McTureous
Kadena Air Base
Camp Laster   OKINAWA
              CITY
Camp   White Beach
Kinser   Naval Facility
Camp Foster/Butler
GINOWAN   MCAS Futenma

NAHA

US Bases on Okinawa

6 AWASE 泡瀬

At about this point on the island, roughly from Kadena (嘉手納町; Kadéna-chō) on the west coast across to Okinawa City (沖縄市; Okinawa-shi) in the center, to Awase (泡瀬; Awasé) on the Pacific side, Okinawa's geography re-forms itself in a most peculiar way. Its east side throws a southern dropping arm into the Pacific Ocean, the Katsuren Peninsula (勝連半島; Katsuren-hantō), and its west coast juts out onto a small point in the East China Sea after Yomitan, Cape Zanpa (残波岬; Zanpa-misaki).

Both sides of the island are worth visiting and it's a coin toss to decide which side first because we'll have to cross back from one to the other in order to see everything, and then proceed further north. We'll start at a center point, Okinawa City Hall. Let's say the coin toss directs us east.

7 KATSUREN CASTLE RUINS 勝連城跡

Okinawa City and its City Hall (沖縄市役所; Okinawa-shiyakusyo) are almost dead center between the two sides of the island. One of the main attractions east of Okinawa City is the Katsuren Castle ruins (勝連城跡; Katsuren gusuku-jōato), which are located at the base of the Katsuren Peninsula, that is, at its northern end. As the crow flies, it's 4.5 miles (7 kilometers) from City Hall to the castle site. By road, down from the heights of Okinawa City, through the Awase district on Naka-gusuku Bay, past the sugar cane mill and over to Katsuren Castle, it's about 6.75 miles (11 kilometers), and you've got a choice of a dozen different routes to get there.

Katsuren is another UNESCO World Heritage Site and it's well deserved because the castle was one of the most important in the Ryukyu kingdom. It's also one of the most scenic to visit. Although it's not as grand as Nakagusuku, it's quite large nonetheless and its setting is also most dramatic. From its apex on a bluff, it overlooks both sides of the Katsuren Peninsula, with Nakagusuku Bay on one side and Kin Bay on the other, both waters of the Pacific Ocean. The castle's "golden age" was the mid-15th century under the powerful Lord ("Anji") Amawari. Though the date of his birth is not known, his death is recorded as 1458.

According to Okinawan legend, Amawari was born to a peasant family near Chatan. He seized power by overthrowing the previous lord of Katsuren. "Overthrow" is quite literally the word; it is said that Amawari threw his lord over the castle ramparts to his death. Through maritime trade, he gained wealth and power and married Momotofumi Agari, daughter of the Ryukyuan King Shō Taikyū (c. 1415–60), based at Shuri Castle.

Anxious about Amawari's growing power, the King Shō Taikyū arranged for a new castle to be built at Nakagusuku and he placed it under the command of Lord Gosamaru. Nakagusuku is sited about midway between Katsuren and Shuri Castles. In 1458, Amawari accused Gosamaru of plotting to overthrow the king and led the royal armies on an attack on Nakagusuku.

Katsuren Castle ruins, located on a bluff overlooking both sides of the Katsuren Peninsula.

Okinawan Tombs

The word for a tomb in Japan is *haka* (墓) but in Okinawa there is a special kind, appropriately called *kameko-baka* (亀甲墓) or turtleback tomb. The resemblance is fairly easy to see. Less obvious is that the tomb is supposed to resemble a woman's womb, and the small rectangular opening located in the center front the woman's vagina. This serves as the entrance for placing the urns of the deceased inside. Buddhists believe that the dead should return back from where

they originally came. A tomb can hold many generations of ancestors. Traditionally, a dead body was placed inside for two or three years. The tomb was then reopened and the bones were cleansed and washed with *awamori* liquor (page 12). Placed into an urn, they were then returned inside. Today, the bone washing ritual no longer exists. Dead bodies are cremated and the ashes are placed in an urn that is deposited in the tomb. Each year in the spring (the exact date varies with the lunar calendar), Okinawans commemorate Shiimii (清明祭; known as Seimei Sai in Japanese), one of the island's most important religious ceremonies. Preparation begins a few days before the actual date when family members clean the area around the tomb. This helps to appease the spirits of ancestors whom Okinawans believe are constantly watching over them. On the day of Shiimii, large quantities of food are prepared and brought to the tomb, along with flowers and *awamori*. Paper "money" is burned, prayers are said, music is played, food is eaten and *awamori* is drunk. The occasion is festive and may go on all night. By paying respect to the dead, the ancestors are appeased and, in turn, asked to watch over and protect the living.

It is said that out of loyalty to the king, Gosamaru refused to fight back and killed himself rather than betray his benefactor. Subsequently, one theory holds that Amawari plotted to overthrow the king, but his plan was discovered by his wife, the king's daughter. Learning of the plot, the king attacked first and defeated Amawari who was executed. An alternate theory holds that entire affair—the rivalry between Amawari and Gosamaru—was in reality a plot by the royal government in order to remove the two of them, since both were viewed as powerful rivals and potential threats to the royal succession. No matter the historical truth, the tale of Gosamaru's suicide and Amawari's downfall is among the most popular in Okinawan historical lore.

There's no admission charge to visit the Katsuren Castle and on a sunny day it's a wonderful place for a picnic. There are stone or wooden steps all the way up, and after a fairly steep climb you'll be rewarded with a million dollar view.

8 WHITE BEACH NAVAL FACILITY

If we continue south on the Katsuren Peninsula, it's a little less than 3.75 miles (6 kilometers) to its final tip at the White Beach Naval Facility. White Beach is a very active US Navy Base and you'll need a military ID to enter, but if you are able to enter you may get a chance to see naval warships and submarines, which frequently make it a port of call. There are two piers at the naval base but additional ships moor offshore. Most people who visit White Beach, however, come to stay in one of the rental cabins or trailers and enjoy the beach because this is a prime R&R facility open to all service members and their guests.

The Navy occupies the western side of the tip. Around the corner, on the eastern side, and just over a mile (2 kilometers) north, is Heshikiya Port (平敷屋港; Heshikiya-kō). That's the jumping off point for ferries to Tsuken Island. We'll discuss the port and the island further below when we cover the Okinawa shotō.

Similarly, 1.75 miles (3 kilometers) north of Heshikiya Port, and staying on the east side of the Katsuren Peninsula, we'll come to the 3-mile (5-kilometer)-long Kaichu-doro Causeway (海中道路; lit. "Sea Center Road"). The causeway is the route to the Henza, Hamahiga, Miyagi and Ikei Islands, each one connected by another and, for some, another, bridge. We'll discuss the causeway and these islands and their smaller "sister" islands, further below.

There's nothing more of any particular interest on the Katsuren Peninsula and, for that matter, there's not much more on this side of the island all the way up for the next 20–25 miles (32–40 kilometers), so we'll depart and cross over to the west coast. From the Kaichu-doro back to Okinawa City Hall, it's 8.5 miles (13.5 kilometers) by various routes, but there's no reason to return there. Rather, we'll go straight across, more or less due west, over the top of Kadena Air Base, then north to Yomitan Village (読谷村; Yomitan-son) and the Zakimi Castle ruins site (座喜味城跡; Zakimi gusuku-jōato). It's a total of 15 miles (24 kilometers). The castle is 1 mile (1.5 kilometers) due north of the Yomitan Town Hall.

9 YOMITAN VILLAGE 読谷村

Locally, on Okinawa, Yomitan (読谷村; Yomitan-son) is well known as an agricultural producer of sugar cane, chrysanthemums and purple sweet potatoes. In fairness, it must be said that many places in Okinawa and the Ryukyus grow sugar cane, so that's

not unusual. More unusual, however, is the chrysanthemum trade. It's the leading cash crop of the town. Unlike mainland Japan where it's too cold in the winter to grow chrysanthemums, farmers here can raise their flowers all winter long for off-season blooms. They use vast quantities of overhead strung lamps at night both for extra heat and to force blooming. You'll see all colors of the rainbow in the fields when driving through Yomitan at certain times of the year.

Finally, Yomitan takes special pride in its production of purple sweet potatoes (紅いも; *beni imo*). Thought to have been brought to Okinawa from Taiwan over 1,000 years ago, you'll find hot baked and steamed purple sweet potatoes everywhere in Okinawa. They're a healthy sweet treat loved by everyone. Every fall, Yomitan hosts the Beni Imo Hometown Festival (紅いもの里; beni imo no sato) and holds a Miss Beni Imo Contest (紅いも娘; Beni imo musumé). What do Okinawans do at the Beni imo Festival? What do you think? Eat purple potatoes and wash them down with copious amounts of Orion Beer.

10 ZAKIMI CASTLE RUINS SITE 座喜味城跡

Yomitan's leading ancient attraction is the Zakimi Castle (座喜味城; Zakimi gusuku). It's a UNESCO World Heritage Site, designated along with the others in 2000. The castle was built by Gosamaru. Mentioned earlier for his role at Nakagusuku, he was a legendary warrior who played an important role in uniting the many warring kingdoms of Okinawa

May 5, Children's Day

Until 1948 the 5th day of the 5th month on the lunar calendar was celebrated as Boys' Day, Tango no Sekku (端午の節句; also called the Feast of Banners). The 3rd day of the 3rd month, Hina matsuri, (雛祭; also known as Doll Festival) was celebrated by and for girls. After World War II the Japanese government redesignated the two days as one Children's Day, to be celebrated on May 5th on the Roman calendar. It's now called

Kodomo no hi (こどもの日). For this day, parents put up *koi-nobori* (鯉幟), carp-shaped wind streamers, which are meant to symbolize strength and courage. Families spend time together and pray for their children's health, growth and happiness. This photo was taken on Yomitan's Hijagawa River (比謝川), the initial landing site of Allied Forces in the Battle of Okinawa.

The ruins of Zakimi Castle.

An aerial view of Cape Zanpa.

under one king. As a reward for his loyalty, Gosamaru was declared Lord ("Aji") of Zakimi Castle. His role was to keep an eye on rival lords to the north, namely at Nakijin Gusuku. Nakijin is the last of the UNESCO-designated castles on Okinawa and we'll visit it later when we reach the top of the island.

Large cut stones are a precious and valuable commodity. According to legend, Gosamaru is said to have had the stones from his former castle in Yamada moved one by one to Zakimi by forming a human chain of workers. Later, Gosamaru's reputation as a great castle builder was further enhanced by his completion of Nakagusuku, the largest castle on Okinawa after Shuri. He left Zakimi for Nakagusuku in order to be closer to his king.

⑪ CAPE ZANPA 残波岬

From the Zakimi Castle site, we'll drive almost due north 4 miles (6.5 kilometers), as far as we can go in Yomitan, to its northwesternmost point at Cape Zanpa. There are three things of interest here: the Okinawa-Zanpamisaki Royal Hotel, Zanpa Beach and a lighthouse at the tip of the cape, all three visible in the aerial photo above right.

The Zanpamisaki Royal is a 475-room luxury hotel with an 18-hole golf course. It has a large outdoor pool as well as hot soaking bath and spa facilities. It's popular with Japanese tour groups who come in on weekly packages and therefore get the benefit of competitive group rates. If you check in on your own, rooms start at $200–$250 a night for a standard twin. That's rather typical of most all the luxury hotels on this side of the island. The Zanpamisaki Royal is the first of a long string of top hotels that, starting here, run all the way up the western shoreline until

just before Nago. The Onna Coast, as it is known, is the prime beach and resort area of Okinawa. We'll mention a number of these hotels as we pass them by further below, but the Zanpamisaki Royal can be said to be the beginning.

The second attraction on the cape are the twin side-by-side white sand beaches called Zanpa Beach (残波浜; Zanpa-hama). It's one of the few beaches on Okinawa where you don't need water booties. In other words, on these beaches white sand means white sand, not sand with rocks and broken shards of coral, which unfortunately is the norm on many beaches on Okinawa. Zanpa Beach's really soft white sand is thus popular with couples with kids.

The third attraction is the picturesque Zanpa Lighthouse (残波岬灯台; Zanpa-misaki tōudai). Of course, it's just a light-

The lighthouse at the tip of Cape Zanpa.

house, but it's a scenic one, high as it is standing on the Zanpa cliffs right at the end of a narrow, windswept point. For 150 Yen you can exercise your leg muscles and knee joints and climb to the top. Up there it's exactly what you would expect, a great view.

12 MAEDA POINT 真栄田岬

Our next stop is Maeda Point (真栄田岬; Maeda-misaki), just over 5 miles (8.5 kilometers) to the east following the coastal road. Along with the Sunabe Seawall, Maeda Point is the most popular dive spot on Okinawa, some would say too popular. It wasn't always this way, but a few years ago the local authorities decided to "improve" the site. A large pay parking lot was built, along with a new restaurant-snack bar, gift shop and dive school. Ever since, every hotel on the island brings its minivans full of mainland Japanese tourists here to dive. After being featured on a TV program, diving at Maeda Point is now on everyone's checklist of "things to do." It's still a great place, but you might want to come on a weekday as on weekends there's hardly a parking space.

The point itself is a large rough-hewn coral bluff. It's very scenic. There's a cement set of stairs running down about 330 feet (100 meters) that delivers divers to the water. Unless it's dead calm, which it often is not, entry in the sea can be tricky. It's sharp rock, covered with sea urchins, and sometimes pounding surf. On really rough days, it's closed. It may, in fact, be safe enough under water, but most accidents have happened merely from people entering and exiting. Getting gear on and off, especially flippers, can be a real challenge. Once you're in, there's a short section over coral stone flats, perhaps 165 feet (50 meters). It's no more

The stairs leading down to Maeda entry point.

Renaissance Okinawa Resort.

than 10–15 feet (3–5 meters) deep. But once past there, there's a wall, a strait vertical drop of at least 100–165 feet (30–50 meters). It's good diving and there are all kinds of fish. A few thousand feet along the reef's edge, east from the entry point, is the Blue Cave. It was this attraction that was so prominently featured on the TV special.

It's a narrow cave, maybe 10–15 feet across, a water depth of about 15–30 feet (5–10 meters) and a cave height above the water line, perhaps also 15–30 feet (5–10 meters). That's big enough, but not so big. Imagine a hundred or more people in here. You need an underwater traffic cop to direct the streams of divers coming in and going out. Nonetheless, especially on a quiet day, it's an easy cave to dive and enjoy. It's beautiful and it's perfectly safe, two good reasons why it's so popular.

If Maeda Point is closed due to high waves, head around the corner a few hundred feet west to Maeda Flats. As the name suggests, this section of coast is never more than 3–10 feet (1–3 meters) deep and stretches out thousands of feet offshore. It's an excellent place for beginning divers and youngsters. In many places you can stand up. Although there's not the diversity of fish, especially large ones, as on Maeda Point, nevertheless there's a lot of action to be found with the smaller creatures. One more thing, there's a decent beach, something that doesn't exist at Maeda Point.

From Maeda Point we're going to hug the coast, almost always driving along Route 58. The road takes us north and east all the way to Nago. You'll see references to this beautiful section of shoreline as the Onna Coast since it is centered on the village of Onna (恩納村; Onna-son). The "crow flies" distance from

The Blue Cave along the reef at Maeda Point.

the tip of Maeda Point to Nago City Hall is almost 16 miles (26 kilometers). Our driving route along the shore takes us through the villages of Yamada, Nakadomari, Maeganeku, Fuchaku, Tancha and then, about halfway, Onna. After that, it's Seragaki, Afuso, Nakama, Kise, Koki, Kyoda, Sukuta, Yofuke and, finally, Nago. There are no major sights here, but it's a pretty drive and passes by virtually every top waterfront hotel along the way. The distance by road is just under 22 miles (35 kilometers) and takes about an hour, depending on traffic.

Not long after leaving Maeda, only 2–3 miles (3–5 kilometers), you come to the first of the beaches, Malibu, Renaissance and Moon, each separated by less than

three-quarters of a mile (1 kilometer), and the first batch of four resorts, the Renaissance Okinawa Resort, Hotel Moon Beach, Sun Marina Hotel and Rizzan Sea-Park Tancha Bay Hotel. Most people would probably agree that the Renaissance is the most grand of the lot. It has its own private beach and a great outdoor pool. But in fairness to the others, they all have their own private beaches and they all have good pools. For $200–$300 a night, it's what you would expect; they are all quite deluxe. Although none of them has a golf course on site, all of them have privileges or can arrange play at a nearby club. There are several top flight golf courses within a stone's throw of these four hotels. One, in particular, the Kafuu Resort Fuchaku, is an enormous luxury hotel-condo golf complex, perhaps the largest on Okinawa.

A few miles further up the coast, shortly after Onna village, you come to one of the best hotels on the island, the ANA Inter-Continental Manza Beach Resort. It's perched on its own private peninsula. It might be easier to ask what doesn't it have? Pools, private beach, deluxe dining, spa and sauna? Hotels in this class have virtually everything one could ask for.

From the beach at the ANA Inter-Continental Hotel Resort, or from Onna village, you can see a slightly smaller version of the famous "Wedded Rocks" (夫婦岩;

The private beach and outdoor pool of the Renaissance Okinawa Resort.

Méoto Iwa) found in the sea off the main island of Japan, Honshu. They're "wedded"— tied to one another by a "shimenawa" rope. And on the adjacent Cape Manza you'll find Manza-mo (万座毛) a picturesque high bluff overlooking some great coral rock formations, including one said to resemble an elephant's trunk.

A couple of miles further along and it's the village of Seragaki, with several more hotels, among them the Manza Beach Hotel, Miyuki Beach Hotel, Panacea and Oriental Hills. You'll find prices a little more affordable here. These properties run anywhere from $150 to $250 per night for a standard twin room. The beaches along this stretch of coast include Miyuki, Seragaki and Mission. Away from shore, less than three-quarters of a mile (1 kilometer) inland, you'll find the Atta Terrace Golf Resort, another enormous first-rate golf course complex.

Continuing a few more miles further north, shortly after Akama village, you come to the most deluxe resort collection of all, the Kariyushi Beach Resort Ocean Spa and Okinawa Marriot Resort and Spa, and just before Kise village the Busena Terrace Beach Resort. They're all gorgeous. Which one to choose may be a question of who's offering the best package deal, for you're now in the $300–500 per night range, and at these rates it's worth shopping around.

The lobby of the ANA InterContinental.

The ANA InterContinental Manza Beach Resort.

If money is no object, many consider the Busena Terrace Beach Resort to be the best hotel on the island. Like the ANA Inter-Continental, it's on its own exclusive peninsula, and in addition to the usual 400 or so deluxe rooms offers a couple dozen private ocean villas. It's where the premiers, presidents, prime ministers and potentates stayed at the 2000 G-8 Summit, and if it's good enough for them, then it should be good enough for you and me.

Here's something a little different for those who wish to explore the ocean but perhaps are fearful of it. Go undersea without getting wet. You won't need a scuba tank or a snorkel here. Located at the end of a long wooden pier and then down a 50 foot (15 meter) spiral staircase, the Busena Terrace Underwater Observatory is a reverse aquarium. Instead of the fish being in a tank and you're looking in, here you're in the fishbowl and the fish are outside. It's a submarine glass-enclosed viewing station with 360 degree views. The windows in the observatory allow visitors to see tropical sea life swimming around in their natural habitat. On the walls between the windows are pictures with the names of all the types of fish that one might see. It's a good place to get acquainted with reef life in Okinawa without any diving lessons at all.

Going up the coast a bit further, there are only a few smaller hotels, such as the Kise Beach Palace and the Okinawa Suncoast in Koki. After here, you pass through the villages of Kyoda, Sukuta and Yofuke, but there are no more hotels or resorts. The final stretch of coast until you reach Nago, perhaps the last 3 miles (5 kilometers), is almost all rocky and, besides, it's just too far from Naha and the airport for most tourists to come.

Busena Terrace Beach Resort pools and beach.

Busena Terrace Underwater Observatory.

We'll pause here, for this is our boundary from central Okinawa to north Okinawa. We started just above Naha, more or less at a line we drew across the island from the east coast town of Nishihara across to the west coast town of Urasoe, with the American Consulate at the center. Now we'll draw a line from just below Nago on the East China Sea side, east across the island to a particularly narrow point, the inside rim of Oura Bay (大浦湾; Ōura-wan). This line is only 3.75 miles (6 kilometers) wide but the island will get much wider very soon as we head north. As the crow flies, from the US Consulate to any point along this central-northern dividing line, it's 27 miles (43 kilometers), but by road it's anywhere from 35 to 40 miles (56 to 64 kilometers). There are several routes. One runs along the east coast, one along the west, and the expressway can be said to run mostly through the island's middle. Either coastal route takes about two hours to drive whereas the expressway takes less than an hour.

Manza-mo, the area above the Manza cliffs, was named by an 18th-century Ryukyuan king and means "a field large enough to hold tens of thousands of people."

Chapter 7

OKINAWA MAIN ISLAND: THE NORTH
沖縄本島北部
Natural attractions, fabulous fish

Colloquially known as Yanbaru, the northern section of Okinawa Main Island (沖縄本島北部; Okinawa-hontō Hokubu) is, with the exception of the Churaumi Aquarium, easily the least-known part of the island. Even to Okinawans in Naha, and perhaps even to some in Nago (名護市; Nago-shi), much of the north is isolated, remote and wild. A large percentage of it is uninhabited. We're roughly talking about the section of the island from Nago to Cape Hedo (辺戸岬; Hédo-misaki) and we'll include the relatively large western extension of the Motobu Peninsula (本部半島; Motobu-hantō).

Our line separating the central and northern sections of Okinawa Island can be said to start on the east coast, at the innermost indentation of Oura Bay (大浦湾; Ōura-wan), and extends west to three-quarters of a mile (1 kilometer) below Nago. Conveniently, there's a road that forms this almost perfect east–west delineation for us. We'll start our line where Route 331 almost touches the inner part of Oura Bay, then runs a bit south until it meets Route 329. From there the road crosses the island in a fairly straight line northwest to just south of Nago, at the junction of Routes 329 and 58. Crossing the island here, it's almost exactly 5 miles (8 kilometers) by road; as the crow flies, it's 3.5 miles (5.5 kilometers). Most everything of interest below this line, all the way back to slightly above Naha, we've mentioned previously in our Central Okinawa chapter. Now, in this chapter we'll cover the last remaining portion of the island, the North.

From virtually any point along our Route 329 line north to Okinawa's end at the tip of Cape Hedo, it's a tiny bit more than 25 miles (40 kilometers) as the crow flies. By road, the distance varies widely. There's a choice, as this uppermost section of the island is entirely encircled by a coastal road. If we take the route following the east coast, Route 70, starting at Oura Bay north to Cape Hedo, it's just under 50 miles (80 kilometers).

However, if we cross the island and travel north to Hedo Point on the west coast road from the junction of Routes 329 and 58, following Route 58 all the way along the East China Sea, it's 35 miles (56 kilometers). And that does not include the 5 miles (8 kilometers) from Oura Bay to the Route 58/329 intersection below Nago.

The distances between the east and west coast routes are very different because the roads are different. The west coast road is a highway and it tracks a very straight path north. In contrast, most of the east coast route is over a small local road and it twists and turns all the way up the Pacific Coast. Both routes are scenic, and naturally many people will make a day of it by going round the cape, up one side of the island and then down the other. A complete circuit of the

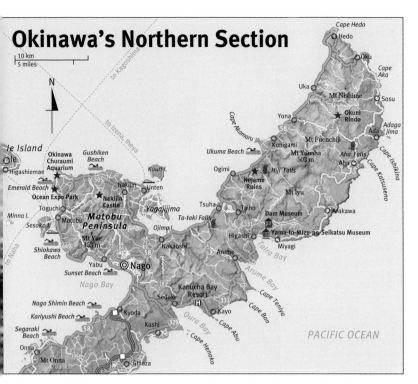

Okinawa's Northern Section

north section of Okinawa, starting and ending at Nago, is 90 miles (144 kilometers). Count on most of a day to accomplish this.

Unlike some of the wildly varying topography in the southern and central portions of the island, the 25-mile (40-kilometer)-long northern piece of Okinawa is boringly uniform in its width. By and large, it's 7 miles (12 kilometers) across from east to west. It fluctuates a little bit, but not much. There are several brief sections that are as wide as 9 miles (14 kilometers), and for one instant, pinched between bays on both coasts, it narrows to 3 miles (5 kilometers), but only for a moment. Almost all of the 7 by 25 miles (12 by 40 kilometers) north end is covered by mountains and dense vegetation, literally jungle. In fact, a sizeable chunk of it is occupied by the Marines. It's their jungle warfare training center, Camp Gonsalves.

Have we forgotten something? Oh yes, in addition to the long northern top of the island, there's Okinawa's largest land extension, the Motobu Peninsula. It begins at Nago and extends west about 7 miles (12 kilometers) to the town of Motobu near its end. In overall size and shape, the peninsula is fairly circular, with a narrowing at its base where it joins the main part of Okinawa Island. It's about 8 miles (13 kilometers) from north to south or east to west. There are nine small inhabited islands all around the peninsula and ferries to them leave from three local ports. Several can be reached by bridges or causeways. The most well-known attraction on the Motobu Peninsula, indeed the most well-known attraction in all of Okinawa, is the Churaumi Aquarium. Naturally, we'll be stopping by there, too.

Like the northern section of the island, most of the Motobu Peninsula is covered in mountains and jungle; however, it's not nearly so uninhabited. In fact, it's full of small villages and farms. One of the crops, as elsewhere in the Ryukyus, is sugar cane, but there are also pineapple farms and other specialty crops, such as aloe cactus for producing skin lotions and bird-of-paradise farms for the cut flower trade. There's one more *gusuku*, if you haven't seen enough, and there's a leper colony. This, of course is not a tourist attraction. It's one of only

Cherry Blossom Season

Japanese people take the seasonal blooms of the cherry tree very seriously. Television cameramen and reporters will stand by, waiting for the first unfurling of a blossom. During the spring, each evening on the news the Japanese Meteorological Agency gives its official forecast and bloom prediction and the public tracks the *sakura zensen* (cherry blossom front) as it moves northward from one end of Japan to the other. The blossoming begins in Okinawa around the end of January and moves north through the Ryukyus. It typically reaches the bottom of the mainland, at Kagoshima, at the end of February. Then, by the end of March, it's blooming time in Kyoto and Tokyo. By mid-April it proceeds into northern Japan until it finally arrives in Hokkaidō around the beginning of May. Japanese turn out in large numbers at parks, shrines and temples with family and friends to hold flower viewing parties, at which they will recite poetry about cherry trees. Much saké may be imbibed. Cherry blossoms are deeply symbolic in Japanese culture. The brilliance of their blooms represents the beauty of youth: their ephemeral nature, the transience of life, and death. There are many types of flowering cherries and several hundred cultivars are recognized. Their blossoms range from almost pure white with a touch of pink to the deepest rose red. Flowers may come in single or double varieties. The classic petal, reminiscent of clouds or snow, and found in Tokyo and Washington, DC, is the Yoshino (染井吉野; *Somei-yoshino*; Latin: *Prunus × yedoensis*).

several in the world, along with the Father Damien, Hansen's Disease colony on the island of Molokai in Hawaii. The Okinawa colony is open to the public. It is run by missionaries and you might come across it while driving around. Only remember that it is someone's home.

① NAGO 名護市

Let's begin in Nago (名護市; Nago-shi), Okinawa's third largest city. It has a population of approximately 60,000 which, of course, is really not very large. It's a pleasant enough place with a large public beach. It's nestled against some fairly steep hills and spills down to meet the East China Sea on

The Orion Beer Brewery in Nago is in the foreground. The harbor and beach are center rear.

Nago Bay (名護湾; Nago-wan). There's a port but it's mostly for local fisherman and light industry. It's not a commercial port and there is no ferry service from it to anywhere. Nago hosts two big events every year. In the fall, mid-November, the city hosts the Tour de Okinawa bicycle marathon. In the spring, there is the Sakura (桜 or 櫻; さくら) or Cherry Blossom Festival. The Okinawa Sakura is known throughout Japan as it marks the official beginning of the cherry blossom season. Avid blossom viewers will start in Nago, Okinawa, one of Japan's southernmost places, follow the blooms up to the mainland, then on to Tokyo and from there north all the way to Hokkaido. The expected peak blooming dates are widely reported in the media and TV camera crews move from place to place following the season.

Without question, Nago's most popular attraction is the Orion Beer Brewery (オリオンビール株式会社; Orion Bīru Kabushiki Gaisha). It's pretty easy to find. Just look for the big tanks. Tours are free but by appointment. The brewery runs several every day throughout the year. Although the tours are only conducted in Japanese, they'll give you a little English-language placard which explains each step in the brewing process as you walk from point to point in the brewery. At the end of the tour—here's the highlight— a full-sized free draft of beer, your choice of

The Orion Beer Brewery in Nago.

Getting under way from Motobu Port.

brew. The only caveat: there must be a designated driver in your group. He or she will be given a soft drink or tea.

② MOTOBU PENINSULA 本部半島

From Nago, before heading north, let's branch out west onto the Motobu Peninsula (本部半島; Motobu-hantō). Starting from the Municipal City Hall, it's a little over 9 miles (14 kilometers) along the peninsula's southern shore (Route 449) to Motobu Port (本部港; Motobu-kō). The drive is a bit like Dr Jekyll and Mr Hyde, nice but not always so nice. Essentially, if you keep your view to the left, looking south, it's a beautiful seaside route along the East China Sea the whole way. There are several good beaches although there are no showers or other public facilities. But the parking is free and there are no crowds.

That's the good side. If you turn to the right and look north, it's not so pretty. It's a long series of stone quarries, ripped-open mountainsides and cement factories. Just about every road and masonry building in Okinawa originates here, and at certain times, weekdays mostly, the heavy truck traffic and road dust can be a nightmare. If it's been raining, watch it, for then the rock dust on the road mixes with the water and it's like driving on ice. There have been many accidents and a number of fatalities along this stretch of road.

③ MOTOBU PORT 本部港

In any case, you'll soon enough reach the port at Motobu. There are two ferry services sailing from here. First, the alternating daily "A" Line and Marix Lines to and from Naha

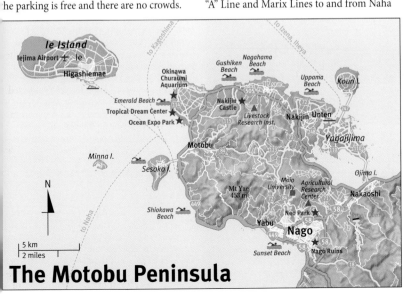

The Motobu Peninsula

and the Amami Islands stop on their way coming and going. As mentioned earlier, you can board at Motobu instead of Nago. It saves two hours sailing time and about $15 per person plus more for any vehicle. The other service is local. Ferries to and from Ie Island (伊江島; Ié-jima) dock here. There are several each day. We'll discuss Ie later on when we discuss the Okinawa-shotō (surrounding islands).

4 SESOKO 瀬底島

From the port, it's a little less than a mile (1 kilometer) west to the bridge over to Sesoko (瀬底島; Sésoko-jima), which we'll also mention later, along with all the outlying islands. From the bridge, it's not much more than a mile (2 kilometers) into Motobu Town. Follow the water and only a dozen or so blocks from the Motobu Town Hall is Motobu's port, somewhat confusingly called Toguchi Port (渡久地港; Toguchi-kō). It's from Toguchi Port, not Motobu Port, that ferries sail back and forth to Minna Island (水納島; Minna-jima). Again, we'll discuss the ferry schedule and that island when we cover Okinawa's east and west coast surrounding islands.

The bridge from Motobu to Sesoko Island.

The famous Okinawa Churaumi Aquarium.

5 OKINAWA CHURAUMI AQUARIUM 沖縄美ら海水族館

From either Toguchi Port or the Motobu Town office, it's about 3 miles (5 kilometers) along the coast road to the very end of the peninsula and the parking lots of the Okinawa Churaumi Aquarium (沖縄美ら海水族館; Okinawa Churaumi Suizokan). It can be very busy on weekends and if you're visiting at that time, there will probably be guys in orange vests telling you where to go. Sometimes you have to hike a pretty good distance from the outer lots to the aquarium.

The aquarium is, in fact, but one attraction in what is officially known as the Okinawa Ocean Expo Park (沖縄海洋博公園; Okinawa kaiyō-haku kōen). Some of the other things to visit are a native Okinawan Village Museum, which is said to be an authentic reproduction of an old Ryukyuan community, the Oceanic Culture Museum, which features a gigantic early Pacific-Asian sailing vessel and a number of Polynesian-type canoes, the Tropical Dream Center, which displays over 2,000 types of orchids, and the Tropical & Subtropical Arboretum.

Ie Jima, as seen from the Churaumi Aquarium.

To be perfectly frank, I'd give them all a miss and just stick with the aquarium. But that naturally is up to you. Everyone has different tastes and what appeals to some doesn't always appeal to others and vice-versa. Since you're already all the way up here, you can have a look around and decide for yourself. If you are at all interested in tropical plants, the one additional attraction you might wish to consider is the Tropical & Subtropical Arboretum (熱帯・亜熱帯都市緑化植物園; Nettai Anettai Toshi Ryokka Shokubutsuen). It's a 22-acre (9-hectare) arboretum and botanical garden featuring

Churaumi Aquarium and Ocean Expo Park

Located at the end of Okinawa's Motobu Peninsula and overlooking scenic Ie Island, the Churaumi Aquarium (美ら海水族館; Churaumi Suizokan) is the second largest aquarium in the world after the Georgia Aquarium in Atlanta. Churaumi means "beautiful ocean" in the Okinawan dialect. In addition to the two million gallon Kuroshio Tank pictured here, and a large shark tank, there are over 70 other specialized tanks, sealife exhibits, an outdoor dolphin theater, manatee pools and a sea turtles display. It's one of the most popular tourist attractions of Okinawa.

Sea horse (Genus Hippocampus).

The spectacular Kuroshio Sea main tank.

Lion fish (Pterois volitans).

A false killer whale (Pseudorca crassidens) performing at the Sea Mammal Exhibit.

A "bloom" of a white-spotted jellyfish (Phyllorhiza punctata).

some 30,000 plants covering more than 300 species. It's the only such park on Okinawa and it's free. Of course, if you like plants, then maybe the orchid display is worth a look too, but it's not free. It costs about $10 per person (half for students).

The aquarium is also not free and some find it a bit expensive. It runs 1,800 Yen per person (students less, several rates). Two thoughts. First, this is Japan and everything's expensive. Second, have you visited any aquaria in the US lately? How about the National Aquarium in Baltimore, one of America's finest? Tickets there range from $25 to $30 per person depending on the type of ticket, which makes the Churaumi seem like a pretty good deal. It's a very fine aquarium and well worth the visit. In addition to the enormous main tank, which sports the world's largest acrylic panel, 27 feet high by 74 feet wide (8.2 meters high by 22.5 meters wide) with a thickness of 24 inches (60 centimeters), there are dozens of other lesser tanks, some big, some small, full of around 750 types of exotic sea creatures from a variety of environments. It's a comprehensive learning experience.

6 NAKIJIN CASTLE RUINS 今帰仁城跡

The Churami Aquarium is located at the Motobu Peninsula's westernmost point, quite close to the top of the peninsula. From here, we'll head due east, riding along the peninsula's northern edge on the Motobu Loop Road, which in this section is Route 505. It's a little less than 4 miles (6 kilometers) until the signs for Nakijin Gusuku. Then turn right, a bit more than three-quarters of a mile (1 kilometer) and you're there.

All that remains of Nakijin Castle, perched on an isolated, rocky outcrop at the northernmost tip of the Motobu Peninsula, are its encircling walls.

Nakijin Castle (今帰仁城; Nakijin Gusuku) is the northernmost *gusuku* on Okinawa Island. Like the others we've seen, it is a UNESCO World Heritage Site. From its remaining encircling walls, it appears to have been a very large complex. The standing ramparts are impressive, but what is perhaps most striking is the palpable impression of isolation. Whatever grandeur the fortress may have had, its perch on a rocky outcropping surrounded on almost all sides by steep vertical drops, including one to the sea, give it a sense almost of emptiness. Even the panoramic view over the East China Sea seems windswept and cold. Yet up until the time Nakijin Castle reached the zenith of its power in the early 1400s, it was evidently a great place of worship. Several *utaki* (御嶽; lit. "sacred place" in Okinawan) sites of worship have been unearthed by archeologists in the fortress.

Recall that the most sacred *utaki* on Okinawa is the Seifa Utaki on the Chinen Peninsula in southern Okinawa. What make these places holy, what forms of early Shinto worship their believers may have practiced, seems so alien, so lost in the fog of time and the distance of history. It seems wholly disconnected. Maybe not to everyone, but to this visitor the castle seemed occupied only by ghosts—and none too benevolent, like the spirits of souls unassuaged.

7 UNTEN PORT 運天港

From the castle we'll retrace our steps back three-quarters of a mile (1 kilometer) to the north coast loop road (Route 505), then continue east 4 more miles (6 more kilometers) to Nakijin Village (今帰仁村; Nakijin-

Unten Port at center, with Yagaji Island on the right separated from the Okinawa mainland by a narrow sea channel and a small inland bay.

son). There's nothing in particular that we're seeking here, it's just a little village, but it's the nearest point of reference to where we're headed. Approximately 3 miles (5 kilometers) further east (for there are a number of little roads taking you there) is the port of Unten (運天港; Unten-kō). Two ferry services sail out of here daily, one to the island of Izena (伊是名島; Izéna-jima), the other to Iheya (伊平屋島; Ihéya-jima). These lovely twin isles are 20 and 25 miles (32 and 40 kilometers) by sea due north respectively and are covered below in the Okinawa-shotō (surrounding islands) chapters.

The new western bridge connecting the Motobu Peninsula to Yagajijima.

⑧ YAGAJIJIMA 屋我地島

We are actually only 720 feet (220 meters) over the water from a very interesting and remote place, but we won't be able to get there for a while. Due east from Unten Port is the little island of Yagajijima (屋我地島; Yagaji-jima). At this point, it's separated from the Okinawan mainland by a narrow sea channel. Further south it's separated by a small bay. The island is connected to the mainland by two bridges, one on the east, and a new one on the west. Directly across the channel, on a little jutting point of land, are the graves of two French seamen who died while visiting here in 1846. It's called Oranda Baka (オランダ墓; Okinawan pronunciation of "Hollanders' Grave"). Although we're very close to it, it's unreachable for the moment, unless we start swimming. We'll visit the gravesite when we visit Yagaji Island.

After leaving Unten Port, and after 1.75 miles (3 kilometers) of local roads, we'll return to the Northern Motobu Loop Road, Route 505, and head southeast. At the intersection where the local road joins 505, you'll see signs and a brand-new highway (Route 248) running due east. The road was built to connect to the new west-side bridge to Yagaji. Formerly, the island's only road access was via its east-side bridge. Now there are two. We'll visit the island and its two adjacent neighboring islands later. For now, it doesn't make much difference which way we return to Route 58 and the way north. If we stay on the Motobu Loop Route 505 until it ends at the intersection of Route 58, it's 7.5 miles (12 kilometers) from Unten Port or if we take the new bridge and cut across Yagajijima and Oujima, it's 6 miles (10 kilometers). In either case, the intersection at Route 58 marks the northeastern end of the Motobu

The ferry to Iheyajima berthed at Unten Port.

Peninsula. The Route 58 Highway comes up 4 miles (6 kilometers) from Nago, although it starts much earlier, in Naha. It more or less follows the island's west coast all the way to Hedo Point.

Let's express the distance around the Motobu Peninsula more succinctly. If we start in Nago, take the southern coastal loop road west to Motobu Town, then continue north to the Churaumi Aquarium, then return east via the northern coastal loop road to Nakijin, then continue to the junction of Route 58 and take it south to Nago—a nice big clockwise circle—it's a total of 31 miles (50 kilometers). Add about 4.5 miles (7 kilometers) for the round trip from Nakijin to Unten Port if you wish to go there. Thirty miles (48 kilometers) is not a great distance, yet driving on Okinawa is rarely comparable to a cruise down a US Interstate Highway. Figure on at least 3–4 hours to make the circuit. And, of course, that's only a circuit. If you wish to explore the mountain roads in the interior of the peninsula, you can easily spend a day. There are good views and, perhaps surprisingly, good cafés in the most remote places on the Motobu, so don't be worried about delving into this little explored part of the island.

9 CAPE AKAMARU 赤丸岬

From the Route 505/58 intersection it's just a little over 25 miles (40 kilometers) north to Cape Hedo. From Nago it's 30 miles (48 kilometers). It is a lovely drive all the way up the west coast as the road hugs the shoreline almost the entire distance. A little more than halfway, 14 miles (22 kilometers) from the intersection, you'll come to the village of Okuma (奥間; Okuma), and 1 mile (1.5 kilometers) to its west a small promontory capped with a bulbous headland that juts out into the sea. It's Cape Akamaru (赤丸岬; Akamaru-misaki) and here you'll find two resorts. They were originally one. One is open to the public, the other is a military facility.

The cape was requisitioned at the end of World War II by the US Army to serve as a recreational facility. With the addition of several sorts of lodging facilities, including cabins, Okuma Beach, as it was then known, served in that role for over 30 years. In May of 1977, one section of the resort, half the southern beach, was returned to Japanese local administration. The photograph of the cape below was taken from the east. Its general orientation pushes out to the west, so the beach on the right-hand side is the north beach and that on the left is the south beach. The end of the cape is still controlled by the US military. It's separated from the rest of Okuma by a road and a fence. It's a joint operation run by Moral, Welfare & Recreation (MWR) for the various branches of the armed services and is now known as the Okuma Military Recreational Facility.

It's a great place to go. If you're a military ID holder and live on or near any of the bases to the south, it's far enough away that you'll feel like you've gone away someplace, yet it's really only about a two-hour drive

Cape Akamaru and the village of Okuma.

Okuma Military Recreational Facility.

from home. The facilities are good (cabins, restaurant, beach, small golf course, etc.), and they have every type of water sports activity available for adults and kids. It's a great family destination. There's a large camping area too, if that's your style.

The eastern half of Okuma's southern beach is the portion returned to Japan. It's operated by a subsidiary of Japan Airlines and called the JAL Private Resort. Although it's called "private," it's open to everyone. Since it's no longer a military facility, no one needs an ID to come here. It was established using the original lodging facilities built by the military. Although it's been completely upgraded over the years, it's still advertised by JAL to "provide affordable luxury hotel accommodations." In other words, it runs around $200 a night instead of the $300 or more a night you'll pay in the top-end resorts a little further south on the Onna coast.

10 HIJI FALLS 比地大滝

By far the most popular day trip from either of the Okuma resorts is to Hiji Falls (比地大滝; Hiji Ōtaki). From the entry gate at the Okuma Military Recreational Facility, it's almost 1.75 miles (3 kilometers) to the parking lot at. You'll pass just below the village of Okuma and about halfway there you'll cross Route 58 at a stoplight. Follow the river to the falls. There's an entrance fee of 500 Yen.

From the entrance gate of the falls, it's a 1-mile (1.5-kilometers) hike along a well-marked and well-traveled path. The trail follows the Hiji River (比地川; Hiji-gawa). Opinions vary on the hike itself. It's easily one of the most popular short hikes on the island as it has a very pretty waterfall at its end. But, after all it's a mile and coming and going, that's two miles, and those two miles

AL Private Resort at Okuma.

Okinawa's vast northern Yanbaru Forest.

re up and down more than a couple of dozen sets of stairs. So if you're in your 20s or 30s, it's a piece of cake. Figure on 20 minutes each way. Oldsters, those not in such great shape, or those with bad knees and families with young children are going to have a tougher time. Figure on 40 minutes. Bring a water bottle.

Nature enthusiasts will appreciate the hike. It's reported that there are over 1,200 species of subtropical plants and it's possible you might see several rare animals like the Okinawa Rail (Yanbaru-kiuna), a flightless bird; Pryer's woodpecker (Noguchi-gera), a single species in a single genus; and several types of salamander, turtle and frog, all unique to the Yanbaru Forest. You won't be disappointed when you reach the falls as the water supply in the north runs fairly consistently year round. The cascade measures 85 feet (26 meters) high, making it the highest waterfall in Okinawa. Swimming and diving are prohibited. There have been many accidents (and several deaths) here, but you are allowed to wade in the cool waters at the base of the falls.

Incidentally, from the moment you arrived at the Hiji Falls parking lot or, for that matter, when you crossed Route 58 coming east, you entered Okinawa's vast northern jungle forest, the Yanbaru (やんばるの森; Yanbaru no mori). The word descriptively translates from Okinawan dialect as "mountain area with dense forests." With the exception of a few northern villages, almost the entire top one-third of Okinawa Island is covered by this great forest. About one-quarter of it, the eastern side, is occupied by the Marines. It's the Camp Gonsalves Jungle Warfare Training Center. This section is a restricted zone and only has a few public roads crossing through.

If the little hike to Hiji Falls only whetted your appetite for more, armed with a good map or GPS you can explore east from here. Almost all of the north is criss-crossed by narrow roads and jeep tracks. You might want a four-wheel drive vehicle, a dirt or mountain bike or a sturdy pair of legs. Three miles (5 kilometers) east from the Hiji Falls parking lot, almost dead center on this section of the island, is Mt Yonaha (与那覇岳; Yonaha-daké), Okinawa's highest point at 1,634 feet (498 meters). It's a favorite place for hikers. Upon reaching the summit, you'll find two aluminum ladders that lean against the trees. Climb up and now you've

The 85-foot (26-meter) cascade at Hiji Falls.

got the highest view on all of Okinawa. You can reach the peak from the end of the track. The other, more common entrance to the northern hiking trail is from the north, about 6 miles (10 kilometers) south of Route 2.

11 **ŌKUNI-RINDO** 大国林道

Let's say that you've returned from the Hiji Falls parking lot to the intersection of Route 58 below Okuma Village. That's 1 mile (1.5 kilometers). From this point it's a 15-mile (24-kilometer) straight shot north to Cape

Habu Snakes (Genus Trimeresurus)

Why aren't these guys an endangered-species? I don't know, but I do know that the only safe way to handle them is in a jar of *awamori* liquor, as shown here. *Habu* (波布) is the generic Japanese name used to refer to about a dozen venomous snakes in the pit viper family. They're dangerous and can be deadly. They can be irritable and strike fast. Maybe their only good characteristic is that they're nocturnal and thus not usually encountered during a day's outdoor activities. They are fairly easy to recognize due to their enlarged triangular-shaped heads. They average around 4–6 feet (1.5–2 meters) and have a heavily built body. Their various species are found throughout all the Ryukyus with the notable exceptions of Yoron, Okinoerabu and Kikai, a fact that residents of those islands never fail to remind you of. Good islands for snake-a-phobes. It's easy to get overly worked up about these creatures. Stay out of the trees, jungles, sugar cane fields, old tombs and caves, especially at night.

Ōkuni-rindo Forest Road

How about taking a roller coaster-like ride through the Yanbaru jungle? Sometimes said to be the best kept secret in Okinawa, a drive on the Ōkuni-rindo (lit. "big country forest road") takes you through some of the most rugged mountains and deepest jungle forest on the island from the comfort of your air-conditioned car. But it's not for those with squeamish stomachs or kids with motion sickness. It's an up and down, twisting, zigzag mountain road running the whole length through the center of the top of Okinawa. It's per-

fect for those who would like to experience the nature and beauty of the Yanbaru Forest but might not appreciate the heat, humidity, insects or *habu* snakes of a mountain hiking expedition. Ōkuni-rindo's southern end is at Route 331, near Ōgimi village (大宜味村; Ōgimi-son). Although it's possible to drive on a number of jeep tracks all the way to Oku (奥), the northernmost village on Okinawa, most people will be content with the 22 miles (35 kilometers) from 331 to Route 2, just above Mt Yonaha, in Kunigami (国頭村; Kunigami-son). The road provides the nearest access to the hiking trail for Yonaha. If you find the going too rough, there are places to bail out and either head east to Route 70 or west to 58. One of the side roads goes past Hiji Falls, taking you back to Okuma.

Hedo. Along the way you'll pass the western end of Route 2 and you can make an interesting side trip from there. From the traffic light at the junction of Route 58 and the Hiji Falls road, it's 4 miles (6 kilometers) north to the tiny village of Yona (与那; Yona). Look carefully and double check your map, for it's pretty easy to miss the right-hand turn on to Route 2 if you're going too fast. You can drive right by without seeing it.

Route 2 is Okinawa's northernmost road connecting the west coast (Route 58) and east coast (Route 70). Route 2 is 7.5 miles (12 kilometers) long from the junction with Route 58 to the intersection with Route 70. Midway across, at almost exactly 4 miles (6 kilometers) from either side, there are two intersections with the northern and southern ends of the hairpin, zigzag mountain road Ōkuni-rindo (大国林道). You can take a hair-raising 9-mile (14-kilometer) northern spur from here to Oku (奥) or the 20-mile (32-kilometer) stomach-wrenching southern ride all the way to Ōgimi (大宜味), or get off near Hiji Falls and return to Route 58 and then Okuma.

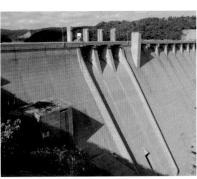

Aha Reservoir Dam.

Aha Falls, popular for outdoor swimming.

12 AHA FALLS 安波滝

If, instead of taking any part of the Ōkuni-rindo you cross the island over the mountains on Route 2, you'll reach Route 70. Turn right there and go south about 1.5 miles (2.5 kilometers) until you see a sign for Tanaga-gumui (タナガーグムイ). Turn right again on to a small access road. You can park beside the road and hike to what is commonly called Aha Falls (安波滝; Aha-taki). Unlike the mile-long hike at Hiji, this one's only a few thousand feet, but they're straight downhill. Even in dry weather, it's a slippery, muddy trail down to the pool and the falls. Some good news is that there's no charge.

Here's the story about the two names. Tanaga-gumui is a pond below a waterfall on the Fuku River (福川; Fuku-gawa). From the falls and pond the river runs approximately three-quarters of a mile (1 kilometer) south until it ends on a small bay of the Pacific Ocean at the little village of Aha (安波; Aha). In the local dialect, Tanaga-gumui means "pool of freshwater prawns." There were, at one time, large quantities of delicious freshwater shrimp in this pool, but they were fished out years ago and are now extinct. Downstream, on the same bay

at Aha, another river flows and empties. This one comes from the Aha Reservoir Dam (安波井堰; Aha-iseki), about 1.75 miles (3 kilometers) to the west.

So, in fact, what's called Aha Falls has nothing to do with the Aha River or Dam. There's no longer any waterfall there since it was dammed some years ago. But even though the Fuku River is not the Aha River, both rivers end on the bay at Aha village and hence English speakers started calling it Aha Falls because that's much easier to say than Tanaga-gumui, which is what the Japanese call the place.

Like Hiji Falls, Tanaga-gumui is a popular hike and considered one of the best places for a cool outdoor freshwater swim. Its clear waters are fed by its scenic cascading waterfall. Because the pool is deep in most places, a popular activity is to dive off the rocks above the pond. Unfortunately, there are also submerged rocks that are not visible. A number of US service members and others have been seriously injured here, and several have lost their lives. It's forbidden to dive in this pool, although that prohibition doesn't seem to stop too many people. The swimming is fine. Just be careful.

13 CAPE HEDO 辺戸岬

Let's return to where we started this side trip, back to the west side of the island at the junction of Routes 58 and 2 at Yona village. From the intersection it's just a bit over 10 miles (16 kilometers) up to Cape Hedo (辺戸岬; Hedo-misaki), the northernmost tip of Okinawa. Hedo Point, as it's also called, is the meeting place of the Pacific Ocean and East China Sea. The cape's cliffs rise 230 feet (70 meters) above the blue waters and it's possible to see Yoron Island (与論島; Yoron-tō) 14 miles (22 kilometers) to the north on a clear day. On the top of the cliffs there's a memorial stone inscribed (in Japanese) with words of praise in commemoration of the 1972 return of the island back to Japan from US military control.

Far below, on windy days, the crashing waves of the sea and ocean can spray all the way to the top and you'll need a raincoat. Few people would think of swimming at such times. Here's the hidden danger: even on the calmest days, at certain times, generally the

This monument at the northernmost point of Okinawa, Hedo Point, commemorates the end of US occupation and the return of Okinawa to Japanese sovereignty in 1972.

turning of the tides, the waters swirl below with powerful undersea currents due to the mixing of the ocean and the sea. It's no place for beginners, it's a place for experienced divers, and even they have to take care.

So where are we in terms of distance at this northernmost point of Okinawa? From the memorial stone at Hedo Point all the way south to the monument atop the cliffs at Cape Kyan, it is 65 miles (104 kilometers) as the crow flies. Via the west coast, tracking along the East China Sea the whole way on Route 58 (and several other roads below Naha), it's 80 miles (128 kilometers). It could possibly be driven in about three or four hours if there was not too much traffic. Driving on the east coast, staying along the Pacific Ocean as much as possible (a combination of Routes 70-331-329-331-3), it's a long 115 miles (184 kilometers). Driving that route could easily take five hours.

Taking the toll expressway its entire length, using local roads below Naha and Route 58 above Nago, does not reduce the miles between Capes Hedo and Kyan compared to taking Route 58 the whole way. In fact, it adds some. But it would shave at least an hour off the driving time, maybe an hour and a half. Of course, what's the hurry if you're sightseeing?

14 ADA 安田

Having enjoyed the view, now it's time to leave the Cape, and head . . . is there anywhere but south? Of course not, but now we'll drive along Okinawa's eastern shoreline facing the Pacific Ocean, along Route 70. It's a quick 6 miles (10 kilometers) to Oku (奥), the northernmost village of Okinawa. It's a small place but dramatically sited

Cape Hedo, the northernmost tip of Okinawa.

between mountains to its rear and a fine natural harbor in front. The village is known for its great display of carp wind streamers every year on May 5th, Children's Day (こどもの日; Kodomo no hi). From Oku we'll continue south almost another 10 miles (16 kilometers) to the turn-off for Ada (安田). We won't stop here now but we'll come again when we visit the offshore islands of Okinawa, for Ada is the site of the first islet south of Hedo Point, Adakashima (安田ケ島; Adaka-shima). Incidentally, if you do wish to stop now, it's only one 1 (1.5 kilometers) east down the mountain to Ada and its enormous white sand beach.

It's only a little over a mile (2 kilometers) from the intersection of the Ada road to the junction with Route 2 described a little earlier. If you wish to do so, you could cross back over the island at this point and pick up the Ōkuni-rindo in 4 miles (6 kilometers) or go 8 miles (13 kilometers) to the East China Sea at Yona and catch Route 58. Continuing south, however, from the Route 2 intersection, it's 1.5 miles (2.5 kilometers) further to Aha Falls and another mile to Aha village.

Staying on Route 70 all the while, now it's 17 miles (27 kilometers) south from Aha to Higashi village (東村; Higashi-son). From the village it's less than three-quarters of a mile (1 kilometer) to the end of Route 70, where it meets Route 331. Taking 331 north for 5 miles (8 kilometers) brings you across the island to Route 58. From there it's not quite 7.5 miles (12 kilometers) north to Okuma or 11 miles (18 kilometers) south to Nago. But we're not crossing over now, we're staying on the east coast and heading south.

15 KANUCHA BAY RESORT

From the end point of Route 70 where it meets Route 331 we'll go south on 331 another 12 miles (20 kilometers) to the Kanucha Resort, otherwise known as the Kanucha Bay Hotel & Villas on the north shore of Oura Bay (大浦湾; Ōura-wan) and we'll stop here for a breather. By the way, without any stops or side trips along the way, from the check-in desk in the lobby of the Kanucha Bay Hotel back to the monument stone at Cape Hedo, it's a little over 48 miles (77 kilometers).

We said earlier while visiting the deluxe resorts on Okinawa's Onna coast on the central western side of the island that there were very few top properties on the island's east coast, and that's true. And we also said that most people would agree that the Busena Terrace Beach Resort was the top resort hotel on the island, but that's only half true. Because, in fact, most people would rank the Kanucha Bay Hotel & Villas equally high, if not higher, than the Busena Terrace. Without getting into an argument over which is the best, it's a fair statement that there are at least two "top of the top" properties on Okinawa Island: the Busena Terrace and the Kanucha Bay.

However, we can't discuss the Kanuch Resort without mentioning its location. First, it's on the island's east coast, where there are almost no fine resorts. There's a reason for this. There are few resorts on Okinawa's Pacific shore due to the generally higher surf and dangerous waves. The bottom line is that the ocean is usually rougher on this side of the island. But, here, there's an exception and this is not a problem. The resort is not sited directly on the Pacific but, rather, on Oura

The Pacific shoreline on northern Okinawa.

The splendid white beach at Ada village.

The Kanucha Resort, otherwise known as Kanucha Bay Hotel & Villas.

The Kanucha Golf Course, a challenging 18-hole championship course amid sea and forest.

Bay, a great natural inlet from the ocean and thus the waters are as safe as anywhere on Okinawa. Naturally, the hotel, on the water as it is, runs all the usual water sports activities from its long and private beach.

Second, it's far from Naha, from the airport, even from Nago. The fact is that it's far from everything. Along with the two Okuma resorts, it's easily the most remote resort on Okinawa Main Island. Well, that bit of geography doesn't seem to stop anyone from coming. It only makes it a slightly longer journey to reach the destination. The hotel runs shuttle buses for its guests to and from the airport throughout the day. They take the expressway and it's 50 miles (80 kilome-

ters) door to door and it takes an hour and a half. That's not the end of the world. It can take almost as long, sometimes longer depending on the traffic, to reach the resorts on the western Onna coast.

The Kanucha Resort is a perfect example of what is often said, but not always true: "Build it and they will come." Yes, maybe. Arguably, this statement is only true when you make it worth someone's while. Only then will they come, for if they come and it's a disappointment, word gets out pretty quickly and then nobody comes. Here, they've accomplished their mission. The guests who come are going to stay and enjoy themselves, for they have everything on site.

Bill Clinton House

Here's an extraordinary story. Multimillionaire Japanese businessman Takeharu Shiraishi, founder of the Kanucha Resort and many other enterprises, loves America, democracy and US Presidents, especially Presidents Lincoln, Roosevelt and Clinton. He's visited the US over 50 times. So he built an exact replica of Bill Clinton's Hope, Arkansas, boyhood home at Kanucha Bay. He found furniture from antique shops in Arkansas and Texas, including a Singer sewing machine and a 1947 Frigidaire refrigerator. "Just turning down Clinton Avenue made me cry," says guest Beckie Moore, executive director of the real house in Hope, opened to the public in 1997. "It's such a generous gesture that's probably never been done before and probably never will be again—the house of a US president built in another country." Regardless of your politics, and whether or not you like Bill Clinton, it is a generous gesture and one that deserves respect. You can visit the house when you come to the Kanucha Resort & Villas.

And when any guests might wish to go sightseeing in Naha, or visit other places on the island, they'll pick up a rental car at the resort and go. So the reality is that no one is so isolated, unless they wish to be.

The resort is an expansive complex, sprawling over the hills overlooking the Pacific Ocean on Oura Bay. It's so large that the property runs an internal set of shuttle buses taking guests to and from its many restaurants, gorgeous sheltered beach, several large swimming pools and tremendous 18-hole golf course, which boasts stunning views over the sea and surrounding mountains. There are over 300 rooms and villas in 19 different styles, in a half dozen different buildings and settings. Figuring out the daily rates by type of room or style of building, by differing meal plans and by varying seasonal rates takes a finance degree from a university. But don't worry, everything is at least $400–500 a night and upwards. So, in the supposed words of J.P. Morgan, "If you have to ask the price, you can't afford it."

Here's a last bit, because otherwise readers will think I'm working for the place on commission—and I'm not. In addition to the main hotel and all types of villas, there's a full-scale model of Bill Clinton's boyhood home in Hope, Arkansas. It was built in his honor for the G-8 Summit. So if you haven't yet made it to Hope for the tour, there's hope—you can do it here. And it's free, probably the only thing that is free on this resort.

16 CAPE HENOKO 辺野古崎

If you check your road map you'll see that we'll leave the Kanucha Resort by picking up again on Route 331 and continuing east 4 miles (6 kilometers) around the inner end of Oura Bay until its end where it meets Route 329. If you recall, that was our dividing line from the island's central and northern portions. So we're going to end our coverage of the northern section of Okinawa here, except that we're going to cheat just a tiny bit and mention one last place a little south of the line because it logically fits into our dsicussion of the North.

At the junction of Routes 331 and of the 329 there's a choice. Go right, northwest 4 miles (6 kilometers) until you reach Route 58 on the west coast and then less than three-quarters of a mile (1 kilometer) more and you're in Nago, or take Route 329 south

A holiday cottage at the US Marine Corps Camp Schwab, Oura Bay.

3 miles (5 kilometers) to just before the village of Henoko (辺野古; Henoko). Here, if you're a military ID holder, enter Camp Schwab and check in to the Cottages at Oura Bay, some of the most deluxe, spacious and comfortable lodgings you'll see anywhere. Without doubt this is one of the nicest R&R facilities, if not the nicest, on Okinawa. Marine Camp Schwab occupies all the tip of Cape Henoko (辺野古崎; Henoko-zaki) and what a delightful spot it is. It's ringed by beautiful beaches on both sides of the cape, but most people will swim on the more sheltered side on Oura Bay.

You can't go wrong visiting here, and strangely enough, one of the pleasures, looking out directly across the bay 2 miles (3 kilometers) to the gorgeous Kanucha Resort, is thinking: "How nice this place is and I'm paying 1/10th the rate." For here, it's about $50 a night instead of $500. I don't know about you, but that gives me a warm and fuzzy feeling all over.

This is where we'll end our visit of Okinawa-hontō (Okinawa Main Island). Let's have a quick look at the map of Okinawa's surrounding islands (Okinawa-shotō) before embarking on our circular tour around them, for there are many islands and it's going to take some time.

As mentioned earlier, we'll begin at Cape Hedo and work our way around 360 degrees clockwise. There are close to 20 islands and islets along the east coast, although fewer than 10 are inhabited. Okinawa's west side, however, has many more and they range much further out to sea. Altogether, there are over 40, with about 20 of those inhabited. So, what are we waiting for? Let's get going, the islands await.

Chapter 8

ISLANDS EAST OF OKINAWA 沖縄諸島
Scattered islets, quiet resorts

1. **Adakashima** 安田ケ島
2. **Abuōrujima** 安部オール島
3. **Nagashima** 長島
4. **Tairajima** 平島
5. **Ikeijima** 伊計島
6. **Miyagijima** 宮城島
7. **Henzajima** 平安座島
8. **Hamahigashima** 浜比嘉島
9. **Ukibarushima** 浮原島
10. **Minamiukibarushima** 南浮原島
11. **Yabuchijima** 薮地島
12. **Aginamiiwa** アギナミ岩
13. **Gonjiyaniwa** ゴンジヤン岩
14. **Tsukenjima** 津堅島
15. **Kudakajima** 久高島
16. **Kumakajima** クマカ島
17. **Adochijima** アドチ島
18. **Tamataiwa** タマタ岩
19. **Ādjijima** アージ島
20. **Ōjima** 奥武島

Although Cape Hedo was the ending place of our coverage of Okinawa-hontō, it's the starting place for our clockwise exploration of the other islands in the Okinawa-shotō, "the near islands" (沖縄諸島). The first close-in island on the eastern side of Okinawa, just a bit south of Hedo Point, is Adakashima and it's not much of a start, for it's just a little speck of a place.

1 ADAKASHIMA 安田ケ島
Ten miles (16 kilometers) south of Hedo Point as the crow flies, or about 16 miles (26 kilometers) by the coast road is the town of Ada (安田; Ada). Most of northern Okinawa is uninhabited. Ada is one of only a handful of villages on the northeast section of the island. It's a very small fishing village with approximately 150 residents. About

1,150 feet (350 meters) offshore is a little green uninhabited island, Adakashima (安田ケ島; Adaka-shima). It measures close to 1,640 feet (500 meters) long and up to 660 feet (200 meters) wide in several places. It actually has a couple of nice beaches, so it may be worth the swim if you're a good swimmer or worth the paddle if you're a keen kayaker.

2 ABUŌRUJIMA 安部オール島
The Pacific Ocean side of Okinawa has far fewer islands than does the East China Sea side, so we'll travel about one-third of the way down the island's eastern shore (35 miles/56 kilometers) from Ada on the coast road to Oura Bay (大浦湾; Ōura-wan) to find our next islands—all three of them and all tiny and uninhabitable. First, on the bay's northern shore, 11 miles (18 kilometers) east of Nago and just 1.25 miles (2 kilometers) east of the luxury golf resort, Kanuchu Bay Hotel & Villas, is the little village of Abu (安部; Abu). At the northeasternmost extremity of the bay, at the end of Cape Gimi (安部崎; Abu-zaki or Gimi-zaki), is a rocky little island, Abuōrujima (安部オール島; Abuōru-jima). It's perhaps 1,310 feet (400

Adakashima, the first islet in our clockwise circuit of Okinawa Island.

Abuōrujima, one of several uninhabited islets at Oura Bay.

A colorful bridge above pristine waters connects Miyagijima and Ikeijima.

meters) long and 500 feet (150 meters wide). It's only 500 feet (150 meters) offshore from the cape and at low tide you can walk there.

3 NAGASHIMA 長島

Directly west across the mouth of Oura Bay, 3 miles (5 kilometers) over water but 10.5 miles (17 kilometers) by road around the bay is Oura Bay's opposite, southern promontory, Cape Henoko (辺野古崎; Henokozaki). At the end of Cape Heneko are two more islets, Nagashima (長島; Naga-shima) and Tairajima. Both are about 2,300 feet (700 meters) offshore. Naga means "long" and that's a good way to describe this one as it's actually a 1,400-feet (425-meter)-long string of three mini-islets and a few connected rocks. Most of it is only around 100 feet (30 meters) wide, but at its widest it's 330 feet (100 meters). On the largest of the three islets there's a little beach and then a 330-foot (100-meter) path leading to the isle's highest point, on its eastern end, where there is a light beacon.

4 TAIRAJIMA 平島

About 1,150 feet (350 meters) south of Nagashima ("Long" Island) is Tairajima (平島; Taira-jima; "Flat" Island). There's not really too much to say about this one either. It's more or less round and about 490 feet (150 meters) in diameter. Incidentally, both of these islets are just off Cape Henoko, which is controlled by the US Marines. It's part of Camp Schwab, formerly called Camp Henoko, and still the home of the Henoko Ordnance Depot, an ammunitions storage facility on base. Unless you've got military ID, it's a restricted area.

5 IKEIJIMA 伊計島

If we had a ship, we'd set sail south and then a bit west from Cape Henoko and its two little islands to our next destination. By sea it's a little less than 9 miles (14 kilometers) to Ikeijima, the first and most northerly of a small group of islands. But we don't have a boat, so we'll drive, staying on Okinawa's eastside coastal road, Route 329, for the

Uninhabited Nagashima ("Long Island") at left and Tairajima ("Flat Island") at right lie directly on the mouth of Oura Bay, just off Cape Heneko.

Ikeijiima's Big Time Resort.

Ikei Beach, a pleasant beach with calm waters.

The end of the line, the northern tip of Ikeijima.

most part. By this route it's southwest counter-clockwise all the way around Kin Bay (金武湾; Kinbu-wan or Kin-wan), then southeast down almost to the end of the Katsuren Peninsula (勝連半島; Katsuren-hantō), then east over the almost 3-mile (5-kilometer)-long Kaichu-doro Causeway (海中道路; lit. "Sea Center Road" or, more figuratively, "Road through the Sea") to Henzajima, continuing northeast and across another bridge to Miyagijima, then north and across another bridge to Ikeijima and its final tip—a true "Land's End." Altogether, the route by road from Cape Henoko at Camp Schwab to the end of Ikeijima (伊計島; Ikéi-jima) is 40 miles (60 kilometers).

If you have a look at an aerial shot of Ikei Island you'll see that it's a uniformly laid out rectangular grid about three-quarters of a mile (1 kilometer) wide and 1.25 miles (2 kilometers) long. Its area is 6.75 square miles (1.75 square kilometers) and its circumference 4.5 miles (7 kilometers). The island's population is close to 400. It has a small village and port (伊計港; Ikei-kō) on its

southern side by the bridge that connects it to Miyagijima, a small resort on its northern end and sugar cane fields in between. The resort is the attraction for most visitors. It's not too fancy but (for Japan) not too expensive, around $150 a night. It's called the Big Time Resort and it has a main building with about 60 rooms surrounding a large indoor atrium, a nice outdoor swimming pool, a good, relatively inexpensive restaurant and some 30 private cottages spread around the complex. It's a quiet spot, almost isolated. It's one of a very few resorts on Okinawa's Pacific side and that's not by accident.

Although the hotel has several small, white sandy beaches on very secluded coves, there's a reason why not too many people swim here, at least not out too far. This "Land's End" is a promontory and the meeting place of the waters of Kin Bay and the open Pacific. Twice a day, with the turning of the tides, the waters swirl and it can be dangerous. Several people have been swept away and drowned just offshore at this location.

For a much safer alternative, try Ikei Beach. It's at the bottom of the island, just past the bridge when coming from Miyagi. It's on the west side, that is, the Kin Bay side of the island. It costs a few hundred Yen to park here, but they have all the water sports equipment and other facilities that you could wish for, including a good cafeteria style restaurant.

6 MIYAGIJIMA 宮城島

Turning around and heading south from Ikei, we'll re-cross the Miyagi–Ikei Bridge and have a look at Miyagijima (宮城島; Miyagi-jima). It's more or less an oval about 1.25 miles (2 kilometers) across and a bit less than 1.75 miles (3 kilometers) from north to

Miyagi's best beach is at the island's northern end.

Henzajima is mostly covered with oil tanks.

outh. Its total area is 2 square miles (5.52 square kilometers). Circling most of its perimeter, one gets the impression that it's a very rugged little island, comprised mostly of steep hills, which leads one to think that here cannot be much agriculture. But if you take one of the tiny one-lane roads and drive up the hills to the island's center top, you'll find that it is, in fact, a little plateau, almost completely covered in sugar cane fields.

Miyagi has several small villages, the largest of which, Tobaru (桃原; Tōbaru), is a decent sized port. Tobaru's on the island's southern end, along a sea channel that separates Miyagi from Henzajima. Because of the channel, the port has equal access to both the Pacific and Kin Bay. There are a couple of small beaches along Miyagi's eastern side but they're well off the beaten track and hard to get to. The best beach is at the northern end, a little before the bridge to Ikei. It's on the island's western side, on Kin Bay. Like Ikei Beach, it has nice public facilities and you'll pay a few hundred Yen to use them.

7 **HENZAJIMA** 平安座島

The channel that separates Henzajima (平安座島; Henza-jima) from Miyagijima is quite narrow, only 10–30 feet (3–10 meters) wide for most of its 1-mile (1.5-kilometer) length. But for the channel, Henza and Miyagi would be one island. Henza is fairly square, perhaps 1–1.5 miles (1.5–2.5 kilometers) in any one direction. Its surface area is 2 square miles (5 square kilometers). The island's only village, Yonashirohenza (与那城平安座; Yonashiro-henza), is at its southern end. It's quite large, with about 1,800 residents. The village, which is also called Henza Town, has a fairly large harbor for a village of its size. Other than the village and the port, the other 90 percent of the island is an oil refinery and tank farm. Altogether, there are about 70 great round oil tank behemoths occupying almost every square foot of the island. It's impressive to see though not possible to visit. For security reasons, almost the entire island is a restricted zone. Other than the village, the only public access is the road along the island's east

The Kaichu-doro Maritime Museum is located in the middle of the 2.75-mile (4.5-kilometer) span.

The Kaichu-doro causeway, the "Road through the Sea," connects Okinawa-honto's Katsuren Peninsula to Henzajima, shown on the left. The long bridge at the rear connects Henza to Hamahigajima on the right.

side leading north to Miyagijima. Thus, there is very little for the tourist on Henza.

By road, it's 7.5 miles (12 kilometers) from the northern tip of Ikei to Yonashirohenza. From there, there's a choice of two bridges, both long. The longest, Kaichu-doro, is 2.75 miles (4.5 kilometers) and links Henza–Miyagi–Ikei Islands to the Katsuren Peninsula on Okinawa-hontō. This magnificent causeway, a minor tourist attraction in its own right, has a sightseeing area, a maritime cultural museum, restaurant and gift shops, plus a large safe parking area, all in the middle of its span. On its northern Kin Bay side, there are vast shallow areas of sea. A quirk of topography keeps this area forever windblown, and for this reason you'll always find windsurfers and para-kitegliders here. It's fun to watch. The other bridge from Henza Town is a less than one mile (1.4-kilometer)-long span to Hamahigashima. We'll go there before returning to the Okinawan mainland.

8 HAMAHIGASHIMA 浜比嘉島

This small islet, roughly triangular in shape, is about 1 mile (1.5 kilometers) across at its widest and 1.25 miles (2 kilometers) long from north to south. That gives it an area of slightly more than 1 square mile (2.5 square kilometers) and a circumference of 4.5 miles (7 kilometers). Hamahigashima (浜比嘉島; Hamahiga-shima) has a population of about 450, who reside in three small villages, each with its own port. Just as you come over the bridge from Henza, three-quarters of a mile (1 kilometer) to your right (west) is Hama

The Kaichu-doro causeway has several tourist attractions in the middle of its span.

(浜; lit. "beach"). It has the longest beach on the island. It's almost three-quarters of a mile (1 kilometer) of clean white sand and it has free showers and parking. As you can imagine, it's popular, but it's never overcrowded because most people don't know about it.

If, instead of turning right after you've crossed the bridge, you turn left (east), in three-quarters of a mile (1 kilometer) you come to Higa (比嘉), an equally small fishing village. Higa doesn't really have a beach of its own but its mini-luxury resort does. On a bluff overlooking the village and the ocean is the Hamahigashima Resort, a lovely, elegant property. It's small, only about 30 rooms, but that's what's nice about it. It offers beautiful spacious sleeping rooms, a fine dining room and a beautiful "infinity" pool overlooking the Pacific Ocean. It is a "designer" property, with everything just so—modern, clean and stylish. It runs about $200 per night for a double room. Most packages include breakfast and dinner.

There's a path and a set of stairs leading down to the beach, only about 500 feet (150 meters) away. The beach is 660 feet (200

Hamahiga Island on the right, populated by three small fishing villages, boasts a mini-luxury resort and white sand beaches. The bridge spans the sea between the island and Henza.

meters) long. Around the corner there's another beach, this one another 660 feet (200 meters) long. In fact, if you follow the second beach to your right (south), in another couple of hundred meters you'll come to the island's third village, this one a mere hamlet of perhaps two dozen homes. It's about as laid back and as charming an island as you can find.

Incidentally, although this islet and the resort front the Pacific Ocean, here the beaches are protected by a barrier reef about miles (5 kilometers) offshore. This natural breaker and the relatively shallow waters surrounding Hamahiga Island help ensure peaceful and safe swimming. Looking out over the sea, in the distance, 1.75 miles (3 kilometers) southeast offshore from Hamahiga, we find two small, uninhabited islets: Ukibaru and South Ukibaru. Let's have a quick glance at them.

The small and stylish Hamahigashima Resort is oriented so that every room has a gorgeous view over the Pacific Ocean, allowing guests to watch the morning sun rise.

⑨ **UKIBARUSHIMA** 浮原島

Ukibaru (浮原島; Ukibaru-shima) is one of the prettiest little uninhabited islets you'll ever come across. It's a near perfect circle, 2,000 feet (600 meters) in diameter. It's almost completely surrounded by clean, fine, white sand. Thick vegetation covers the island's interior except for its very center which, almost by magic, comprises more clean, fine, white sand. A better, more sheltered spot for camping you could not find, or invent. Charter companies offer diving and snorkeling trips to Ukibaru and other east coast islands out of Okinawa.

⑩ **MINAMIUKIBARUSHIMA** 南浮原島

Some 4,250 feet (1,300 meters) southwest of Ukibaru Island is "South" Ukibaru Island. It's sort of a long, thin oval, with a hole punched in one side for a natural cove and beach. From end to end, Minami-ukibarushima (南浮原島); Minami-Ukibaru-shima) is about 1,975 feet (600 meters) long. And it's narrow; most of its width is 500 feet (150 meters). Both Ukibarus are within the barrier reef that shelters Hamahiga, Henza and the lower Katsuren Peninsula from the open Pacific Ocean.

From Hamahiga we'll cross back over the bridge to Henza Town, then back over the Kaichu-doro Causeway. That returns us to Okinawa-hontō, specifically the Katsuren Peninsula, a 1.5-mile (2.5-kilometer)-wide by 5-mile (8-kilometer)-long arm of Okinawa that juts out into the Pacific. From the end of the causeway it's less than a mile (1.5 kilometers) southeast (to the left) to Yakena Port (屋慶名港; Yakena-kō) and our next islet, Yabuchi.

Bridge to Nowhere? There's a short span from Yakena to Yabuchijima.

11 **YABUCHIJIMA** 薮地島

There's a small run-down harbor, Yakena, and a little 790-foot (240-meter) bridge from the Okinawa mainland to Yabuchijima (薮地島; Yabuchi-jima). Half the time the bridge is so occupied by fishermen and their parked cars and gear that you can barely get your car across. So it's really not much of a bridge for vehicular traffic. It's more of a fishing pier. There's not much traffic to Yabuchi anyway because it's hardly inhabited. In fact, it's questionable whether it's inhabited at all. The paved road ends almost as soon as you're on the island. Then it's a dirt path, partially covered in vegetation. Pushing your way through the jungle you catch a glimmer here and there of a shack or tarpaulin covered shed, some with cattle inside. And there's a cultivated field here and there. But residences? None look habitable. So it's hard to say. If there is a resident year-round population on this island, it can't be more than five or ten people. Yabuchi may be the least inhabited islet in the Okinawa-shotō. It's an irregularly shaped piece of land less

The Bridge to Nowhere goes nowhere. Shortly after crossing onto Yabuchi, the road ends.

than a mile (1.3 kilometers) in length and anywhere from 980 to 1,970 feet (300 to 600 meters) in width. It's area is a quarter of a square mile (0.61 square kilometers). However, if you like your beaches quiet, it's got one. There is a rocky beach, maybe 660 feet (200 meters) long, on the island's southern shore. There's usually no one there.

If we leave Yabuchi Island, cross the bridge back to Okinawa, and again make a left, that is, head south, in 1 mile (1.5 kilometers) we'll arrive at a larger and somewhat more prosperous harbor, Heshikiya Port (平敷屋港; Heshikiya-kō). In addition to fishing craft, it is the location of the marine terminal for the ferry to Tsuken Island. But before boarding the ferry, there's one more spot of an island nearby, although it's going to be inaccessible to many persons for it's at the very end of the Katsuren Peninsula, which is a military base.

12 **AGINAMIIWA** アギナミ岩

Aginamiiwa (アギナミ岩; Aginami-iwa) is immediately south of and adjacent to Heshikiya Town and its port is the very end, the last tip, of the Katsuren Peninsula. The tip is about a third of a square mile (a square kilometer) and completely occupied by the US Navy. It's White Beach Naval Facility, a staging area for Marines and their equipment. It's a port of call for nuclear-powered warships and submarines, which frequently dock here. White Beach is also a popular recreational facility for US Service members and their guests. In addition to its beach, there are both indoor and outdoor swimming pools, water sports equipment (seadoos, kayaks, etc.) for rent, a variety of cabin and cottages and a restaurant and bar. About 1,050 feet (325 meters) offshore from the

Aginamiiwa, a small set of islets off the final tip of the Katsuren Peninsula at White Beach Naval Facility.

beach, at the very end of the tip, begins a set of rocks extending another 985 feet (300 meters) further south. There are six or seven of them, depending on the height of the tide.

There's really not much, just a bunch of rocks, usually called *iwa* instead of *jima*, for they really are just rocks with some vegetation. They're so small that they barely qualify as "islets." At low tide you can walk out to them. The first two are each about 100–130 feet (30–40 meters) across in any one direction. The next three range from 30–65 feet (10–20 meters) in size and the last, largest islet is about 325 by 440 feet (100 by 135 metrs) in area. It's probably safe to say that it's a good fishing spot as there are always Japanese fishermen out here, either perched on the rocks or anchored in their boats.

13 GONJIYANIWA ゴンジヤン岩

Approximately 2,620 feet (800 meters) due east of Aginami-iwa and around 2,625 feet (625 meters) southeast of the White Beach facility's white beach, is one more large rock,

Gonijiyaniwa (ゴンジヤン岩; Gonjiyan-iwa). It's about 230 feet (70 meters) across from east to west and perhaps 130 feet (40 meters) wide from north to south. It's almost devoid of vegetation.

14 TSUKENJIMA 津堅島

At its very closest to mainland Okinawa, Tsukenjima (津堅島; Tsuken-jima) is a little more than 2.5 miles (4 kilometers) from its northern end to the beach at White Beach Naval Station. But from Heshikiya Port (平敷屋港; Heshikiya-kō) to Tsuken Port (津堅港; Tsuken-kō) it's a tad further, about 5 miles (8 kilometers). In either case, you get the

The Tsuken Carrot Observatory, with the Harbor Lighthouse at left rear.

Along with Kudaka, Tsuken is one of the two "big" islands in Nakagusuku Bay. Tsuken's little sister islet, tiny Afuiwa, is just to the left at top.

A passenger and vehicle ferry (left) and a passenger express (right) serve Tsuken's transport needs.

picture, it's not far. Depending on the time of year, there are five or six ferries a day out of Heshikiya Port that make the round trip. The fast passenger express ferry takes about 10 minutes one way. The slower ferry runs several times a day and takes about 25 minutes, but it carries vehicles. That's worth remembering if you plan on bringing your bike, car or motorcycle.

Tsuken is a small, low-lying island known for its wonderful carrots. For whatever reason, good soil conditions or just tradition, Tsuken is the most famous place in Okinawa for carrot growing. You'll find them in all the produce markets, usually marked as "Tsuken Carrots." Compared to US carrots, they're quite different. They are shorter and much thicker, not long and narrow as the ones we're used to. They have . . . what can I say, a carrot flavor.

Tsuken Island is quite rectangular in shape, about 1.25 miles (2 kilometers) long and 1 mile (1.5 kilometers) wide. Its area is a bit less than 0.73 square miles (2 square kilometers) and its circumference is 4 miles (7 kilometers).

Kamiya-sō Minshuku on Tsukenjima.

Surrounding the port is the island's only village. The population of Tsuken is 550 and most of the inhabitants live there. As mentioned, the island is mostly flat. The highest point is 125 feet (39 meters) and that spot is in town. On this high point is a small park. It's usually deserted, but in the park is Tsuken's premier sight—a giant carrot! You can enter the big carrot sculpture and climb to the top on its interior spiral staircase. There's a nice view of the village and port. On a 10-point scale of the world's greatest tourist sites, with the Grand Canyon, Niagara Falls and Mt Fuji perhaps being scored in the 9s or 10s, maybe the Tsuken Carrot is a 0.001. Nonetheless, it's still kind of cute.

On account of Tsuken's proximity to Okinawa and its frequent ferry service, many people visiting the island will make it a day trip. However, it is possible to spend an enjoyable night or a weekend. There are two side-by-side waterfront *minshuku* inns just under a mile (1.5 kilometer) from town. They share a wide sandy beach on the Nakagusuku Bay side of the island and offer all the marine activities one might desire. The larger of the two, with about a dozen rooms, is called Kamiya-sō (神谷荘; phone 098-978-3027) and runs about 5,500 Yen per person. The other is smaller and a little less expensive. It also has campsites available with running water and hot showers. Sites go for 1,000 Yen. Either place will pick you up at the Marine Terminal when you arrive if you call ahead and make reservations.

Tsuken had a small role during World War II. During the Battle of Okinawa, the island was staged by the Japanese Imperial Navy as a first line of defense of the Okinawa mainland. It consequently became a site of bloody combat with many casualties. In town

Visitors can walk to Afuiwa, a tiny islet off the northeast corner of Tsuken Island, at low tide.

there are several memorial stones with the names of the dead engraved on them. At war's end, the island's residents were forced to move to the Haebaru area of Okinawa. They were not allowed to return to their homes until 1950.

On the northern end of Tsuken there is a large deserted beach and just across a short channel is another tiny spot of an island, Afu Rock. Let's go there.

AFUIWA (アフ岩; Afu-iwa). This dot of an islet is only 740 feet (225 meters) off the beach at the northeast corner of Tsuken. You can walk there in about knee-level water at

low tide or swim at high tide. Afu Rock is around 500 by 820 feet (150 by 250 meters) in width and length. It's uninhabited and perhaps a little dangerous. There's a fair amount of fused, rusting ordnance sprinkled about, what looks like to be a few batches of unfired 120 mm shells. It's always said in Okinawa that you never touch metal or metallic objects that you can't identify, either on the ground or in the water when diving. For some unexplained reason, the little stretch of water between the islands is often full of very large "chocolate chip" starfish.

As the crow flies, over or across open water, it's a little more than 5 miles (8 kilo-

General Simon Bolivar Buckner Jr

Awarded his 4th General's star posthumously, then Army Lieutenant-General Buckner led the ground campaign of the amphibious assault known as "Operation Iceberg" that launched the Battle of Okinawa (page 93). It was the greatest, most prolonged, most deadly and most successful sea–land–air conflict in American military history. Buckner was born in 1886 and went on to attend the Virginia Military Institute and win an appointment to West Point (class of 1908) from President Theodore Roosevelt. His pedigree was impeccable. His father was Confederate General Simon Bolivar Buckner Sr (1823–1914), also a West Point graduate (1844) and named in honor of the greatest of all South American heroes, El Libertador Simón Bolívar (1783–1830). During the Civil War he was forced to surrender to General Ulysses S. Grant. He later became the Governor of Kentucky (1887–91).

Buckner Jr was killed on June 18, 1945 during the closing days of the Battle of Okinawa. He had been watching combat operations when he was mortally wounded by fragmentation from a Japanese artillery shell. He was the highest ranking US military officer killed by enemy fire during World War II.

This aerial view of Kudakajima shows its flat topography.

meters) south from Tsuken to our next island Kudaka, but there's no commercial ferry service between the two. Rather, we'll have to return to shore and drive around Nakagusuku Bay to get there. Kudakajima could be said to be Tsuken's twin. Both are located in the Pacific Ocean, each near the respective ends of the twin peninsulas that form Okinawa's largest bay, Nakagusuku (中城湾; Naka-Gusuku-wan, lit. "Central Fortress Bay"). The bay's northern extremity is defined by the Katsuren Peninsula. The southern end is demarcated by the Chinen Peninsula (知念半島; Chinen-hantō). Sailing from Heshikiya Port, at the Katsuren Peninsula's southeastern end, to Azama Port, which is at the northeastern end of the Chinen Peninsula, is 11 miles (18 kilometers) over water. But we'll have to drive it; by road, around the bay, it's 27 miles (44 kilometers).

During World War II and in the years immediately following, the bay was called "Buckner Bay" by Americans in honor of General Simon Bolivar Buckner Jr, who was killed not that far from the southern end of the bay in central south Okinawa (page 145). There's a memorial plaque to him at the location of his death (page 92).

The Kudakajima ferry, which docks at Azama on the northeastern side of the island.

15 KUDAKAJIMA 久高島

Southern Okinawa's Chinen Peninsula holds at least three things of interest: the Ryukyu Golf Club, one of the finest clubs on Okinawa with a course high up on the bluffs in the central part of the peninsula; a superb one-third of a mile (half-kilometer)-long "double" beach on Chinen's northeastern side, at Azama, and adjacent to the beach, Azama Port (安座真港; Azama-kō). If you're planning on taking the Kudaka ferry, it's important to go to Azama because you can easily go to a much larger port on the northern end of the peninsula by mistake. The two ports are only 1.5 miles (2.5 kilometers) apart. The ferry to and from Kudaka docks at Azama, which is on the northeastern point of the peninsula. The larger port, on the most northern tip, is for private fishing craft. It's not the terminal for the ferry.

The ferry runs six, sometimes seven times a day, about every two hours, starting at 9:00AM. Kudakajima (久高島; Kudaka-jima) is less than 2 miles (3.5 kilometers) from Okinawa but from port to port it's a little further, 4 miles (6 kilometers) east from Azama Port. It takes 15–20 minutes to get there. The ferry arrives at Tokujin Harbor (徳仁港; Tokujin-kō), which is at the very southernmost end of the island, just below and adjacent to Kudaka's only village. Only about 250 people live on Kudakajima. The island is 2 miles (3 kilometers) long and is narrow, anywhere from 500 to almost 1,970 feet (150 to almost 600 meters). That gives it an area of 0.53 square miles (1.37 square kilometers). This is indeed a small island! Its circumference is 4.85 miles (7.8 kilometers). It's completely flat. The highest point is 55 feet (17 meters). You can rent a bike and tour Kudaka in about an hour or two.

Sea Snakes

Sea snakes are neither fish nor eels and therefore do not have gills. They are air-breathing reptiles and must come to the surface to breathe. They are not very large, generally about 4–5 feet (1.2–1.5 meters) in length, and have paddle-shaped tails. They are completely adapted to their aquatic lifestyle although some come on to land to lay their eggs. Sea snakes are mostly found in the warm tropical waters of the Indian Ocean and the western Pacific. They do not occur in the Atlantic. There are more than 60 species divided into 17 genera, but what they all have in common is that they are highly venomous—often lethal. The two most common types found in Okinawan waters are the Black-banded sea krait (*Erabu umi-hebi*; エラブウミヘビ; Latin: *Laticauda semifasciata*) and the Blue-lipped sea krait (*Hirou umi-hebi*; ヒロウウミヘビ; Latin: *Laticauda laticaudata*). Fortunately, both are generally mild-tempered and it's extremely rare for them to strike unless they are somehow provoked.

Uganhama Utaki, a small sacred cave with a spring and a stone urn filled with offerings.

Cape Kaberu at the northern end of Kudakajima illustrates well the island's rocky shoreline.

Kudaka is primarily an agricultural island, mostly growing sugar cane. There's one central paved road in the middle of the island and it runs the entire length of Kudaka from the port and town to the top northern end at Cape Kaberu (カベール岬; Kabēru-misaki).

Parallel to the central road, on Kudaka's Pacific Ocean side, that is, the east coast, there's an unpaved but perfectly passable road giving access every few hundred meters to the Ishikihama coast (伊敷浜; Ishiki-hama). The advantage of the beaches on this coast is that they are protected by a great reef formation. There's almost no surf at all. Disadvantages? Most of the Ishiki Beach shoreline is rocky although there are some sections that are nice.

In fact, there are a number of nice beaches here and there scattered all over Kudaka, and one of the nicest is very close to the harbor. You can literally step off the ferry and walk a few hundred feet and you're on Megihama Beach (メーギ浜; Mēgi-hama). It's on the island's west coast, between Tokujin Port and the fishing port. You can't miss it. In fact, you'll see it when arriving on the ferry. Funny thing though, you may hear that Kudaka is known for its sea snakes. Sure enough, on a casual snorkeling trip there, right at the harbor, I saw more Erabu sea snakes than in any other place at any other time in over 10 years of diving in Okinawa. So it's true, they are there. Of course, they're generally harmless so this isn't too big a deal. They are actually quite fascinating to watch.

Kudaka is said to be the "Isle of the Gods" and many Japanese and Okinawan tourists make a day trip to this island because of its sacred sites. In Okinawan mythology, it's the place that Amamikiyo or Amamiko (アマミキヨ or アマミコ), the creator goddess of the Okinawa Islands and the goddess of ancestor

The small uninhabited islet of Kumakajima lies off the eastern end of the Chinen Peninsula.

worship, descended from the sky and first set foot. Amamikiyo is credited with bringing an abundant harvest. The Amami Island group takes its name from this goddess.

The most sacred spot on the island is Kubo Utaki (クボー御嶽; Kubō Utaki, also pronounced and spelled フボー御嶽; Fubō Utaki). It's a grove, perhaps a couple of hundred square meters in size, about two-thirds of the way up the western side of Kudaka, between the road and the Uganhama shoreline (ウガン浜; Ugan-hama). There's a short path from the road to the entrance to the site. Visitors walk to the entrance, pray, leave coins, burn incense and depart. No one is allowed to enter the site. There is a small plaque, in Japanese only, that gives a brief description of the place, but that's it. This is truly something you probably have to be Okinawan to appreciate.

Only a few hundred meters south of the Kubo Utaki site, also on the Uganhama

coast and close by to a small secluded beach, is another interesting little sacred spot, and this is one that you can visit. You can even drink it! You'll see a sign for Uganhama Utaki. Follow the path down a fairly long flight of concrete steps. At the bottom is a small cave near the base of the rocks, and inside is a cool, fresh water spring. Try the water. It's delicious. There's something resembling a stone urn full of coins and incense sticks in the cave. From here, it's only a few meters to your own private beach. There's rarely anyone around and the sand is perfect. It's clean and smooth, not ridden with sharp bits of broken coral.

We'll leave Kudakajima now, but notice on our return, about halfway back to Okinawa-hontō on our left, a little over a mile (2 kilometers) south, is a small islet. This is Kumaka Island. We'll discuss it next.

16 KUMAKAJIMA クマカ島

An uninhabited islet, (Kumakajima (クマカ島; Kumaka-jima) is 1.5 miles (2.5 kilometers) offshore from Okinawa's Chinen Peninsula and just over 2 miles (3 kilometers) from Kudakajima's harbor, in other words, more or less midway between the two. Basically, it's an ovular sandbar with a central rocky section covered in vegetation. Including its sand, the islet is about 500 feet (150 meters) long by 200 feet (60 meters) wide. Not including its sand, the rock and vegetative hard core of the islet is a rough circle about 200 feet (60 meters) in diameter. There's a derelict bunker on its southern side, built during World War II. During the summer, private boats from Chinen Harbor take beach-goers out here for the day.

Immediately beyond the tsunami barriers, the first small island on the right is Adochijima; to its left rear is Tamataiwa; to their right rear is Komakajima; and to Komakajima's rear left is Kudakajima.

The causeway and gated entrance to Adjijima, one of Okinawa's most unusual tiny islands because it is privately owned. A helipad is marked on the causeway in front of the gate.

17 ADOCHIJIMA アドチ島

Returning to Kudakajima and Azama Port, it is 5 miles (8 kilometers) south on the coastal road (Route 331) to Yamazato (山里; Yama-zato), a small village. It would appear that the village is particularly prosperous—or at least well-regarded in the Prefecture's legislature—because it has on its shoreline a substantial collection of modern infrastructure amenites: a sports field, a nice-sized port and a white sand beach with ample parking, showers and changing rooms. All of these facilities are man-made; they've been constructed and they're not old. Moreover, the whole complex is protected by a couple of large concrete tsunami barriers as seen in the photo.

From the barriers you could swim or perhaps walk at low tide to Adochijima (アドチ島; Adochi-jima), a small, green uninhabited islet just offshore. It's about 1,640 feet (500 meters) off the coast of Okinawa, but only around 410 feet (125 meters) from the end of the port's tsunami breakers. It is a fairly symmetrical rectangle, about 660 feet (200 meters) long by 230 (70 kilometers) wide. It has a nice beach on the side that fronts Yamazato's harbor. It's completely covered in dense vegetation.

18 TAMATAIWA タマタ岩

Perhaps a bit less than a mile (1.25 kilometers) east of Adochi, maybe a third of the way from the shore to Kumakajima, you'll

A tiny island in the Pacific Ocean: Adji is one of the few inhabited islands of Okinawa that is not open to the public. It's someone's private oceanfront estate.

The popular island of Ōjima is reached by a bridge (center right) from the mainland.

find a little set of rocks, Tamataiwa (タマタ岩; Tamata-iwa). Altogether, there are about a dozen of them, none larger than about 65 feet (20 meters) across. As they could be easily enough run into on some early morning or nighttime sailing, there is a signal light warning beacon on one of them.

19 ĀDJIJIMA アージ島

From Adochi or Tamata we return to shore and walk south along the beach almost exactly three-quarters of a mile (1 kilometer)

to our next islet, Ādjijima (アージ島; Ādji-jima). This must be one of the most unusual tiny islands, perhaps the tiniest, in all the Okinawa-shotō, for it is privately held. It is someone's residence. Its causeway is short, only about 165 feet (50 meters), but it includes a small bridge allowing the tidal waters to pass underneath. At low tide it's reachable over a sandbar but at high tide it's completely surrounded by water and then the causeway is the only land link. As small and as close to shore as it may be, it nevertheless

This aerial view of Ōjima shows that it is quite circular in shape and rather heavily populated.

is an island. At the end of the causeway/ bridge, there's a gate, and it's locked. What appears to be a helipad is directly in front of it. At the top of the gate it says アーヂ島, an alternative spelling for Adjijima.

The island is a well-formed oval, 410 feet (125 meters) long from north to south and about 200 feet (60 meters) wide from east to west. Immediately after entering the gate, Adji's causeway, which is its driveway, splits into two, right and left, and becomes a ring road encircling the island. A branch of the ring road veers up the little hill towards the center of the island and the residence. The island is private and not open to the public. What little can be seen from the shore or from the sea reveals a quite substantial home and several other buildings. It may be a family compound. There is also a dock on the ocean side. If you like islands, or you like privacy, this may well be your kind of place. I know that it's my kind of place. Now, if only that lottery ticket I bought would pay off!

20 ŌJIMA 奥武島

From the causeway at Ādjijima, then back to the coast road (Route 331), it's 4 miles (6 kilometers) west and just a little south to the next island, Ōjima (奥武島; Ō-jima). If you're coming directly from the port at Azama, it's the same road southwest about 7 miles (12 kilometers) along the Chinen Peninsula's eastern shore. Here, we'll visit the final, most southern east coast Okinawa islet, Ōjima. There's a short bridge, maybe 260 feet (80 meters) long, connecting it to the mainland. It's a tiny island, quite circular in shape, and around 985 feet (300 meters) in diameter. That converts to less than 0.027 of a square mile (1/10th of a square kilometer). The islet has a good-sized harbor, a large baseball sports field, a couple of hundred homes and one apartment building. There is a ring road surrounding the island, a decent beach and one very good *soba* restaurant just on the left as you come over the bridge.

Ōjima is small and it has a particularly attractive "feel" about it. For some reason, it always seems welcoming when you're here. People are relaxed and friendly. It's hard to define, but there is something special about the place. Because there are a couple of really, really small, yet inhabited, islands, Ōjima may not necessarily win the prize for the smallest inhabited island in the Ryukyus.

But on a population per square mile basis for small islands, it should win the prize for the most people on a small island in the Ryukyu-rettō. For other than the ball park, there's barely a square foot that's not covered in housing. Why oh why oh why oh—why does everyone want to live on Ōjima? Start again. Why everybody wants to live here is hard to know, but oh they do so. It must be popular for a reason. Maybe it's the place that has the best *soba*?

Our mangled affair with alliteration over, we'll leave Ōjima and take the coast road southwest through the Itoman (糸満; Itoman) section of Okinawa. This constitutes the very southern end of Okinawa Main Island and is often referred to as Shima-jiri (島尻). *Shima* means "island" and *jiri* means "bottom"—and it really means bottom as in one's bottom, butt, buttocks, etc., so it quite literally means "Okinawa Island's bottom." We'll take this route as far as it will take us, to its end at Cape Kyan (喜屋武岬; Kyan-misaki). Altogether, it's just a bit under 11 miles (18 kilometers).

At Cape Kyan is, naturally enough, the Kyan Monument, a lighthouse, and some great views over the Kyan cliffs to the ocean beyond. From here we can go nowhere but north. We've visited all the islands on Okinawa's Pacific Ocean side and reached the island's southern end. Now we'll head north along the island's west coast and visit the islands on Okinawa's East China Sea side. There are many, many islands on this side of Okinawa-hontō, far more than on the Pacific Ocean side.

Cape Kyan Lighthouse on Okinawa's southern tip.

Chapter 9

THE KERAMA ISLANDS 慶良間諸島
Wondrous whales, delightful dives

1. **Kamiyamajima** 神山島
2. **Kuefujima** クエフ島
3. **Nagannujima** ナガンヌ島
4. **Maejima** 前島
5. **Kuroshima** 黒島
6. **Tokashikijima** 渡嘉敷島
7. **Zamamijima** 座間味島
8. **Akajima** 阿嘉島
9. **Gerumajima** 慶留間島
10. **Fukajijima** 外地島
11. **Ōjima** 奥武島
12. **Kubashima** 久場島
13. **Yakabijima** 屋嘉比島

The Kerama Islands (慶良間諸島; Kerama-shotō) comprise a mini-archipelago of some 20 islands located off Okinawa's west coast between 12 and 24 miles (20 and 38 kilometers) west of Naha and Itoman. They are just as frequently referred to as the Kerama-guntō (慶良間群島) or Kerama-rettō (慶良間列島). Four of the islands are inhabited: Tokashiki, Zamami, Aka and Geruma. A fifth, Fukaji, houses the airport. Since no one permanently resides there—it is only sometimes inhabited by day—technically it's considered uninhabited.

The Keramas are popular with day visitors from Okinawa and tourists from mainland Japan. They are especially popular with divers because their waters are crystal clear and their magnificent coral formations have not been destroyed or stolen by collectors. The Keramas are also one of the prime viewing areas for humpback whales and almost all whale watching excursion boats from Okinawa come to these islands. Every year, in early spring, starting in February and continuing through March, the humpbacks' migration route takes them through these beautiful, warm waters.

Although the Kerama Islands have neither large luxury hotels nor fancy resorts, and there are no golf courses, there are many small hotels, *minshuku* inns and hostels. Almost all serve food and beverage. If yours does not, it's not a problem, for there are many small restaurants and cafés. If you're looking for a peaceful, beautiful destination and don't need to be entertained, and if you like diving or snorkeling, then you may have found your paradise, for these small islands, so close to Okinawa, have a lot to offer.

Other than a long swim or sailing your own ship, there's only one way to reach the islands: commercial ferry service. Until a

The Tokashiki passenger and vehicle ferry.

Full house on the Ferry Zamami.

few years ago there were also daily flights from Naha but they were discontinued. It's an open question whether flights will begin again. The small airport on Fukaji Island has, for now, been abandoned.

There are two different sets of ferry services for the islands. One sails to Tokashiki, the other goes to both Aka and Zamami. All passenger ferries for the Keramas use the sea terminal at Naha's Tomari Port (泊港; Tomari-kō; also called Tomarin).

Subject to some seasonal variation, such as additional service in summer, in general for Tokashiki there are three sailings a day, two on the *Marine Liner Tokashiki Express* fast boat and one on the ferry *Kerama*, which takes motor vehicles. The fast express ships leave Naha daily at 9:00AM and 4:30PM. Each sailing takes 35 minutes to reach the island and 25 minutes to unload and reload. The ferries then leave at 10:00AM and 5:30PM, respectively, for the 35-minute return to Tomari Port. In addition, the passenger and vehicle ferry leaves Naha every day at 10:00AM. It takes 80 minutes, arriving at Tokashiki at 11:10AM. The ship then waits until 3:30PM or 4:00PM, depending on the season, before returning to Naha, arriving at 4:40PM or 5:10PM respectively. All ships arrive and depart at Tokashiki Port (渡嘉敷港; Tokashiki-kō), which is on the island's east side, facing Naha.

There is also a fast passenger service and slower passenger and vehicle service to and from Aka and Zamami. In general, the *Queen Zamami III*, which is the fast boat, carries passengers only, no vehicles, and departs Tomari Port twice daily at 9:00AM and 4:00PM. The early sailing goes directly to Zamami, arriving at 9:50AM. Ten minutes later, at 10:00AM, it sails over to Aka, which takes 10 minutes. Another 10 minutes later, now 10:20AM, the ferry departs Aka and returns to Naha, arriving at 11:10AM.

The afternoon sailing of the *Queen* plies a slightly different route. Leaving Naha at 4:00PM, the ferry first goes to Aka, arriving at 4:50PM. Ten minutes later, at 5:00PM, it continues over to Zamami, arriving at 5:10PM. Ten minutes after that, at 5:20PM, it departs and heads back for Naha, arriving at 6:10PM.

If you wish to bring your car or motorbike/cycle/scooter over to the islands, you need to take the slower boat, the ferry *Zamami*. In this case, there is at least one departure, often two, per day. The ferry leaves Naha at

Whale Watching in the Keramas

Humpback whales (*Megaptera novaeangliae*) visit the Keramas every year from January to April. Many tours are available. Those who wish to get up close and personal might choose a tour using Zodiac-type boats. Those prone to seasickness or apprehensive of rocking in the open ocean in a small boat might prefer a tour using larger craft. Either way, it's an exciting experience for children and adults. The shape and color of every humpback's dorsal fin and tail are unique, as individual in each animal as are fingerprints to humans. In general, their body is black on the upper side and mottled black and white on the underside. Flippers range from all white to all black. Adult males measure around 40–50 feet (12–15 meters) and females a little less, about 30–40 feet (9–12 meters). Weight varies from 25 to 40 tons. Females give birth to a calf every 2–3 years after a gestation period close to 12 months. A newborn calf is 10–15 feet (3–4.5 meters) long and weighs about two tons. Some years ago, scientists discovered that humpbacks sing complex songs, each lasting 10–20 minutes and repeated continuously for hours at a time. Since singing appears to be exclusively male, it's thought to be part of mating behavior. Man and killer whales are the major predators of humpbacks. Sharks also attack them. It is believed that there are approximately 75,000 humpback whales alive today, about 15–20 percent of their original population before 19th- and 20th-century whaling decimated their numbers.

The Queen Zamami III hydrofoil.

The Marine Liner Tokashiki Express.

10:00AM and takes 90 minutes to reach Aka, arriving at 11:30AM. After unloading and reloading, the ferry leaves Aka at 11:45AM and sails to Zamami, arriving at noon. There the ferry docks until 3:00PM when she departs and returns to Aka, arriving at 3:15PM. Again taking on new passengers, the ferry leaves at 3:30PM and returns to Naha 90 minutes later, arriving at 5:00PM.

During most of the busy season (summer and certain holidays), there is an additional ferry departure leaving Naha Tomari Port at 2:30PM. The ship arrives at Aka 90 minutes later, at 4:00PM. Discharging and reloading passenger, vehicles and freight, she departs Aka at 4:15PM and arrives at Zamami Port at 4:30PM. She leaves the island at 5:00PM and returns directly to Naha at 6:30PM, not stopping at Aka on the way back.

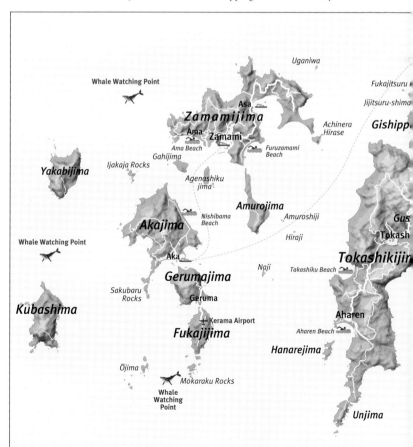

The Zamami passenger and vehicle ferry.

A danger spot, the Kamiyama reef outcropping.

As mentioned earlier, there used to be an airline service to the Keramas. Until 2006 there were several flights a day between Naha and Kerama Airport (慶良間空港; Kerama Kūkō). Unfortunately, the air route was suspended because it wasn't profitable. Given

Hatejima

Nakajima

Maejima

to Naha

N

2 km
1 mile

The Keramas

the relatively frequent ferry service, there evidently was not enough demand for the 10-minute flight. At present, there also does not seem to be any hurry to reinstate the flights, so the airport now sits empty and forlorn. It is located on the tiny island of Fukaji.

Fukajijima is connected by a short bridge to the next island, Gerumajima, which, in turn, is connected by another bridge to the next island, Akajima. From Akajima there are several daily ferries leaving for Zamami but not for Tokashiki. To reach Tokashiki from either Akajima or Zamamijima, it's necessary to return to Naha and take a ferry out from there. Of course, since these islands are very small and the distances between them equally small, it's entirely conceivable that a local fisherman or sailor will take you from one to the next, most likely for the price of the fuel required.

In addition to the four inhabited islands, the Kerama group includes a couple of dozen miscellaneous isles, islets and rocks. We'll mention most of them. Although all the lesser islands are uninhabited, they, or the waters around them, are visited by private watercraft carrying people seeking a secluded beach, an idyllic picnic site or a good diving or snorkeling location.

We'll visit this archipelago in a westward path, coming out from Naha. As a group, starting from Maejima in the east to Yakabijima and Kubashima in the west, they span almost 14 miles (22 kilometers). From north to south, starting at either the top of Zamamijima or Kuroshima to the bottom of the Ōjima rocks or Unjima, it's about 8 miles (13 kilometers). You'll soon see that these approximate 110 square miles (286 square kilometers) of the East China Sea are quite busy indeed—full of little islands popping up all over the place.

Low-lying Kamiyamajima comprises more than a square kilometer of hazardous shoals.

1 KAMIYAMAJIMA 神山島

The first place we'll mention isn't really much of a *jima*, an "island." It's better described as a shipping and navigation hazard. It's a combination of three or four islets, reefs and sandbars 6 miles (10 kilometers) northwest from Tomari Port. Depending on the height of the tide, you might see most it or you might not. Several small islets are always above the waterline and have some permanent vegetation but much of Kamiyamajima (神山島; Kami-yama-jima) is often submerged.

From the perspective of the sea, Kamiyama appears to be one long island and sandbar with a light beacon planted on its far eastern end. An aerial view, however, shows that it is, in fact, several islets and sandbars surrounded by a shallow reef. The constituent parts are variously shaped as rounds, rectangles or crescents and range in size from a few thousand feet to almost three-quarters of a mile (1 kilometer) in length. None are much larger than a couple of hundred feet across. Again, depending on the tides, the island's highest points rise to 15–30 feet (4.5–9 meters).

Outcroppings like this are no joke. In 1963 112 people aboard the passenger ferry *Midori-maru* drowned when she went down after hitting a reef here. Most Kerama-bound ferries, and those sailing to Tonaki and Kume, usually steer well below the Kamiyama shoal, to its south. Northbound ferries, those headed for Aguni, the Amamis or Tokyo, sail above the shoal. Keep your eye open and you should see it. It spans well over a square kilometer. By the way, the name literally translates as "God's Mountain Island," quite a name for such a dangerous place.

2 KUEFUJIMA クエフ島

The size of this landmass also depends on the height of the tide. The Kuefujima (クエフ島; Kuéfu-jima, also called Kuéfu-tō) outcropping may be one long sandbar or two. It's less than 1.25 miles (2 kilometers) southwest from Kamiyamajima. At neap tide (or any low tide), the islet may be as long as 1,640 feet (500 meters), running east to west. At spring tide, it divides in half and each portion of the sandbar may be about 325–550 feet (100–150 meters) long. At all times, it's never much wider, north to south, than about 80–100 feet (24–30 meters). And it's never much taller than 7–10 feet (2–3 meters). It's merely a place to run aground. In fact, how is deserves to be called a *jima* at all is a mystery, for it's really no island, nor even an islet. It's simply a sandbar.

3 NAGANNUJIMA ナガンヌ島

Here's another hazardous reef waiting for the unwary sailor, the last of this set of three marine outcroppings. The Nagannu shoal is not as large as the Kamiyama, nonetheless, it's a combination of two or three islets and several connecting sandbars, nicely protected by a submerged reef. Nagannujima (ナガンヌ島; Nagan-nu-jima) is about 1.25 miles (2 kilometers) west after the Kamiyama reef and the same distance northwest from the Kuefu sandbar. Naturally, it's also potentially dangerous and large ships give it a wide berth.

Nagannujima is about three-quarters of a mile (1 kilometer) long from east to west and about 500–650 feet (150–200 meters) wide. It's never much higher than about 15 feet (5 meters). Several sections are covered in

The size of the Kuefujima sandbar (front) and Kamiyama islet (rear) depends on the height of the tide.

…everal areas of Nagannujima, another hazardous …hoal, have permanent vegetation. The islet is a …opular destination for day-trippers.

…Maejima, the first "real" island in the Kerama …nini-archipelago, is actually three islets strung …n a north–south row.

…permanent scrub vegetation. Interestingly, …his mini-islet is set up for day-trippers from …Naha's local luxury hotels. There are fresh-…water showers, cabanas and chaise-longues …available. Would-be Robinson Crusoes pack …a lunch and refreshments and come out here …for peace, quiet and clean water swimming, …something they can't find in Naha's Harbor. …There's a pier on the island's southern side …where light craft can tie up.

4 MAEJIMA 前島

…Not counting the three preceding island …reefs, sandy islets or sandbars, we now come …to what can only be described as the first …"real" island west of Okinawa-hontō. The …name Maéjima (前島; Maé-jima) translates …as "Anterior Island," which is quite logical …considering that it's located in front of the …other Keramas. The island is 14 miles (22 …kilometers) due west of Naha's Tomari Port. …Maejima is actually a small collection of …three islets, the center one being a double …isle, arranged in a north–south row. …Altogether, the three islets extend 3 miles …(5 kilometers) in length. The largest islet,

Mae, is the most southerly and is 1.75 miles (3 kilometers) long. No part of any of them is ever much wider than about 1,640 or 1,970 feet (500 or 600 meters). Maejima is quite steep and tall given its small size.

Nowadays it is difficult to believe that anyone could live on Mae, but prior to World War II it was indeed inhabited. It was known as a prime bonito tuna fishery. The residents had a water collection system that made habitation possible, but it was destroyed in a typhoon and Mae was abandoned not long afterwards. It has remained uninhabited ever since. Maejima has two named islets just above it to the north, Nakajima and Hatejima.

NAKAJIMA (中島; Naka-jima). Only about 400 feet (120 meters) separate the northern tip of Maejima from the southern tip of Nakajima. Its name suitably means "Middle Island." Altogether this little uninhabited double islet is about three-quarters of a mile (1 kilometer) long, it's in two pieces connect-ed by a sandbar. The first section is more or less a rectangle about 2,700 feet (825 meters) long from north to south and 820 feet (250 meters) wide from east to west. The second northern section is roughly a 2,150 square foot (200 square meter) rock. Although from a distance Naka looks like two islets, techni-cally, since these two are connected, they are considered to be one.

HATEJIMA (ハテ島; Haté-jima). Separated from the northern top half of Nakajima by about 660 feet (200 meters) of water, Hatejima, also known as Hateno (ハテ之; Haténo), is the last islet in this mini-group. It's sort of round, anywhere from 1,150 to 1,640 feet (350–500 meters) in diameter, depending on where it's measured.

The northern side of uninhabited Kuroshima, the most northerly of the Keramas, is known for its dark-colored stone.

Tokashiki from the south, with Un Islet at the bottom and Banari Islet at left center.

A welcoming committee for passengers at Tokashiki Port, where the ferries dock.

5 KUROSHIMA 黒島

You'll find this uninhabited islet about 3 miles (5 kilometers) west and a little north of Maejima. That location makes Kuroshima (黒島; Kuro-shima) the most northerly of the Keramas. It's a small place, roughly rectangular or oblong in shape, about three-quarters of a mile (1 kilometer) long and 985 feet (300 meters) wide. Its name translates as "Black Island," a reference to the appearance of its dark-colored stone. Ferries headed out to Kume and Tonaki ply the waters just above this islet.

6 TOKASHIKIJIMA 渡嘉敷島

The northern end of Tokashiki (pronounced "To-kash-key") lies a bit less than 3 miles (5 kilometers) southwest of Kuroshima, 4.5–5 miles (7–8 kilometers) west of Maejima and 19 miles (30 kilometers) due west from Naha. It is the first inhabited island of the Kerama group when sailing out of Okinawa. It's also the largest island in the Kerama group at about 6 square miles (15.3 square kilometers). It can be described as a long, narrow rectangle or oval, measuring almost 5.5 miles (9 kilometers) in length from end to end, north to south, and anywhere from 1 to 1.5 miles (1.5 to 2.5 kilometers) wide, east to west. That gives it a circumference of not quite 12 miles (20 kilometers).

It's a very hilly island and very scenic. Most of Tokashiki is from 325 to 650 feet (100 to 200 meters) high and covered with tropical vegetation. The highest point is Mt Akama (赤間山; Akama-yama) on the island's north end. You can drive to the top. At a height of 745 feet (227 meters), it gives visitors a 360-degree panoramic view of the sea all around and the adjacent Keramas to the east and west. It's the highest peak in

the Keramas. Incidentally, at most of the scenic vista viewing places on all the inhabited Keramas, you'll find *tenbō-dai* (展望台), observation posts or lookouts. They're nice places for a stop or even a picnic as they're covered from the elements by a roof.

Tokashikijima (渡嘉敷島; Tokashi-ki-jima) has approximately 725 residents scattered in several villages. The two largest are Tokashiki Port (渡嘉敷港; Tokashi-ki-kō), where the ferries dock, and Aharen (阿波連; Aharen), which is on the other side (west side) of the island and has the largest and best beach. There are several hostels and *minshuku* inns in Tokashiki, 20 or so in Aharen and one in the little village of Tokashiku (渡嘉志久;

Tokashiki Port, where the ferries dock.

Tokashiki's World War II Mass Suicide Site.

In this photo looking east, tiny Jijitsurujima is on the far left (north) and far larger Gishippujima is on the right (south).

Tokashi-ku). Most tourist facilities are in Aharen. Everyone caters to the dive trade and all the *minshuku* are hooked up with local dive shops, of which there are many. There are several quite large Japanese Youth Camps on the island, one in the north and one in Tokashiku, but these will not be of interest to most Western visitors.

Tokashiki has a tragic historical note. At the onset of the Battle of Okinawa, the island was blasted by the preliminary air assault and then subject to ground invasion by US forces, all a prelude to the invasion of Okinawa-hontō the next day. Overwrought with fear, fueled by insane propaganda, half the island's residents committed suicide rather than be captured alive. There is a small monument to them called the Mass Suicide Site (集団自殺之地; Shūdan jisatsu no chi). It's just below Tokashiki's highest point at Mt Akama, a very short distance above the island's largest youth camp on the northern end of Tokashikijima. There is also a little war memorial not too far away and a history and culture museum in Tokashiki village.

Tokashiki main island is itself surrounded by a half dozen miniscule satellite islands. We'll mention them starting from the north and traveling around the island clockwise.

JIJITSURUJIMA (地自津留島; Jijitsuru-jima). The most northerly of the little set of islands surrounding Tokashiki is about a 100-foot (30-meter) swim due north of Gishippu, which itself is due north above Tokashiki. This tiny northern islet is known as Jijitsuru. That's a mouthful, but it kind of rolls off the tongue. It's a mostly round, green little place, about 330 feet (100 meters) in diameter from almost any point. It has a rocky shoreline which offers no beaches.

GISHIPPUJIMA (儀志布島; Gishippu-jima). This uninhabited islet is located just below Jijitsuru and is about 750 feet (225 meters) off the northern shore of the Tokashikijima "mainland." It's a long, thin, green-covered, oval-shaped islet with some pretty beaches on each side. The island is almost 1 mile (1.5 kilometers) long from north to south and about 1,310 feet (400 meters) wide east to west at its widest center point. That gives the island a shoreline of a little over 2.5 miles (4 kilometers) and an area of a bit less than half a square kilometer. It's comparatively hilly; the island's highest point is 374 feet (114 meters) above sea level.

GUSUKUJIMA (城島; Gusuku-jima). Popularly known as "Fortress Island," Gusukujima lies directly in front of the approach to Tokashiki's Port, hence its name. This little round, green, uninhabited would-be defender lies about 1,640 feet (500 meters) off the island's east coast and ranges from 1,070 to 1,150 feet (325 to 350 meters) in diameter. During a low tide, it's easy to walk out to it because it's then connected to the Tokashiki "mainland."

Gusukujima ("Fortress Island") is considered the "guardian" of Tokashiki Port.

Unjima and its lighthouse at left, the sharply pointed Shiro Rock at right.

Many of Tokashiki's small beaches are inaccessible by road and you'll need your own watercraft to reach them. Once there, you'll have the place to yourself.

UNSEIWA (運瀬岩; Unsé-iwa). This is a nondescript little rock roughly 2,790 feet (850 meters) due east off the southeast end of Tokashiki. The only reason it's worth noticing is to avoid it while sailing. It is more or less an oval and measures about 50 by 100 feet (15 by 30 meters). You might perhaps be able to swim out to this mini-islet if this section of Tokashiki were accessible, but it's not, at least by land. The same is true of the island's northern end. Most of the island is a dense, uninhabited jungle, with its few villages connected by good roads. The only way to reach many of the small secluded beaches sprinkled around the edges of Tokashiki is by your own watercraft.

UNJIMA (ウン島; Un-jima, but usually called Un-tō). There's a scenic paved road all the way to the very bottom of Tokashiki. There you'll find a parking lot, restrooms and two nice beaches, one on each side of the island. From the parking area there is an excellent hiking path that goes 1,150 feet (350 meters) south and up to an observation platform at the very southern end of the island. The view is fabulous. You'll see the Aka and Zamami ferries go by to your south.

Only a narrow, shallow 130-foot (40-meter)-wide channel separates Tokashikijima from Unjima, which lies just below it. However, from the heights of the observatory, it would be quite a rocky and dangerous scramble to get down to the shoreline.

Un Island is a relatively large, rocky, green islet. It's nearly three-quarters of a mile (1 kilometer) long from north to south and ranges about 985–1,150 feet (300–350 meters) wide, east–west, along most of its length. It is uninhabited. There are the remnants of a primitive road, now more of a hiking path, running the entire length of the islet from end to end. At the southern end, at the top of the islet's highest point, there is a lighthouse. At more or less the center of the island, just off the road/path, there is a helicopter landing pad for servicing the light beacon.

SHIROIWA (白岩; Shiro-iwa). At the southern end of Un Island and separated by a 500-foot (150-meter) channel lies one more islet. It is a sharp large rock protruding out of the sea like the tip of a spear and it marks the southernmost point of the Kerama Islands. It is Shiro, or "White Rock." It's an oval, about

Hanarijima, or "Solitary" Island, at the western side of Tokashiki, a collection of rocks.

There are beautiful beaches all over Tokashiki but two of the best are at Aharen and Tokashiku.

The glass-bottomed Yellow Submarine sailing out of Tokashiki's Aharen Port.

525 feet (160 meters) long from east to west and roughly 165 feet (50 meters) wide from north to south. It is an inhospitable looking place and devoid of vegetation. From the many waves breaking all around Shiro, it is evident that there are a number of other rocks just under the sea's surface waiting for the careless mariner.

HANARIJIMA (離島; Hanari-jima). Rounding the southern end of Tokashiki and coming around the western side there's one final islet about 2,620 feet (800 meters) offshore from the village of Aharen, its beach and the fishing port. It's actually a collection of a number of rocks but three are quite large. All are more or less connected by sandbars and that's why the islet bears but one name. Overall, it measures almost exactly 1,970 feet (600 meters) long from top to bottom and about 985 feet (300 meters) from side to side at its widest point. The largest islet of the big three is the one at the center; it's about 985 feet (300 meters) in diameter in all directions. The topmost northern islet measures about 985 by 740 feet (130 by 225 meters). The southern islet is about 330 feet (100 meters) across. The single name of the three main islets, plus all the adjacent rocks, translates as "Solitary" or "Isolated" Island and can also be pronounced as Banarijima.

That about does it for Tokashiki and its immediate neighbors. Therefore, we are finished here. Let's travel west to Zamami and have a look over there.

At their very closest points, only 1.25 miles (2 kilometers) separate the northernmost tip of Tokashiki from the easternmost point of Zamami. But unless you can swim the distance—or hire a local fisherman to take you—you'll have to backtrack on the ferry to Naha, wait, maybe overnight, and take another ferry out to Zamami. So close, yet so far away.

⑦ ZAMAMIJIMA 座間味島

This is the second largest of the Kerama Islands and the most popular. There's relatively frequent ferry service and there's a good deal of tourist infrastructure on the island. Zamamijima (座間味島; Zamamijima) is 23 miles (37 kilometers) as the crow flies from Naha Tomari Port to the port at Zamami, but sea routes as they are, with Tokashiki blocking the way to the east, it's closer to 30 miles (50 kilometers) sailing distance. The fast ferry takes 50 minutes, the slower vehicle ferry 90 minutes.

Zamami's geography makes it a particularly difficult island to describe as it has no easily defined shape. A map gives a better picture. Let's try saying it this way: from east to west it spans a little over 3 miles (5 kilometers). From north to south it covers almost 2.5 miles (4 kilometers). That might equal 8 square miles (20 square kilometers) but take away all the little bays, coves, inlets, peninsulas, capes and points in between and it looks more like a mangled slice of Swiss cheese. Thus, its area is only 2.5 square miles (6.66 square kilometers) although its circumference is an extraordinary 15 miles (24 kilometers)! Talk about a contorted coastline. It makes Zamami a very interesting island on which to drive around. It's relatively hilly too; the highest point is 528 feet (161 meters).

The easternmost cape of Zamami Island.

Zamami Port from the Takatsukiyama Lookout. The upper portion of the photo shows, from left to right, the northern tip of Aka, Gahijima, the Ijakaja Rocks and Yakabijima.

The Unajinozaki Observation Platform.

On arrival at Zamami Port (座間味港; Zamami-kō), you'll be greeted by a half-submerged humpback whale statue in the harbor, a little reminder that you're in whale watching country. Zamami village is home to more than 600 of the island's 700 residents and is the main place for *minshuku*. There were over 30 at last count and almost an equal number of dive shops. Although Zamami is the main center for the island's tourism industry, there are several *minshuku* in each of the island's two other tiny villages, Ama (阿真) and Asa (阿佐). These really little places are right on the shore and it doesn't get any more laid-back than this. Asa, strangely enough, has the biggest and newest "hotel"

in the Keramas. It's called the Kerama Beach Hotel and it's quite nice. However, it's $150 a night whereas the *minshuku* run $30–50 per person per night.

The best way to see Zamamijima is to rent a bicycle or scooter and drive around. You can visit the whole island in a few hours. There are good beaches everywhere, but two of the best-known are Furuzamami (古座間味ビーチ; Furu-Zamami bīchi) and Ama (阿真ビーチ; Ama bīchi).

Wherever you go, you'll find strategically sited observation platforms. The Takatsukiyama Lookout (高月山展望台; Takatsuki-yama tenbō-dai) offers a good bird's eye view over Zamami Port, the Kerama Strait, Aka and the other islands to the south. It's 450 feet (137 meters) above sea level. The Inazaki Observation Tower

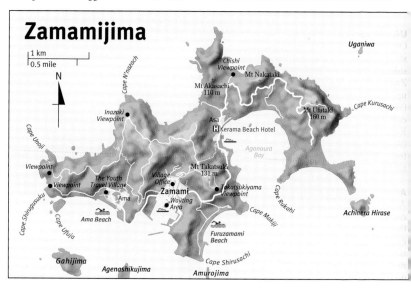

《稲崎展望台; Ina-zaki tenbō-dai) on Cape Ina gives a good perspective of Zamami Island and the sea to the north. Both the Unajinozaki (女瀬ノ崎展望台; Unaji-no zaki tenbō-dai) and Kami-no hama tenbō-dai (神の浜展望台; lit. "God's Beach Lookout") viewing platforms on Zamami's westernmost cape have spectacular views out to Yakabi, Kuba, Tonaki and, in clear weather, Kume. These two platforms are also superb places for watching the sunset.

If you're on Zamami during the whale migration season, you'll most likely find a whale "spotter" at one or more of these observatories. They station themselves at these high points and scan the seas with high-power telescopes or binoculars. Once a spotter sights a pod of humpbacks or sees their water spouts, he or she will call the captain on board the whale watching ship with his radio or cell phone to alert him to the whales' location. It's these spotters who pretty much ensure that tourists get a sighting of whales, for they usually have paid about $100 for a half day's outing and would like to get their money's worth.

To the north and east of Zamami there are a couple of minor but named rocks, and immediately to the south there are three fairly good-sized islets worth describing. In fact, the ferries must skirt around several of them in order to approach the island's harbor. We'll list them below, from north to south, then east to west.

UGANIWA (男岩; Ugan-iwa; also called Otoko-iwa, lit. "Man Rock"). This sheer stone spike is visible at the far right-hand side in the photo opening this section on Zamami Island (page 161). It's a straight-up, sharply pointed slab of rock 2,950 feet (900 meters) due north of Zamami's north-easternmost point at Cape Kuruzaki (黒前崎; Kuru-zaki). Ugan is approximately 300 feet (90 meters) in diameter and roughly 410 feet (125 meters) tall. It's an impressive sight. Locals call it "Penis Rock."

ACHINERA HIRASE (アチネーラ平瀬; Achinēra Hirasé). This large rock and a couple of sidekick stones are located less than 500 feet (150 meters) off the south-easternmost tip of Zamamijima. The islet is essentially round, about 820 feet (250 meters) in diameter and covered with thick green vegetation. It's abruptly sheer and

Looking west from Tokashiki, starting at the bottom is Amuro, then Agenashiku, Gahi, the Ijakaja Rocks and Yakabi. The eastern tip of Zamami is at top right and the northern tip of Aka at far left.

rocky, it has no beaches and it is uninhabited. There is a handful of rocks surrounding it and they measure anywhere from 80 to 165 feet (25 to 50 meters) across.

AMUROJIMA (安室島; Amuro-jima). Amuro is the easternmost and largest of the Zamami islets. Its northern tip almost touches the southernmost point of Zamami. They are separated by about 1,150 feet (350 meters). This uninhabited isle is quite long, 1.25 miles (2 kilometers) from north to south. The top half of Amuro is about 660 feet (200 meters) wide and the bottom half is mostly around 1,970 feet (600 meters). Its coastline circumference measures 3.25 miles (5.5 kilometers) and its area is a quarter of a square mile (0.62 square kilometers). Its highest point is 325 feet (99 meters) above sea level.

Here's a caution. For some reason, the information available on this islet always includes the fact that it is populated by Habu snakes. As that's true for almost all the Ryukyus, why single out this one? Are there many more on Amuro than other places? It's not clear, but I don't wish to find out so I'll just view this islet from the shore of Zamami.

AGENASHIKUJIMA (安慶名敷島; Agéna-shiku-jima). This mini-islet is a little over three-quarters of a mile (1.3 kilometers) west of the top portion of Amuro and three-quarters of a mile (1 kilometer) south of the dock at Zamami Port. Agenashiku is quite small. It's a narrow oval in shape, almost 1,970 feet (600 meters) long and 590 feet (180 meters) wide. It is 0.08 square kilometers in area, about a bit more than one and a quarter miles (2.1 kilometers) around, and

Agenashikushima, with Zamami Port in the background, has a collection of half a dozen rocks to its southeast.

Gahijima, as seen from the Kami-no hama tenbō-dai ("God's Beach Lookout") on Cape Shirugusuku, Zamami Island.

its highest point is 170 feet (51 meters). It has a collection of about a half dozen rocks immediately to its southeast. Some are as large as 130–165 feet (40–50 meters) across. At one time the central flat portion of Agenashiku Islet was cultivated with sugar cane. It's no longer worth the trouble and the island was abandoned many years ago.

GAHIJIMA (嘉比島; Gahi-jima). Continue due west about 2,130 feet (650 meters) from Agenashiku and one arrives at Gahi. The islet is poised almost exactly between Zamami's

Keramashika (ケラマジカー)
Found only on the three Aka Islands plus Yakabi, Kerama deer (*Cervus nippon keramae*) were brought from Kagoshima Prefecture 400 years ago. They are small, about 75 kilograms (165 lbs) in weight and dark brown or even black with white rumps. Only bucks have horns, which they shed in the early spring to grow new ones. The deer are considered a pest by farmers but are loved by tourists. They are protected. The best chance of sighting one is early morning or late afternoon, before sunset.

southwesternmost cape of Shirugusuku (白城の崎; Shiru-gusuku no zaki; lit. "White Castle Cape") and Aka's northernmost point, Cape Kurozaki (黒崎; Kuro zaki; lit. "Black Cape"). Alternatively, measured from the dock at Zamami Port, it is just over 1 mile (1.7 kilometers) to the southwest.

Gahi is actually a little collection of one larger central islet and three smaller ones, all connected by sand. Its overall dimensions are approximately 985 by 1,800 feet (300 by 550 meters), with the primary central rock measuring around 740 by 985 (225 by 300 meters). The three other islets measure anywhere from 245 to 495 feet (75 to 150 meters) in diameter. All are green, covered by thick, dense subtropical vegetation. The westernmost islet has a trail leading up to a small knoll where you'll find the lighthouse. The overall circumference of Gahi, including the sand, is close to 1 mile (1.5 kilometers) and it has an area of one-tenth of a square kilometer. Its highest point is 165 feet (50 meters) above sea level.

8 AKAJIMA 阿嘉島
This is the third largest of the Kerama Islands with an area of 1.5 square miles (3.8 square kilometers). Akajima (阿嘉島; Aka-jima) is located less than 1.25 miles (2 kilometers) to the southwest of Zamami. Were it not for a fairly large indentation, a bay, on its west coast, it would be a near perfect square. From almost any end to any other end, east–west or north–south, it measures about 1.25 miles (2 kilometers) across. It has a circumference of 7.75 miles (12.3 kilometers) and its highest point is 614 feet (187 meters) at Mt Naka (中岳; Naka-daké; lit. "Central Peak"). The population is about 350, most of whom live in Aka Port (阿嘉港; Aka-kō), the only

village on the island. There are over 20 *min-shuku* and 15 dive shops in the village.

The closest points of land between Aka and Zamami are slightly less than 1 mile (1.5 kilometers) apart, from Aka's northernmost little tip at Cape Kuro (黒崎; Kuro-zaki) to Zamami's southwestern end at Shirugusuku (白城の崎; Shiru-gusuku no zaki; lit. "White Castle Cape"). The ferry distance from port to port, however, is about 3.5 miles (5.5 kilometers). That's still not far, of course, and it only takes 10 minutes. All the Naha–Zamami ferries stop at Aka, either coming or going and, in addition, there is a local passenger-only speedboat, the *Mitsu Shima*, that sails between the two islands four times a day during the summer season. Motor vehicles cannot be accommodated but bicycles can.

Almost every shoreline on Akajima is a white sand beach. The largest, Nishihama (西浜 or ニシハマビーチ; Nishi-hama-bīchi, also pronounced Nishi-bama-bīchi) occupies almost the entire northeastern coast. Not as long, nor as nice, but convenient because it's right in front of Aka village, is Maihama Beach (舞浜ビーチ; Mai-hama-bīchi). Also not far from town, going east, and just to the north of the port is Aka Beach (阿嘉ビーチ; Aka-bīchi).

For more beaches, try going around Aka's southwest corner. After taking in the view from the Amagusuku Observatory (天城展望台 or アマグスク展望台; Ama-gusuku tenbō-dai) and retracing your steps just a little, you will come to Hizushi Beach (ひずしビーチ; Hi-zushi-bīchi).

If you keep going north from there on the island's most interesting drive, a little over 2.5 miles (4 kilometers) and the farthest you can go on Aka, you will first pass by the

Sailing into Akajima Port.

Akajima Port and bridge.

Nakadake Observatory (中岳展望台; Naka-daké tenbō-dai), then the Kushibaru Observatory (後原展望台; Kushi-baru tenbō dai). Both of these are excellent short hikes. At the very end of the road you'll come to a modest parking area and the finest of all Aka's beaches, Kushibaru Beach (後原浜; Kushi-baru hama). It's also sometimes written as Kushi-hara Beach (クシバル海岸; Kushi-baru bīchi or Kushi-baru kaigan).

The white sand Maihama Beach runs along the full length in front of Aka village.

At low tide there are sandy patches around the Ijakajajima rocks and it's possible to walk around them.

No matter which beach you may choose, or no matter where else you may visit on the island, and no matter the time of year you may come, try to get out either early in the morning or just before sunset, for these are the times of day you are most likely to spot Kerama deer. They're really just about everywhere on Aka, Geruma and Fukaji, but they are shy and will bounce back into the bush the moment you come along. A bicycle is the ideal vehicle as long as you keep quiet. They are plentiful, so you're almost guaranteed to see them. The problem is trying to get a good photograph. They are quick and will disappear faster than you can imagine.

The last features we'll mention about Aka are its immediate neighbors. Just offshore, Akajima has several interesting collections of rocks. One's to the north, another is close by the western coast, and the last forms sort of a kite's tail due south. We'll visit them north to south.

IJAKAJAJIMA (伊釈加釈島; Ija kaja-jima). This little boating hazard is less than three-quarters of a mile (1 kilometer) northwest of Aka's northernmost beach. It's an uninhabitable collection of a half dozen rocks, the largest of which is about 330 feet (100 me-

ters) by 660 feet (200 meters). Altogether, from end to end, the set measures around 1,640 feet (500 meters) in length and 660 feet (200 meters) wide. At low tide there are sandy patches and it's possible to walk from one to the next. At high tide, they are separate islets. Most of them are about half-covered in scrub vegetation.

KUSHIBARUIWA (後原岩; Kushi-baru iwa). This set of stones numbers about a half a dozen but from the beach at Kushibaru appears to be three. They start only 410 feet (125 meters) offshore. The full length of the group is about 740 feet (225 meters). At the most, the width is approximately 245 feet (75 meters). The largest rock is about 295 feet (90 meters) across, the rest range from 80 to 165 feet (25 to 50 meters) in size. There is a bit of vegetation on the top of the largest one, but the rest are barren.

Without the aid of a boat, the beach and the stones at Kushibaru are the closest one can get to Yakabi, the other deer island which lies a bit further offshore. We'll mention that island further below.

SAKUBARUIWA (サクバル奇岩; Sakubaru-iwa). Just as the tail of a kite hangs below its

The largely barren Kushibaru rocks.

Sakubaruiwa is almost an extension of Aka Island.

attached quadrilateral, so too does the tail-end of Aka. The Sakubaru Rock formation starts at the very bottom tip of Aka and extends almost three-quarters of a mile (1 kilometer) further south. Altogether, it's a large group of more than a dozen uninhabitable islets. They're almost an extension of Aka and, in fact, at low tide you can walk out on them quite far. At their widest point, they are about 985 feet (300 meters) across, but for most of their length they are only 330 feet (100 meters) wide. The first one begins less than 30 feet (10 meters) from the shore of Aka and, in fact, it's often directly connected by a sandbar.

The Sakubaru Rocks vary in size considerably. The smaller ones are approximately 165 feet (50 meters) across, the larger up to 660 feet (200 meters) in dimension. An excellent view of them can be had from the Amagusuku Observatory (天城展望台; Amagusuku tenbō-dai) or from the Aka Bridge (阿嘉大橋; Aka ōhashi; lit. "Aka Great Bridge").

The Aka Great Bridge linking Aka and Geruma.

9 GERUMAJIMA 慶留間島

Gerumajima (慶留間島; Geruma-jima) is the fourth inhabited island in the Keramashotō. It's directly south of Akajima and separated from it by only about 985 feet (300 meters). This gap was bridged in 1998 so that it's now possible to drive to Geruma from Aka on the "Aka Great Bridge." Formerly, a small ferry shuttled passengers and vehicles across for a fee.

Geruma Island is a most uniform square, about three-quarters of a mile (1 kilometer) in length or width. Its area, therefore, is just about three-quarters of a mile (1 kilometer) or 1.15 square kilometers to be exact. It has an almost 3-mile (5-kilometer) circumference and it is tall, its highest point being 515 feet (157 meters). The island has about 75 residents, almost all of whom live in the one tiny village and port at the very bottom (southern end) of the island, Geruma (慶留間港; Geruma-kō). There are two *minshuku* inns in the village.

If you're looking for a peaceful place to visit, Geruma is an excellent choice. In addition to the friendly *minshuku*, there is a good restaurant in town. If you like to hike, Geruma has one of the most interesting trails in these islands. It starts just north of the village as a small paved road off the main road, to the left. From there, it ascends rapidly. It's a good hike. After about three-quarters of a mile (1 kilometer) of twists

and turns, more or less straight up, the pavement ends and a hiking trail begins. This quickly leads to a small Shinto shrine. From the shrine the path continues all the way around the northern end of the island, all along its highest bluffs. The view of Aka, Zamami and Tokashiki is magnificent, the best you'll find.

After taking in the view, the path continues right around the top so that you'll end back nearby the little shrine without having to retrace your steps. From there it's back down the paved road. You can drive to the top if you have a vehicle and start your hike where the pavement ends. That's an easy hike as it's almost completely flat.

Geruma Port, located at the island's southern end.

Takara House, a preserved Okinawan-style house.

The small bridge that connects Geruma Island to its southern neighbor, Fukaji Island.

A much shorter and less strenuous hike runs from the village to the only observatory on the island, Azanamui (アザナムイ展望台; Azana-mui tenbō-dai). It has a nice view back towards the village and the bridge to Fukaji. Like all the public lookout sites, it's free.

Geruma has one "sight," Takara House (高良家; Takara-ke). It's a preserved old Okinawan-style house protected as a Japanese cultural relic. There's a 300 Yen admission charge. It's right in the center of town, so you can't miss it.

Although Geruma may only be a small island, it has good connections. In the north it's attached by a large bridge to Aka and at its southern end, just below the village, it's connected by a little bridge to Fukaji.

Fukajijima is the little island that holds what used to be the Kerama Airport (慶良間空港; Kerama Kūkō). It's still there, but it's not functioning. We'll go there next.

10 FUKAJIJIMA 外地島

Fukaji is located directly south of Geruma. Only 260 feet (80 meters) of water separate the two islands, and since that narrow sea channel was bridged quite some time ago, it's been possible to drive from Fukaji to Geruma and then from Geruma to Aka.

Fukajijima (外地島; Fukaji-jima) is an oval in shape, with two rather pointy ends. It's about a bit less than a mile (1.6 kilometers) long from north to south and around 2,460 feet (750 meters) wide at its widest point. It has been calculated to have a

shoreline circumference of 2.75 miles (4.6 kilometers) and its highest point is 250 feet (76 meters) above sea level. The island is mostly a natural plateau and thus its flat top was chosen for a convenient landing strip. The island was the Kerama Airport for about 10 years until just a few years ago when it closed. Even though the flight from Naha was only about 10 minutes, as opposed to the ferries which take an hour to an hour and a half, not enough passengers were willing to pay the premium for the speed. So now the airport no longer functions. Strangely enough, it's not been fully abandoned. The terminal's open, the lights are on, and the air-conditioning is working, which means the building is being maintained. But for what end, who knows?

Even before the airport's closure, the island was considered uninhabited as its only occupants were airport staff. They were present by day, but at night they went home to Geruma or Aka Islands. Some flew back home to Naha every night. Since no one permanently resided there, Fukaji was and is considered uninhabited.

Fukaji has one minor, but historic, site and one observation platform, Gaichi (外地展望台; Gaichi tenbō-dai). Let's hike to the observatory first. The entire airport runway, terminal and parking lot are enclosed by chain link fencing to keep the Kerama deer from wandering on to the runway. From inside the airport parking area, and just across from the terminal, there's a gate with a latch. Most people assume that it's not open to the public. In fact, it's the entrance to the path to the top of the one little hill on Fukaji. Open the latch and start hiking. It's not a long hike and it's not a steep climb, only about 820 feet (250 meters) in total, but from the top you'll get an excellent view back over to Geruma village and out over the southern and western seas. It only takes 5–10 minutes and it's worth the short climb.

About the only road on Fukaji is the 1,640 feet (500 meters) that runs from the Geruma Bridge to the airport. However, if you look closely, just after crossing over the bridge, on your right, there is a small road straight back down to the shore. It's about 400 feet (150 meters) in all and ends at a concrete boat ramp. At the bottom of the little road, near the ramp, and now almost under the bridge, is a small World War II commemoration stone. Its date reads March 26, 1945.

The land battle known variously as the Battle of Okinawa, Operation Iceberg and the Typhoon of Steel began on Easter Sunday, April 1, 1945. It took place over an almost three-month period and claimed several hundred thousand lives.

In fact, the campaign began a few days beforehand—at this very spot. The first Americans ashore were soldiers of the 77th Infantry Division, who landed here on Fukaji Island in the Kerama Islands on March 26. It took five days to secure all the islands. The 77th Infantry lost 27 men and another 81 were wounded. Japanese dead and other casualties numbered over 650; most would not surrender. The operation provided a protected anchorage for the fleet close to

The first landing site of the Battle of Okinawa.

the Okinawa mainland and eliminated the threat from suicide boats from the Keramas. The inscription on the plaque, in English and Japanese, reads: "Men of the 77th Division salute as the American flag is raised for the first time on the Japanese homeland."

If these stones could speak, what tales could they tell?

Fukaji has a few close-by neighbors. One satellite islet is directly to its south and nearly adjacent, the others are a bit further away to the west. All of them are uninhabitable.

The well-maintained but non-functioning Kerama Airport on Fukaji Island.

Fukaji Island's closest and largest southern neighbor, the Mukarakujima Rocks, comprise a dozen or so uninhabitable and uninviting rocks.

The Ōjima Rocks to the west of the Mukarakujima Rocks, likewise their neighbor comprise a collection of rocks though some are partially vegetated.

MUKARAKUJIMA (ムカラク島; Mukaraku-jima). Fukaji's closest and largest neighbor is a rather foreboding-looking set of uninhabitable rocks directly in front of the island as you approach on a southern flight path. The islets start less than 30 feet (10 meters) from the southern end of Fukaji and extend almost 2,620 feet (800 meters). They vary in size from about 330 feet (100 meters) across to the largest, which is approximately 1,150 feet (350 meters) in diameter. There are perhaps a dozen rocks altogether, but it's difficult to say where one ends or another begins as some are connected to one another by patches of sand.

⑪ **ŌJIMA** 奥武島

A little less than 1 mile (1.5 kilometers) due west of the Mukarakujima Rocks, which lie below Fukajijima, is Ōjima (奥武島; Ō-jima). This Ōjima should not be confused with the two other nearby Ōjimas (same Kanji characters), one alongside southeastern Okinawa, the other next to Kume Island further west. The Keramas' Ōjima is really more a collection of rocks than a single island. None are very big.

UBUIWA (ウブ岩; Ubu-iwa). The largest islet of the Ōjima group is individually referred to as Ubu-iwa. Ubu Rock is a partially vegetation-covered stone oval about 740 feet (225 meters) long and 985 feet (300 meters) wide. It's comprised of one fairly large rock about 410 by 740 feet (125 by 225 meters), which is connected by a nice sandy isthmus (twin north and south beaches!) to another rock (really a bunch of rocks) about 330 by 500 feet (100 by 150 meters). Because they're connected, even if vaguely, they are

collectively considered one island. Within an area that extends over 330 feet (100 meters) due south, there are at least a half dozen more mini-islets, some as large as 65 by 130 feet (20 by 40 meters) across, that are considered part of Ubu. It's a tricky area in which to sail.

KUBAIWA (クバ岩; Kuba-iwa). Some 410 feet (125 meters) due north of Ubu, there's an isolated rock called Kuba. It's also an oval in shape and measures about 590 feet (180 meters) long by almost 330 feet (100 meters) wide. It is also partially covered in thick green scrub vegetation. Kuba's mass is all rock. For this reason, there are no beaches here.

NAKAIWA (ナカ岩; Naka-iwa). About 2,130 feet (650 meters) southwest of Ōjima (Ubu and Kuba Islets) and their immediate adjoining rock neighbors, is another little group of four of five rocks which are collectively known as Nakaiwa. The span between the most northerly Naka rock and the most southern is about 1,640 feet (500 meters), with most individual stones about 65–100 feet (20–30 meters) in diameter. The southernmost islet of the group is the largest. It measures about 330 feet (100 meters) across in any given direction. Depending on the height of the tide, a number of the adjacent unnamed rocks lie just above or below the waterline and thus appear or disappear with its rising and falling. It's also a dangerous area for mariners.

YUBUIWA (ユブ岩; Yubu-iwa). Approximately 820 feet (250 meters) southeast of the Naka rocks is this group of six or seven more rocks which bear the name Yubu. The northernmost is the largest one. It measures about 575 feet (175 meters) long by 260 feet (80 meters) wide and is, in turn, surrounded by a handful of smaller stone islets. There's almost no vegetation on any of them. About 820 feet (250 meters) to the south is another little group. The three or four mini-islets in this group measure 30–80 feet (10–25 meters) in diameter. In the grand scheme of things, a 30-foot (10-meter) rock may appear insignificant, but it is not. Any fixed rock at sea can be large enough to punch a hole in any ship, big or small. Rock islets like those that comprise Ōjima have a funny habit—they don't move when you hit them. Along with Unjima and Shiroiwa (the islets due south of Tokashikijima), the Ōjima Rocks vie for the most southerly location of the Keramas.

12 KUBASHIMA 久場島

Kuba Island is located a little more than 1.75 miles (3 kilometers) northwest of Ōjima, 2.5 (4 kilometers) southwest of Aka, or 3 miles (4 and a half kilometers) due west of Geruma and Fukaji. Kuba and its northern neighbor Yakabi are the two westernmost islands in the Kerama group. As the crow flies, they are each approximately 25 miles (40 kilometers) west of Naha on Okinawa Main Island. Both are uninhabited and designated as protected reserves.

Kubashima (久場島; Kuba-shima) is a fairly uniform rectangle with a pointy top. It is over 1.5 miles (2.2 kilometers) long from north to south and almost exactly three-quarters of a mile (1 kilometer) wide for nearly all of its length. Its area is a bit more than half a square mile (1.55 square kilometers) with a 4.5-mile (6.8-kilometer)

circumference. It's hilly, rising to 886 feet (270 meters) above sea level. Both Kuba Island and Yakabi Island are completely covered in dense vegetation.

13 YAKABIJIMA 屋嘉比島

Not quite 1.75 miles (3 kilometers) due north of Kubashima is Yakabijima (屋嘉比島; Yakabi-jima). Measured from several points, it is 1.25 miles (2 kilometers) north-west of Aka, 1.75 miles (3 kilometers) south-west from Zamami's closest point, and 3.5 miles (5.5 kilometers) from the port at Zamami.

The shape of Yakabi Island is more or less a pretty well-formed oval, 1.25 miles (1.8 kilometers) long and three-quarters of a mile (1 kilometer) across at its center. It is half a square mile (1.26 square kilometers) in area and 3.25 miles (5.3 kilometers) in circumference. Like Kuba, it is tall; its highest point is 702 feet (214 meters) above sea level and its top is considered sacred. It's a *Utaki* (御嶽; lit. the Okinawan term for a sacred place).

During World Wars I and II, copper was mined on Yakabi, but the production was small and the mines were closed after the end of Second World War. Although the island is not populated by humans, it's a home for Kerama deer (page 164).

That wraps up our look at the Kerama-rettō. From here we'll have to return to Naha in order to drive to, or catch other ferries to, the other islands off the western coast of Okinawa Main Island. Some are close, just offshore, others are quite a bit further west. Some, like Kume, are fairly well known and popular, others, like Tonaki and Aguni, are little known to tourists. We'll visit them all and you can decide which ones you might like to visit.

Both Kuba Island (left) and Yakabi Island (right) are protected reserves and are closed to the public. Yakabijima, in particular, is a refuge for Kerama deer.

Chapter 10

ISLANDS WEST OF OKINAWA 沖縄諸島
Golden beaches, remarkable rocks

1. **Edzunajima** エーヅナ島
2. **Rukan-shō** ルカン礁
3. **Senagajima** 瀬長島
4. **Tonakijima** 渡名喜島
5. **Kumejima** 久米島
6. **Torishima** 鳥島
7. **Agunijima** 粟国島
8. **Sesokojima** 瀬底島
9. **Minnajima** 水納島
10. **Iejima** 伊江島
11. **Ōjima** 奥武島
12. **Yagajijima** 屋我地島
13. **Kourijima** 古宇利島
14. **Izenajima** 伊是名島
15. **Iheyajima** 伊平屋島

In addition to the Kerama Islands (discussed in Chapter 9), there are many other islands off Okinawa's west coast. We'll cover all except the Keramas in this chapter. Starting from Cape Kyan, it's not far before reaching the first one, only 2.5 miles (4 kilometers) north from Kyan-zaki to Nashiro (名城; Nashiro), a small village. Just 30 feet (10 meters) offshore, there's a straight line of three mini-islets that look as if they're trying to run away from the coast.

1 **EDZUNAJIMA** エーヅナ島

This tiny group has only one name but it's really three islets. Depending on the height of the tide, the first two are more often one as they're connected to each other by a fairly good-sized sandbar which can reach to within 3 feet (1 meter) of the mainland. But disregarding the sand, only considering the islet's vegetation-covered rocky portions, the first islet starts about 100 feet (30 meters) from shore. It's about 130 by 165 feet (40 by 50 meters) around. From its western-facing side, it's about 115 feet (35 meters) over sand, sometimes water, to number two islet that

The Edzuna Islet trio, just north of Cape Kyan.

is somewhat larger, an oval around 130 by 245 feet (40 by 75 meters). Then, it's just 65 feet (20 meters) further west, over water—no sandbar here—to number three island, the largest. It's a poorly drawn circle roughly 410 feet (125 meters) in diameter, completely covered in vegetation, with almost no sandy sections. There's nothing particularly special about Edzunajima (エーヅナ島; Edzunajima) except it's very easy to reach. You can walk there from the shore.

From here we'll continue north through Itoman City (糸満市; Itoman-shi) 6 miles (10 kilometers) to just below Naha Airport where we'll find our second island on this coast. Following this section of shoreline takes us over and through several large man-made islands. Built up from dredging and landfill, these reclamation projects are now populated by industrial and commercial buildings as well as residences. There's nothing especially interesting about them, except they're large and have increased Okinawa's total surface area by many square miles. There are similar such man-made islands in the Awase section of Okinawa on the other side of the island, on Nakagusuku Bay.

2 **RUKAN-SHŌ** ルカン礁

If we had a boat, we could make a detour on the sea before continuing from Edzuna Island up to our next island, Senagajima. If we set out straight west just about 6 miles (10 kilometers) from Edzuna, we'd come to the Rukan Reef. The shoal is a collection of rock, coral formation and sand. It's far more of a shipping hazard than it is an island and, as such, it's clearly marked on navigation charts. Altogether, Rukan-sho (ルカン礁; Rukan-shō) takes up about half a square kilometer of what would otherwise be smooth sailing over open waters.

3 SENAGAJIMA 瀬長島

On the weekends this otherwise uninhabited little isle is the hottest spot in town for at least three reasons: a large four-leaf clover set of baseball diamonds, a popular beach and a shoreline for collecting shellfish, and *the* place for watching jets come into Naha Airport. Senagajima (瀬長島; Senaga-jima) was originally a tiny village before World War II but was transformed into an American military ammunitions depot for the next 30 years. Only after Okinawa's return to Japan did the island revert to Japanese authority and become a place for outdoor recreational activities. A couple of years ago there were plans to take the island as part of a Naha International Airport expansion project but public protest killed the idea.

Senaga is a most oddly shaped semi-oval about 1,640–1,970 feet (500–600 meters) in diameter in any one direction and maybe 1 mile (1.6 kilometers) in circumference. There's a paved ring road that circles the island and a semi-paved path to the island's center top. It's not high and it's not much. The north, south and west coastlines are undeveloped but the center high point of the island has become home to a new luxury airport hotel. At low tide people walk over the reefs collecting sea life. The island's eastern side has the beach, ball fields and, in the summer, lots of concession stands for lunch, snacks, ice cream, drinks, etc. No one permanently lives on Senaga, so technically it's an uninhabited island, but there are plenty of people by day and in the evenings in the summer. It's a relaxing place for Naha residents to escape city life. In the winter it's pretty quiet.

The island is connected to the mainland by a 2,300-foot (700-meter)-long causeway and here's where the airplane viewing action is. The Naha flight approach landing lights are built over water for about three-quarters of a mile (1 kilometer) immediately before

Senagajima is a popular recreation island noted for its baseball diamonds, white sand beach and, at low tide, shoreline reefs.

the airport's 1.25-mile (2-kilometer)-long single runway. The causeway runs perpendicular to the approach. There is plenty of safe parking along it and people just park their cars and wait for the planes to come in. From about 7:00AM until 10:00PM every day, Naha Airport handles around 300 take-offs and landings. That's 15 hours or 900 minutes or about one every three minutes, so you don't have to wait very long. The Senaga Causeway is the best place in Okinawa to view jets and other aircraft landing. It's only 1,970 feet (600 meters) before the airport's runway and they literally fly in right over the top of you! The Senaga Island Causeway is where Okinawan parents bring their children to watch the planes.

To leave Senagajima we'll cross back over the causeway to Okinawa mainland. From here we'll travel north just under 4 miles (6 kilometers), passing the airport along the way, then come to downtown Naha. At its beginning we'll pass by the first of Naha's three ports, appropriately called Naha Port (那覇港; Naha-kō). It's a commercial shipping port, a Naval port (US and Japan) and the ferry port for the "A" and Marix Lines to the Amami Islands and Kagoshima.

About 1.75 miles (3 kilometers) further north we'll come to Tomari Port (泊港; Tomari-kō). That's where we'll stop for the moment as it's the terminus for ferries to the Keramas and many other of the Okinawan East China Sea islands. If we were to continue from here northbound on the road through Naha, in about 1 mile (1.6 kilometers) we would come to Naha's third port, called New Port (那覇新港; Naha Shin-kō), which many still call Aja Port (安謝港; Aja-kō). It's the terminus for the long-distance ferries north to Tokyo, Osaka and other mainland cities.

Naha Airport take-offs and landings.

The Kume Line ferry leaving Naha Tomari Port.

FERRIES TO TONAKI AND KUME

We'll start at Tomari Port and board one of the morning ferries outbound to some of the other islands off Okinawa's west coast. There are many in addition to the Kerama Islands. One of the most popular, and lovely, is Kume. Let's go there next.

Here's the general scheme. Year round, every day except in bad weather, there are two daily sailings for Kumejima and one for Tonakijima. There is some extra service in the summer months. Every morning at 8:30AM the Kume Line ferry (passengers, vehicles and cargo) departs Naha heading west. Thirty-six miles (58 kilometers) later, or two hours and 15 minutes, at 10:45AM, the ferry arrives at the small island of Tonakijima. Unloading and reloading passengers and freight takes 15 minutes. At 11:00AM the ferry departs and sails another hour and a half for 30 miles (48 kilometers) to Kumejima, arriving at 12:30PM. There she docks for an hour and a half.

At 2:00PM the Kume Ferry departs and sails 60 miles (96 kilometers) directly back to Naha, not stopping at Tonaki along the way. She arrives at Tomari Port three hours and 15 minutes later, at 5:15PM, where she moors for the night. The next day, and every day, the ferry repeats this schedule.

Kumejima Airport terminal building.

Meanwhile, at 2:00PM another Kume-bound ferry departs Naha and sails directly there, arriving non-stop at 5:15PM. She'll dock and stay overnight at Kume. The next morning, at 8:30AM, this ferry will depart Kume and sail two hours to Tonaki, arriving at 10:00AM. Fifteen minutes later, at 10:15AM, she'll depart and sail the two and a quarter hours bringing her home to Tomari Port at 12:30PM. She'll leave again at 2:00PM on her afternoon direct run to Kume, thus starting the cycle all over again.

The net result of this daily scheduling of two ships serving two islands is:

- two ferries a day from Naha to Kume, one at 8:30AM, one at 2:00PM
- two ferries a day from Kume to Naha, one at 8:30AM, one at 2:00PM
- one ferry a day from Naha to Tonaki, at 8:30AM
- one ferry a day from Tonaki to Naha, at 10:15AM
- one ferry a day from Tonaki to Kume, at 11:00AM
- one ferry a day from Kume to Tonaki, at 8:30AM

In addition, for those in a hurry or those prone to seasickness, it is possible to fly into Kume. Kume Island has a good-sized airport and you can fly there from Naha. Both Japan Transocean Air (JTA) and Ryukyu Air Commuter (RAC) operate daily flights from Naha. It only takes 40 minutes and costs about $120 one way. In the summer season, JTA also operates several direct flights a week from Tokyo's Haneda Airport. The Kume Airport is located at the far westernmost point of the island. Unfortunately, Tonaki has no airport, so the only way to reach that island is by sea.

The full length of Tonakijima from the east, with the Kume Line ferry passing in front.

④ **TONAKIJIMA** 渡名喜島

Sailing west out of Naha's Tomari Port, Tonakijima (渡名喜島; Tonaki-jima) is the first stop on the morning ferry to Kume. Sailing time is about two and a half hours. It's not quite 40 miles (64 kilometers) or a little more than halfway to Kume. The island lies a bit north of Naha's latitude; it's due west more or less from Okinawa City.

Tonaki is very small. It's shaped somewhat like a crescent with a bump on its southern end. It's longest north–south dimension is 2.3 miles (3.7 kilometers) and its greatest east–west width is 1.25 miles (2.2 kilometers), but that's misleading. Most of the island's width is three-quarters of a mile (1 kilometer) or less. Its area is only 1.3 square miles (3.46 square kilometers) but it has a rather long circumference of 10 miles (16 kilometers).

Most of Tonaki is too hilly and rocky for agriculture. Its highest point is Mt Ufu (大岳; Ufu-daké, also called Ō-také) at 587 feet (179 meters) above sea level. There are approximately 600 residents, almost all of whom live at the port town, Tonaki village, also known as Sonota (その他; Sonota). The village is located at the island's midsection, which is the only low ground. It's a saddle straddling the island, connecting the village to the sea on both sides. There are several

minshuku inns located in the village. The operators will meet you at the harbor if you make a reservation. The village is tiny enough that nothing is more than a couple of hundred meters distant.

The harbor is on the west side of the island. The east side is too shallow for a port but it has a good beach. There are beaches on the west coast as well. The lower southern two-thirds of the island is ringed by a paved road. The northern one-third only has jeep tracks and hiking trails.

From Tonaki Port you can see the next island we'll pass by. It's a bit less than 2.5 miles (4 kilometers) to the northwest.

IRISUNAJIMA OR IDESUNAJIMA (入砂島

or 出砂島; Irisuna-jima or Idésuna-jima). This poor little teardrop of an islet is used as an aerial bombing target range by the American Air Force from Kadena Air Base. It is an equal opportunity bomb site, however, as the Japanese Self-Defense Forces training out of Naha Air Base use it as well. Visiting the island is prohibited because it's littered with unexploded ordnance.

It is located 2.25 miles (3.6 kilometers) northwest of Tonaki Port. At its greatest length it's 1,400 feet (700 meters) long, at its widest 2,300 feet (425 meters) across. Its

"Get on Sand Island"/"Get off Sand Island," used by the US as an aerial bombing target range.

"Sand Island," a pockmarked bomb site.

highest point is probably 10–15 feet (4–5 meters). If you zoom in on it from a satellite camera like Google Earth, you'll see that it is completely pockmarked from the many explosions it has endured.

The latter two Kanji characters of its name mean "Sand Island." The first character—and

this is cute—one means "Get in," the other "Get out." So, it's either "Get on Sand Island" or "Get off Sand Island." Both names are correct. Someone must have a sense of humor. Naturally, it is uninhabited and uninhabitable.

5 KUMEJIMA 久米島

For many visitors, Kumejima (久米島; Kumé-jima) is the most beautiful of all the small islands in the Okinawa archipelago, if not the most beautiful island of all the Ryukyus. The entire island has been designated a Japanese Prefectural National Park. It was untouched by the Battle of Okinawa and much of its architecture and a number of its homes are as they have been for centuries. You'll see more traditional terra cotta clay-tiled red-, orange- and white-roofed houses here than on any other island in the Ryukyu Archipelago.

Sailing 60 miles (96 kilometers) west from Naha direct or 30 miles (48 kilometers) from Tonaki, the ferry soon enough comes to Kume. The ship arrives at Kanegusuku Port (兼城港; Kané-gusuku-kō), part of the island's largest town, Gushikawa (具志川; Gushi-kawa). The port and town are on Kume's central western side. The airport (久米空港; Kumé-kūkō) is about 3 miles (5 kilometers) to the west, at the very end of the island's western coast. Although there are some small hotels and *minshuku* right in town, many visitors will probably wish to stay near Eef Beach (イーフビーチ; Īfu-bīchi) in Nakazato Town (仲里; Naka-zato), about 4 miles (6 kilometers) away on the eastern side of the island.

Because the island is popular with Japanese travelers, it offers far more choice in hotels, restaurants and other accommodations than other islands comparable in size.

Kumejima's best, the Cypress Resort Hotel.

In all, Kume sports three luxury resort hotels, several standard class hotels and more than a dozen *minshuku*.

Top of the line is the newly renovated and reopened Cypress Resort Hotel (サイプレス リゾート; Saipuresu-Rizōto), located less than 1.25 miles (2 kilometers) from the airport and 1.75 miles (3 kilometers) from Gushikawa Town. Some might object because of its relatively isolated location, but the hotel commands its own expansive place right on Shinri Beach (シンリ浜; Shinri hama). In fact, guests don't even have to walk the hundred meters to the beach. A swimmer or chaise longue dweller can enjoy the view overlooking the ocean and beach from the comfort of the hotel's ultra modern infinity pool. Altogether, the Cypress is about as elegant a place to stay as one could wish for and it's probably the island's nicest place to have a drink and watch the sun set over the ocean.

Kume's two other top properties are the Kume Island Resort (formerly the Nikko Resort) and the Eef Beach Hotel. Both are first class but neither can really be said to be "luxury." All three of these hotel resorts have rates that can vary from as high as $350 a night (twin occupancy) to as low as $100 or $150, including breakfast. The vast price differences can be explained by time of year (seasonal rates) and whether the hotel is booked as part of a package. It's always worth checking with local travel agencies to see what sort of deals are available. Remember that your fellow Japanese hotel guests have almost always paid less than you because they booked the resort as part of a package.

If no reasonable deals can be found at the big hotels, it's worth checking out the rates at one or more of the many *minshuku* or lesser-priced hotels on the island. There's a fairly

Kumejima

| 2 km |
| 1 mile |

to Tonaki

Hateno Hama Beach

Hateno Hama-jima

to Tonaki, Naha

Namiji Restaurant (波路)

You can't miss it. Namiji's right off the beach (Īfu-bīchi) on the main drag in town. It's packed every night and there's usually a line of patrons waiting outside the door for a table (or sushi bar space). So why are people waiting when there's lots of other restaurants on the same street? How about the freshest, finest seafood? And how about the mouthwatering sushi and sashimi, and friendly service and reasonable prices? How about the Shikwasa beer? That last one's tricky. You'll have to go to find out for yourself. But try it, it's delicious.

large number of both *minshuku* and smaller hotels in Gushikawa and even more in Nakazato. Those in town have the advantage of being near the ferry dock and those in Nakazato are within a block of Eef Beach. In fact, most are lined up, along with many restaurants, along Eef Beach Street (イーフビーチ通り; Īfu-bīchi dōri). Japanese pensions generally run around 4,000–5,000 Yen per person per night, breakfast (and sometimes dinner) included.

Although Kume is often described as a "small" island, to anyone familiar with the Ryukyus that's a relative statement. For in this chain of several hundred small islands and islets, all things considered it's a pretty big island. In fact, it is Okinawa Prefecture's fifth largest. Describing its shape is a little tough. How about a large lopsided mushroom or a giant tooth, specifically a molar with a single root? Kume is another one of these islands where a picture is worth a thousand words. From its northern top to its very southernmost pointy tip, it is 7 miles (12 kilometers) long. And coincidentally, from end to end, east to west, across the island's widest points, it is also 7 miles (12 kilome-

ters). Its area is just over 25 square miles (63 square kilometers) and its circumference is approximately 30 miles (48 kilometers). Kume Island's official website lists a 2011 census population figure of 8,626 inhabitants. That's exceptionally large compared with many other "small" islands.

Kumejima has just about everything you might wish for on a peaceful tropical paradise. It has both mountains and the sea. The island is volcanic in origin, breathtakingly mountainous, yet is fringed by coral reefs and pure white sand beaches. Let's circle the island in a clockwise direction starting in town at the Marine Terminal, right by the Kanegusuku Port ferry dock. There, they'll give us a little guide map which lists the island's top sights. It's only in Japanese but it has pictures of all the major sights. You can use it to point out where you wish to go when asking directions from strangers.

From the terminal we'll work our way along the west coast towards the airport, then from there north and east along Kume's rugged and very mountainous north shore. After visiting the island's highest viewpoints at Kume's northern top, we'll go south and east, eventually arriving at the Eef Beach area. Finally, we'll drop straight south towards Kume's very southern bottom tip, Cape Shimajiri (島尻崎). After taking in the viewpoints from there, we'll have to

Cape Shimajiri at the southern tip of Kumejima.

Minshuku Kumejima, one of the nicest minshuku on Kume Island, is right in town, one block from the ferry terminal.

backtrack a bit north as we'll run out of road. We'll then return in a westerly direction back to Gushikawa Town.

In all, we'll drive about 30–40 miles (50–60 kilometers), and although that doesn't sound like much it will take the better part of a day. In fact, one could easily break up the sightseeing on Kume into two or more days depending on how many things you might wish to see and how much time you might like to spend on the beach as part of an excursion around the island.

The first "sight" you'll notice, right in front of the Marine Terminal, is "Male Rock," a stone phallus rising on top of tiny Mt Garasa Islet. Since it is an island in its own right, we'll describe this place a little further below when we visit the offshore satellite islands surrounding Kumejima. As Male Rock is more easily seen from the western side of Garasayama Island, you'll have to walk a block or two to get a proper (or is it an "improper"?) view. In doing so, you'll pass right by the Minshuku Kumejima (民宿久米島). It's a brightly painted three-story blue-and-white building that you can't miss.

From Kanegusuku Port it's 1.5 miles (2.5 kilometers) north through Gushikawa, passing by the village office, to the Uezu Residence, also called Uezu Old House

Otoko-iwa (男岩) and Onna-iwa (女岩)

Perhaps these two places explain why Kumejima is considered such a romantic island. Kume has two rather unusual natural fertility symbols: Otoko-iwa ("Male Rock") and Onna-iwa ("Female Rock"). The male fertility symbol is an upright phallus on Garasayama Islet, just offshore at Kanegusuku Port. Onna-iwa, the female symbol, is more commonly known as Mīfugā" (ミーフガー). That word translates as "Vagina Rock" as this is the shape of its opening. The formation is said to have powers to help women conceive. You may see women praying there. Mīfugā is on Kume's northern shore, visible from Gushikawa Castle. Every spring thousands of white lilies bloom around the rock.

(上江州家; Uezu-ke, pronounced Uwae-shū-ka). This section of town is named Uezu.

Built in 1726, the Uezu family home is a designated Japanese National Heritage site and a treasure and it's an example of pure Okinawan style. It was built to house the Uezu family who were descended from the lords of Gushikawa Castle. In the Ryukyu kingdom they held a social rank called *pechin*, a status similar to a samurai. For generations the Uezus were the heads of the local administrative district. Today, the house, its interior and courtyard, are preserved as they were 300 years ago. It's an archetype of a fine Okinawan dwelling: the extended red tile roof, the support posts

Uezu Old House, one of the oldest traditional residences of any Okinawan Island.

perched on stone, all surrounded by coral stone walls and Fukugi trees. It's a lesson in traditional design perfectly suited to its environment. For those who have visited other Ryukyu Islands, it's similar to the Nakamura House on Okinawa, the Takara House on Geruma in the Kerama Islands and the Miyara Donchi House on Ishigaki. Like those other preserved homes, there's a small admission charge of a few hundred Yen to enter the house.

From here it's just over three-quarters of a mile (1 kilometer) northwest through the Uezu neighborhoods to our next stop, the massive "Five-Branched Pine." We're now above Gushikawa Town and near the public reservoir, which is also a park. There are signs leading tourists to this next attraction, the Goeda-no matsu tree (五枝の松).

For an admirer of trees, the Goeda-no matsu (*goeda* means "five-branched" and *matsu* is "pine") is truly a spectacular sight. It's simply enormous, spreading outward in all directions from its original central trunk in a radius of 25–40 feet (8 to 12 meters). Over time some of its branches bent to the earth from their own weight and took root, thus becoming new trunks. Although an everyday event for a banyan, this is unusual for a pine. The Goeda-no Pine presently has five main trunks and is still growing. Perhaps in another 200 years it will be twice its present size. Under healthy conditions Japanese black pines may live a very, very long time. We may not see it 200 years from today, but maybe our great-great-great-grandchildren will, should they visit here. I hope mine will.

From either the Uezu House or the great pine tree it's about 1.75 miles (3 kilometers) southwest to the coast and our first chance for a beach break, for all along this stretch

of shore there are sandy sections eventually leading to the more than 0.75-mile (1-kilometer)-long Shinri Beach (シンリビーチ; Shinri bīchi). Mentioned earlier, the Cypress Resort Hotel occupies the far western section of Shinri Beach but all of it is open to the public. It's a safe beach as this entire section of coast is fronted by a natural barrier reef. It breaks up the waves and shelters the shoreline. It's not a particularly good snorkeling beach but it's a good one for children and not so strong swimmers.

From Shinri Beach or the Cypress Hotel it's about 1.25 miles (2 kilometers) further northwest to Kume's Airport. Mentioned earlier in this section on the islands west of Okinawa-hontō, this modern airport has several flights a day to Naha and in summer direct flights to Tokyo's Haneda Airport. It's very convenient.

The airport occupies the far westernmost tip of Kumejima, so from here it's only east that we can go, east and a bit north. If you follow the road through the long avenue of windswept pine trees, in a little over three-quarters of a mile (1 kilometer) you'll come to a tiny village, Kitahara (北原; lit. "North Field"). It's really just a collection of one or two shops, a number of private residences and a very elegant but small Shinto shrine on the right-hand side of the road.

Goeda-no matsu (五枝の松)

Resembling an enormous bonsai tree, this spectacular specimen of a Japanese black pine (*Pinus thunbergii*) has records dating to 1839 but it may be much older than that. It stands 20 feet (6 meters) tall and has five trunks. It is claimed that the tree was planted in honor of the Ryukyu harvest gods. It is one of the most famous pine trees in Japan and many songs have been written about it in Okinawan folk music.

Almost directly across from the shrine, on the left side of the road going east, you might just catch out of the corner of your eye a small blue sign: 馬の角 ("Horse's Horn"). What's a horse's horn? The horn of a unicorn, of course. A left and a right and a left again (follow the signs) and you'll come to yet another ancient preserved Okinawan house, this one surrounded by a peaceful though heavily overgrown garden. It's a tiny museum, but more often than not it's closed.

Inside the museum is the usual collection of silk garments, some vintage photographs, several old ceramics and a few artifacts and other memorabilia. But what this particular house museum also holds is a small glass-covered wooden case and mounted therein an unusual, exceptional object.

Have you ever seen a unicorn's horn? Not many people have. There is a note alongside explaining that it was a treasured gift bestowed upon the ruler of this house from a visiting Chinese dignitary. In reality it is thought to be the tusk of a narwhal whale and, indeed, only a short bit of one. Nevertheless, the spiraled tusk of a narwhal is as rare an item as is the spiraled horn of a unicorn. As a rule the horn is kept out of sight, hidden away in a storage credenza, but if you ask the museum's guardian he will open the armoire, unfold the fabric enclosing the box, and let you have a look. It's not sacred, but it's rare, old and treasured. You'll see from the guardian's demeanor that the unicorn horn remains a venerated object. Treat it, and your visit, with respect.

Continuing our drive northeast, in a little less than three-quarters of a mile (1 kilometer) we'll come to a sign for the Yajagama Cave (ヤジャーガマ; Yajā-gama). The cave's name is also listed in Kanji characters (鐘乳洞; Kane chichi hora Dōkutsu; lit. "Breast Bell Cave," Stalactite Cave). From the sign it's a short distance to a small parking area and the cave entrance. There's no admission fee and there's usually no one around.

From the parking lot it's a short climb down some slippery steps and then into a quite large grotto. This large hall is perhaps 65 feet (20 meters) across and equally tall. It's dark but there's a small natural skylight high at the top. This is only the beginning and now you'll need your own flashlight and a hard hat. At the far right of the main entrance cavern there's a little opening, perhaps 18 inches (half a meter) wide and

Horse's Horn

Lying upon a silk pillow and framed in a wooden shadow box is the horn of a unicorn. Given with great ceremony more than 300 years ago by an emissary from China when Kumejima was a small kingdom in its own right, at the time of its presentation it was considered one of the most rare and priceless possessions in the world.

5 feet (1.5 meters) tall. This is the actual entrance to the cave. In fact, it's pretty scary and it's certain that the cave is full of bats and probably a lot more. For the intrepid, know that it's not a terribly long cave but don't go in alone and leave word with someone that you plan on visiting this cave.

From the Yajagama Cave it's another 1.5 miles (2.5 kilometers) northeast following the coast road along the northern top of Kume to the 15th-century Gushikawa Castle Ruins (具志川城跡; Gushi-kawa gusuku jōato). It's mostly reconstructed stone walls that you'll find here, but archeological excavation and restoration work are going on all the time. There is no admission charge to this *gusuku*.

From the castle ruins it's only a couple of hundred meters further down the hill to the shoreline and the "Female Rock" (女岩; Onna-iwa), otherwise popularly known as Mīfugā (ミーフガー; lit. "Vagina Rock"). It's clearly visible from the castle. There's a large paved parking lot and the site almost always has visitors. Incidentally, Mīfugā may be temperamental. The area underneath her opening is littered with fairly large stones that have come crashing down and there are warning signs to watch for falling rock. She may not always appreciate the attention paid to her private, personal space.

To reach our next destination we'll have to backtrack almost 1 mile (1.5 kilometers) up the hill to the main coast road (Route 242), then we'll continue east following the signs nearly 1.5 miles (2.5 kilometers) to a parking

Looking out from the Yajagama Cave, a large, dark grotto filled with stalactites and bats.

Tachijami Rock or "Standing God Rock," a stone monolith 130 feet (40 meters) tall.

area where we'll arrive close to the Tachijami Rock (立神岩 or タチジャミ; lit. "God Established Rock" or "Standing God Rock." It's a stone monolith approximately 130 feet (40 meters) tall. There's a similar standing God monolith, similarly named and even larger on the island of Yonaguni. From the parking lot we'll hike down a path about 985 feet (300 meters) until we reach the shore and that's where we'll come to the stone. While you're here, you can also check out the Tachijami Waterfall (タチジャミの滝; Tachijami-no taki) as it's not far. However, more often than not, unless it's been raining, the falls will be dry and it's not worth the trouble to find them.

From the parking area at Tachijami Rock return to the main road, then continue southeast a little over 1 mile (1.6 kilometers). You'll pass through the tiny towns of Uegusuku (宇江城; Ué-gusuku) and Hiyajo (比屋定; Hiyajyō) along the way. Just after Hiyajo, on the left, you'll see a sign for the Sundial Stone (ウティダ石 or 太陽石;

Utinda-ishi). It's less than 330 feet (100 meters) down a side street from the main road (Route 242). The Japanese-only inscription states that it was used as a time measuring device for the villagers for 500 years. It's not too much, just a sort of large rock with some writings on it. There are a lot of such things in Japan. Shortly before this, along the same route, you also would have passed by the sign for the Tropical Fish Pools (熱帯魚の家; Nettai-gyo no ie). If you've never seen saltwater pools isolated at low tide, usually full of small tropical fish, you might be interested, otherwise you may wish to give this spot a pass too.

From the Sundial Stone continue just under 1 mile (1.5 kilometers) to the next big attraction, which is almost impossible to miss. It's the view from the heights of the observatory atop the Hiyajo Banta Cliffs (比屋定バンタ; Hiyajyō Banta). If you have merely driven by the signs for the fish pools and the sundial, it's about 1.75 miles (3 kilometers) in all southeast from Tachijami to

The view northeast from the observatory on top of the Hiyajo Banta Cliffs.

The Japanese Military Radar Installation situated beyond the castle ruins on Mt Uegusuku.

Hiyajo Banta. You'll pass the village of Hiyajo and the sundial about halfway along the way.

The observatory and accompanying gift shop and refreshment stand are poised some 650 feet (200 meters) above the beautifully clear northern sea directly on the main coastal road (Route 242). On a clear day you can see Kume, Torishima, Aguni, Tonaki, the Keramas and, sometimes, the Okinawan mainland. It's quite a view.

If you like high places you're in for a treat, for the next stop is 1,017 feet (310 meters) above sea level, the highest point of the island, Mt Uegusuku (宇江城岳; Ué-gusuku daké). Bring a sweater or a jacket, for it's at least 5–10 degrees cooler up here than anywhere else on Kume.

The way up starts on the right, off Route 242, almost immediately after the Hiyajo Banta Observation Platform. There's a sign for the Uegusuku Gusuku Ruins (宇江城城跡; Ué gusuku gusuku jōato), for that's where we're going. You can see the outline of the castle from almost everywhere on Kume. It's perched on the very top of the peak. In all, it's not quite 1.75 miles (3 kilometers) from the Hiyajo Banta Cliffs to the ruins. Some sections of the road are narrow and/or extremely steep, thus it's not a road for the faint of heart.

The fortress itself is not much, a partially restored ruin at best, but that's really not the attraction. The attraction is the commanding view of the entire island, which is breathtaking. It doesn't seem like 1,000 feet; it feels more like 10,000. It's like being in an airplane, and it gives one pause to contemplate the poor souls driven by the Kume king centuries ago to heft this pile of stones up this mountain.

To the north and west you'll see the airport, to the east Tonakijima and the Keramas, to the south you'll first see several of Kume's next highest peaks, including the 758-foot (231-meter)-high Mount Ō (大岳; Ō-také; lit. "Big Peak"), and then you'll see all the way to Gushikawa Town, Eef Beach and the tiny adjacent islands of Ō, Ōha and Haténo-hama. Oh, one last thing. Rumor has it that Habu snakes like to live in the rock piles that constitute the reconstructed walls of the ruins. It might be a good idea to stay off them.

In leaving this mountaintop fortress we'll drive back down the same route we took up. It's less than 1.75 miles (3 kilometers) to Route 242. From there we'll continue slightly less than a mile (1.5 kilometers) to a sign for the Aka Waterfall (阿嘉のヒゲ水; Aka no higé-mizu). If it's been raining, it might be worth the rather long and steep climb down to look up at the falls. At their best they are tall, narrow and wispy. If it has been dry, they don't exist and you probably should skip it. The fall's name translates as "Long Red Beard," a reference to the underlying color of the rock face over which they flow.

Continuing southeast, either not quite 1.5 miles (2.5 kilometers) from the Aka Waterfall parking lot or 2.5 miles (4 kilometers) from the Uegusuku Ruins/Route 242 intersection, you'll come to the little town of Maja (真謝; Maja). Almost immediately after entering Maja, on your right, you'll come across Tengogu (天后宮), a modest Shinto shrine. It's no big deal but it's a peaceful spot. Its Kanji characters read Tianhou, meaning "Queen of Heaven Palace" or "Queen's Sky Palace." A "palace" may be a bit of a stretch for this little place but, nonetheless, it's a prized shrine for the village.

Uegusuku Gusuku Ruins, perched on the top of Mt Uegusuku, Kume Island's highest point.

Tengogu, a small prized Shinto shrine in the town of Maja.

A little further down the same road and you'll have passed out of Maja and into Une (宇根; Uné). It's hard to know exactly where one village ends and the other begins, but it's 1,970 feet (600 meters) from the Tengogu Shrine to the sign for Uné-no-dai-Sotetsu, (宇根の大ソテツ), a 250-year-old stand of 20-foot (6-meter)-high cycads (sago palms). They are just off the road, to the right, growing in a manicured private yard, centered by a traditional Okinawan residence and displaying over a dozen beautifully crafted bonsai trees. It is open to the public and there is no admission charge although there is a dish for the offering of coins to help pay for the estate's upkeep.

Before you can say "I've seen a lot of sago palms in Okinawa, enough already," yes, it's true that there are many sagos in the Ryukyus. After all, the plant is indigenous to these islands. However, this display is different. It's a group of probably the largest sagos you will likely ever come across. Sagos, by their nature, are so slow-growing that it's unusual to see them this large. Someone, or rather some generations of caretakers, have watched over and nurtured these giant cycads for more than two centuries. It's a remarkably peaceful garden spot.

Lastly, shortly before the cycad display, you would have passed by the Maja Fukugi Tree Display (真謝のチュラ福木; Maja no Chura Fukugi). It's a straight line of Fukugi trees planted literally in the middle of the road.

From the sago palms and Une, it's less than three-quarters of a mile (1 kilometer) east to the port, Madomari-kō (真泊漁港; lit. "True Night Fishing Port"), and the furthest

east one can go on Kume Island. From here it's about 2.25 miles (4 kilometers) southwest to Eef Beach (イーフビーチ; Īfu-bīchi) and the hotels and resorts you'll find there. There's a choice of several routes. One hugs the southern shoreline and passes the bridge to Ōjima along the way, another runs through the village of Nakazato (仲里; Nakazato) and passes by the town office. Either road will take you in about five minutes to the Eef Beach Hotel, the Kume Island Resort, several other smaller hotels and a large handful of *minshuku*.

Kume is justifiably famous for its fine beaches. There are a number of them, but the best known is Eef Beach. Several years ago, in a global survey, it was voted as one of the 100 most beautiful beaches in the world. It's a 0.75-mile (1-kilometer)-long white fine sand beach on the island's southeast side. It's just below, and not far from, the bridge over to Ōjima, and has more hotels, restaurants and *minshuku* than any other place on Kume. For most tourists this is the most popular place to stay when visiting the island.

If you get bored on Eef, or just wish to check out some other beaches, on the other side of the island, along the southwest coast, there are three more. Closest to Eef (though it's not close) is Ara Beach (アーラ浜; Ārahama), then Gushikawa Beach (具志川浜; Gushikawa-hama), then Shinri Beach (シンリ浜; Shinri-hama). They all provide a change of scenery, but frankly none of them are as nice as Eef Beach. Ara Beach is the most private. It's so isolated that you'll usually have the whole beach to yourself.

Eef Beach Hotel
The Īfu-bichi hoteru is one of the most popular choices on Kume Island. Located right on the beach, you can step out of your room and you're there.

Eef Beach, one of nicest beaches in Japan or any-where, is more than three-quarters of a mile (1 kilometer) of pure white sand. It has a gentle grade and fronts on crystal-clear, warm waters.

Tonbara Rock, a remarkable solitary, upright stone "monument" well offshore of Cape Shimajiri or "Bottom of the Island Cape," at the southeastern-most tip of Kume Island.

If you're lucky you might even chance upon sea turtles as they lay and bury their eggs. We purposefully haven't yet mentioned the tatami-stone beach on Ōjima (page 187) or the 3.75-mile (6-kilometer)-long Hateno-hama sand island beach (page 188) because we'll cover them individually further below as they're located on separate islands.

Although we've explored most of Kume's best-known sights, there is still one more very fine excursion and it's not far. Due south 3 miles (5 kilometers) from Eef Beach, you'll come to the bottom of the island and the end of the road. The route follows the eastern coastline of what is essentially a great penin-sula, the largest on Kume. It's so wild that there are no roads whatsoever on the entire western side of it. With the exception of a few cattle farms, almost all the peninsula has been declared a natural reserve.

The island ends at Cape Shimajiri (島尻崎; Shima-jiri-zaki; lit. "Bottom of the Island Cape"), and here begin the possibilities for

several hikes up some pretty steep hillsides. At one point you'll come to the Bird's Beak Rock (鳥の口; Tori-no kuchi). It's sort of an upright stone monument that resembles the open beak of a seabird looking like it's ready to grab on to something. Out to sea, well offshore to the south, you'll see Kume's great solitary stone, Tonbāra-iwa. At the top of another hill you'll find a panoramic viewing station and one of the most dramatic views of rock and ocean cliffs to be seen anywhere. Look back a few pages, it's the photo featured on page 178. Is it any wonder that people find this island so beautiful?

To get back to Eef Beach it's necessary to turn around and take the same route north 3 miles (5 kilometers) instead of south. To return to the ferry port or the airport from any of the hotels on Eef Beach it's about 4 miles (6 kilometers) due west to Gushikawa and the marine terminal at Kanegusuku. An alternative route, a total of 7.25 miles (11.5 kilometers) west from Eef, through the town and straight to the airport, goes essen-tially from one end of the island to the other, east to west.

Although it may seem as if we're taken in every sight on the island, we have not. There are other small monuments, museums or attractions of some interest here and there all over Kume. There is simply not enough time or space to mention everything worth seeing and, conversely, not everything is worth seeing. In clockwise order, beginning near the Kanegusuku Port, some of the things we've passed by for one reason or another have been:

- Kumejima Cultural Nature Center (久米島 自然文化センター; Kumé-jima shizen bunka sentā).
- Kumejima Firefly Pavillon (久米島ホタル 館; Kumé-jima hotaru-kan).
- Horse Mackerel Museum (あじま〜館; Ajimā-kan).
- The "Mystery" Slope (おばけ坂; Obaké-zaka; lit. Ghost Hill) on the way to Gushikawa Castle.
- Kumejima Silk Production Pavilion (久米 島紬ユイマール館; Kumé-jima tsumugi yuimāru-kan) in Maja Village.

We'll leave Kume now, but probably not for the night, for the next several islands we'll visit are all little satellites and are but a few short minutes away from the mainland. Moreover, we'll have to return because there are no hotels or *minshuku* on any of them.

The Otoko-iwa ("Male Rock") dominates the skyline above "Crow Mountain Island."

GARASAYAMAJIMA (ガラサー山島; Gārasa-yama-jima lit. "Crow Mountain Island"). Named for the crows (カラス; *garasu*) that gather here in the evenings, you may notice this tiny islet when arriving on the ferry. It's only 410 feet (125 meters) offshore from the Kanegusuku Port Marine Terminal and is partially incorporated in the tsunami barrier that protects the harbor. It's not much. It's oval-shaped and only 330 feet (100 meters) long from north to south and less than 30 (48 kilometers) from east to west.

What might catch your attention, however, is the phallus-shaped rock standing erect out of one end of the islet (page 179). It is known as Otoko-iwa or Otoko-yama (男岩 or 男山; lit. "Male Rock" or "Male Mountain") and it's one of two fertility symbols on Kume. The other is female, called Mīfugā" (ミーフガー), otherwise known as Onna-iwa" (女岩; lit. "Female Rock"). It's on the northern end of the island.

ŌJIMA (奥武島; Ō-jima). This small island, less than 1.25 miles (2 kilometers) due east of Eef Beach and Kumejima, is connected to the mainland by a 1,640-foot (500-meter) bridge. It is famous for its Tatami-ishi (畳石; lit. "tatami mat stones"), a remarkable natural volcanic phenomenon. In the last few years tourism has increased on the island and its presence is seen by the addition of a sea turtle museum and an *onsen* spa resort.

Ōjima's general shape is that of a triangle, with its base south and apex north. Across its southern bottom, at its widest points, it is 1 mile (1.6 kilometers). From the center of its base to its northernmost tip it is half that, 2,460 feet (750 meters). It is, in fact, a quite regular pyramid. The island has an area of a quarter of a square mile (0.63 square kilometers) and a circumference of 2.25 miles (4 kilometers). You won't need any oxygen on Ōjima. Its highest point is 49 feet (15 meters) above sea level. It has an official population of 30, but even that small number is difficult to discern. Other than a derelict hotel or apartment house (it's hard to know what it was), there doesn't seem to be much real housing on the island. However, there is a public campground.

In any case, regardless of whether anyone actually lives on Ōjima, most visitors don't come here to stay. They come to visit the Tatami-ishi pentagon- and hexagon-shaped stones that look like giant tortoise shells. These strange rocks are on the south coast of Ōjima and spread along the beach for about 575 feet (175 meters) and offshore for about 80 (25 meters). Altogether, there are some 1,000 of them. Obviously, more of them be seen at the lowest tides. The stones are a protected natural treasure of Okinawa Prefecture. Although that probably means that no one is allowed to dig them up, or remove or damage them in any way, visitors are allowed to walk on them and take photographs. There's no charge.

Because of their resemblance to either the interlocking sections that make up a turtle's carapace or a room full of traditional Japanese floor mats, they are called both "turtleshell rocks" and "tatami-stones." Although by no means common, this unusual natural phenomenon is seen in several places around the world. It is caused when andesite- or basalt-type lava, extruded from a volcanic eruption, gradually cools to rock and splinters or crystallizes along what are called columnar joints. Such formations are rare. The erosion of millions of years by ocean waves has worn down the rocks to nearly flat. Now they look as if someone had manufactured them, but of course they are natural works of art.

The beach on which the rocks are found extends east for more than three-quarters of a mile (1 kilometer), the entire southern shore of the island. On shore, immediately above

Tatami Mat Stones

There are over 1,000 of these naturally formed volcanic basalt five- and six-sided stones. There are somewhat similar formations, due to similar conditions, around the world, most famously at Northern Ireland's Giant's Causeway, the Cape Stolby cliffs on Russia's Kunashir Island in the Kuriles, several islands in the Penghu Archipelago in the Taiwan Strait, Devils Postpile National Monument in California and, most spectacular of all, Devils Tower National Monument in Wyoming.

Ōjima and Ōhajima

Viewed from a high point in Tonnaha Forest Park (登武那霸園地入リ口) on Kumejima, these two islets are just offshore. Ōjima, on the right, may be reached by the bridge visible in the foreground. You'll need to take a boat for Ōhajima, at left rear.

Sea Turtles (海亀 or ウミガメ)

Umigamé, as they are called in Japan, can be any one of seven living species. Although part of the same taxonomic order in which land turtles and tortoises are found, they represent an ancient line of marine reptiles that branched off from their land cousins over 110 million years ago. Sea turtles may be found in all the oceans of the world except the Arctic and Antarctic. Although completely adapted to a seafaring life—they even mate in water—sea turtle females must come on shore to lay their eggs. This is the most vulnerable time for them and their hatchlings. It is estimated that for every 100 eggs laid, one turtle will grow to an adult and reproduce. For a host of reasons—habitant encroachment, natural predators, pollution, fishing nets and turtle meat poachers—all sea turtle species are considered threatened or endangered, several critically so. In particular, the leatherback, Kemp's ridley and hawksbill may not survive into the next century. The green, olive ridley, flatback and loggerhead are endangered, but not yet critically so.

the rocks is the relatively new Kumejima Sea Turtle Museum (久米島ウミガメ館; Kumé-jima Umi gamé-kan). It opened on Ōjima a few years ago and has exhibits and displays on the life cycle of these intriguing creatures. The museum has been successful in breeding several endangered species of sea turtles.

Even more recently built, Ō Island can now claim possession of a luxury spa. Called the Bade Haus Kumejima (バーデハウス久米島; Bāde-hausu Kumé-jima), this European-style public bath has soaking tubs, a large central pool, an outdoor patio area and a small café. Men and women mix (with swim attire) in the central pool and segregate in the private and massage sections. Depending on the spa package you choose, figure on around $30 for the day.

ŌHAJIMA (オーハ島; Ōha-jima; also called Ōhaji). The sandy beach on the southeastern-most corner of Ōjima is but 500 feet (150 meters) from the sandy beach on the south-westernmost corner of Ōhajima. The two islets sit side by side off Kume Island's central eastern coast, Ō a triangle to the west, Ōha a square to the east.

Ōhajima is about 1,640–1,970 feet (500–600 meters) across from north to south or east to west. It has an area of 0.37 square kilometers and a circumference of slightly more than 1.5 miles (2.5 kilometers). Its highest point is 26 feet (8 meters). Although at first glance Ōha appears uninhabited, a closer inspection reveals that there is a small private dock on the island's central west side and that there are three or four dwellings perhaps 325–500 feet (100–150 meters) in from the shore. The population could well be five or ten people.

The island is not connected to Ōjima, Kume or any other place by bridge, so it is

necessary to take a boat (or swim) to get there. Most of the island is ringed by beaches. There are no roads or vehicles on the island, although there are several paths from house to house and to the dock. Ōha Island is completely covered in dense subtropical vegetation.

ICHIYUNZAIWA (イチユンザ岩; Ichi-yunza iwa; also pronounced as Ichunza iwa). You'll find this set of rocks about 820–985 feet (250–300 meters) due north from the north-ernmost little tip of Ōhajima. Depending on the height of the tide, there are anywhere from five or six to a dozen of them. Of the three largest islets, the easternmost measures about 165 by 300 feet (50 by 90 meters) and is oblong in shape. To its southwest there is a long narrow one, around 100 feet (30 meters) wide and over 425 feet (130 meters) from end to end, north to south. Only 165 feet (50 meters) above it is the northernmost and largest islet in the group. It measures about 590 feet (180 meters) from north to south and roughly 330 feet (100 meters) from east to west. It is an oval in shape but with a number of asymetrical cut-outs and indentations. Of the many other tiny islets, most measure anywhere from 5 to 10 to 20 meters across. Almost all of the islets, large and small, are entirely covered with dense green vegetation. Some are connected by sandbars but that depends on the tides.

The collection of these rocks is part of a much larger shoal that eventually extends out several miles. The best-known portion is the bright white sandbar known as Hatenohamajima. We'll go there next.

Hatenohama Island, offshore from Ō Island at the end of Kume's east coast is, in reality, a great long sandbar rather than an island.

This aerial shot shows Kume to the west, Hateno Beach to the east and Ō and Ōha in the middle.

Torishima, the uninhabited "Bird Island" as seen from Kume's Hiyajō Banta.

HATENOHAMAJIMA (ハテの浜島; also spelled はての浜島; Haténo-hama-jima). Beginning about 2,130 feet (650 meters) offshore from Ōhajima and then extending east about 4 miles (6 kilometers), this "island" is really a great long sandbar. It is never wider than about 660 feet (200 meters). It is, in fact, a combination of three or four sandbars, each carrying its own name, but the term for the overall group and the name for the largest and longest of them is Hateno-hama (ハテの浜). The words quite logically translate as "Beach at the End," and surely that's what it is, a beach at the end of Kume's east coast running straight back towards Okinawa.

There are no dwellings, hotels or buildings of any kind. It's uninhabited and uninhabitable. During the summer months a port-a-san type toilet is brought out and parked on the beach. Enterprising Kume residents sometimes bring out beach umbrellas to rent as there is no shade.

Solitary Tonbara Rock stands sentinel at the southernmost tip of Kume Island.

Hateno Beach is reachable by private boat. All the hotels on Kume have connections with operators who offer day excursions out to the islets. The water at Hatenohama is amazingly clear and warm, partly because it is so shallow. Glass-bottom boat tours also go out. If you like long strolls along the beach, this is a good place. Bring cold drinks, fresh water and sunscreen lotion with you! If you fly out to Kume, you'll almost always get a good view of Hatenohama from the air as you approach the island.

TONBARAIWA (トンバーラ岩; Tonbāra iwa). Roughly three-quarters of a mile (1 kilometer) off the southernmost tip of Kume Island lies this solid bastion of stone (page 185). It stands isolated and alone, a silent sentinel for what cause or claim, who knows? The rock measures approximately 820 feet (250 meters) in diameter and about 660 feet (200 meters) high. It supports a bit of green vegetation at its top. There's really not too much to say about it other than it's impressive in its own commanding way. Surely there are some birds or other creatures living on this place, but it's more than certain that it's not inhabitable by man.

6 **TORISHIMA** 鳥島
This uninhabited "Bird Island" is primarily a block of undersea limestone topped with a sandbar. It long ago produced phosphates commercially. It is 18 miles (29 kilometers) north of Kume Island. Its other name is

Uninhabitable Torishima from the air.

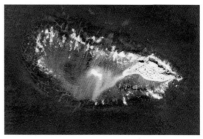

Torijima Shabakujo (鳥島の射爆場) or the Torijima Firing Range. It has been used as a bombing training site by the US Air Force and Marines based in Okinawa since the end of World War II. Torishima (鳥島; Torishima) is extensively pockmarked by bomb craters. No one is allowed there.

It is roughly an oval in shape, about 1,475 feet (450 meters) long east to west, by 500 feet (150 meters) wide north to south. Its area is approximately 0.04 square kilometers and its circumference is a little more than three-quarters of a mile (1 kilometer). It's taller than it appears in the top–down view photo. Its highest elevation is 80 feet (25 meters). All in all, it's not much of a place although Japanese fishermen report good fishing nearby and regularly protest their exclusion from its surrounding waters. The island is often referred to as Kumé-Torishima to avoid confusion with Iōtorishima (硫黄鳥島; Iwō-torishima; lit. "Sulphur Bird Island") some 125 miles (200 kilometers) to the northeast, near Tokunoshima.

Approximately 24 miles (38 kilometers) due east of Torishima is Aguni, the next island we'll visit, but of course we can't get there from here. In fact, we've got no business out here at all. It's a restricted area. From Kume we'll take the ferry or fly back to Naha and then ferry or fly to Aguni.

7 AGUNIJIMA 粟国島

Aguni Island is about 30 miles (48 kilometers) northeast of Kume and 14 miles (22 kilometers) north of Tonaki, but neither island has commercial connections to the island. There is not enough demand for an inter-island passenger ferry service, so everything is consolidated at hubs like Naha.

The entrance to Aguni's limestone cave temple.

As the crow flies and by the sea route Agunijima (粟国島; Aguni-jima) is almost 40 miles (64 kilometers) northwest of Naha. There is one round-trip sailing a day on the Aguni ferry. It leaves Tomari Port at 9:55AM and takes two hours to reach the island, arriving just before noon. The ferry docks at Aguni Port (粟国港; Aguni-kō) until 2:10PM when it returns to Okinawa, arriving at 4:10PM. Aguni also has a small airport (粟国空港; Aguni-kūkō) and there are several flights a day from Naha. Flying time is only 20 minutes.

Aguni's shape is somewhat that of a rounded triangle or perhaps most of the top half of an oval. It's a small island, about 2.25 miles (4 kilometers) across east to west at its widest southern end and a little more than 1.5 miles (2.5 kilometers) at its longest north–south points. It has a surface area of 3 square miles (7.64 square kilometers) and a shoreline of 10.5 miles (17 kilometers). Although there are no great mountains, the island's highest point is only 315 feet (96 meters). It would not be accurate to describe it as "flat," for a good percentage of Aguni is very hilly, and indeed a good part of its shore is lined with very dramatic cliffs.

The Aguni passenger and vehicle ferry.

Dramatic cliffs at Aguni's Cape Fuden.

Aguni Sea Salt (粟国の塩)

Who would have thought that making salt was so complicated? It's true that ordinary sea salts are simply made by the evaporation of sea water, usually in large man-made or natural pans, followed by its collection. But Aguni salt is no ordinary salt. First, the cleanest waters from the East China Sea are piped in from a good distance offshore to the main plant. There, the seawater is pumped up to the top of the tower and trickled down on to the leafless branches of young bamboo stalks, hanging upside-down. This is repeated continuously over the course of about a week. Due to the cinder-block perforations in the tower, the sea breezes gradually carry away the moisture, resulting in *kansui*, or strong saltwater that has been condensed to six or seven times its original volume. Moreover, the salt adheres to the branches, crystallizing thicker and thicker. At the appropriate time, the super-saturated water and crystals are harvested and loaded into the firing pan to be boiled down with other ingredients. At this stage, the salt develops a unique flavor, salty, of course, but much more so. It's actually delicious. Now it's time for sorting out any impurities and packaging. The Aguni Plant ships to buyers all over the world. As might be imagined, such salt is not cheap. Aguni-no-shio may be found on all the gourmet spice and seasoning internet websites. It sells for $20–$25 for an 8 oz or one-cup package.

The main processing building.

Like the German braumeister or the French vintner, the Aguni "saltmaster" boils and blends the raw salt with vinegar and other fine (and secret) ingredients in a reduction pan over a wood-fired furnace.

Working on the salt before packaging.

Salt refinement on upside-down bamboo stalks.

Sesoko Island, which has several excellent beaches, is linked by bridge to the Motobu Peninsula.

There is a small village at the port, Hama (浜), but most of the island's approximately 950 residents live in Aguni village (粟国村; Aguni-son) or Higashi (東; lit. east), which is about three-quarters of a mile (1 kilometer) to the west. The port and the villages lie on the island's south central side. There are a couple of *minshuku* at the port and at least half a dozen in town. Aguni Airport is on the island's top northeastern side, about 1.25 miles (2 kilometers) from the port or village.

For whatever reason, lack of knowledge—everyone goes to Kumejima or the Keramas—Aguni is infrequently visited. That's a shame because it's a very beautiful island. However, if you thought Kume was peaceful, Aguni is downright somnolent. There simply isn't much going on. That's the way it is on some of these small islands. Nonetheless, it's a lovely place, covered in wild cycad palms. Its western end, almost uninhabited, features great cliffs at the Mahana Observatory (マハナ展望台; Mahana Tenbō-dai) on Cape Fuden (筆ん崎; Fuden-zaki). Near the lookout there's a scenic lighthouse and a great windmill that generates 25 percent of Aguni's electricity. This is the island's highest point. The cliffs rise almost 330 feet (100 meters) straight up from the sea.

Near the island's north shore there's a fairly large limestone cavern. It could also be described as a great sinkhole, for it is a large depression in the earth. A Shinto priest spent most of his life on Aguni and the cave holds his ashes. It's called Hora tera-tera Shōnyūdō (洞寺—テラ—鍾乳洞) and is considered a sacred place.

Aguni has one large beach, Ugu (ウーグの浜; Ugu-no-hama), also called Nagahama (長浜ビーチ; Naga-hama bīchi). It occupies the lower half of the island's east side and is about three-quarters of a mile (1 kilometer) long. You'll probably have the whole place to yourself as there's almost never anyone there. By the way, it also happens to be yet another one of those unusual Ryukyuan

beaches that is covered in "star" sand (星砂; *hoshi-zuna*) (page 78).

There's not much tourism on Aguni so the main livelihood of most of the island's residents is agriculture. Most of Aguni's level sections are devoted to sugar cane and you'll see signs advertising the black sugar cane candy they make here. In addition, there is one industry on the island and it is famous throughout Japan: sea salt (page 191). Called Aguni-no-shio (粟国の塩), it's found in many of Tokyo's most famous restaurants. It is also found on many fancy cuisine and connoisseur websites. It's a super premium product. The salt works is up on top of the island on the north shore. The owner is usually around, and if you are interested he'll show you around. It's a fascinating process and the results are truly tasteworthy. There's a good deal more to it than you might otherwise think.

We'll now return to mainland Okinawa and proceed by car up to the Motobu Peninsula. Both Aguni and Kume are as distant as the next islands are close. Some of the next few we can even reach by bridge. For those where we'll need a sea ferry, we'll depart from other ports. There are no further islands that we can reach from Tomari Port, so we are finished here.

⑧ SESOKOJIMA 瀬底島

There's no need to take a ferry to this islet. Sesokojima (瀬底島; Sésoko-jima) is one of Okinawa-shotō's close-in islands and there is a bridge connecting it to Okinawa's Motobu Peninsula. The bridge is 9 miles (14 kilometers) northwest of Nago on Route 449. It's fairly close to the end of the peninsula, about 3 miles (5 kilometers) before the Churaumi Aquarium.

Sesokojima is a small island, only 1.25 square miles (3 square kilometers) in area. It is not quite 1.75 miles (3 kilometers) long from north to south, but its width varies considerably. The top half, by the bridge, is slightly more than 1 mile (1.8 kilometers) across, but from there it narrows down. The lower half starts at around three-quarters of a mile (1 kilometer) in width and tapers to about 1,640 or 1,970 feet (500 or 600 meters) across for its most southern one-third. There are about 350 people living on Sesoko.

It is a lovely island, green and peaceful, with scenic views in all directions. There are several *minshuku* and there is the start of a large luxury hotel. That project, unfortunately, went into bankruptcy, so all you see now is an enormous half-finished construction site. It looks like it would have been a nice place. Maybe it will be rescued by some developer. Most visitors come for the day to enjoy one of several excellent beaches. One is small, right by the end of the bridge on the islet's east side. The other is large, three-quarters of a mile (1 kilometer) long, on the west side of the island. There is also a public golf course on Sesoko, popular with Japanese golfers. The hotel construction site and the golf course are located on the island's west side.

9 MINNAJIMA 水納島

Minna isn't just Minna, it's "mini." Minnajima (水納島; Minna-jima) is a very small island. From its western cape to the beach on its easternmost point it's a little less than a mile (1 kilometer) across. From its furthest northern point, near the dock, to its southernmost point, it's 2,460 feet (750 meters). Altogether, its surface area is only 0.47 square kilometers. One glance at the map shows you its easily recognizable shape, a crescent. Minna is also low. Its highest point is 26 feet (8 meters). It's so flat and low that the Okinawan authorities evacuate the residents when large typhoons are predicted as a precaution against the possibility of a tsunami surge overwhelming the island.

To get to Minna Island take the ferry from Toguchi Port (渡久地港; Toguchi-kō). That's the port in Motobu Town, not Motobu Port. It's a small passenger-only ferry. In the winter months the ferry sails twice daily, morning

The north side of Minnajima, its pier on the right.

and afternoon. From April to June, and then again from September to November, the ferry sails three times a day. During the summer months, when many sunseekers come out to the island's beach, the ferry runs six times a day (ten times in August). It only takes 30 minutes one way.

The island is so small that there are no roads. Since vehicles aren't needed, you can leave yours behind at Toguchi Port. Parking is free at the ferry terminal. The ferry arrives at Minna-kō (水納港), which is merely a pier. There are a couple of paths on Minna. You can walk the whole island in about an hour. There's a small village about 400 feet (150 meters) from the pier and perhaps two dozen houses. The population is around 50. There is an elementary school in the village. A recent report stated that the school had 10 students.

Minna is surrounded by a ring of trees. Once inside the ring you'll see that most of the island is planted with sugar cane. There's a path from the village to the island's cove, which is one of Minna's most interesting features. The cove is completely sheltered and great for exploring tidal pools. It is too shallow to allow entry of any but the very smallest of watercraft. If it's a beach you would prefer, then virtually the whole northern shore is one great beach, appropriately called Minna Beach (水納ビーチ; Minna-bīchi). Visiting the island from Okinawa makes a nice day trip. You can legitimately claim that you've been "offshore" all day.

Crescent-shaped Minnajima, ringed by a beach and trees, has a sheltered cove full of tidal pools.

Iejima Easter Lily Festival

Ie's spring Lily Festival is justifiably famous for the blinding white vistas of what is claimed to be over 1,000,000 growing lilies. Without having personally verified that count, it's safe to say that there are many, and what a spectacular sight it is. With the cooperation of the weather, not too hot, not too cold, the blooms can last up to three weeks.

KAMOMEIWA (カモメ岩; Kamomé-iwa). As miniscule as Minna may be, it nonetheless possesses a little satellite islet of its own. Just 820 feet (250 meters) due south of the mouth of Minna's cove is this little rock. The islet is a rectangle about 330 feet (100 meters) long from end to end, east to west, and about 96 feet (30 meters) from north to south. It's a green island, completely covered in vegetation. Translated, its name means "Seagull Rock" but there are no seagulls. Instead, a type of tern (アジサシ; *ajisashi*), similar to a seagull, flocks and breeds on Kamome during the summer months. When the tide is low you can walk to the islet. However, don't do this during the breeding season. The terns will become alarmed and fly at you to protect their territory and nests.

10 IEJIMA 伊江島

Compared to Minna, Iejima (伊江島; Ié-jima) is a giant, but naturally that's a relative term. It is a bit over 5 miles (8 kilometers) from east to west and 1.75–2.25 miles (3–5.5 kilometers) from north to south. Its middle section narrows down to about 1.5 miles (2.5 kilometers). In all, its area is a respectable 9 square miles (23 square kilometers). From almost any angle, except from the air, Iejima looks round. In actuality, it's nearly a perfect peanut shape or a figure eight.

Ie Island lies just off the northwestern tip of Okinawa's Motobu Peninsula. At their closest points, the two islands are separated

by only 3 miles (5 kilometers). However, to reach Iejima you take the ferry from Motobu Port (本部港; Motobu-kō). From there to Ie Port it's a little further, 7 miles (12 kilometers). For most of the year there are four ferries per day. However, at peak times in a number of summer months there are five. During the annual Easter Lily Festival there may be as many as nine sailings per day on the weekends. It only takes 30 minutes. Parking is free at the ferry parking lot at Motobu Port.

As it is a passenger and vehicle ferry, you can take your car or bike if you wish. Of course, that's an additional fare, but you could spend that same amount of money taking taxis on the island. It all depends on how much you wish to see on Ie and how long you plan to stay. The ferries arrive at Ie's small port Ie-ko (伊江港; Ié-kō). The harbor and its adjacent village are on the southeast shore of the island, maybe three-quarters of a mile (1 kilometer) from the Triple YYY Resort. If you're only going for the day, a couple of short taxi rides will not cost much. You can also rent a bicycle or a car on the island. It is also possible to fly to Iejima, though perhaps not so simple.

Clearly visible in aerial photos are Ie's three landing strips. The far western one is closed to the public. It's part of a small US Marine training facility that occupies the northwest one-eighth of the island. The central landing strip was the original Japanese military airfield from World War II. It was long ago abandoned in favor of the new and present airstrip. The old strip continues to be used as a local road connecting the north and south ends of the island. The current easternmost airstrip is the modern Iejima Airport (伊江島空港; Ié-jima-kūkō). Up until a couple of years ago there were several flights a day to Ie from Naha. Flights only

Iejima's three parallel landing strips.

Ie Island's rich productive farmland as seen from the top of Mt Gusuku.

take about 25 minutes. However, they were discontinued as there was simply not enough demand. It's still possible to fly to Ie, but only by charter. For a small group, it's not that expensive. Call Air Dolphin (098-858-3363).

For a relatively small place Ie has a large population, a little over 5,100. Why is this island so highly populated whereas others, equal in size or larger, are so empty? Of course, there is tourism, but the real answer lies in agriculture. Other than the marine training base, almost every square meter is planted with some type of desirable agricultural product. With one exception, Gusukuyama, which we'll mention below, the island is mostly flat, easy for farming. Most fortuitously it also has exceptionally rich soil. You'll see all kinds of crops, not just sugar cane, on Iejima. Local farmers grow sweet potatoes, peanuts, chrysanthemums, hi-grade tobacco for the Japanese cigarette industry and "logan," a traditional Okinawan vegetable.

One of the island's best-known products combines two of its farm goods, sugar cane and peanuts, into brown sugar-coated peanuts. Try them, they're a real treat. Farmer-ranchers also raise a variety of the black Ishigaki/Kōbé beef cattle. You'll see them grazing here and there. Thus, Ie Island supports a fairly large population, which is not the case on some of the other Ryukyu Islands. Although many residents congregate in Ie village, adjacent to the port, wherever you turn you find houses and people living all over this pretty little island.

Ie has several worthwhile sights, but its most famous attraction is seasonal: the spring Lily Festival. Easter lilies (テッポウユリ; *teppo-yuri*) are from southern Japan and the Ryukyus and several islands specialize in them. Ie is one of them. Every year, from

about the middle of April until the beginning of May, hundreds of thousands of lilies bloom at Lily Field Park (リリー・フィールド公園; Ririfirudo kōen), located alongside the northeastern shore. It's a marvelous spectacle and people from all over Japan flock to see it.

For many visitors the island's most famous year-round and permanent sight is Castle/Fortress Mountain, otherwise known as Mt Gusuku (城山; Gusuku-yama), although we're not finished with its names because *gusuku* is an Okinawan term. People from Japan would pronounce the first Kanji character as *shiro*, as in Shiro-yama ("Castle Mountain"). If that's not enough, Ie residents, in their dialect, call it Ijimatatcchū (イージマタッチュー), which similarly translates as "Ie Fortress Mountain."

Regardless of which name is used, it's an abrupt solid stone peak rising straight up from the surrounding fields, close to town. It is not a volcano, just an unusual thrust of rock. Its officially recorded height is 565 feet (172.2 meters) and you can experience every one of those feet/meters while climbing to the top. There's a staircase, thoughtfully provided, mostly carved into the rock all the way up. There are handrails along the way as well and these are most useful. You'll find people of all

Iejima Castle/Fortress Mountain (伊江島城山)

One of Okinawa's nicest close-in islands, Ie is easily reached by multiple daily ferries. Rising almost 575 feet (175 meters) from the center of one side of the island, Gusukuyama ("Castle Mountain" or Mt Gusuku), is Ie's best-known natural landmark. It's a great climb, with steep, handrailed stairs all the way. At the summit there's a 360-degree panorama over Iejima and the surrounding islands. With a sacred shrine at its base to pray for safe navigation, Mt Gusuku is known as Ie's guardian angel.

The Monument of Hokon is dedicated to Ie Island's casualties in the Battle of Okinawa.

Niiya-teiya Cave was used as a bomb shelter by 1,000 Ie residents during the invasion of the island.

ages and degrees of fitness grasping the rails, huffing and puffing and gasping all the way to the peak's topmost point. The best that can be said, which is always said of such places, is that you'll be rewarded with a wonderful view when you get there—if you don't die of a heart attack first.

For military visitors or students of World War II or journalism, Ie's most noteworthy sight will be the understated but moving memorial to Ernie Pyle. This renowned and courageous war reporter was struck down just days after the beginning of the Battle of Okinawa. The memorial's plaque reads: "At this spot the 77th Infantry Division lost a buddy Ernie Pyle 18 April 1945." After the war Ernie Pyle's body was moved to the Memorial Cemetery of the Pacific overlooking Honolulu. Ie's memorial to him is only

a few hundred feet west from the ferry dock when you arrive. A little further up the hill, through town, is the Japanese War Memorial dedicated to the other 3,500 people (soldiers and civilians) killed on Ie Island in the conflict. It's called the Monument of Hokon and there's a memorial service for these victims every year on April 21st.

There are a few other things worth mentioning about Ie. There is a fairly large seaside cave, Niiya-teiya (ニイヤテイヤ洞; Niiya-teiya-hora), to explore. It's on the southwest side of the island. It was used as a bomb shelter by over a thousand people during the World War II invasion of the island. For this reason its other name is Sennin-hora (千人洞; lit. "1,000 Person Cave"). There is a large stone inside known as Bijuru (ビジュル or びじゅる) or "Stone

Ernie Pyle (1900–1945)

Sadly, this being Okinawa, there are also tragic wartime notes on Iejima. Pulitzer prize award-winning journalist Ernest Taylor Pyle was one of 3,500 killed on this tiny island in the Battle of Okinawa. Only days into the campaign that was to precede the end of World War II, he was shot by a sniper. He'd been riding in a jeep at the front with the troops, something he had a habit of doing. Pyle is considered to have been the greatest war correspondent of the World War II, if not all wars. His love for the ordinary soldier and his disdain for pomp and circumstance were immortalized in the motion picture *G.I. Joe.* That film featured his coverage of the Italian campaign, another of the most difficult battles of the war. Pyle also covered the campaigns of North Africa, Sicily and France. Just before the Battle of Okinawa, he covered the landing at Iwojima. The site of the Ie ambush is marked by a small memorial and plaque. Each year, on the Sunday closest to April 18th, the American Legion marks the anniversary of his death with a wreath-laying ceremony.

The view of the East China Sea from the Wajii Cliffs observation platform on the northern side of Ie.

This aerial view shows tiny Ō at bottom left, Yagaji at mid-center and Kouri at center far right. The northern end of the Motobu Peninsula fills the upper left-hand side of the photo.

of Power." Legend has it that if a woman lifts this stone she will soon become pregnant.

On the central northern shore, a little west of Lily Field Park, is the Wajii (湧出), a freshwater spring that gushes out of the cliffs overlooking the East China Sea. It was, and still is, an important water source for the Ie islanders. Today, however, it's the spectacular view from the heights above the cliffs that's more appreciated and visited by tourists. There's an observatory platform (湧出展望台; Wajii tenbō-dai) that's been built on the top and the vista is fabulous.

Lastly, Ie is popular with visitors in part because of its well-developed tourist infrastructure. This is an island where there are a variety of things to do and see and there are nice places to stay. There are several hotels and over a dozen *minshuku* in all price ranges. There are also more than two dozen restaurants and half a dozen dive shops. For a little splurge, on the southeast corner of the island you'll find the very pleasant Triple YYY Resort. It's a not too big and not too overpriced hotel. It has its own beach, a good section of the much larger Ie Beach (伊江ビーチ; Ie-bīchi), an outdoor swimming pool and jacuzzi, and an indoor sauna. The rooms are spacious and the restaurant is excellent. If you are looking for a relaxing weekend out of the mainstream of Okinawa Main Island, this could be your place. One more thing, if you're a golfer, there's the Iejima Country Club, the longest "short course" in Okinawa. It bills itself as a par 58, 18-hole course or a par 72, 9-hole course.

From Iejima we'll take the ferry back to Okinawa and drive either around the top of the Motobu Peninsula on Route 505 or via the southern road, Route 449, towards Nago

and then head north on Route 58. Whichever route we choose, our next starting point is located at the junction of Routes 58 and 110. From here we'll be visiting the following three islands, Ōjima, Yagajijima and Kourijima, all of which are connected by roads and bridges to Okinawa mainland.

11 ŌJIMA 奥武島

This is yet another islet named Ōjima. You may have noticed that we have visited several islands that share this name. They all use the same Kanji characters which translate incomprehensibly—and nonsensically—as "Austrian Military (or Weapons) Island." The islet has nothing to do with either Austrian weapons or the Austrian military. Ōjima (奥武島; Ō-jima) is just a set of characters that makes no modern sense literally translated. However, there is one obscure meaning of the Chinese characters and they can be translated as a "traditional place to mourn the dead." This phrase has some resonance for this place, as we'll see below.

The crossing from Okinawa-hontō to Ōjima is less than 260 feet (80 meters) over a connecting bridge. The tiny islet is more or less oblong-shaped, with a long bottom left inward hook. Its overall size is about 1,640 feet (500 meters) long and 1,310 feet (400 meters) wide, except that its southwestern end extends another 985 plus feet (300 plus meters), giving it a total size of some 2,950 feet (900 meters) at its very longest. It is relatively hilly, much of it rising about 30–65 feet (10–20 meters). Its main function is to serve as a land bridge between Okinawa and the next larger islet, Yagaji.

Ōjima is at left, the bridge to Okinawa at right.

The bridge connecting Ōjima to Yagaji.

It would be completely accurate to state that Ōjima is uninhabited. However, those morbidly inclined might be tempted to quip that it's inhabited by quite a few—but they're not quite up to contesting their status, as Ō's (very) permanent residents are the occupants of the multitude of tombs on the island. That's really all you see on Ōjima: turtleback tombs and a few others. It's difficult to know whether this is purely traditional, mere coincidence or a matter of local zoning. Whether anyone could purchase a lot and build a home or, indeed, given the neighbors, whether anyone would want to purchase a lot and build a home is an open question. For all

In the 1800s the Okinawan name for all Western people was "Hollander," pronounced "Oranda," for one of their first associations with Europeans was with the Dutch. "Baka" means tomb. Thus, Oranda Baka translates as Hollander's Grave.

intents and purposes, this is a cemetery island and maybe not such a desirable spot for an overnight camping trip with the kids.

Whatever your sentiments on visiting a "dead" island, soon enough, in less than half a mile (less than a kilometer), you're off, for the bridge to the next island, connecting Ōjima to Yagajijima, comes straightaway.

12 YAGAJIJIMA 屋我地島

We'll next cross on to the island of Yagajijima (屋我地島; Yagaji-jima). Its southernmost point is connected to the northernmost tip of Ōjima by a 985-foot (300-meter) bridge. Yagaji is not very regularly shaped. It's probably best to say that it is a little longer than 2.5 miles (4 kilometers) from north to south at its greatest length and about 1.75 miles (3 kilometers) across from east to west at its widest. Its total surface area over its most irregular shape has been calculated at 3 square miles (7.81 square kilometers). No part of it is very high, and indeed its low profile helps make it a fully cultivated agricultural islet.

In fact, it's so well developed and there are so many roads criss-crossing the island that it's easy to get lost while driving around. Virtually every square foot of this islet is fully exploited and everywhere you turn there is a farm of one sort or another growing all manner of exotic crops. You'll see aloe cactus, bird-of-paradise flower farms, chrysanthemums and, of course, sugar cane and other crops.

Up until only a few years ago Yagaji was a dead end, literally and figuratively. Once you turned west on to the island from Route 58 on Okinawa Main Island (and crossing over Ōjima), there was no place to go other than to circle around the islet and return via the same way you entered. Perhaps this isolation

A view of Kourijima from Yagajijima. The two islands are linked by the bridge shown at right, built in 2005.

had something to do with the placement of the National Sanatorium Okinawa Airakuen (国立療養所沖縄愛楽園; Kokuritsu Yoryojo Okinawa Airakuen), a Hansen's Disease-leprosy colony. For it is here, at the north-easternmost point of the islet, that the colony was established in the early part of the 20th century. The number of residents at the sanatorium has varied over the years, from close to 1,000 in the post-World War II period to as few as several hundred today.

As is the case in many other countries, Japan has had a complex and sometimes controversial relationship with this disease, and like others its history includes severe stigmatization and forced segregation of patients to isolated leprosariums. Okinawa's colony was established by Japanese Episco-palian missionary Keisai Aoki (青木恵哉; 1893–1969) under the leadership of Hannah Riddell (1855–1932), an Englishwoman who devoted her life to the sufferers of leprosy in Japan. Aoki was stricken with the disease when he was 16 years old. He was baptized and began missionary work in 1918. He had written to Riddell and it was she who suggested that he go to Okinawa. At the time there were lepers living in caves as their pitiful dwellings had been burned by the islanders. They sought refuge on the then remote and isolated Yagaji Island and built what was to become the Kunigami (later Okinawa) Airakuen Sanatorium. The colony still functions. It's affiliated with several religious organizations on Okinawa.

There's one more remote and isolated place on Yagaji, Oranda baka (オランダ墓), two side-by-side tombs of French seamen who died near here over 150 years ago. In June of 1846, a fleet of three French ships sailed into Unten Port, at Nakijin, to conduct trade with the Ryukyu kingdom. They stayed

about one month. During that time two crew members took ill and died and were buried on a small cape, Untenbaru, on Yagajijima. Their names, the names of their ships and the dates of their deaths are in-scribed on their tombstones.

There's a stainless steel plaque at the gravesite which gives this information in three languages, Japanese, English and French. It's a rather touching little place, just across the saltwater channel that sepa-rates Unten Port from Yagaji. It's actually not that easy to find. Another way to describe its location is to say that Cape Untenbaru is the northwesternmost point of Yagaji Island.

Earlier, we said that Yagaji was a dead end. This is no longer the case. In the past 10 years two modern bridges have been con-structed that have formed new links with other places in Okinawa. One bridge con-nects Yagaji's western end to the Motobu Peninsula, the other extends from the north-ern end of Yagaji to the island of Kouri. We'll go there next.

⑬ KOURIJIMA 古宇利島
Opened to the car-loving Japanese or, rather, Okinawan, public by the 2005 bridge, Kourijima (古宇利島; Kouri-jima) is a tradi-tional small island of about 350 inhabitants It's almost perfectly round, roughly 1.25 miles (2 kilometers) in diameter, 1 square mile (3.11 square kilometers) in area and 5 miles (8 kilometers) in circumference. It's actually quite a high island, more or less a plateau, almost all of which is just over 330 feet (100 meters) tall. Its only village and harbor face south to Yagaji Island and the Motobu Peninsula. Formerly, its port hosted a small ferry that connected it to Okinawa, but that's no longer necessary due to the bridge. The rest of the island is sparsely

A view of Yagajijima from the plateau-like Kourijima, with the linking bridge on the left.

populated but intensively cultivated. There's a ring road that circles the island and you can drive it in about 10 minutes. The main agricultural products are sugar cane and purple sweet potatoes.

Kouri has one nice beach, right next to the port, which is called Chigunu (ちぐぬ浜; Chigunu-hama). The island's specialty product is a type of sea urchin. You'll see them for sale in the shops in the village and by roadside vendors. Called *shirahige-uni* (シラヒゲウニ), they are collected just offshore in the surrounding clear clean waters. They taste of the sea—salty, fresh and delicious.

For many visitors, half the fun of visiting Kouri is getting there. It's a long bridge, almost 1.25 miles (2 kilometers) over the sea. When it first opened a few years ago, there were bumper-to-bumper traffic jams of Okinawans waiting their turn to see the island. Many of these visitors had lived on Okinawa all their lives yet never visited this small place. The traffic jams are over but Kourijima remains.

From Kouri we'll retrace our steps back over the bridge, on to Yagajijima, then head south and west about 1.25 miles (2 kilometers) and take the brand new bridge that connects the west coast of Yagaji to the Motobu Peninsula, thus putting us back on Okinawa mainland. From here, it's about 1 mile (1.5 kilometers) north to Unten Port and our ferry connections to the next, and final, group of islands making up the Okinawa-shotō.

Altogether, since starting this clockwise circuit of Okinawa main island's near neighbors, we've gone around almost 360 degrees. The last little group of about a dozen islands and islets lies approximately 15–25 miles

(24–40 kilometers) north of Unten Port and the Motobu Peninsula. It is also accurate to say that they are about 25–28 miles (38–45 kilometers) west of Yoron-tō and around 20 miles (32 kilometers) northwest of Cape Hedo. Three in the group are inhabited. The two largest, Izena and Iheya, are each served by twice-daily ferry connections, all out of Unten Port. There is no active airport service on either island, so the ferry is the only way to reach them.

14 IZENAJIMA 伊是名島

One of the two largest islands in this mini-cluster of islands, Izenajima (伊是名島; Izéna-jima), is the more southerly and closer to Okinawa. As the crow flies, it's just over 14 miles (22 kilometers) from the northernmost spot on the Motobu Peninsula to the southernmost point on Izena, but the ferry takes the shipping route from Okinawa's Unten Port (運天港; Unten-kō) to Izena's Nakada Port (仲田港; Nakada-kō) and that's more like 20 miles (32 kilometers).

Year round, other than when cancelled due to severe weather, there are two daily ferry round trips to Izena. The first sailing leaves Unten Port at 9:00AM and arrives just under an hour later on Izena at 9:55AM. The ferry docks for less than one hour, then departs at 10:30AM for the return trip to Okinawa, arriving back at Unten Port at 11:25AM.

The ship rests at home port until 1:30PM when it departs on its second daily sailing to Izena, arriving at Nakada Port at 2:25PM. The ferry docks until 3:30PM when it begins its final journey of the day, back to Unten Port, arriving at 4:25PM. The Izena ferry is large and comfortable and takes passengers, vehicles and freight.

Notice that with this schedule it's possible to make a quick one-day visit to Izena, something that's not possible with Izena's immediate neighbor, Iheya. A 9:00AM departure from Okinawa's Unten Port puts you on Izena just before 10:00AM. Granted your visit will be short, only five and a half hours, but with a bike, scooter, car or taxi, you can see most of the island in this time if you wish. You can return to Unten Port on the 3:30PM ferry.

In shape Izenajima is mostly round, a bit longer than wide. In size it's a little less than 3 miles (5 kilometers) in length from its central northern tip to its central southern tip. From east to west the island's size varies from about 1.75–to 3.75 (3–6 kilometers) wide. Its area is 6 square miles (15.3 square kilometers) and its coastline circumference is 10 miles (16 kilometers) long. Although most of the island is fairly flat and cultivated with sugar cane, there are a few high points. The two highest are Mt Ufu (大野山; Ufuyama, also called Ōno-san) at 394 feet (120 meters) on the northwest end, and Mt Chijin (チヂン岳; Chijin-daké) at 390 feet (119 meters) in the southeast.

Izena is primarily a farming island of about 1,760 occupants. As is the case with so many of the smaller Ryukyus, that's a rather dramatic decline. Its population in 2003, less than 10 years ago, was almost 1,900. During the 1970s, it was approximately 3,000 and in the 1960s it was 4,400. Because of the declining population on both Izena and Iheya, there are no longer schools operating beyond junior high. Parents of high school age children must board them on Okinawa during the week. They can come home only on weekends.

There are five distinct villages on the island and all are very small. Nakada (仲田), which is located on Izena's central east coast, and where the port is located, isn't really much larger than the others, but it has almost all the *minshuku*, more than half a dozen. A particularly nice one, the Mishima (美島 or みしま) is only 330 feet (100 meters) from the dock. The others are close by, all a short walk from the marine terminal, which incidentally houses an excellent restaurant. It's no trouble finding a place to stay or eat on Izena. The main administrative town, Izena village, is only three-quarters of a mile (1 kilometer) away, more or less in the center of the island. There are several fairly large *minshuku* there as well. The village also holds a very nice small museum of island ethnography. It charges a modest 200 Yen admission.

On the island's northwest coast, about 1.5 miles (2.5 kilometers) from Izena village, there is an airstrip and a decrepit air terminal. It functioned as a working airport for a few years but closed due to lack of traffic. The airstrip is maintained to a degree that it could be used in an emergency. Likewise, there is a helipad in Izena Village that can be used for medical evacuations or other emergencies.

Izena's best sights are in the southeast, below Izena village. They include the Mountain Forest Park (伊是名山森林公園; Izéna-yama-shinrin-kōen), which has several very beautifully sited observatories, a few nice short hiking trails and a couple of very sacred and interesting *utaki* sites. The best-known observatory is Gitara (ギタラ展望台; Gitara tenbō-dai) at Izena's very southernmost tip. It's a very scenic spot overlooking Izena's most dramatic display of huge rocks.

Ajacent to Gitara, at the southeasternmost section of Izena, you'll find the Futamigaura Seashore (二見ケ浦海岸; Futami-gaura kaigan), a beautiful wild and rugged section of coastline. It has a good view over to the islet of Yanaha.

Less than a mile (2 kilometers) to the west, on Izena's southwestern end, you'll find the

The Izena passenger and vehicle ferry makes two daily round trips between Unten Port and Isena.

In this aerial photo from the west, Gushikawa is on the left, Izena at center and Yanaha on the right.

Umigitara Islet, seen at low tide from Gitara Observatory, with Yanaha in the background.

Takara-no Shima minshuku, located right on Izena Beach, is very popular with Japanese visitors.

island's best beach (伊是名ビーチ; Izéna-bīchi). If you really like the beach and would prefer to stay here, you're in luck as there is a very nice *minshuku* right on it. It's called Takara-no Shima (宝の島; lit. "Treasure Island") and it's very popular with Japanese visitors.

Izena has a few satellite islets surrounding it, mostly to the south, but there's one on the east coast near the harbor and a fairly large one to the north. The northern one, Gushi-kawa, lies actually midway between Izena and Iheya. We'll describe it as we get to Iheya.

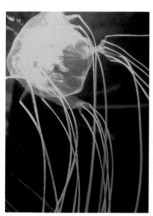

Box Jellyfish or Sea Wasp

Most of the roughly 2,000 species of jellyfish around the world are harmless, but not all. Jellyfish capture their prey using nematocysts, a type of specialized stinging structure. Although most stings are mild enough to not be too bothersome for most people, some, such as the Portuguese Man o' War (*Physalia physalis*), are particularly painful, but rarely fatal. However, one group (class Cubozoa) stands out as truly dangerous, even lethal. Commonly known as "box" jellyfish, they differ most visibly from ordinary jellyfish in that their medusae (their "umbrellas") are cube-shaped, not round or dome-shaped. Their umbrella's underside contains a mechanism whereby they can concentrate and expel water in a jet-like fashion, thereby increasing their speed and allowing them to hunt their prey. Most regular jellyfish merely drift in the ocean currents. Box jellies have a more highly developed nervous system than others and possess true eyes. Most ordinary jellyfish can only distinguish between light and dark. The most venomous species of box jellyfish are found in the tropical waters of the Indo-Pacific, which includes Okinawa. There are at least three dozen different species spanning half a dozen taxonomic families, but one of the most common and dangerous is *Chironex fleckeri*, commonly known as the "sea wasp." It is an infamous lethal species living in warm coastal waters from northern Australia to Vietnam. The amount of venom in one animal is enough to kill 60 adult humans. Its closely related cousin *Chironex yamaguchii* is the one most usually found in Okinawan waters where it is known as the Habu jellyfish (ハブクラゲ; *Habu kurage*). Their bodies are transparent and thus almost impossible to see in the water. They are not large, only about 5–6 inches (12–15 centimeters) in body dimension, with about 3–4 feet (1.5 meters) of trailing tentacles. The stinging cells of the *Habu kurage* contain poison clusters that burst, releasing strings of stingers into an unwary swimmer that can cause permanent scarring. The venom can cause the victim to stop breathing and even cause cardiac arrest. The box jelly's toxins attack the heart and nervous system. Some people go into shock and drown. Some die of heart failure before making it back to shore. Fortunately, most victims survive although none will ever forget their encounter with the sea wasp.

Crescent-shaped, uninhabited Yanaha seen from the southern tip of Izena.

Yanoshitajima, Hinpunkusashi and Kamikusashi, satellite islets of Izena, itself a satellite of Yanaha.

King Shō En (尚円)

Izena's most famous son was born to a peasant family in 1415 but was destined to become the founder of the Second Shō Dynasty and King of the Ryūkyū Kingdom in 1469. He died in 1476 after only a seven-year reign. He was succeeded by his brother. A sister, who he appointed as a high priestess, established a lineage of high priestesses that continued until the 20th century. Shō En's remains are in the royal mausoleum near Shuri Castle in Naha. There is a prominent tomb for his parents on Izena.

UMIGITARA (海ギタラ; Umi-gitara). This dramatic rock stands just off the southernmost tip of Izena's coast. You can walk to it at low tide. It's more or less round, and measures approximately 100–115 feet 30–35 meters) in diameter. Its width is about the same as its height.

YANAHAJIMA (屋那覇島; Ya-naha-jima). One mile (1.5 kilometers) south of Umigitara Rock and Izena's southern end we'll find the largest uninhabited islet of Izena. Yanaha is a not too badly formed crescent in shape, close to 1 mile (1.5 kilometers) long from north to south and anywhere from 985 to 1,640 feet (300 to 500 meters) wide along almost any point of its east to west distance. It's a flat island almost completely ringed with sandy beaches. It has an area of a little less than one-third of a square mile (1 square kilometer), yet a circumference of 3 miles (5 kilometers). Its eastern cove side inside the crescent rises to a sandy hill with an altitude of 40 feet (12 meters) and is completely covered in vegetation, including many sago palms. Yanaha's western outside crescent side is almost barren except for some scrub pandanus trees.

Because the island was inhabited up until World War II, there are the remains of a couple of small roads and the vestiges of an old reservoir and well that were used at the time. They can be found in the center of the island. Yanaha is used today as a camping site by Okinawan Boy Scouts and others. It's open to the public, so anyone may land here and pitch a tent.

YANOSHITAJIMA (屋ノ下島; Ya-no-shita-jima). This is really no more than one fairly large vegetation-covered rock, along with some bordering rock friends, occupying a little dry space some 660 feet (200 meters) off the northwest tip of Yanaha Islet and 1.25 miles (2 kilometers) south of Izena Beach. The biggest islet of the little group is round in shape and about 200 feet (60 meters) in diameter.

HINPUNKUSASHI (ヒンプン クサシ; Hinpun-ku-sashi). A mere 1,360 feet (415 meters) to the northwest of Yanoshita Rock is this little batch of pointy stones, more a boating hazard than an island. The largest is almost 230 feet (70 meters) in diameter. Most are about 80 feet (25 meters), big enough to cause a problem if sailing blind at night.

KAMIKUSASHI (カーミ クサシ; Kami-ku-sashi). Here's one more, and the largest of these three sets of rocks orbiting about Yanahajima. It's about 2,700 feet (825 meters) north of Hinpunkusashi or 1,820 feet (250 meters) southwest of Izena Beach. It's actually a triple-rock islet in one, each one connected to the next, approximately 660 feet (200 meters) in length overall, the largest of the group about 230 feet (70 meters) on its own.

URUGAMIJIMA (降神島; Uru-gami-jima; lit. "God Descending Island"). How's that for a name? We've moved from Yanaha and its neighbors off the southern coast of Izena to Izena's eastern shore, and here, just below the harbor at Nakada, we'll find this uninhabited islet and maybe, if we're lucky, we'll find God descending on to Earth.

If our Deity is to appear, it has to be said that He or She hasn't been too picky about their landing place for it must be admitted that God Descending Island isn't any big deal. It's just your usual run-of-the-mill offshore rock. This one is about 1,640 feet (500 meters) east of the southern end of Izena and a little more than three-quarters of a mile (1 kilometer) southeast of Nakada Port.

For better or worse, Urugami Island is a barren rock, with no particular vegetation to speak of. Its size is approximately 660 feet (200 meters) long by perhaps 330 feet (100 meters) wide.

GUSHIKAWAJIMA (具志川島; Gushi-kawa-jima). This uninhabited islet lies midway between Izena and Iheya, about 1.3 miles (2.2 kilometers) north of the top of Izena and 1.25 miles (2 kilometers) below southern-most Iheya. It's a long, narrow island, a little more than 1 mile (2 kilometers) in length from east to west and anywhere from 325 to 1,310 feet (100 to 400 meters) in width from north to south. It's surface area is a

Urugamijima ("God Descending Island") is little more than a barren rock off Izena's southern coast.

Uninhabited Gushikawajima, midway between Izena and Iheya, is surrounded by sandy beaches.

little more than 0.42 square kilometers and its circumference a little more than 2.5 miles (4 kilometers). Much of Gushikawa is surrounded by sandy beaches but the main central section is covered in vegetation. The island has a fresh water spring that used to serve its residents. It was populated from the 1800s until it was abandoned in 1970. There is a dock on the north side of the island. As is the case with all these uninhabited islets, there is no public transportation to reach them. You'll need your own boat if you wish to visit.

15 IHEYAJIMA 伊平屋島

Although the bottom of Iheyajima (伊平屋島; Ihéya-jima) is only about 2.75 miles (4.5 kilometers) north of the top of Izena, there is no ferry service between the two. To reach Izena from Iheya, or vice versa, it's necessary to return to Okinawa and take another ferry back out. From the northernmost tip of Okinawa's Motobu Peninsula to the south-ernmost point of Iheya, it's 20 miles (32 kilometers). By the most direct sea route however, it's a little further, just a bit over 25 miles (40 kilometers). That's the sailing distance from Okinawa Unten Port (運天港; Unten-kō) to Iheya's port at Maedomari (前泊港; Maedomari-kō). It takes an hour and 20 minutes.

Like Izena, Iheya is served by a twice daily scheduled ferry service. The first ferry leaves Unten Port every day at 11:00AM and arrives at Maedomari at 12:20PM. There's a 40 minute unloading and loading time, after which it departs Iheya at 1:00PM making the return trip to Okinawa, arriving at 2:20PM.

The ship begins its second sailing of the day to Iheya, departing Unten Port at 3:00PM and arriving at Iheya's Maedomari Port at 4:20PM. There it moors until the next morning when it departs Iheya at 9:00AM, and returns to Okinawa Unten Port at 10:20AM.

Iheya is served twice daily by the Iheya passenger and vehicle ferry from Okinawa's Unten Port.

Accordingly, the two daily departures from Unten Port to Iheya are at 11:00AM and 5:00PM. The two daily sailings from Iheya to Unten are at 9:00AM and 1:00PM.

As a result of this schedule, it's not possible to make a meaningful one-day visit to Iheya since 40 minutes really does not do the island justice. You'll have to spend the night. That's, of course, no big hardship because Iheya is a particularly beautiful island, easily worth a day or two of your time.

Iheya is long and narrow with dramatically high mountains for an island of its size. From end to end, it's about 9 miles (14 kilometers) north to south, and anywhere from three-quarters of a mile to 1.75 miles (1–3 kilometers) wide from east to west. Its surface area is not quite 8 square miles (20 square kilometers) and its circumference is almost 25 miles (40 kilometers). Over 80 percent percent of the island is a mountain range over 660 feet (200 meters) tall. Its highest point is Mt Kayō (賀陽山; Kayō-san) at 294 meters (965 feet). In between its many mountains, Iheya's relatively small portions of arable land are fully cultivated and there are especially productive valleys planted with rice and sugar cane.

The population of Iheya is approximately 1,350. That's down from around 2,000 in the 1970s and 3,000 in the 1960s. It's sometimes hard to discern where one village leaves off and another begins, but there are perhaps four or five distinct villages scattered about, but most are on the central or southeastern side of the island. Many of Iheya's residents live in the island's largest village, Iheya village, which for all practical purposes encompasses Maedomari, the port. It is located on the central east coast. For a small town, it's spread over quite a distance and it's not accurate to call it compact. It's a pleasant town with a half dozen *minshuku* and several good restaurants. Note, however, that none of the *minshuku* are very close to the port and so

walking upon arrival is not a very good option. All will pick you up at the ferry terminal when you arrive if you make a reservation beforehand. There is also some lodging on Noho. We'll discuss that islet further below. For those camping (and thus will not get picked up by a *minshuku*), there are car and bicycle rentals at the harbor so you can get your vehicle on arrival and go.

For the Ryukyu sightseer interested in the beautiful scenery of some of the smaller islands and interested in a traditional way of life perhaps not so commonly found today on a "big" busy island like Okinawa, Iheya has it all. Although mountainous, it is, in fact, an agricultural island. And there's some tourism, but not much.

What really stands out is the island's natural beauty, which is quite exceptional. It has several excellent, almost deserted beaches; high vistas crossed by excellent hiking trails; Noho, an attached, interesting smaller island to its south; and a particularly scenic northern cape famous for being covered in Chinese fan palm trees. We'll start at the top and work our way south and west.

Cape Dana (田名岬; Dana-misaki; also pronounced Tana-misaki), the northeastern

Ferries arrive at Maedomari Port Marine Terminal.

Maedomari Port on Iheya's central east coast.

An aerial view of mountainous Iheyajima from the east. Nohojima is at far left (south).

tip of Iheya, rather dramatically terminates with a 308-foot (94-meter)-high mountain capped with a lighthouse. It's called Dana Kubayama (田名のクバ山; Dana-no Kubayama). There's a small road that leads to the summit. It boasts two remarkable things, a spectacular view that includes the ocean to the north and east and a good part of the island to the south and west, and thousands and thousands of Chinese fan Areca palm trees known as *kuba* in local Iheyan dialect. The trees are treasured as special places where gods descend. It's unusual to find such a dense group of them and this holds special *kami*, thus it is an *utaki* sacred place of worship. In fact, this species of palm is typical, but not common, in the Ryukyus, and for whatever reason—a stray seed dropped by a passing bird or a seedling floated onshore that took hold—they have flourished and congregate here. It's a unique natural sight.

A few hundred meters below the cape, on the Iheya's northwest shore, you'll find Shioshita Beach (潮下浜; Shio-shita hama, also called Suga-hama) It's a nice stretch of white sand populated only by sea birds and crabs. If you're looking for a place to get away from it all, you'll find it here.

Only a little below Shioshita Beach you'll come to a very interesting section of coast.

View of Iheya from Cape Dana in the northeast.

It's a fine stretch of shore populated by a mas of great stones of volcanic basalt. Two in particular stand out. First, a little west away from the end, perhaps three-quarters of a mile (1 kilometer), you'll come to Muzoumizu (無蔵水; also spelled Nzomiji; lit. "Collection of Water"). It has a freshwater spring at its top, which in itself is extraordinarily unusual. Naturally, it's a place of legend. It is said that a long time ago a fisherman went out to sea from here. He was lost and all gave up hope except his wife who waited patiently for years, drinking from this spring. The presumed widow was beautiful and many tried to marry her but she

A mass of volcanic balsalt stones on Shioshita Beach, also called Suga-hama, on Iheya's northwest shore.

Iheya Rice Paddy Scarecrow
There's an artist on Iheya. He or she has planted over a dozen scarecrows like this, each with its own quirky personality.

The cave is unusual, for you must first climb before you can descend. It's up a steep little rock mountain, where a staircase is provided, and then down into its depths. The entrance is through a quite narrow slice of rock. Those a bit on the hefty side will not be able to enter. Once inside, it's clean white sand all the way down to its bottom. It's about 80 feet (25 meters) deep and there's one large hall about 30–50 feet (10–15 meters) across. There is an altar and people come here to pray. There are mythological Okinawan legends about this cave. It was supposedly the hiding hole for Amanoterasu-ōmikami, a sun goddess who hid herself for she could not bear to watch the other gods quarreling.

About 1.25 miles (2 kilometers) below the beach and cave you'll come to the next big "sight" of Iheya, a huge pine tree called Nentō Hira-matsu (念頭平松). It's a Ryukyu black pine estimated to be about 250 years old. It is 26 feet (8 meters) high and has a central trunk with a diameter somewhat larger than 3 feet (1 meter). Its crown is roughly 80 feet (25 meters) across. It's called the "Umbrella Pine" and that name comes

Exterior and interior of Kumaya Cave, the subject of several mythological Okinawan legends.

remained chaste, always waiting. Years later he miraculously returned—and the expression in Japanese—which does not translate very well, is that this water gave his wife sustenance and hope. People with little hope, but with faith and determination, climb this rock and drink from the fount.

The second spectacular rock is another three-quarters of a mile (1 kilometer) further west and just a bit offshore. It's called Yahe-iwa (ヤヘー岩). Since it is, in fact, a little island, we'll mention it separately below when we discuss Iheya's surrounding islets.

Cross the island from its northwestern-most end to its northeasternmost and right below the cape at Kubayama you'll find two places of interest: the Kumaya Seacoast (クマヤ海岸; Kuma-ya-kaigan) and Kumaya Cave (クマヤ洞窟; Kuma-ya-dōkutsu). In Iheyan dialect, Kumaya means a "hiding hole," a reference to the cave. Note that Kumaya is also frequently spelled くまや. Although the beach is not Iheya's finest, it's still an interesting walk along the shoreline and there are a few short sandy sections. Close nearby there are showers and toilet facilities, making it a good camping location.

Muzou-mizu ("Collection of Water") Rock, so-named for the unusual freshwater spring at its top.

Yonezaki Beach, which has the finest white sand on Iheya, is particularly popular with campers.

from the way its branches grow on all sides like an umbrella that is spread wide open. The Nentou-Hiramatsu Pine Tree, along with Kume's Five-branched Pine, are known as the two most famous great pines of Okinawa.

Coming now to about the center of the island, you'll find the Koshidake Forest Reserve (腰岳森林公園; Koshi-daké Shinrin-kōen). It's a park that includes a good seaside hike and summer cabins that can be rented. You can hike from the forest to the sea. The hike is not long but leads from near the Koshidake lighthouse to the Katasumi Shrine in Gakiya, near Iheya village. Thus, it's a trail across the island. There's a scenic spot where both the sea and the mountains can be seen from the Koshidake lighthouse.

In the springtime the hillsides bloom with multicolored azaleas and sweet-scented wild gardenia. In every level place you'll find the ubiquitous white Easter lilies and all shades of pink to red Amaryllis.

Only a few more miles south and west and you'll reach the bottom of the island, called Shimajiri (島尻; lit. "butt of the island"). It's a very narrow tip with Iheya's best beaches on both sides of it. It's called Yonezaki Beach (米崎ビーチ; Yoné-zaki bīchi). Here you'll find the finest white sand on Iheya and the finest free camping site. There are many designated camp sites and ample free parking. There are good public showers and toilet facilities. Many Japanese and Okinawans come to Iheya just for this idyllic location.

Nentō Hira-matsu, aptly nicknamed the "Umbrella Pine" for its spreading branches, is a 250-year-old-Ryukyu black pine. It is one of Okinawa's two famous pines, the other being Kume's Five-branched Pine.

The Noho Great Bridge connects mainland Iheya and Noho Island to its south.

Yonezaki Beach used to be the end of the road but in 1978 a 203-foot (62-meter)-long bridge was built connecting mainland Iheya to little Noho Island. The old bridge was replaced by a new larger bridge, Noho ōhashi (野甫大橋; lit. Noho Great Bridge) in 2003/4 to accommodate heavier truck traffic. Let's cross this bridge when we come to it and go to Noho.

Noho's friendly and hospitable Minshuku Noho.

NOHOJIMA (野甫島; Noho-jima). This is the third inhabited islet in our final set of islands comprising the Okinawa-shotō. It's less than 330 feet (100 meters) south of Iheya and used to be separated from its much larger neighbor, but over 30 years ago a bridge was constructed linking the two. It's difficult to say whether Noho Island more resembles a square or a rectangle. It's not very uniform one way or another. It's a tiny postage stamp of an island, less than a mile (1.3 kilometers) at its longest, more or less east to west, and a little less than three-quarters of a mile (1 kilometer) from north to south. Its total surface area is less than half a square mile (1.06 square kilometers) and much of it is cultivated with sugar cane.

Depending on whether they are home or not, Noho has a population of about 140. Most residents live in the one small village which you reach as soon as you cross over the bridge. By the way, if you make the very first right-hand turn after the bridge, which is just before entering the village proper, you'll find Noho's very friendly and hospitable *minshuku*. It's called, logically enough: Minshuku Noho (民宿のほ). It's a nice place to stay as there is an excellent beach just across the street. Tatami-style rooms are reasonably priced and your meals are includ-

ed in the rates. They take some special pride in serving the very freshest of fish in the evening meal. In the summer they use their large manicured lawn for outdoor music concerts and barbeques. It's nothing fancy but it's a most relaxed environment and you'll discover that some of your fellow guests have been coming here for years.

Here's another little surprise for such a small island. Noho has a delightful little Salt Museum. It's called the Noho Salt Museum (倶楽部野甫の塩; Kurabu Noho no shio). The owner has traveled the world visiting salty places. He's studied the subject, he's taken pictures, he's got samples which he's prepared into exhibits and he'll be glad to show you around. They also sell the very finest sea salt at the museum shop.

At Noho's southwesternmost tip you'll find the Shimazaki Seashore (島崎海岸; Shima-zaki kaigan), a great scenic spot. You'll have a beautiful view to a group of large offshore rocks and there are mangrove trees where the shore meets the sea. From here you can see Izena and, on a clear day, Okinawa. Some 2,780 feet (850 meters) across the island to its southeasternmost end you'll find a nice, although small, beach, some large rock formations and a good view to Gushikawa Islet. Also at this southernmost point you'll see an ancient freshwater well. You can peer down its shaft. It's deep, much deeper than you might have assumed. The well is virtually in the shadow of the modern electricity generating windmill.

FIFI-GAMA (フィーフィーガマ; Fīfī-gama). As Iheya is to Okinawa (a satellite island), and Noho is to Iheya (a satellite islet), Fifi-gama is to Noho (a satellite rock). It's little, only about 250 feet (75 meters) long by 82 (25 meters) wide and it lies 410 feet (125 meters) off the nicest beach on Noho, on the northern end of the island, across the street from the Minshuku Noho. There is a small cave on the islet, said to be the home of Fifi, the Noho dialect's name for Kijimunā (キジムナー), the mischievous Okinawan spirit.

Kijimuna are the subject of Okinawan fairy tales and, among many other characteristics, are said to be great fishermen. They are spirits of the woods and forests and most commonly live in banyan trees. They are supposedly about the size of three to four-year-old children but have especially large heads and are covered in red hair. Many tales

The small but delightful Noho Salt Museum.

have them playing tricks or pranks, fooling humans, but occasionally they befriend them. Unfortunately, these friendships usually end badly, with the Kijimuna insulted or offended in some way, and then they leave to hide again in the forest.

YAHEIWA (ヤヘー岩; Yahé-iwa). This rather dramatic solitary rock, which is also known as Yahégusuku (ヤヘーグスク or ヤヘー城; lit. "Fortress Yahe" or "Yahe Castle"), is

In this aerial view of Cape Kyan, the true southernmost point of Okinawa Main Island is at the upper right corner. The lighthouse and peace monuments are midway along the rocky Kyan cliffs.

located about 165 feet (50 meters) off the northwest shore of Iheya. It's roughly 165 feet (50 meters) in diameter and almost equally tall. It's a "pure" rock, devoid of vegetation. It is uninhabited and uninhabitable. There are ruins on its top. Although it seems much too small to have been a *gusuku* ruin, it's possible that it could have been a watch post or signal station of some kind. Only a little stonework remains to be seen, but you can walk across from the beach to the rock at low tide and have a look.

We began our discussion of the Okinawa-shotō some 75 islands ago with Adakashima, a tiny islet at the northeasternmost point of Okinawa. We'll end it here with this tiny islet, Yahé-iwa, just a large rock, in fact, offshore from Okinawa's northwesternmost island of Iheya. We've completed a full circle, having gone around almost 360 degrees beginning and ending near Okinawa's northern tip, Cape Hedo.

That completes our look at Okinawa-hontō and the Okinawa shotō. It's a large group of islands and it's taken quite some time to visit them all. We'll next set sail (in fact, we'll have to fly) about 186 miles (300 kilometers) southwest to the Miyako-shotō, or the Miyako Archipelago. It's a beautiful, though much smaller group of islands, especially when compared to the number of islands surrounding Okinawa Main Island. Altogether, there are only eight major islands in the Miyako group.

Before leaving the Okinawa Islands, however, it might be worth reflecting on this, the largest group of islands in the Ryukyu Archipelago, and offering some guidance. The fact is that most people simply won't have the time—weeks or months—required to visit all these islands. For most visitors a trip to Okinawa may mean sightseeing Okinawa Main Island, Okinawa-hontō, and that's it. So if a traveler had just a few extra days and could visit only one small island in the Okinawa-shotō group, which one might it be? In other words, let's choose one island and let it be representative of all the other little islands.

It's a tough call because it's difficult to say which of the many islands in the Okinawa Archipelago is the most beautiful or the most interesting, for every one is beautiful and everyone is interesting in its own way. Each island is a little different from the others and all have something to offer. However, if you

Yaheiwa, a dramatic solitary rock devoid of vegetation, has unidentifuable ruins on top.

Fifi-gama, a satellite rock off Noho, has a small cave, said to be the home of an Okinawan spirit.

could visit only one, you'd be well advised to consider Kumejima. It's only a few hours away by ferry or a very short flight. It's mountainous yet has great beaches. It has a well-developed tourist infrastructure, that is, nice hotels and restaurants, and it has a number of minor sights worth seeing.

A similar choice might be Agunijima, but it is less developed and has much less infrastructure. The island is more remote, more wild and windswept, but it's dramatically beautiful. Looking for calm, peaceful, perhaps not so wild but still beautiful? Then perhaps Iheyajima?

Here's another island to consider, and although it's not in the Okinawa group, it's close by—Yoron-tō. Its beaches are second to none and the island has an excellent tourist support structure.

Ask others who have visited these small islands. Get a few opinions and try to work out what's right for you, but whichever you may choose, you can't go too far wrong. They're all beautiful.

Chapter 11

THE MIYAKO ISLANDS 宮古諸島
Pristine waters, rich coral reefs

1. **Miyakojima** 宮古島
2. **Irabujima** 伊良部島
3. **Shimojijima** 下地島
4. **Taramajima** 多良間島
5. **Minnajima** 水納島

As often as you'll see references to the Miyako Island group as Miyako-shotō, you will just as frequently see the group listed as Miyako-rettō (宮古列島) or Miyako-guntō (宮古群島). All three terms are used. The Miyako group lies about halfway between Okinawa and Taiwan, some 186 miles (297 kilometers) southwest of Naha, Okinawa, and around 75 miles (120 kilometers) northeast of Ishigaki in the Yaeyama group. Less visited and less crowded by tourists than the Yaeyamas, the Miyakos are nonetheless popular with divers. The islands have some of the finest diving locations in the Ryukyus, with crystal-clear turquoise waters and pristine coral reefs. These clear waters are welcomed by non-divers too. Many beach-goers come to the Miyakos for the warm waters and clean, white sandy shores that are found throughout the islands.

Altogether, there are eight islands in the chain with a combined area of 79 square miles (205 square kilometers). Miyako is directly connected by bridges to two smaller islands, Ikema in the north and Kurima in the south. In addition, there's tiny Ōgami Islet to the northeast and the relatively large twin islands of Irabu and Shimoji to the west. Sometime in 2014 these latter two islands will also be connected by a great bridge to Miyako. That makes six islands, all quite close to one another. The last two of the eight, Tarama and Minna, are around 40 miles (60 kilometers) to the west.

By and large, all the islands are flat or moderately hilly. None are mountainous. The highest point of all the islands is Miyako's Mt Yoko (横岳; Yoko-daké), at just under 375 feet (115 meters). The islands

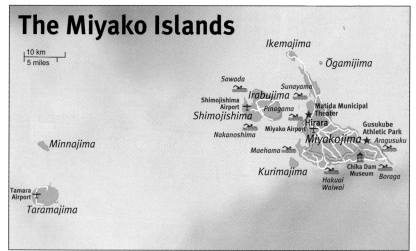

The Hirara–Irabu passenger ferry.

Local ferries at Hirara Port.

Miyako Airport on the west side of Miyakojima.

are almost entirely composed of coral and Ryukyu limestone. More than half the total area is devoted to agriculture, mostly sugar cane, but also some tobacco and other products. The population of all the islands in the chain is about 53,000. Miyakojima is by far the largest island both in terms of area and population. Its main city, Hirara (平良市; Hirara-shi), has some 35,000 residents and serves as the transportation hub for ferries and flights to the other islands in the group as well as a center for hotels, restaurants, diving supplies and other tourist services.

Miyako Airport (宮古空港; Miyako Kūkō) has daily direct flights to Tokyo's Haneda Airport (3 hours) and Osaka's Kansai Airport (2.5 hours). There are several flights a day to Naha Airport on Okinawa Main Island (45 minutes) and to Ishigaki (30 minutes). There are also daily flights to Tarama (25 minutes), a small island midway between Miyako and Ishigaki. The airport is 3 miles (5 kilometers) from downtown and it takes 5–10 minutes to get there. All the local rental car companies have counters or facilities at the airport terminal and in town.

Because of the frequent and convenient air service, there was a consequent lack of demand for the ferry service. In 2008 the Okinawa–Miyako–Ishigaki passenger and vehicle ferry was discontinued. It is no longer possible to sail to Miyako or the Yaeyamas. Local ferries still connect some of the lesser islands in the Miyako chain to Miyakojima.

The most famous Miyako-shotō natural annual event is the Yaébishi (やえびし), named for Yabiji Reef (八重干瀬; Yabiji-sera), a huge coral reef north of Ikemajima, at the top end of Miyako. Every year, in early March, during the lowest spring tides of the year, a vast coral reef appears from beneath the sea, seemingly rising like the legendary city of Atlantis. It's magnificent but, unfortunately, the reef becomes a magnet attracting coral hunters and shellfish gatherers. Hordes of "collectors" come equipped with crowbars and rock hammers to smash and pry away anything they can get their hands on.

The most famous man-made event is the annual Miyako "Strong-Man" Competition (全日本トライアスロン 宮古島大会; Zen Nihon torai asuron Miyako jima taikai), a triathlon that attracts more than 1,500 athletes from all over Japan and overseas. Held around the third week of April, it's comprised of a 4-mile (6-kilometer) swim, 95 miles (152 kilometers) of cycling and a 26-mile (42-kilometer) running marathon. The event, reserved for those who really wish to prove how fit they are, can take up to 14 hours.

Coral hunters and fish collectors at Yabiji Reef during the lowest spring tides in March.

☐ **MIYAKOJIMA** 宮古島

Miyako Island (宮古島; Miyako-jima) lies approximately 235 miles (376 kilometers) east of Taipei, Taiwan, and 175 miles (280 kilometers) southwest of Naha, Okinawa. Roughly triangular in shape, Miyakojima is about 19 miles (30 kilometers) long from its southeasternmost point to its northernmost tip. Across its base, east to west, it's 12 miles (20 kilometers) wide. At not quite 62 square miles (160 square kilometers) in area, it is the southern Ryukyu's and Okinawa Prefecture's fourth largest island. The island's circumference measures 70 miles (112 kilometers) and its highest point is 375 feet (115 meters) above sea level. It is the largest and most populous island in the Miyako Island group. Most of the island is planted with sugar cane.

Miyako's capital and only real city is Hirara (平良; Hirara), a very pleasant place of 35,000 residents. It's located on the central west coast of the island and surrounds the harbor (宮古港 or 平良港; Miyako-kō or Hirara-kō). If you're staying in any of the hotels or *minshuku* inns in town, you can walk, as it's a compact city. Although there is no longer any long-distance inter-island ferry service to Okinawa or Ishigaki, Miyako's port is still the place of shipping, cargo, freight and commerce. After all, it's an island and islands need constant replenishment of a myriad of supplies. Miyako's Airport is only about 3 miles (5 kilometers) from downtown and takes 5–10 minutes by car or taxi to get there.

There are several large resort hotels not far from town and several dozen smaller hotels and *minshuku* in town. If you're not eating at your hotel, there are many restaurants in Hirara. For some reason, Miyako is famous for having more bars and nightclubs per person than any other place in Japan. The nightlife scene is very popular. Drinks of choice include Okinawa's Orion beer and *awamori* (泡盛), which in Miyako is usually 30 percent alcohol.

Awamori, incidentally, is at the center of a Miyako drinking custom known as Otōri (オトーリ). Otōri usually involves 5–10 people but there is no set number. Each person in turn acts as "toastmaster" and makes a short speech related to the evening's celebration or particular event being observed. He or she pours *awamori* for the neighboring person and each around the group fills his or her small *awamori* glass. All drink. The next person then repeats the process. This can go on all night. It's said that it's never polite to leave. The only escape is feigning a trip to the restroom and then running or stumbling out the back door.

Miyako is an interesting island and there is more to see and do than it might at first appear. It can take a day or two to see it all and it's large enough that you'll probably want to rent a car, scooter or bike to get around. That's easily done as there are numerous vehicle rental places in Hirara. If you are planning on touring the island by car or bike, it's most efficient to circle it counter-clockwise. That way you'll see the south and east coasts in morning light and the northern and western shores in the afternoon and evening light.

To accomplish this, in one relatively long day, we'll track along all three sides of the triangle-shaped Miyako. Starting in Hirara and driving south we'll then follow the island's southern coast from west to east. That's about 21 miles (34 kilometers). Then we'll drive from the southeastern tip at Cape Higashi-Henna to Miyako's northern end at Cape Nishi-Henna, which is also approximately 21 miles (34 kilometers). From there we'll head south along the island's west coast, ending back at Hirara, about another 9 miles (14 kilometers).

Starting in Hirara, you might begin with the Hakuai Monument (博愛記念碑; Hakuai kinen-hi). Designated as a "Monument of Humanity," this large memorial stone is dedicated to German–Japanese friendship. It's inscribed with thanks from German Kaiser Wilhelm I (1797–1888) to the people of Miyako. It's located in the center of town, not far from the port, but tucked away in an overgrown park and looking a bit forlorn.

In 1873, the *J. R. Robertson*, a German merchant ship, ran aground off Miyako in a typhoon while sailing from Australia to China. The islanders took care of the sailors for a month and then sent them home via China. In 1876, another German ship arrived, this one carrying the stone expressing the gratitude of the German emperor. The inscription is in both German and Chinese, the lingua franca of the Ryukyus at the time, but hard to make out. It describes the distress and rescue of the shipwreck.

Ever since that time there has been a particular bond between this small island and Germany. In 2000, at the time of the Okinawa G-8 Summit, then Chancellor Gerhard Schröder and his wife made a special visit to Miyako to renew the friendship alliance between these two far-apart places. On July 21 of 2000, a road was dedicated to Chancellor Gerhard Schröder-Strasse (シュレーダー通りの碑; Shurēdā-dōri no ishibumi), which runs out past the airport on the way to the Ueno German Culture Village.

A little to the north of Hirara, near the waterfront, perhaps less than three-quarters of a mile (1 kilometer) northeast from the ferry terminal, you'll find the tomb of Tuyumya Nakasone Genga (仲宗根豊見親玄雅; Nakasoné Tuyumiya Genga), a feudal lord who unified Miyako Island into the Kingdom of the Ryukyus in the late 15th century. Tuyumya is an Okinawan honorific, not a name. Genga Nakasone is a hero celebrated for having spared the people of Miyako from the death and destruction that would have resulted from attempts to resist an invasion, instead having chosen to unify with the Yaeyamas and ultimately the Okinawan monarchy. Nakasone originally built the tomb for his father. It is designated as an important Japanese cultural property.

Less than three-quarters of a mile (1 kilometer) north of there, on the same road, is the Nintō-zei ishi (人頭税石) or "Head Tax Stone." It's a small pillar standing in what appears to be someone's yard. Before the Meiji Period (明治時代; Meiji-jidai), 1868–1912, it is said that a tax was levied on every islander taller than the 4.5-foot (1.4-meter)-tall stone. Other reports state that the tax stone was employed until 1903. A third version has it that the entire story is a fiction. If the story is true, it is said that men paid their tax in millet, a type of grain, and women paid their tax with cloth.

Backtracking south about 1 mile (1.6 kilometers), we'll return to the harbor area and then continue just past it to the first of many beaches that we'll find on Miyako. Painagama (パイナガマビーチ; Painagama bīchi) may not be Miyako's most famous beach but it's a perfectly good one and it's the closest to town. It's within walking distance of downtown Hirara, only a few blocks from the center and a couple of blocks south of the port. It's not too big but it has a clean, white, wide sand frontage, freshwater showers and changing facilities. Just across the street from the beach is a popular seafood restaurant.

From Painagama it's less than 1 mile (1.5 kilometers) west to a much larger beach, Sunset Beach (サンセットビーチ; Sansetto bīchi), which is the main attraction of a fairly large public park. As at Painagama, there are public showers and men's and ladies' rooms.

A road dedicated to Gerhard Schröder-Strasse and German–Japanese friendship.

The tomb of Tuyumya Nakasone, a feudal lord who unified Miyako with the Ryukyus.

The Head Tax Stone, a small pillar said to have measured the height of people for tax purposes.

Painagama Beach, the closest beach to Hirara.

Monument of the Five Brave Men who reported the Russian fleet entering Japanese waters in 1905.

Also, as its name indicates, it's popular at sunset for it faces directly west, looking out across the water to Irabu Island. Just below Sunset Beach is the road that leads to the new bridge across to Irabujima. It's quite spectacular and at 2 miles (3 kilometers) in length from shore to shore, it's the longest over the sea bridge in Japan. It's been in construction for the past five years and is scheduled to open in 2014.

We won't take it now. Instead, we'll pass by and continue through the little port village of Hisamatsu (久松) to the "Monument of the Five Brave Men" (久松五勇士顕彰碑; Hisamatsu-go-yūshi-kenshōhi). It's next to the Hisamatsu Fishing Port, about 1.5 miles (2.5 kilometers) south of Painagama Beach.

The "Five Braves" is quite a story. At the risk of great oversimplification, on the night of February 8, 1904, Japan started the first great war of the 20th century, the Russo-Japanese War (日露戦争; Nichi-Ro Sensō), by launching a surprise torpedo attack on the Russian warm water port and concession at Port Arthur, located at the end of Liaodong

Peninsula in the south of Chinese Manchuria. The Battle of Port Arthur (旅順港海戦; Ryojunkō Kaisen), as it came to be known, caused great damage to the Imperial Russian Naval Far East fleet and the Russian psyche. When word of the attack reached Moscow, Tsar Nicholas II (1868–1918) was stunned by the news. Being a man of great rigidity and stubbornness, it is said that he simply could not believe that Japan would commit an act of war without a formal declaration of war. In any case, the Tsar ordered the Baltic squadron to sail halfway around the world, 18,000 nautical miles (33,000 kilometers), from the Baltic Sea to the Pacific Ocean via the Cape of Good Hope.

On May 25, 1905, five Japanese fishermen from Hisamatsu Village sighted the Russian fleet steaming north past the east coast of Miyako. At that time Miyako had no telegraph connection with mainland Japan, so the men rowed 15 hours over 60 miles (96 kilometers) to Ishigaki, then ran five hours to reach the telegraph station there. The message alerting the Japanese Imperial Navy

The Tsushima Strait connects the East China Sea to the Sea of Japan.

Port Arthur and exercised control over Manchuria and Korea. The Russians were forced to sue for peace. The Russo-Japanese War ended with the signing of the Treaty of Portsmouth on September 5, 1905 at the Portsmouth Naval Shipyard in Kittery, Maine. For his efforts as mediator, American President Theodore Roosevelt was awarded the Nobel Peace Prize.

For the Russians, the war represented a nadir in their military history; an extra-ordinary humiliation at the hands of the Japanese; the beginning of the end of the Russian monarchy; and the nascent beginning of the Russian Revolution. For the rest of the Western world, the Japanese victory represented a rise in the power and prestige

"Ghosts from the Crushing Defeat"
Created in 1904 or 1905, this colored woodcut print by Japanese artist Kobayashi Kiyochika (小林 清親 1847–1915) shows Tsar Nicholas II waking from a nightmare of his destroyed military equipment from their defeat in the Russo-Japanese War. The writing in the upper left purports to tell the stories of the battered cannons, telegraph, locomotive and battle-ships. Under the title "The Tsar Sees His Forces Returning," the original of this work is held by the Library of Congress, Washington, DC.

was sent. This deed of patriotic loyalty and bravery is what the monument celebrates.

Unfortunately for the Russians, at this stage Port Arthur had fallen and the goal of the fleet was merely to reach Vladivostok safely and await further instructions. Of the three sea routes available to them, the commanding admiral had chosen the shortest and most direct, passing through the Tsushima Strait between Japan and Korea. This, however, was also the most dangerous route as it passed very close to mainland Japan. And, of course, by now the Japanese were on full alert as they knew that the fleet was approaching.

On May 27–28 of 1905, the Japanese engaged the Battle of Tsushima (対馬海戦; Tsushima-kaisen) and annihilated the Russian fleet. All eight of their battleships, numerous smaller vessels and more than 5,000 Russian sailors were lost, while the Japanese lost three torpedo boats and 116 men. Only three Russian vessels escaped to Vladivostok. After the battle the Japanese army occupied all of Sakhalin Island and

Miyakojima Tokyu Resort Hotel, the best hotel close to Hirara, on Yonaha-Maehama Beach.

The "Great Bridge" that connects Miyakojima to Kurimajima to its southeast.

Ueno German Culture Village, Miyako's most famous international attraction.

of an Asian power that heretofore was unimaginable. For Japan, it was to set the stage for two great world wars over the next half a century.

After leaving the Hisamatsu Memorial, follow south along the coast road that parallels Yonaha Bay (与那覇湾; Yonaha-wan) for approximately 5 miles (8 kilometers) until you reach the Miyakojima Tokyu Resort Hotel (宮古島東急 リゾート; Miyakojima Tōkyū rizōto), the best hotel close to Hirara. You'll pass the southern end of the airport; the Upukaa Mangroves Promenade-Boardwalk (マングローブの遊歩道; Mangurōbu no puromunādo) at Kawamitsu Village (川満; Kawamitsu); the massive Okinawa Sugar Refining Plant; and the village of Shimoji (下地) along the way.

The Tokyu Resort Hotel is deluxe in all respects and sited directly in the middle of one of the most beautiful beaches of Miyako, the Yonaha-Maehama Beach (与那覇前浜ビーチ; Yonaha-Maehama bīchi), located on the island's southwest corner. It is several kilometers of soft white sand. Public access, apart from the hotel, is available in either direction, less than three-quarters of

a mile (1 kilometer) north or south. At the southern access, next to Maehama Port (前浜港; Maehama kō), there are public showers. The beach has great views of across the water to Kurima Island (来間島; Kurimajima) and the nearby "Great Bridge" that connects to it.

From the hotel to the Kurima bridge (来間大橋; Kurima-Ōhashi), it's about 1 mile (1.6 kilometers) southeast. We'll discuss Kurimajima a little further below after we've rounded Miyako, but you could cross over the bridge and visit the island in less than half an hour. From the bridge, if we track east along the southern coast road, past the Emerald Coast Golf Club, in about another 4 miles (6 kilometers), we'll come to Ueno village (上野村; Ueno-son) and Miyako's most famous international attraction, the Ueno German Culture Village (うえのドイツ 文化村; Ueno doitsu bunka-mura).

It is part resort, hotel complex, conference center, amusement park, museum, shipwreck memorial, Brothers Grimm fairy tale "Haus" for children, and part kitsch. There's even a full-scale reproduction of the Marksburg Castle of the Rhine River. And if that's not enough, there are a couple of sections of the

Shigira Golden Hot Springs Spa.

Cape Higashi-Henna, Miyako's southeasternmost point.

Shigira Bayside Suite Allamanda, a combination of several deluxe hotels and resort facilities.

Shigira Bay Country Club Golf Course, part of the Shigira Bayside Suite Allamanda complex.

Berlin Wall. The whole place is a bit over the top, but its inspiration and the operative word for both the Kaiser Wilhelm Memorial Stone in town and the German Culture Village is *hakuai* (博愛), which means philanthropy, for it was on a coral reef just offshore from Ueno where in 1873 the German ship the *Robertson* foundered and sank. The villagers rescued the crew, cared for them and after a month sent them home to Germany. Ever since that time, this village and Miyakojima have enjoyed a special friendship with Germany.

Staying on the southern coast road, it's less than three-quarters of a mile (1 kilometer) due east to Miyako's newest luxury attraction, the Shigira Golden Hot Springs Spa (シギラ黄金温泉; Shigira ougon onsen). It's a beautiful hot springs resort with both separate bathing and spa facilities for men and women and several large common pools for men and women together. Swimsuits are required in the mixed areas. Sauna, massage, fitness rooms and a restaurant—all first class—are available. The resort is open daily until 10:00PM. You won't find a better hot springs facility in all the Ryukyus.

Less than three-quarters of a mile (1 kilometer) east along the coast road leads to the most deluxe and the most expensive hotel resort on the island, the Shigira Bayside Suite Allamanda (シギラベイサイドスイート アラマンダ; Shigira beisaido suito ar amanda), which is part of the Shigira Bay Country Club (シギラベイカントリークラブ 宮古島; Shigira bei kantorī kurabu Miyako jima). It's a combination of three, soon to be four, separate hotels, each with its own swimming pool and resort facilities. All have restaurants and all share use of the 18-hole golf course. One hotel is all suites, each with its own private swimming pool, the only such hotel in Japan. There is also a wedding chapel and couples from all over Japan come here to be married. Prices for regular rooms start around $500 a night and go up from there. Suites are in the $1,000–$2,000 range.

From the country club we'll follow along Miyako's southern shoreline, which forms the base of this triangle-shaped island, for the next 6 miles (10 kilometers). We'll pass the dramatic cliff-faced Muigaa and Nanamata coastlines and then the Takenakayama Observatory (中山天文台を取る; Také naka yama tenbō-dai) along the way. Seashell lovers and collectors will want to stop at the very fine Seashell Museum (宮古島海宝館; Miyako jima Kaihō-kan), which is in the village of Bora (保良). It has thousands of beautiful specimens from all over the world. Just below Bora is another beach also considered one of Miyako's nicest, Boragaa (保良川 ビーチ; Boragaa bīchi). As is usually the case at most of Miyako's public beaches, showers and toilet facilities are provided.

From Boragaa Beach it's a little less than 3 miles (5 kilometers) due east, still along the coast, to the very southeasternmost point of Miyako, Cape Higashi-Henna (東平安名崎; Higashi-henna-zaki). Regardless of how much time you spend at the beach, don't miss this cape. Higashi-Henna-zaki is an extremely narrow, 1.5-mile (2-kilometer)-long arm jutting out into the Pacific Ocean. It's especially scenic and is consistently listed as one of the most beautiful spots in Japan. There's a

An aerial view of scenic Cape Higashi-Henna, a long arm jutting out into the Pacific Ocean.

There are over 40,000 tropical trees and plants at the Miyakojima City Tropical Botanical Gardens.

141-foot (43-meter)-high lighthouse at the tip of the promontory.

As the crow flies, it's exactly 18 miles (29 kilometers) from Miyako's southeasternmost point at Cape Higashi-Henna to its northernmost point at Cape Nishi-Henna (西平安名崎; Nishi-henna-zaki). Although we're not crows, since the road hugs the shoreline quite closely it's still a fairly direct shot from one cape to the other. Thus, the road distance is only a little longer, approximately 21 miles (34 kilometers). It's a beautiful drive along Miyako's eastern shore, bordered by the Pacific Ocean the whole way.

Only about 3 miles (5 kilometers) northwest of Cape Higashi-Henna, just past the Ocean Links Golf Club, you'll come to what many people think is Miyako's finest beach, the Yoshino Shore (吉野海岸; Yoshino-kaigan). Close to another mile (1.6 kilometers) after Yoshino is the beautiful Aragusuku Coast (親城海岸; Ara-gusuku kaigan), which also has a good beach. Yoshino has freshwater showers and toilets for visitors. Aragusuku has toilets only.

From the beaches our next stop is almost 9 miles (14 kilometers) northwest at the Miyakojima City Tropical Botanical Gardens (宮古島市 熱帯植物園; Miyako-jima-shi Nettai Shokubutsu-en). Although they are only 2.5 miles (4 kilometers) due east of downtown Hirara, many people find it easier to visit the gardens while touring on this side of the island. The park is one of Miyako's more popular attractions, perhaps because it is free!

Established in 1964, the park now has over 40,000 trees and plants from 1,600 tropical species from all over Asia and around the world. The red-blooming flamboyant trees (*Delonix regia*), also commonly called royal poinciana, are particularly beautiful in April and May.

Six miles (10 kilometers) north of the gardens along the east coast you'll come to the tiny village of Shimajiri and then Shimajiri Port (島尻港; Shima jiri-kō). This small harbor is the arrival and departure point for the ferry service to Ōgami Island (大神島; Ōgami-jima). We'll mention the island below.

From Shimajiri it's less than three-quarters of a mile (1 kilometer) further north to the Shimajiri Mangrove Forest (島尻マングローブ林; Shima jiri Mangurōbu-rin). It's the largest colony of mangroves on the island

The numerous species at the Shimajiri Mangrove Forest can be viewed from boardwalks.

A horse at the Miyako Pony Farm, a ranch and breeding station for this increasingly rare horse.

and a number of different mangrove species are represented. There are boardwalk paths through the mangroves which permit access over what would otherwise be impassible swamp, water and mud.

From the Mangrove Forest it's not quite 2.5 miles (4 kilometers) north to the top of the island, which ends in a rather unusual fashion. The northernmost point of Miyako splits, like the fish tail of a mackerel, and each end of the tail runs out over a 0.75-mile (1-kilometer)-long narrow peninsula. Up through the middle you'll pass by Karimata (狩俣; Kari mata), a small village, and then come to the Yukishio Saltworks (雪塩製塩所; Yuki shio seien-sho). The salt processed here is famous for containing the most natural minerals of any sea salt in the world. There are factory tours, which are free, and naturally you can buy the salt itself in the gift shop. Also worth trying is the ice cream, which rather remarkably has an enhanced flavor because of the addition of salt.

Leaving Yukishio, the left (west) fork of the split leads to the Miyako Pony Farm (宮古馬; Miyako uma), a ranch and breeding station for the rare Miyako horse, one of eight breeds of horse considered native to Japan. They are small, somewhat similar to the Mongolian horse, and their lineage goes back centuries. In the middle of the 20th century there were over 10,000 of them but today there are less than 100.

Continuing out on to the end of the peninsula leads to the Karimata Wind Farm (狩俣風力発電所; Kari mata Furyo kuha tsuden-sho), a collection of wind turbines that generate electricity. The idea, of course, is to lessen the island's dependence on fossil fuels.

The very tip of the left side of the peninsula is Cape Nishi-Henna (Japanese: 西平安名崎; Nishi-henna-zaki). Altogether, although it's really only about 8 miles (13 kilometers) north of Hirara, it's taken all day to reach here. That's somewhat the nature of these small islands. There really is a lot to see. From here, if we backtrack, pass the Yukishio Saltworks and take the right-hand side fork (east), we'll travel less than three-quarters of

Karimata Wind Farm, a collection of wind turbines that generate electricity for the island.

The main attraction at the Miyako Underwater Park is the underwater viewing station.

The natural stone arch at Sunayama Beach, one of Miyako's most picturesque beaches.

a mile (1 kilometer) to what also used to be a dead end, but no longer. Ever since 1992 the end of this fork is the starting point of a great bridge, the Ikema-Ōhashi, which connects mainland Miyako to the little island of Ikema. We'll discuss Ikemajima further below.

To complete our circuit of Miyako, we'll turn around and head south along the western shore of the island a little less than 3 miles (5 kilometers) until we reach the

Miyako Underwater Park (宮古島海中公園; Miyakojima kaichū kōen). It's a fairly popular tourist attraction that combines a short hiking trail along a sheltered cove, some free outdoor exhibits on marine life and an underwater viewing station, which has an admission charge.

From the Miyako Underwater Park we'll continue south about 4 miles (6 kilometers) following along Miyako's west coast, rounding Oura Bay (大浦湾; Ōura-wan), then a little more than 1 mile (1.6 kilometers) west—follow the signs—to Sunayama Beach (砂山ビーチ; Suna-yama bīchi; lit. "Sand-Hill Beach"). It's one of Miyako's most picturesque beaches and has a large natural stone arch that is widely photographed. There are men's and women's changing rooms and showers at the parking lot. From there it's a bit of a hike up over the sand hill for which the beach is named.

Our round the island tour is about over. From Sunayama it's only 2.5 miles (4 kilometers) straight south to downtown Hirara or the port. You'll pass the Nintō-zei Head Tax Stone and the Tuyumya Nakasone Mausoleum about three-quarters of a mile (1 kilometer) before reaching town.

Miyako main island is surrounded by, and in many cases attached to, several smaller satellite islands. Let's mention them now.

KURIMAJIMA (来間島; Kurima-jima). Kurima is a small islet less than one mile (1.5 kilometers) off the southwestern end of Miyako. It's a fairly uniform oval- or egg-shaped islet, about 1–1.25 miles (1.5–2 kilometers) in diameter from any given cross-island points. It has a surface area of about 1 square mile (2.84 square kilometers) and a circumference of 4.5 miles (7 kilometers). The island's population is estimated at 200.

This aerial view of flat, low-lying Kurimajima shows its almost oval shape and sugar cane fields.

The Ikema Great Bridge connects the northern-most tip of Miyako with tiny Ikema Island.

Unusually, the Ikema Wildlife Sanctuary encompasses a large freshwater pond and marshlands.

The bridge connecting Kurima to Miyako is about 7.5 miles (12 kilometers) south of Hirara City. The island has been connected to the mainland for more than 15 years by the 1-mile (1.5-kilometer)-long Kurima Great Bridge (来間大橋; Kurima Ōhashi).

Kurima is mostly flat and almost entirely planted with sugar cane. If you're looking for privacy, you'll find it on any one of several attractive, secluded, small beaches on the western side of the island. One of the best is Nagamahama Beach (長間浜; Nagama hama). You'll probably have it all to yourself.

Kurima's eastern side, that is the side facing Miyako, has some modest cliffs and on the island's highest point, 197 feet (60 meters), you'll find the quite elaborate three-story Ryugu-jo Observatory (竜宮城展望台; Ryūgū-jō tenbō-dai). It was designed to resemble the supposed undersea palace of Ryūjin (龍神), the dragon god of the sea in Japanese mythology. It has a wonderful view of all Kurima, plus the bridge back to Miyako, plus the white sand Yonaha-Maehama Beach and the Tokyu Resort Hotel.

IKEMAJIMA (池間島; Ikéma-jima). The northernmost tip of Miyako used to end at Cape Nishi-Henna (西平安名崎; Nishi Henna-zaki). That changed in 1992 when the Ikema Great Bridge (池間大橋; Ikéma-Ōhashi) was completed. It artificially extended Miyako's reach all the way to Ikema and replaced the local ferry service. At 4,675 feet (1,425 meters) long, the Ikema-Ōhashi was the longest bridge in Japan at the time of its opening, but it wasn't long before that record was broken and longer bridges were completed, including the Kurima Bridge at the other end of Miyako.

Ikemajima is a small box-shaped islet less than 1 mile (just 1.5 kilometers) above Miyako's northern end. At its longest, it's more than 1.25 miles (2 kilometers) and at its widest about 1 mile (1.5 kilometers). The island's area is about 1 square mile (2.83 square kilometers) and its shoreline circumference is 3.75 miles (6 kilometers). Its highest point is reported at 92 feet (28 meters).

The island's only village, Ikema (池間) is at the southern end, near the bridge. Ikema's port used to be the ferry terminus. Now it's

The 1-mile (1.5-kilometer)-long Kurima Great Bridge connecting Kurimajima and Miyakojima.

Ōgamijima ("Great God") Island has an observation platform at the top with a good view.

only a local fishing harbor. Virtually every one of the island's 800 residents lives in the village. The rest of Ikemajima is planted in sugarcane, except the center.

Unusually, Ikema has a fairly large central freshwater pond and several dozen acres of surrounding marshland. It's called the Ikema Wildlife Sanctuary (池間鳥獣保護区; Ikema chōjū hogo-ku). A marked dirt road leads to the marsh and there's a viewing platform at the parking lot. The marsh is unusual because the composition of most coral limestone islands in the Ryukyus usually allows water to escape by draining away. In fact, holding freshwater drinking supplies in reservoirs on most islands in Okinawa is generally a challenge. If they are not solid concrete, they must be lined with some type of impermeable barrier in order to hold water. For whatever reason, this marshland maintains its water year round. Many birds find this critical to their survival and nest here.

There are several small beaches on Ikema, one on the southeast corner, near the bridge and port. Another, perhaps the nicest, is at the very top northern end. It's called Ikemajima Block Beach (池間島ブロックビーチ; Ikéma-jima Burokku bīchi).

From 3–9.5 miles (5–15 kilometers) north of Ikema and approximately 4.5 miles (7 kilometers) across is the Yabiji Reef (八重干瀬; Yabiji) (page 214). This is where every spring the seasonally lowest tides of the year expose vast sections of the reef and hordes of tourists and local collectors march out of ships on to the reef. The exposed reef phenomenon is known as Yaébishi (やえびし).

ŌGAMIJIMA (大神島; Ōgami-jima). This rarely visited little islet is just over 2.5 miles (4 kilometers) north of Shimajiri Port (島尻港; Shima-jiri-kō) near the northern end of Miyako Island. There is a local passenger-only ferry service that connects Ōgami to Miyako with four round trips per day. The ferry only takes 15 minutes one way.

Ōgami, whose Kanji characters mean "Great God," is oval in shape, 2,460 feet (750 meters) long from north to south and about 1,640 feet (500 meters) wide from east to west. For the most part, the island is covered in wild vegetation. The population is reported to be about 30. The few dwellings are scattered from the port, located at Ōgami's southern end, to the center of the island. The island has one fairly large hill in the center. It's about 66 feet (20 meters) high. On top there's an observation platform with a view.

2 **IRABUJIMA** 伊良部島

The twin islands of Irabu and Shimoji are located 4 miles (6 kilometers) west of Miyako's Hirara port. They nest so closely to one another that it's easy to think of them as one but they are, in fact, separated by a narrow sea channel (crossed by six bridges), so they are two distinct islands. Irabujima (伊良部島; Irabu-jima) is the larger of the

The Miyako–Irabu passenger and vehicle ferry.

Toguchi Beach is famous for its perfect sand.

The longest bridge in Japan connects Irabujima at left and Miyakojima at right.

Makiyama Observatory, built in the shape of a giant bird of prey on the highest cliffs of Irabujima, allows splendid views of the surroundings.

two and closer to Miyako. Its main port is Sarahama (佐良浜港; Sara-hama-kō) and it is served by commercial ferries from Hirara. It's on the island's central east coast. A combination of high-speed passenger ferries and slightly slower passenger and vehicle ferries sail from Miyako every hour or 90 minutes all day long. The fast ferries take 15 minutes, the vehicle ferries take 25. Sarahama is the largest village on Irabu and although most people visit the island on a day trip from Miyako, it's possible to spend the night as there are several *minshuku* in town. As rapid and as convenient as the ferry service is, it will soon be obsolete. For the past five years, construction of what is soon to be the longest bridge in Japan is nearing an end.

Irabu's shape is quite that of an egg, lying down a little to the left. At its greatest length it's 5 miles (8 kilometers) long. At its greatest width, it's almost 3 miles (5 kilometers) across. Its total surface area measures 11 square miles (29 square kilometers). It is the second largest island of the Miyako chain and is mostly covered with sugar cane. In addition to Sarahama, there's Irabu Village (伊良部), which is only slightly smaller. It is on the southwest coast of the island. Apart from these two villages, there is almost no part of Irabu that is not cultivated.

Irabu has a couple of beaches. The best is Toguchi Beach (渡口の浜; Toguchi-no-hama), famous for its perfect sand. You'll hear it said that the sand on this beach is so fine and white that it is like walking on flour, and this is true. It's located at the southwest corner of the island, right where Irabu bumps up against Shimoji Island. There's a parking lot, showers and toilet facilities. There's also a beach shop with a café that serves cold Orion beer (オリオンビール; Orion bīru) and the best bowl of Okinawa *soba* (沖縄そば) that you'll find anywhere.

On the northwest shore of the island, also where Irabu meets Shimoji, you'll find Sawada Beach (佐和田の浜; Sawada-no-hama). Its extra long slope and rocky bottom preclude it from being a very good swimming or diving beach. It's really better known for its scenery and its sunsets. It is covered by a collection of great rocks deposited by a tsunami several hundred years ago. At low tide you can walk through this rock field if you wish. There are also showers and toilets.

Irabu's big "sight," which is visible all the way from the west coast of Miyako, is the Makiyama Observatory (牧山展望台; Makiyama tenbō-dai). It's perched near the southeastern end of the island just across the sea strait from Hirara, on the highest cliffs of

Cape Shiratori, the northernmost tip of Irabujima, is the site of three observatories.

Funausagibanata Observatory, one of the three observatories at Cape Shiratori is in the shape of a giant grey hawk native to Irabujima.

Irabu. It's a concrete lookout partially constructed in the shape of a giant bird of prey. It's a pretty drive up to the top and, of course, there's a great view from there.

Also attractive and worth seeing is the wild and dramatic scenery of the north end of the island. It's a reserve called Nishikaigan Park (西海岸公園; Nishi-kaigan kōen; lit. "West Coast Park"). The northernmost tip is crowned with three observatories at Cape Shiratori (白鳥岬; Shira tori zaki; lit. "White Bird Cape"). Two are the regular type of round concrete structure, the third is in the shape of a giant grey hawk native to the island. It's the *sashiba* (サシバ; Latin: *Butastur indicus*; also known as the "grey-faced buzzard"). The three observatories are within 1.5 miles (2 kilometers) of one another and a hiking trail connects them. The "hawk" lookout is called Funausagi-banata Observatory (フナウサギバナタ 展望台; Funausagi banata tenbō-dai)

From Irabu it's easy enough to get to Shimoji. The two islands run side by side straddling a narrow channel of seawater for 2 miles (3 kilometers). The channel is never more than around 100 meters wide and it's crossed every few hundred meters by a total of six bridges connecting the two islands. We'll go there next.

③ SHIMOJIJIMA 下地島

Unlike Irabu, which is densely settled and has two villages, Shimojijima (下地島; Shimoji-jima) is almost uninhabited. It's a small island, half devoted to sugar cane and half devoted to an airport, but most of the sugar cane planters and the airport personnel don't live there. They commute from Irabu. The island is almost devoid of dwellings. The few that exist, maybe a dozen, are found on the island's northeast, just across the sea channel from Irabu village. Immediately below these residences there's a public golf course, Sashiba Links (サシバリンクス 伊良部; Sashiba rinku suirabu; lit. "Irabu Hawk Links").

Like Irabu, its larger neighbor to the east, Shimoji has the shape of an egg. It's an oval, also leaning to the left, but less than half the size of its big brother. At its longest north–south axis it's not quite 3 miles (5 kilometers) in length. At its widest east–west points it's 1.5 miles (2.5 kilometers) across. Altogether, Shimoji's area is 3.5 square miles (9.54 square kilometers). Again, like Irabu, it's mostly flat, so flat indeed that in 1979 Japanese aviation authorities decided that it would be a perfect place to expand a small existing airport into a full-length 10,000-foot (3,000-meter) runway into an airline training facility. The Pilot Flight Training Center Foundation (下地パイロット 飛行訓練所; Shitaji pairotto hikō kunrensho) occupies several buildings and a control tower at the airport.

Ever since it was built, both Japan Airlines and ANA have used Shimoji for training pilots on all sizes of aircraft right up to Boeing 747s. Shortly after the long runway opened, in 1980, commercial services, in-

This aerial view is from the north. Shimoji and its airstrip are on the right, larger Irabu is on the left.

Shimoji's Tōri-iké, dark-colored twin ponds, are connected to the sea by limestone caverns.

Nakanoshima Beach on Irabura's western shore is an excellent snorkeling site.

cluding direct flights from Tokyo and Naha, commenced. However, since most accommodations and tourist service are on Miyako, transferring from Shimoji to the ferry port in Irabu and then sailing over to Miyako was unnecessarily time-consuming and inconvenient, especially when you consider that the Miyako Aiport is five minutes from downtown Miyako! Consequently, commercial airline service was never economically viable. Flights were finally discontinued in 1994. Therefore, although you may see jet aircraft taking off and landing, and there is indeed a small passenger terminal and control tower, you can't fly here. The airport remains open today only as a training facility.

Shimoji's best known (and maybe only) tourist attractions are the dark green, almost black, twin ponds of Tōri-iké (通り池). Usually described as "mysterious" because of their exceptionally dark-colored waters, they are saltwater, connected to the sea by underwater limestone caverns. Properly trained SCUBA cave divers explore them.

Because they are connected to the ocean, their water levels rise and fall with the changing tides. When viewed from above, the ponds look like two eyes and are called "dragon eye balls" by the islanders. The twin ponds are located at the far western end of the island, on the west side of the airport runway. The road runs around the southern end of the airport, then up along Shimoji's west coast, then over and around the north end of the runway, which projects out into the sea. It's easy enough to drive there from either direction. From the parking lot it's a short walk to the pools.

The ponds are most uniformly circular, each about 165 feet (50 meters) in diameter. A Shimojijima legend has it that two fishermen caught a mermaid and, being friendly neighbors, they decided to cut her in half and share her. Later, on the night of their catch, they heard sobbing coming from the sea, beckoning her to come back. The mermaid replied that she could not come back as she was cut in half. The voice from the sea told her that three big waves would be sent to bring her home. Not long after, a tsunami came and washed the fishermen's homes away along with the mermaid. When the water receded, all that was left were the twin ponds of Tōri-iké.

There is another place worth mentioning on Shimoji. It's not that great of a beach but it's an excellent snorkeling site, Nakanoshima Beach (中の島ビーチ; Nakanoshima bīchi). It's on the western shore, about 1 mile (1.5 kilometers) south of the Tori iké ponds. The beach is rather rough but it's located on a sheltered cove. There are excellent rock and coral formations just offshore. It's a popular spot with diving boats from Irabu. The large rock in the middle of the cove is Nakanoshima (中の島; Naka no shima; lit. "Center Island").

Finally, about 1,640 feet (500 meters) north of Nakanoshima Beach, just off the same road, you'll come to Obi-iwa (帯岩), an enormous rock, all by itself, pushed up on to the shore. It's hard to imagine how it got there.

④ TARAMAJIMA 多良間島

This small round island lies more or less midway between Miyako and Ishigaki. More precisely, as the crow flies, Taramajima (多良間島; Tarama-jima) is a little less than 40 miles (60 kilometers) southwest of Miyako

An aerial view of Taramajima. Minna Island is just visible in the background.

The Tarama passenger and vehicle ferry makes one round trip per day except Sundays.

and 20 miles (32 kilometers) northeast of the northern tip of Ishigaki. It's a very well-formed sphere with a diameter ranging from 2.75 miles (4.5 kilometers) north to south and 3.5 miles (5.5 kilometers) east to west. Its total surface area is just under 7.5 square miles (20 square kilometers) and its circumference is 12 miles (20 kilometers). Tarama is almost completely flat. Its highest elevation is about 66 feet (20 meters). The island is fully cultivated, mostly with sugar cane. It has around 1,300 residents, most of whom live in the only village, Tarama (多良間村; Tarama-son). The village is less than three-quarters of a mile (1 kilometer) south of Maedomari Port (前泊港; Maedomari-kō), which is on Tarama's central north shore. There are half a dozen *minshuku* and an equal number of restaurants in the village, but that's about all. Not too many tourists come to Taramajima.

Other than by private ship, there are two ways to reach Tarama. There is an almost daily ferry and there is a small airport (多良間空港; Tarama Kūkō). The airport is on the far western side of the island and is served by daily flights from Miyako on RAC Airlines commuter planes. A one-way flight takes about 25 minutes. There are no flights from Ishigaki. If you fly over the south central section of Tarama, you may see the remnants

of the old airstrip. It was abandoned when the new airport was opened in 2003.

In addition to flying, there is a passenger and vehicle ferry from Miyako every day except Sundays. It departs Hirara Port at 9:00AM, and arrives at Tarama's Maedomari Port two hours later. It remains in port until 2:00PM when it departs for the return journey to Miyako. It arrives at 4:00PM.

The sailing distance, port to port, is 40 miles (64 kilometers). Formerly, the ferry continued to Ishigaki, spent the night, then made the return trip the next day. That service was discontinued in 2008. The sailing distance from Tarama to Ishigaki City is about 60 miles (96 kilometers), but that's moot. It wasn't economically viable and commercial services between Okinawa and the Miyakos and the Miyakos and Yaeyamas have been abandoned.

Tarama's biggest (at least its highest) sightseeing attraction is Yaeyama Tōmidai (八重山遠見台; Yaé-yama Tōmi-dai). Because the island is so flat, its highest point is not geological, a hill or a mountain. Rather, it's a 108-foot (33-meter)-high tower on a small hill. The name literally means "Yaeyama Distant One," a reference to the fact that you can see the northern end of Ishigaki Island from this viewpoint. Naturally, you'll get a great view of all Tarama plus Minna 5 miles (8 kilometers) away.

Most of Tarama Island is ringed by good sandy beaches. There are few or no public facilities at them, but you can be fairly certain that they won't be too crowded.

5 MINNAJIMA 水納島

This tiny islet is 5 miles (8 kilometers) due north of Tarama. As close as that may be, unfortunately Minnajima (水納島; Minna-

Tiny Minnajima is completely ringed with beaches.

jima) is an island with no scheduled ferry service and no airport. You'll have to charter a boat out of Tarama to reach it. That should not be too difficult as its few residents do most of their shopping on Tarama, making the longer 40-mile (60-kilometer) trip to Miyako only occasionally.

Minna is very small, its surface area only 1 square mile (2.5 square kilometers). It's a wedge-shaped islet, about 1.75 miles (3 kilometers) at its longest and a little more than three-quarters of a mile (1 kilometer) at its widest, but its width tapers down to 1,640 and 1,970 feet (500 and 600 meters) on its southeastern end. Its shoreline circumference is 4 miles (6 kilometers). Its highest elevation

is about 33 feet (10 meters). Its small port, Minna-kō (水納港), which is really just a pier, is on the southeastern shore.

The island is completely ringed with white sandy beaches. Almost no part of the island is cultivated and most of it is wild scrub vegetation. There are presently five people living on Minna and they are all members of the same family. There are only a couple of sandy tracks, no roads, no village and no school for children. There are no services of any kind on Minna. It's one of those islands that is most likely destined to become uninhabited in the next five to ten years.

That wraps up our coverage of the Miyako Archipelago. From here we'll backtrack to Miyako Island and fly south to our next destination, the beautiful Yaeyama Islands.

Sugar Cane (砂糖黍) Satō-kibi

Native to South and Southeast Asia, sugar cane is today cultivated in all the tropical regions of the world. Taxonomically, the plants are in the tall perennial grass family and fall in the genus Saccharum. There are several dozen species and since all readily inter-breed growers have developed numerous hybrids and cultivars that are commercially productive. Like bamboo, sugar cane has strong, jointed stalks, but unlike bamboo these are densely fibrous, not hollow. Plants grow from 2–6 meters (6–18 feet) tall and are rich in natural sugar. It is this sugar that makes the plant so valuable. Naturally, the primary product is pure cane sugar, but the plants may also be refined into molasses, sugar cane juice or syrup, rock candy or, most famously, distilled into rum. In Japan, a distilled alcohol product made from sugar cane is called *shōchū* (焼酎). In what may have great future promise, sugar cane is increasingly being harvested for its use in producing ethanol alcohol, a gasoline additive or substitute.

Scuba Diving and Snorkeling

One of the more interesting and challenging activities throughout the Ryūkyūs is skin diving, be it snorkeling or scuba diving, for Okinawa has some of the cleanest, clearest waters on the planet. Japanese tourists are very keen on the sport and lessons and rental equipment are available on most every island. You don't need much gear when snorkeling, but to scuba dive you must become certified in order to rent the equipment or to fill your tanks with air.

Chapter 12

THE YAEYAMA ISLANDS 沖縄諸島
Idyllic beaches, fascinating nature

1. **Ishigakijima** 石垣島
2. **Taketomijima** 竹富島
3. **Hamajima** 浜島
4. **Kayamajima** 嘉弥真島
5. **Kohamajima** 小浜島
6. **Kuroshima** 黒島
7. **Aragusukujima** 新城島
8. **Hatomajima** 鳩間島
9. **Iriomotejima** 西表島
10. **Haterumajima** 波照間島
11. **Nakanouganjima** 仲ノ御神島
12. **Yonagunijima** 与那国島

Beginning approximately 75 miles (120 kilometers) southwest of Miyakojima and the Miyako Islands, and very different from them, are the Yaeyama Islands (八重山諸島; Yaéyama-shotō), the most southerly island group in the Ryukyus and in Japan. They are different because the Yaeyamas are volcanic in origin, not coral-based as are the Miyakos. They contain mountains with heavily forested areas, completely unlike the flat coral islands of the Miyako chain. The word Yaeyama (pronounced with four syllables) means "Eightfold Mountains" and refers to their peaks visible from far away at sea.

As a group, the Yaeyama archipelago is quite diverse and spreads out over more than 20 islands and islets. From the most eastern point on the northern shore of Ishigaki to the most western point on Yonaguni, it's 88 miles (140 kilometers). From the most northern point on Ishigaki to the southern end of Hateruma, it's 51 (82 kilometers). Altogether, the surface area of all the Yaeyama Islands combined equals approximately 224 square miles (581 square kilometers). The chain includes two fairly large islands, Ishigaki and Iriomote, which together account for the vast majority of the archipelago's area, 200 square miles (518 square kilometers). The remaining balance of 24 square miles (63 square kilometers) is divided among the other much smaller islands in the group. Despite their

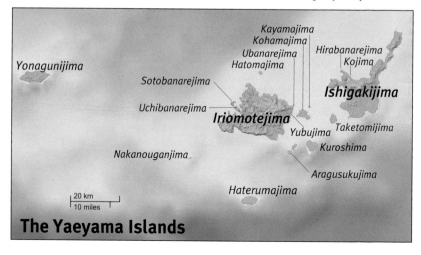

The Yaeyama Islands

Ishigaki Airport is the main entry point for visitors to the Yaeyamas from Okinawa's Naha, the Japanese mainland and elsewhere.

Ferries from Ishigaki Port provide fast, convenient and frequent service to almost all islands in the Yaeyama group.

small size, more than half the islands and islets in the Yaeyamas are inhabited.

As the crow flies, it's 1,210 miles (1,950 kilometers) southwest from Tokyo or 260 miles (415 kilometers) southwest from Naha to Ishigaki Airport (石垣空港; Ishigaki Kūkō), which is about 1.75 miles (3 kilometers) and five minutes from downtown Ishigaki City, the capital of the archipelago and the only city of any size in the group. Flying time from Tokyo is about three and a half hours. From Naha it's about one hour. There are frequent flights from those two cities every day of the year, and service, though less frequent, from a number of other mainland Japan cities as well.

Over the past few years, the Yaeyamas have grown increasingly more popular with Japanese tourists. Currently, Ishigaki's Airport serves almost two million passengers a year, and it's overburdened. Because no aircraft larger than a Boeing 737 can land there, construction started several years ago on a new one, New Ishigaki Airport (新石垣空港; Shin-Ishigaki Kūkō). The expected date of completion is somewhere in 2014. The new airport will also be on the eastern side of the island, but a bit further north, about 10 miles (16 kilometers) from downtown. Whether one is arriving at the present airport or eventually the new one, Ishigaki is not an international airport, so anyone visiting from overseas must fly through, and clear customs in, Tokyo or Naha. Of course, that could also change if flights were to commence from next-door Taiwan, something that has been discussed.

Good air service is important because there are no longer any ferries from Naha,

Miyako, mainland Japan or Taiwan. The last company offering ferry service abandoned its route and went out of business in 2007. It seems, for example, that few persons were interested in the 16-hour overnight sail from Okinawa's Naha.

The total population of the Yaeyamas is about 53,000, and although most of the islands have residents the distribution is by no means even. The majority of the islands in the group have only a very few residents. The greatest number, approximately 48,000, live on one island—Ishigaki. The other 5,000 are spread out over all the other islands. The Yaeyama chain includes Japan's southernmost point, on Haterumajima, and its westernmost, on Yonagunijima. From Yonaguni Island you can receive your favorite Chinese television programs from Taiwan, which is only 68 miles (108 kilometers) to the west. The northernmost opposite extreme point of Japan from Yonaguni is 1,800 miles (2,900 kilometers) away at Cape Sōya (宗谷岬; Sōya Misaki), near Wakkanai on the island of Hokkaidō.

Although there's no boat transport *to* the Yaeyamas, local transportation *within* the group is easy. Ishigaki harbor is the hub and there are frequent ferries to most all the surrounding islands. Travel time, for example, from Ishigaki to Taketomi Island is 10 minutes; to Iriomote 40 minutes; to Kohama around 30. High-speed ferries make the trip to Hateruma in just about one hour. Yonaguni is the most distant and it's considerably longer to sail there, about four to five hours. Moreover, the trip can be rough and there is no daily service. For these reasons, many people prefer to fly. There are daily flights from Ishigaki and it only takes 30 minutes. There also used to be flights to Hateruma, but these were stopped in 2007.

Because local inter-island transportation is so good, many visitors make Ishigaki the base for their stay in the Yaeyamas and take a series of day trips to the other islands from there. Ishigaki has a well-developed tourist infrastructure and has more hotels, *minshuku* inns, restaurants, and car, scooter and bike rental companies than any other place in the island chain.

The ANA Intercontinental Hotel, the best hotel near Ishigaki City, has both indoor and outdoor swimming pools, and its own beautiful beach.

This display map of the Yaeyamas is on the Southern Gate Bridge overlooking Ishigaki Port. The bridge connects to Yashima artificial island.

The Yaeyamas are located only one degree north of the Tropic of Cancer, lying on the same latitude as Miami, Florida. The islands are the first to receive the warm waters of the Kuroshio Current (see page 101) from Taiwan and the Philippines and thus they are the most "tropical" destination in the Ryukyu Archipelago and in Japan. Many people think that, as a group, the Yaeyamas are the most beautiful islands in the country. Without question, they are one of the most exotic.

As Ishigaki is the hub for the Yaeyamas, we'll start there and then move on to the other islands, one by one, westward and southward, as their distances increase from Ishigaki Port.

1 ISHIGAKIJIMA 石垣島

The word Ishigaki means "stone wall," a reference to the coral stone enclosures traditionally built around homes to protect them from typhoon damage. It is the name of the island, the city and the port.

Ishigakijima (石垣島; Ishigaki–jima) is the third largest island in Okinawa Prefecture, after Okinawa and Iriomote, and the second largest of the Yaeyama group. It is 22 miles (35 kilometers) long from north to south and 11 miles (18 kilometers) across from east to west at its widest point. Its land area is 88 square miles (229 square kilometers) and its coastline circumference measures 101 miles (162 kilometers). Ishigaki's population is also relatively large, about 48,000. The vast majority of the island's residents live in or around Ishigaki City (石垣市; Ishigaki-shi), which is also the home of Ishigaki Port (石垣港; Ishigaki-kō).

Ishigaki Island is very beautiful and has a number of excellent beaches and, for an island its size, high mountains, including the highest point in Okinawa Prefecture, Mt Omoto (於茂登岳; Omoto-daké) at 1,726 feet (526 meters). Ishigaki also features world famous Kabira Bay (川平湾; Kabira-wan), home of the Japanese black pearl industry.

Ishigaki City is the southernmost city of Japan. Its northern twin city, at the other end of the country, is Wakkanai (稚内市; Wakkanai-shi), at the very top of Hokkaido Island (北海道; Hokkaidō). Ishigaki City is a very pleasant place with numerous hotels and restaurants and ample shopping opportunities. It's small enough to get around completely on foot, yet large enough to support a very lively nightlife, bar, club and restaurant

scene. Most residents refer to central Ishigaki as Shigaichi (市街地; lit. "urban area" or "city streets"), Chushin (中心; lit. "center") or just Machi (町; lit. "town"). The main districts are Ōkawa (大川; lit. "big river") and Misaki-chō (美崎町; lit. "cape town"). "Very lively" is an understatement. You could spend a few weeks here and find another bar, club and restaurant every night and still keep having fun. It's a very, very lively place.

By day, however, it must be admitted, there are not too many sights in town, although one you'll always find listed in the tourist brochures is Miyara Donchi (宮良殿内), a museum, but still a private residence. It's an example of a traditional, old-style Okinawan house dating from 1819. As such, it is similar to the Nakamura Residence on Okinawa, the Takara House on Geruma and the Uezu-ke old house on Kume. There is an admission charge of a couple of hundred Yen and an old man prohibiting visitors from taking photos. I'd give this attraction a miss and visit the ones on Okinawa or Kume or Geruma instead.

The other big "sight" in downtown Ishigaki is the 730 Crossing Monument (730 記念碑; Nana-San-Maru), named for July 30, 1978 when Okinawa's right-hand side traffic returned to the left-hand side, which is the pattern for Japan. Under American occupation from the end of World War II, Okinawa's

This aerial view of southeastern Ishigaki shows Ishigaki City and the port at left rear, Ishigaki Airport at right rear, Maezato Beach in the center and the ANA Intercontinental Hotel to its right.

You'll find some good shopping at the Ayapani Mall in town, a covered arcade that stretches over two blocks.

traffic system had been changed to the US right-hand side. Although the islands were returned to Japanese control in 1972, it took six more years for the roads to be reversed to their original left orientation. The 730 Monument is a proxy for Okinawa's return to Japan. It's a stone with a traffic arrow carved and painted into it indicating the shift from driving on the American side of the road (right) to the Japanese (left) side.

Only a block from the 730 Monument is the port and marine terminal. Its full name is the Port of Ishigaki Outer Islands Ferry Terminal (石垣港 離島ターミナル; Ishigaki-kō ritō tāminaru) and it's a beehive of activity. Like a busy airport, hundreds of vessels and thousands of people every day transit through Ishigaki harbor.

There's a friendly, helpful tourist information center inside the terminal and there's usually someone there who speaks English. They can supply you with a map of the island and advise on the ferry schedules. You can also rent a car and they'll help you with a hotel booking if you don't already have one.

Before we leave the harbor, we'll mention the first islet, adjacent to Ishigaki Port.

This stone marker, the 730 Crossing Monument in downtown Ishigaki, commemorates July 30th, 1978, the date Okinawa Prefecture reverted back from driving on the right-hand side of the road to the left-hand side, the norm for Japan.

YASHIMA JINKŌSHIMA (八島人工島; Yashima jinkō-shima; lit. "Eight Island Manmade Island"). The section of town where the port is located is called Yashima. Some years back, an artificial island was created from dredging the harbor and it was named after this part of town. It's connected to the Ishigaki mainland by the Southern Gate Bridge (サザンゲートブリッジ; Sazangēto-burijji). Unfortunately, there's not much actually on the island. You'll get a nice view from the bridge back over the harbor, but the island itself is somewhat of a would-be industrial storage lot and wasteland. It's easy to imagine that there were big plans for this place when it was constructed, but it's easy to see that those ambitions have not yet been fulfilled.

The Outer Islands Ferry Terminal at Ishigaki Port, the point of departure for the Yaeyamas.

Yamamoto Restaurant
(やまもと焼肉)

Yamamoto is the hottest spot in Ishigaki City. It is an institution in and the owner is a local celebrity. Patrons get their own little mini-grill, a brazier for preparing their Ishigaki beef and other assorted delights. You really can't visit this island and not try the beef. But, one word of warning, bring your wallet. Prime meat like this is not cheap. Count on paying $100 for two.

The Cape Tamatori Observatory is a good place to stop and admire the view along the east coast road north to the very end of the island.

From Cape Hirakubo, the northernmost tip of Ishigaki-jima, there is a spectacular view of the ocean and the islet of Daichi-Hanare offshore.

Ishigaki Island is big enough that you'll probably want to rent a car or scooter in order to get around. There are plenty of rental places in town. For our discussion below, we'll circle the island in a counter-clockwise direction in order to catch the morning sun on the east side and the afternoon sun and evening sunset on the west.

Leaving Ishigaki City, heading east on Route 390, it's about 2.25 miles (3 kilometers) past the present airport to the ANA Intercontinental Resort Hotel. There is an excellent beach all along this section of coast, Maezato (マエザトビーチ; Maézato bīchi). Although the ANA Hotel occupies a portion of the beachfront, Maezato Beach is public and open to anyone. There are freshwater showers there. From the ANA it's only

another 4 miles (6 kilometers) to the small town of Shiraho (白保) and this is where the island's most scenic drive really begins.

For the next 22 miles (35 kilometers), all the way to the island's top at Cape Hirakubo (平久保崎; Hirakubo-zaki), it is one gorgeous vista after another. It's a drive you'll never forget. About halfway up there's a spectacular panorama from the Cape Tamatori Observation Point (玉取崎展望台; Tamatori-zaki Tenbō-dai). As you come up this long, narrow arm of Ishigaki, for the first half of the way you'll have the Pacific Ocean on your right. For the second half, the East China Sea will be on your left. It's one of the most beautiful driving excursions in the Yaeyamas or the Ryukyus, or anywhere for that matter.

Ishigaki Beef (石垣牛) Ishigaki-gyū

He may not know it, but he's highly prized—and delicious. Most people have heard of Kobé beef (神戸ビーフ; Kōbe Bīfu). That's a registered trademark of the Kobé Beef Association and is reserved for Tajima cattle (但馬牛 Tajima-ushi or Tajima-gyū), one of several types of black Wagyū (和牛) cattle raised in Japan. (*Wa* means "Japanese" and *gyū* means "cow"). By law, Kobé beef cattle must be raised in Hyōgo Prefecture. But Wagyū cattle breeds may be raised anywhere, and they are. There are several high-quality

named types, including Mishima, Ōmi, Sanda and Ishigaki. The cattle are considered to produce the finest beef and best steaks in the world, highly regarded for its flavor and tenderness. The cattle are valuable because they are genetically predisposed to yield an intensely marbled beef that contains a higher percentage of omega fatty acids and a high percentage of unsaturated fat. There are several Ishigaki beef restaurants in Ishigaki City. Most employ wood charcoal braziers on the tables where patrons prepare assorted slices of beef to their own liking.

A protected grove of rare Yaeyama palms, found only on the islands of Ishigaki and Iriomote, at the Yaeyama Palm Tree Forest in Yonehare.

About 4 miles (6 kilometers) before reaching the end of the island, you'll pass by another popular beach and this one also has free showers. It's Ishigakijima Sunset Beach (石垣島 サンセットビーチ; Ishigaki-jima Sansetto-bīchi) and, as its name implies, its orientation makes it a good choice for the afternoon sun.

Upon reaching Ishigaki's northern end you'll come to Cape Hirakubo, a "land's end." The cliffs and the sea here are especially romantic. It's a sort of wind-blown, lonely place and, for Ishigaki, an "end-of-the-world" kind of place. But it's not really all that empty. All around you'll see that the surrounding pastures are grazed by black Ishigaki cattle,

prized for their marbled beef, so in fact, it's a bucolic and pastoral place as well as a scenic and romantic one.

Just offshore from this northern tip you'll see another one of several islets that we'll mention along the way as we circle around Ishigaki Island.

DAICHI-HANAREJIMA (大地離島; Daichi-hanaré or Daichi ritō). This vegetation-covered little rock lies about 1,640 feet (500 meters) offshore straight north from Hirakubozaki. It's only a speck of an islet, more or less oval-shaped, measuring close to 740 feet (225 meters) long north to south and 410 feet (125 meters) wide. It may be inhabited by birds or other creatures but not by man.

The road ends at Cape Hirakubo, so we'll have to turn around and head back. From the cape it's 19 miles (30 kilometers) due south along the western shore of the Ishigaki Peninsula and then a tiny bit west to Yonehara (米原). There's another excellent beach here, Yonehara Beach (米原ビーチ; Yonéhara bichi), one of the most popular on the island. It also has public showers and it's a public campground. A good snorkeling coral reef is a little further offshore and it, too, is a popular place. But watch it, there are warning signs about the current. It's rather notorious for strong currents out beyond the reef, so don't swim out too far.

A southern view of beautiful Kabira Bay. The bay is protected because of the black pearl industry and thus off-limits to swimmers.

Both Western and Asian cuisines are available at the Club Med Kabira Beach and the standards for everything are very high.

The entrance sign to Club Méditerranée Kabira, the most luxurious resort on Ishigakijima, located a short distance northwest of Kabira Bay.

Less than three-quarters of a mile (1 kilometer) away from the beach, inland to the immediate south, is the Yaeyama Palm Tree Forest (ヤエヤマヒルギ林; *Satakentia liukiuensis*; Yaéyama hirugi-rin), a unique jungle preserve of exotic trees. It's free. You can park your car then take about a 20-minute stroll on a good path through thick jungle. It's located at the base of Mt Omoto. The highlight here for tree fanciers is the Yaeyama palm, a unique species only from Ishigaki and Iriomote. They're tall, rising to a height of about 65 feet (20 meters).

From the Yonehara palm forest it's only 4 miles (6 kilometers) straight west to the first view of Kabira Bay (川平湾; Kabira-wan) from its southern end. It's beautiful, but swimming is not allowed. It's protected on account of the black pearl industry based here. Those wishing to see its undersea life can take a glass-bottom boat tour.

Rounding the bay, and driving a little more than 1.25 miles (2 kilometers) along its western side north, you'll come to an entry point on Kabira Bay, a place where boats can put in or take out on a concrete ramp. Here you'll find the Mikimoto Black Pearl Showroom. There are signs, so you really can't miss it. It keeps regular business hours, so if you're there during the day chances are

Kabira Bay Black Pearls

Just like mother-of-pearl, the smooth, lustrous inside layer of the shell of a mollusk, a pearl is formed of calcium carbonate which, in this case, has been deposited in concentric layers around some microscopic, irritating object. Pearls can occur naturally, which is extremely rare, or can be farmed, cultivated commercially, which is far more common. Whether wild or cultured, the most valuable pearls, those considered of gemstone quality, are almost always nacreous and iridescent, that is, they appear to glow from the surrounding

light which changes with the angle upon which they are viewed. Virtually any type of a shelled mollusk can produce some kind of a pearl, but the most highly regarded are pearl oysters from the genus Pinctada, which have been cultivated especially for this purpose. Only about half a dozen species have proven suitable. Pearl oysters are not closely related to either the types of mussels used in freshwater pearl cultivation or to the oysters commonly eaten. Black pearls, often called South Sea or Tahitian pearls, come from the black-lip oyster (*Pinctada margaritifera*). Mikimoto, a brand name of fine white pearls, come from the Akoya pearl oyster (*Pinctada fucata*). The above photograph is from the Mikimoto Company's Pearl Showroom on Kabira Bay. The price for this strand of superb black pearls is 450,000 Yen or about $5,000.

that it will be open. It's worth the stop. Even if you don't wish to buy anything, the showroom includes several informative displays explaining the story of pearls and their cultivation. Not many people can walk away from these black pearls without being impressed. They are truly beautiful.

Immediately offshore from the pearl showroom you'll see a pair of fairly good-sized islets almost blocking the entrance to Kabira Bay. These are Kojima and Majibanari. There are actually tiny third and fourth ones too, but they do not have names and don't merit much discussion.

The swimming pool at Club Méditerranée Kabira.

KOJIMA (小島; Ko-jima). Looking east from the shore, Ko is the larger of the two islands. It's to the right, south. It is green, covered in dense vegetation and uninhabited. The islet is at the northeastern end of Kabira Bay and protects the harbor by effectively blocking most of the bay's opening to the open ocean. Kojima (lit. "Little Island") is more or less an oval and is not so little. It measures 3,610 feet (1,100 meters) from north to south and 1,640 feet (500 meters) east to west at its widest points. From the boat landing it's about 1,150 feet (350 meters) offshore at its closest point. About a quarter of it is visible at the right center of the photo of Kabira Bay on page 237.

Rocky little Hirabanarejima from Cape Kabiraishi.

MAJIBANARIJIMA (マジバナリ島; Majibanari-jima). About 500 feet (150 meters) to the north of Kojima is a much smaller uninhabited islet, also partially blocking passage in or out of Kabira Bay. It also is mostly an oval in shape, about 985 feet (300 meters) from top to bottom and 330 feet (100 meters) across from east to west. The islet is about 660 feet (200 meters) offshore from the western side of Kabira Bay.

Approximately 1.75 miles (3 kilometers) northwest of Kabira Bay you'll come to the end of the road and the Club Méditerranée Kabira. Although it is the most luxurious resort on the island, it can nevertheless be relatively affordable when purchased as part of a package, including airfare. Figure on around $500 for two for the hotel portion with a two-night stay. That includes deluxe dining; the Club Med is known for its very high standards of cuisine.

If you leave the Club Méditerranée Kabira and follow the road northwest 500 feet (150 meters) you'll come to the very end of this

northeasternmost end of Ishigaki: Cape Kabiraishi (川平石崎; Kabira-ishi-zaki). And here you'll come to yet another tiny islet. Only 260 feet (80 meters) or so north of the cape's northernmost point you'll find Hirabanarejima.

HIRABANAREJIMA (平離島; Hira-banaré-jima; also called Hirarijima). It's not too much, just another rocky little isle half covered in scrub vegetation. It's about 740 feet (225 meters) long at its longest, and averages around 330 feet (100 meters) wide for most of its length. It is uninhabited.

Continuing from Hirabanarejima, but now turning south, it's about 1.5 miles (2.5 kilometers) along the inside western end of Cape Kabiraishi before you arrive at a good beach, Sukuji (底地ビーチ; Sukuji bīchi). If coming from the south it's not too far before reaching the end of the peninsula, but it's on the western, not eastern, side. Take the turn at the sign for the Ishigaki Seaside Hotel. The beach has three-quarters of a mile (1 kilometer) of clean, fine, white sand. There are also changing rooms, showers and toilets. The beach is probably best for families as its long, gentle slope is perfect for small children. On the

With its soft white sand and gentle gradient, Sukuji Beach is ideal for families with small children.

The view from Uganzaki Lighthouse on the westernmost point of Ishigaki is spectacular.

other hand, because the water stays so shallow for so long, it's not a good place for snorkelers or serious swimmers.

In addition to the Club Med, which is on the eastern side of Cape Kabiraishi, there are two more large hotels on the western side, one right on Sukuji Beach, the other a few hundred or so feet off of it. The property directly on the beach is the Ishigaki Sea Side Hotel (石垣 シーサイドホテル; Ishigaki shī-saido hoteru). The other property, just a few meters back from the beach, is the Seamen's Club (シーマンズクラブ; Shīmanzu-kurabu). Both are deluxe properties and if you can find an appealing room rate at either one, grab it.

From this point near the end of the Kabiraishi Cape we'll have to retrace our path back to the little village of Kabira and Kabira Bay. From there we'll head south, this time staying on the west side of the island, the East China Sea side.

If you're in a hurry or need to get back to Ishigaki City, from the Club Med it's just a little under 12 miles (20 kilometers) almost due south all the way on Route 79. You can drive it in less than 30 minutes. For the first half of the way the coastal road hugs the western shoreline. It's a scenic drive although not as spectacular as the island's Pacific coast drive.

If you have a little more time, a pleasant side trip along the way back to Ishigaki City will take you out to the island's westernmost point, the end of Cape Ugan (御神崎; Ugan-zaki). From Club Med head south past Kabira, about 4 miles (6 kilometers) altogether, to the village of Sakieda (崎枝), then turn right and continue almost another 3 miles (5 kilometers) due west to the end of the road and the Uganzaki Lighthouse (御神崎灯台; Ugan-zaki tōdai). The view from the heights here is one of the best on the island, like the view at Cape Hirakubo. It's a marvelous vista.

From Uganzaki it's a scenic 6 miles (10 kilometers) south, then east, rounding the cape and returning to the coastal road (Route 79) where you started. At this junction turn right, head south and continue almost 5.5 miles (9 kilometers), then turn right (leaving Route 79) on to a smaller road heading west. Follow the signs about 1.5 miles (2.5 kilometers) to Cape Kannon (観音崎; Kannon-zaki) and the Kannonzaki Viewpoint (観音崎展望台; Kannon-zaki Tenbō-dai). This road takes you southwest along Fusaki Beach (フサキビーチ; Fusaki bīchi), where you can stop for one last swim of the day before returning to Ishigaki City.

At the cape's end, across the road from the Observatory Viewpoint, you'll find a pair of very sad little memorials and a modest Shinto shrine with a grand entrance. The first memorial is dedicated to a group of Chinese laborers killed in the 19th century. The second is to three American Airmen killed in World War II. They are almost adjacent to one another. The shrine is only a couple of hundred meters down the road from the first two memorials.

At first glance the Chinese memorial, Tōjinbaka (唐人墓; Tōjin no haka) appears to be a small, highly decorated temple, but closer inspection reveals it to be the "Tang People's Grave." In 1852 a British ship with an American crew was bound for California. Its cargo was human, some 400 Hokkien Chinese laborers headed for the mining and railroad work of America's west. The ship ran aground off Ishigaki's shore and the men, at

The Tōjinbaka memorial is dedicated to a group of Chinese laborers killed in the 19th century.

The American Servicemen's Memorial is in remembrance of three prisoner-of-war airmen.

this point already maltreated, decided to escape. They fled on to the island and sought refuge. Considered mutineers, they were pursued by the ship's crew. Of the 380 who escaped, most were captured, but 128 were killed. Some headed into the mountains where they starved or committed suicide. Only a lucky few were hidden by friendly

Kannon-dō Entranceway

The temple entrance path at Kannon-dō Shrine displays one of the finest collections of traditional *tōrō* (灯籠 or 灯篭, 灯楼 "light basket/light tower") that you'll find anywhere in Japan. Made of stone, wood or metal, lanterns originally illuminated the holy path (*sandō*; 参道; lit. "visiting road") to Buddha. Later they were adopted by Shinto shrines. There are two main categories of *tōrō*: *tsuri-dōrō* (釣灯籠, 掻灯・or 吊り灯籠, lit. "hanging lamp"), which usually hang from the eaves of a roof, and *dai-dōrō* (台灯籠 lit. "platform lamp," which can be a pedestal, as here, or squat, standing on the ground. *Dai-dōrō* are commonly made of stone, in which case they are called *ishi-dōrō* (石灯籠 lit. "stone lantern").

locals and protected. The memorial was built in 1971 in honor of those who perished.

An equally terrible story lies behind the American Servicemen's Memorial which is nearby the Tōjin Tomb site. Almost at the close of World War II, on the morning of April 15, 1945, a Grumman Avenger, assigned to the carrier USS *Makassar Strait*, was shot down off the coast of Ishigaki by the Japanese Navy. Three aviators parachuted into the sea and swam to a reef where they were captured. All three were tortured, two were beheaded. The third airman was beaten, paraded through Ishigaki City and used for bayonet practice by his guards until he died. The torture and killing of prisoners-of-war were direct violations of the 1929 Geneva Convention on the rules of war and the treatment of prisoners to which Japan had been a signatory.

After the war, the murder of the three airmen led to the conviction of 41 Japanese soldiers and sailors for war crimes. Seven were executed. The memorial was dedicated in 2001. Its twin plaques in English and Japanese tell the story. Here's the final paragraph from the English language plaque: "To console the spirits of the three fallen American service members and to honor their deaths, we jointly dedicate this monument in the hope that this memorial stone will contribute to the everlasting peace and friendship between Japan and the United States, and that this monument will serve as a cornerstone to convey to future generations our keen desire for eternal peace in the world and our determination to renounce war."

From the two unrelated memorials it's about 985 feet (300 meters) south along the same road to the Kannon Temple (観音堂;

Taketomijima

Kannon-dō). At first glance, when you park your car, for instance, you'll be impressed with the stately, even magnificent, traditional stone lantern-lined Shinto entranceway to the temple. And you should be; it is very impressive. Stone lanterns (灯籠; *tōrō*) have been used for centuries in Asia, and particularly in Japan, to line the *sandō* (approach) to a temple or shrine. Along with the *torii* gate, their presence helps delineate the passage from the world of the profane to that of the profound.

Thus, you'll most likely find this lovely *tōrō*-lined *sandō* a real treat and eagerly await the shrine that lies within. But, alas, it's a modest little wooden, clay tile-roofed structure. There's nothing wrong with it, and it may be very holy, so treat it with respect, but as a tourist attraction it's a one out of ten. The stone *tōrō*, on the other hand, are very special, far more impressive than what lies at the end of the road. It's a case where the wrapper is more impressive than the package.

From the Kannonzaki Observatory, the Tōjin Memorial sites and the Kannon-dō Temple, it's only about 3 miles (5 kilometers) southeast to downtown Ishigaki and the end of this circle-island tour. For those interested in mountain hiking in the interior of the island, two of the best places to go are Mt Omoto (於茂登岳; Omoto-daké), 1,726 feet (526 meters) in the central northern section of the island's main body, and Mt Nosoko (野底岳; Nosoko-daké), 925 feet (282

meters) at the beginning of the island's long northern peninsula. Both climbs are well regarded and offer great views.

From Ishigaki City we'll begin our travels to the other islands of the Yaeyama Archipelago. We'll begin with the islands closest to Ishigaki and fan out west, north and south to the others further afield. We'll end at the two most distant islands in the chain: Hateruma in the south and Yonaguni in the west.

2 TAKETOMIJIMA 竹富島

About 4 miles (6 kilometers) due west from Ishigaki Port and 10 minutes by ferry lies the tiny, flat, pancake of an island, Taketomijima (竹富島; Také-tomi-jima). Ferries run daily, shuttling back and forth between the two islands every 30 minutes. They arrive at little Taketomi East Port (竹富東港; Také-tomi higashi-kō) on the northeast side of the island. From the port it's a 0.75-mile (1-kilometer) walk or bicycle/minibus/taxi ride to the center of the island where the only village, also called Taketomi, is located.

Taketomi is basically egg-shaped, about 2 miles (3 kilometers) long from top to bottom, and 1.5 miles (2.5 kilometers) wide. It has an area of 2.09 square miles (5.42 square kilometers) and a circumference of 5.5 miles (9 kilometers). About 320 people make Taketomi their home, and although many of its residents earn their living from

Transportation around Taketomijima is by water buffalo cart, by bicycle or on foot.

the tourist industry, a fair number are employed in the operation of a large cattle ranch occupying the southern one-third of the island or work on a commercial shrimp farm, also in the southern part of Taketomi.

Taketomi Island is famous for being one of Okinawa's best preserved places and for this reason it has been designated a Japanese National Treasure. You only have to spend a few minutes on the island to see why. In its traditional Ryukyuan village, which is the only village (集落; *shūraku*) on the island, there are no buildings permitted over one story high. Hence, all the houses (a number of which are *minshuku*) and shops have the ambience of an ancient small town. In addition, the buildings must employ the traditional Okinawan red-, white- or orange-tiled roof. And, naturally, though it might not be required, you won't find a rooftop that does not sport a *shīsā* lion dog on top, some of which are quite imaginative.

You won't find any ugly cinder block or cement walls here either; they're not allowed. Rather, most houses have their surrounding walls fashioned of hand-cut coral stone, the way it's been for centuries. The town lanes are of similar construction and are usually festooned with blooming hibiscus, bougainvillea or other flowering plants. The streets? No common hot ugly black asphalt, pavement or cement will do. Here it is white coral dust and sand, hard-packed over the years by many feet. Transportation around the island is by water buffalo cart (水牛車; *suigyū-sha*). Bicycles may also be rented, or you can walk. After all, nothing is too far.

Taketomi village has a tiny "downtown," the remnants of an ancient public well, an elementary and junior high school, a post office and a viewing tower called Nagaminoto, the biggest tourist "sight" on the island.

Taketomi's best beach, at Kondoi (コンドイビーチ; *Kondoi bīchi*), is popular for its snow white fine coral sand. Its long gentle grade is good for families with children, but not for snorkelers. In addition, there are two beaches, one on each side of the island, famous for their *hoshizuna* (星砂; lit. "star sand"; see page 78). On Taketomi, as well as a few islands in the Ryukyus, you'll find this unique microscopic wonder. If you look closely, you'll see that the sand is actually composed of star-shaped grains, the remnant exoskeletons of miniature sea creatures known as foraminifera. Taketomi's two

Coral stone walls and white coral lanes complement the traditional Okinawan red-, white- or orange-tiled roofs of the houses.

The 15-foot (4.5-meter) Nagaminoto Tower, Taketomi's highest point, allows a great view over the island.

star sand beaches (星砂の浜; *hoshizuna-no-hama*) are Kaiji-hama (カイジ浜) on the island's southwestern coast and Aiyaru-hama (アイヤル浜) on the eastern side.

Lying on the beach is one of the more adventurous activities on idyllic, peaceful Taketomi. Many visitors are content merely to stroll around the picturesque village or idle away the hours in a quaint traditional Japanese restaurant or café, of which there are many. Although the majority of visitors make a day trip to Taketomijima, it's easy to spend the night as there are at least a dozen *minshuku*. In fact, because a number of the residents offer accommodations in their homes and operate as *minshuku*, the number is probably closer to 20. Spending a night or two can be very relaxing. When all the day-trippers leave on the evening's last ferry, you and a few others will have the island to yourselves. Everyone sits back, enjoys a meal, drinks an Orion and gazes at the stars. There's no pollution here and all the Milky Way's limitless expanse is above.

The tiny islet of Kayama, more or less a rounded rectangle, is ringed by beaches and covered with vegetation. This view of it is taken from sugar cane-covered Kohama islet to its south.

3 HAMAJIMA 浜島

More a sandbar than an island, the tiny almost-islet of Hamajima lies a little less than 3 miles (5 kilometers) northwest of Taketomi, 7 miles (12 kilometers) west of Ishigaki Port and 2 miles (3 kilometers) east of Kayama. Hamajima (浜島; Hama-jima; lit. "Beach Island") does not appear on most maps of the Yaeyamas.

At its greatest length Hamajima is not quite 985 feet (300 meters) across the two ends of its east–west oriented crescent shape. The widest sections of the islet's surface measure from 80 to 165 feet (25 to 50 meters). There are a few patches of rock at the northeastern end of this otherwise completely sand-covered place. There is no vegetation of any kind and it's most definitely uninhabitable—except, perhaps, by some of the rabbits from Kayamajima.

Rabbit Island (ウサギ島; Usagi-tō)

That's the unofficial name for Kayamajima. Up until 20 years ago the island was inhabited, although not by many people. When the last residents left, their rabbits stayed behind. They did what rabbits do—multiply! Today there are more than 1,000 rabbits on Kayama Island.

4 KAYAMAJIMA 嘉弥真島

There is no public scheduled ferry service to this tiny private islet. Kayamajima (嘉弥真島; Kayama-jima) is about 10 miles (16 kilometers) west and just a little north of Ishigaki Port and less than 1.25 miles (2 kilometers) north of Kohamajima. Its shape is more or less a rounded rectangle, about 2,380 feet (725 meters) long and 1,720 feet (525 meters) wide.

The islet is mostly ringed by beaches and is entirely covered in vegetation. It is technically uninhabited, but because it is owned and used by a resort hotel, beach-goers come out for the day. There's a pier, cabanas and other facilities on the island to keep guests comfortable. Kayama is locally famous for its rabbit population. No one knows exactly how many there are on the island, but it's believed there are more than a thousand. They are the descendants of a small population of domestic rabbits originally raised by the island's residents some 20 years earlier when the island was inhabited. They are feral now—and everywhere.

5 KOHAMAJIMA 小浜島

You'll find this small island not quite 11 miles (17 kilometers) west of Ishigaki Port, less than 1.25 miles (2 kilometers) south of Kayamajima and about 2 miles (3 kilometers) east of Iriomote. Kohamajima (小浜島; Kohama-jima; lit. "Little Beach Island") is a calm, lovely place graced with sugar cane farms, a little observatory and two luxury resorts. It is easily worth a day trip from Ishigaki. Frequent daily ferries make the trip in 25–30 minutes.

The island's shape is quite difficult to describe. It's much simpler to illustrate by reference to an aerial photograph. The island's greatest length is just over 3 miles (5 kilometers) from its southeastern tip to

On the links at the Haimurubushi Resort Hotel on Kohama Island.

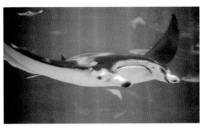

Manta Way, a narrow strait of crystal-clear turquoise waters between Iriomote and Kohama fills every spring with enormous but gentle manta rays. Divers from all over the world come to experience this extraordinary phenomenon.

its southwestern end. Its north–south distance is about 1.5 miles (2.5 kilometers) between most any two points. Its area has been calculated at 3 square miles (7.84 square kilometers) with a coastline of just over 10 miles (16 kilometers). Kohama's population is approximately 585, which is relatively high for an island of its size. Many of Kohama's residents are employed by the resorts located on the island.

Although from a distance when approaching on the ferry, the island appears mostly flat, as you get closer you'll see that it actually is quite hilly. The ferries arrive at and depart from Kohama Port (小浜港; Ko-hama-kō), which is located on the northeast end of the island. There's a little tourist information service there where they'll give you a map. It's also possible to rent a bicycle, scooter or car, which is advisable. On a hot day, walking across this island would be a challenge. Because it is hilly you'll get a workout on a bicycle.

In addition to the five-star resorts there are about 10 *minshuku* on Kohama. If you wish to spend the night and haven't already

made a reservation, the tourist office will phone one for you if you ask. Most are in the island's centrally located little village, Murauchi (村内; lit. "village"), but there are a couple on the southwestern tip of Cape Hoso (細崎; Hoso-zaki) as well. That's also the closet land point to Manta Way, which we'll mention further below.

Incidentally, if you happen to see a crowd of Japanese tourists posing for photos in front of what appears to be a somewhat ordinary old house in the center of town, it's most likely that you've come across what used to be the set of the nationally syndicated NHK (Japan's national television network) TV drama *Chura san* (ちゅらさん). Kohama became famous for a few years, starting in 2001, when the popular daytime drama was shot on the island. At the time, this led to a boom in local tourism. Interest in the house has since died down, but there is always someone who recognizes the set and wants to take photos of it.

In this aerial view of Kohama Island from the north, Manta Way and Iriomote are to the right, Kuro Island is to the rear (south), and tiny Kayama is just barely visible in the lower left-hand corner.

In the north central part of the island you'll come to its highest point, Mt Ufu (大岳; Ufu-daké; also pronounced Ō-také), which, including the observatory at its top is about 330 feet (100 meters) tall. That's pretty high for a "flat" island and you'll get a great view from up there.

Kohama features two deluxe resorts: the Villa Hapira Pana (ヴィラハピラパナ; Vira-hapira-pana) and the Haimuru Mirage Resort Hotel (はいむるぶし; Haimuru-bushi), both of which occupy the island's southeast end and cape, and completely cover it with 18 holes of golf.

The seaside setting and hundreds of acres of golf greens make this a particularly beautiful place. Japanese tourists and golfers fly here from Tokyo and other places in mainland Japan usually on a one-week package. Booking either hotel on your own would set you back anywhere from $300 to $500 a night depending on your choice of room. All accommodations include meals—they have to, there's almost nowhere else to eat on this island other than at *minshuku*. The best beach on Kohama is also found here, Haimurubushi Beach (はいむるぶし ビーチ; Haimuru-bushi bīchi), and although it appears that it is controlled by the hotel, it is technically open to the public. The island's other best-known beach is even larger though it is not maintained as at the resort. It's Tōmaru Beach (唐丸ビーチ; Tōmaru bīchi) and it is close to the ferry port.

Kohama is most famous, both in Japan and internationally, for Manta Way (ヨナラ水道; Yonara Suidō). That's the 3-mile (5-kilometer)-long by 1.25-mile (2-kilometer)-wide strait running between Kohama and Iriomote. Each year, between April and June, and then again from August to October, divers from around the world come to Hosozaki, the Strait and all the way up to Ishigaki's northwestern end to swim with manta rays. The enormous gentle creatures feed on plankton which is abundant in these waters. The experience is known among Japanese divers as the "Manta Scramble" (マンタスクランブル; Manta-sukuranburu).

6 KUROSHIMA 黒島

The next destination in our westward and southward expanding sequence of islands visited from Ishigaki is Kuro. The name means "black," a reference to the island's dark-colored soil. Kuroshima (黒島; Kuro-

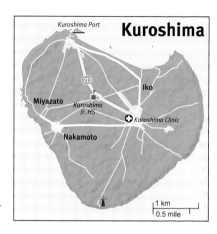

shima) is located a bit less than 12 miles (19 kilometers) southwest of Ishigaki Port. Several ferry companies ply the route, which takes 30 minutes one way. Service varies seasonally, but most of the year there are several daily round-trip sailings with more frequent departures in the summer months.

Kuroshima is invariably described as a "heart-shaped" island and this is as good a description as any. The island measures approximately 2.5 miles (4 kilometers) across at its widest northern section and 2.25 miles (3.5 kilometers) from north to south. It has an overall area of 3.75 square miles (10 square kilometers) and a circumference of 7.75 miles (12 kilometers). The island is completely flat, all of it only a few meters above sea level.

Kuro Island has around 215 residents who are unevenly divided into three small settlements. The first one you'll see is the port, Kuroshima-kō (黒島港), which is located at the island's northwesternmost end. There are perhaps a dozen houses there and several shops where you can rent a bicycle on arrival.

About 1.25 miles (2 kilometers) south of the port, on Kuro's west coast, there is another tiny village, this one holding maybe 20–25 homes and a few larger buildings. The Kuroshima Visitor Center is here and just a little north you'll find the Kuroshima Research Center (黒島研究所; Kuroshima kenkyūjo), also referred to as the Marine Park Institute. Its purpose is the study and protection of marine life in general and sea turtles in particular. You'll also find a small museum on sea life. It charges 300 Yen. Sometimes during the summer months the institute leads guided tours of sea turtle egg laying. You have to inquire, and there's also a charge for this. Adjacent to the Marine Park Institute is the Marine Village Resort, which is a pleasant place to stay.

A little over 1 mile (2 kilometers) due east of the Visitor Center is the island's largest village where the post office and the only gas station are located. The village has some 40 or 50 residences. There are half a dozen *minshuku* as well. All generally include meals, although there is one restaurant-café in town. Somewhat in the middle of these three villages are the Kuroshima primary and junior high schools. Nearby the schools you'll come to the Agarisuji (あがりすじ) tower, a little viewing platform by the road which offers a nice view of this pancake flat island. For the most part, Kuro's very small road system connects these four places, which are all located in the northwestern one-third of the island.

Kuro has two beaches. One is popular for its clean fine sand, the other is better known as a diving and snorkeling site. The best sun-bathing and swimming beach is West Beach (西の浜; Nishi-no-hama). It's located on the northwestern shore, not far from the port. One warning, it's also popular with sea turtles so you must be careful in the spring and summer months not to step on their egg sites. Sections of the beach, or the entire beach, may be cordoned off by the Marine Park Institute. The other beach, a good diving place, is Nakamoto (仲本海岸; Naka-moto kaigan) on Kuro's southwest coast.

The rest of Kuroshima is essentially a large cow pasture, for it is commonly said that on Kuro there are ten times as many cattle as there are people. That's actually an understate-ment. A recent article listed the cattle popula-

Kuro's Marine Park Institute has a small museum on the sea life of the island.

Kuroshima's West Beach is where sea turtles come to lay their eggs in the spring and summer months.

tion as 3,000. Most of the island's residents are employed directly or indirectly in cattle ranching. Kuroshima's main industry is the production of beef. These are not dairy cattle.

7 ARAGUSUKUJIMA 新城島

A little less than 2.5 miles (4 kilometers) due west of Kuroshima as the crow flies you'll come to Aragusukujima (新城島; Ara-gusuku-jima; lit. "New Castle Island"), but before going any further we'll have to mention a few things. One, you can't get there from here. In other words, from Kuro, or almost any other Yaeyama Island, unless you have your own watercraft you must re-turn to Ishigaki Port and take a ferry from there. With a very few limited exceptions, there simply is no demand for an inter-island ferry service. Virtually all ferries operate out of the Ishigaki hub and it's therefore usually necessary to return there before embarking to another island.

Second, it is 15 miles (24 kilometers) southwest from Ishigaki Port to Aragusuku, but there is no ferry service in any case. The island's population is variously reported as twelve, seven, six or even two. Therefore, not only is there is no ferry service, there are no public or commercial services of any kind on the island, that is, no *minshuku*, convenience stores, gas station, schools, post office, etc. Those wishing to visit must go by chartered boat, which can be arranged at Ishigaki harbor. Check with the tourist service. A fair number of people visit here for snorkeling or just for the sake of going where few others go. If you were traveling to Iriomote's Ohara Port, you would pass right by Aragusuku as it's only 4 miles (6 kilometers) southeast of there. But the ferry won't stop along the way (except for the island's residents).

This aerial view shows Aragusuku's twin islets, Kamiji and Shimoji, accessible to each other at low tide.

Here's something else. Aragusuku "Island" is, in fact, two islands. They're close by one another, so close that they're usually referred to as one, but in local dialect they're called Panari (パナリ), which means "separated" or "apart." At low tide you can walk over a shallow coral shoal about 1,475 feet (450 meters) from one to the other. History has it that they were originally one island. In the 17th century a tsunami broke them apart and killed most of the inhabitants.

If not referring to the two islands collectively as Panari, the northern larger islet is named Kamiji, also known as Uechi, and the southern islet is known as Shimoji.

KAMIJIJIMA (上地島; Kamiji-jima). This islet is the larger of the Aragusuku twins. Its Kanji characters literally translate as "Upper" or "Over" Land Island, an obvious reference to its placement above its sister isle to the south. It's usually called Uéchi-jima (うえちじま) or simply Uéchi, but sometimes you'll hear or see Kamiji-jima (かみちじま) or just Kamiji.

It is oblong in shape, about 1.5 miles (2.5 kilometers) in length and around 2,620 feet (800 meters) wide. It's completely flat. Uechi's area is three-quarters of a square mile (1.76 square kilometers) and its circumference is 3.75 miles (6 kilometers). The island has a landing pier on the central western side and this is where the few residents live. There used to be more, but the population has declined dramatically over the past 20 years.

An aerial view of flat, oblong Kamijijima. It has a landing pier in the center of its western side.

SHIMOJIJIMA (下地島; Shimoji-jima). This islet's Kanji translates, rather logically, as "Under" or "Below" Land Island, again with reference to its sister isle to the north. It is uninhabited. It is round, with an approximate diameter of 1 mile (1.6 kilometers). Its land area is half a square mile (1.58 square kilometers) and it has a coastline circumference of 3 miles (5 kilometers). It was farmed with sugar cane until it was abandoned a few years ago. Its land is still privately owned but it's questionable whether it ever will become inhabited again.

8 HATOMAJIMA 鳩間島

About 24 miles (38 kilometers) northwest of Ishigaki Port, or some 12 miles (20 kilometers) also to the northwest, beyond Kohama and Kayama islets, lies this tiny place, Hatomajima (鳩間島; Hato-ma-jima). It is approximately 3 miles (5 kilometers) due north of the center of Iriomote. The island is more or less an oval, very small, about

1.25 miles (2 kilometers) long at its greatest length and not quite three-quarters of a mile (1 kilometer) wide at its greatest width. Its surface area is just under half of a square mile (1 square kilometer) and its coastline is 2.25 miles (4 kilometers) long.

There is a commercial ferry service to the island but it is much less frequent than the service to, for example, Taketomi or Kohama. Scheduled ferries vary seasonally, with at least one round trip per day all year round and up to two or three per day during the summer. Depending on the time of year, some of the ferry services may consist of a mail boat making a stop on Iriomote along the way. Direct travel time one way from Ishigaki Port is two hours.

In a recent census, the island's population was recorded at 49, almost all of whom live on the southern end of the island in the little village of Hatoma Port (鳩間港; Hato-ma-kō). The rest of the island is uninhabited and covered in scrub vegetation. There is a road/path making a circle around the island but it's only partially paved. As is the case with so many small islands in the Ryukyus, Hatoma's population has been declining for decades. It wasn't all that long ago when there were several hundred residents. The tuna fishing industry was an important source of income up until World War II and into the 1960s. Changing fish populations, changing patterns of modern life and changing expectations of young people have all contributed to an over-all decline in many such islands. Japanese Government officials have essentially tried to "close" the island for some years, but diehard residents remain. Presently, there's a public

An aerial view of oval-shaped Hatoma Island, with Hatoma Port at top (south), where its residents live.

school up to junior high, but who knows how long that will last. Ultimately, this island, along with many other very small islands, is destined to become uninhabited and with that, a way of life will pass.

Here's some good news: there are three *minshuku* on Hatoma and visitors are most welcome. All include meals in their rates, which is necessary because there are no restaurants on the island. Hatoma, and the tiny inhabited islets like it, are perhaps the ultimate in a quiet vacation. No one from back home or your office will bother you here because they won't be able to find you.

9 IRIOMOTEJIMA 西表島

With an area of 112 square miles (289 square kilometers) and a coastline circumference of 80 miles (128 kilometers), Iriomotejima (西表島; Iriomoté-jima) is the largest island of the Yaeyamas and the second largest island in Okinawa Prefecture (after Okinawa itself). It is roughly square in shape although tilted on an axis and possessing a broken-off south-western end. It measures approximately 9 miles (14 kilometers) from north to south and 11 miles (17 kilometers) from east to west. Although a relatively large island for the Ryukyus, it is one of the least densely populated with fewer than 2,300 residents. Essentially, Iriomote is Japan's jungle. Ninety percent of it is covered in mountains, dense tropical vegetation or mangrove swamps, and almost the entire island is either locally protected or part of Iriomote National Park. Iriomote's highest peak is Mt Komi (古見岳; Komi-daké) at 1,540 feet (469.5 meters). The island is home to a number of unique species, including the Yama-neko, the Iriomote wild cat, a small rare species of lynx. They are nocturnal and rarely seen by visitors.

This aerial view of Kamijijima's sister islet Shimo-jijima shows its abandoned sugar cane fields.

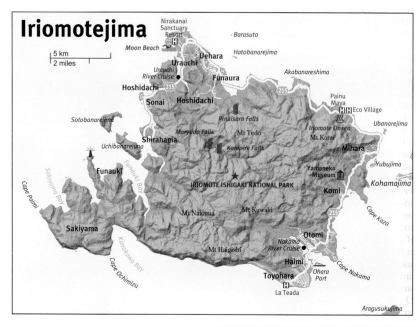

There is no airport or airstrip on Iriomote and the only way on to the island is by public ferry from Ishigaki or private watercraft. As the crow flies, it's 15 miles (24 kilometers) from Ishigaki Port to Iriomote's east coast. Of course, the ferry distance is somewhat longer. There are several ports on Iriomote but the two most commonly used by the commercial ferry services are Ohara Port (大原港; Ōhara-kō) at Iriomote's southeastern end, and Uehara Port (上原港; Uéhara-kō), almost at the northernmost tip of the island.

Note that Ohara Port's actual name is Nakama (仲間港; Nakama-kō), but it's widely referred to as Ohara Port. Of the two ports, Ohara is Iriomote's busiest with the most

Iriomote, the largest island in the Yaeyamas, as seen across Manta Way from Kohamajima.

One of the high-speed Ishigaki–Iriomote ferries.

frequent service to Ishigaki. During the high season, in summer, there are more than two dozen—closer to 30—high-speed ferries a day, with departures every 15–30 minutes. Even during the winter there can be as many as a dozen sailings a day, about one every hour during daylight hours. Note that in the course of a day, several of these ferries will make a stop en route, coming or going, to either Taketomi or Kohama. Thus, here is one of the rare opportunities where it is possible, with proper planning, to travel to one island and continue to another without needlessly backtracking to the central hub, in this case Ishigaki.

Travel time between Ishigaki and Ohara, without any stops, is 35 minutes. Sailing distance is just over 19 miles (30 kilometers). In addition to the foregoing high-speed ferries, three times a week a passenger and vehicle ferry runs between the two islands. It's slower—sailing takes about two hours one way—but it costs about a third less. Obviously, you can bring your vehicle with you on this ferry although that naturally costs more. For all the possibilities and current schedules and prices it's best to check with the tourist information service at Ishigaki Port.

Iriomote's other commercial port, Uehara, at the top northwest side of the island, has somewhat less frequent service than Ohara, but not much less. During the busy summer season there are about 20 daily high-speed ferries between Ishigaki and Iriomote, about one every half hour. In winter cut that number in half, but that's still about one every hour throughout the day. Note that several of these trips will make a stop along the way, in this case to the small island of Hatoma, just above Iriomote. Without the stop, travel time is 40 minutes one way. The sailing distance between Ishigaki Port and Uehara is 23 miles (37 kilometers). Add a few kilometers and an extra 20 minutes if your ship makes the stop at Hatoma. In addition to the fast passenger service there is also a thrice-weekly passenger and vehicle ferry on which you can bring your car, motorbike or bicycle. It takes three hours one way. Since that line also serves Hatoma, there will always be a stop there, either coming or going.

Here's something else, in the fall and winter months the northern end of Iriomote is particularly prone to strong northeasterly winds. Cancellations (欠航; *kekkō*; lit. suspension of service) due to bad weather are very common. If that occurs on your sailing, the Uehara Ferry still runs, but it docks at Ohara. Since the fare is somewhat higher to Uehara, the ferry service will transfer you free of charge on their bus from Ohara to Uehara or will drop you off at any point along the way.

The comfortable cabin of a high-speed ferry.

A small cascade along one of Iriomote's many hiking trails in the island's national park.

Finally, note that when checking ferry schedules for Uehara Port you may find some confusing references to nearby Funaura Port (船浦港; Funaura-kō). Funaura is 1.25 miles (2 kilometers) south of Uehara and up until 2006 was used as the northern port. Therefore, those references are obsolete; Funaura Port today is only used as a private fishing port, not for public services.

Although the vast majority of Japanese tourists visit Iriomote on a day-trip out of Ishigaki, it is entirely possible to stay on the island. There are car, bike and scooter rentals available at both ports and there are *minshuku* all over. There are about 10 in the eastern section of Iriomote, most, but not all, in Ohara. And there are more *minshuku*, over 30, on the western side. Most are in Uehara, but several each are in Funaura, Sonai (祖納), Shirahama (白浜) and Funauki (船浮). If *minshuku* are not your cup of tea, there are several very deluxe small hotels sprinkled about as well. We'll mention them as we visit the island further below.

Unlike most of the Ryukyus, Iriomote is one of the few islands where its perimeter is not entirely encircled by a ring road. Nor is the island criss-crossed by all sorts of local roads. Essentially, there is one road that parallels about two-thirds of the island's

Haemida Beach on southern Iriomote has lovely fine white sand but dangerous currents offshore.

Guided boat tours are offered along the Nakama River, leaving from Ohara Port at the river mouth.

shoreline. It's officially designated as Route 215 but it's commonly known as the Kaichū dōro (海中道路; lit. "marine or sea road"). There are no roads through the interior.

Remember that a third of the island is designated as the Iriomote National Park (西表国立公園; Iriomoté kokuritsu-kōen), the only national park in all of Okinawa, and most of the rest of the island is a protected nature preserve under local law. Therefore, seeing much of Iriomote means either taking one of several river cruises, kayaking, hiking or a combination of these. There are several rivers where cruises are offered and there are numerous hiking trails.

One word of caution about the trails. The most popular hiking excursion on Iriomote is the cross-island hike. It's 12 miles (20 kilometers) long and takes about eight hours. It's fairly well marked and fairly well traveled, but you are crossing jungle and this is home to Habu snakes. After a Japanese tourist went missing a few years ago, hikers are now

requested to submit their plans to the local police. At minimum you should let your *minshuku* or hotel know your itinerary for the day.

We'll visit the island by starting at the bottom southeast corner, a little below Ohara Port, then work our way counter-clockwise, up and around the Kaichū dōro north, then all the way across the top, west to Uehara Port, then a short distance south along the west coast until the road ends at Shirahama Port (白浜港; Shira hama-kō). In addition to the various points of interest along the way, there are about half a dozen small islets just offshore at several places. We'll have a look at them as we pass by.

Assuming that you have arrived at Ohara Port, drive a little less than 1.75 miles (3 kilometers) southwest on Route 215 to Toyohara (豊原) and the La Teada Iriomote Resort (ホテル ラ・ティーダ西表; Hoteru Ra Tīda Iriomoté). It's a nice small hotel that bills itself as a "nature resort." The theme

The Iriomote Wild Cat

In Latin, it's the *Prionailurus iriomotensis*, in Japanese 西表山猫 or Iriomote-yama-neko, which literally is "mountain cat." But no matter how you say it, the Yama-neko is a very rare creature indeed. The one pictured here is at a research station on the island. It's estimated there are perhaps 100 of these cats in existence, but in truth it's hard to tell whether it's a rare species or just someone's house cat got loose. The closest most Iriomote visitors will get to seeing one is on the sign above.

Mangrove Trees

"Mangrove" is the common name for over 100 species of mostly unrelated trees and shrubs that inhabit and help colonize coastlines in many parts of the tropical and subtropical world. What they all have in common is the ability to live in the salt and brackish waters where freshwater rivers and estuaries meet the sea. Although the various families and genera are quite diverse, several of the more popular species are referred to as "black," "white" and "red" mangroves. Even those simple terms encompass over 40 distinct species.

"Looking-glass" Mangrove

Known in Japanese as Sakishima-suo-no-ki, the Latin botanical name is *Heritiera littoralis*. They can be found from tropical East Africa to Southern India to Southeast Asia. Not a common species anywhere, their taxonomic status is quite complex. They are only very distantly related to true mangroves. Their sometimes enormous buttress roots were used by early Iriomote inhabitants for ship rudders. Although the trees appear extremely stable, they are, in fact, extremely shallow-rooted and are sometimes blown over in typhoons. Only their great above-ground roots protect them from this happening more frequently.

here is everything "green" in keeping with the island's ecology. Summer high-season prices for a standard twin run about $250 a night, which includes dinner and breakfast. Larger, more deluxe rooms run about $350. Knock off around $100 from those rates if you're staying in the winter.

Less than three-quarters of a mile (1 kilometer) after the hotel, going west, Route 215 ends, but a minor paved road continues almost another 2.5 miles (4 kilometers). The road ends at a public campground. This entire strip of Iriomote's southern coast is fringed by the longest beach on the island, Haemida Beach (南風見田の浜; Haémida-no hama). There are some beautiful fine, white, clean, sand sections along this coast, but do take note that those signs in Japanese on the beach warn of dangerous currents. The only safe places to swim are in the

shallow lagoon areas between the beach and the outlying coral reef. It's not safe to snorkel or dive on the reef. The campground and the beach mark the southwestern end of the road, so we'll turn around and retrace our steps about 4 miles (6 kilometers) back northeast to Ohara.

The port and village of Ohara lie at the mouth of the Nakama River (仲間川; Nakama-gawa), the second longest of Iriomote Island. Guided river tours are offered here. Alternatively, you can rent a canoe or kayak, or you can hike alongside the river's course on a designated trail. It's a part of the cross-island trail. The Nakama is not long, only about 11 miles (18 kilometers), but its banks contain almost 4 miles (6 kilometers) of mangrove forest and one colony of Yaeyama palms. Towards its upper end you'll see what is believed to be the

Water buffalo carts crossing to Yubu Island from Iriomote.

largest Sakishima-suo-no-ki (サキシマスオウノキ) in Japan. Sometimes called the "looking-glass" mangrove in English, the name's a reference to the silvery scales on the underside of its leaves. The tree appears green from the top and white from below.

Continuing north from Ohara you'll first cross the bridge over the Nakama River, then in just a little over 3 miles (5 kilometers), and less than a mile (1 kilometer) before the tiny village of Komi (古見), you'll come to (here's a mouthful) the Komi-no Sakishima-suo-no-ki gunraku (古見の サキシマスオウ の木群落; lit. "Komi Looking-Glass Mangrove Tree Forest"). Some of the largest and most spectacular specimens of this extraordinary tree are found here. You can walk a very short distance from a parking area to the trees.

After the tree grove and after Komi village, it's less than three-quarters of a mile (1 kilometer) north on Route 215 to a left-hand turn. Take it. The turn leads about 2,300 feet (700 meters) to the Iriomote Wildlife Conservation Center (西表 野生生物保護センター; Iriomoté yasei seibutsu hogo sentā). There is a sign. It's a small museum featuring the wildlife of the island, with special attention to the Iriomote wild cat (イリオモテ ヤマネコ; Iriomoté yama-neko).

A rare and endangered animal, it is estimated that there may be around 100 on the island. There is a breeding cage where cats that have been hit by cars or otherwise injured and captured are rehabilitated before they are released back into the wild. You may get a chance to see one of these felines here. Otherwise, you probably never will as they generally sleep during the day. Wandering around at night, stumbling through the

Water buffalo carts are popular for commuting between Yubijima and Iriomote at low tide.

jungle trying to find one, which is the time when Habu snakes are on patrol, is probably not a very wise idea. The center is open every day except Mondays and holidays from 10AM to 4PM. Admission is free.

Returning to the coastal road, Route 215, we'll continue north just a bit under 1.75 miles (3 kilometers) to a right-hand turn. This small turn-off takes us less than 985 feet (300 meters) to a large sandy parking lot full of tour buses. This is the staging area for the water buffalo cart wagons to Yubu Island. Yubu is the first of several small islands that are scattered around the coast of Iriomote.

YUBUJIMA (由布島; Yubu-jima). Here is our first little satellite isle, this one unique among the surrounding islets of Iriomote in that it is inhabited, albeit by only 23 people as reported in a recent census.

Yubu, which is also pronounced Yufu, is located about 1,070 feet (325 meters) offshore from Iriomote overlooking Manta Way, the 1.5-mile (2.5-kilometer)-wide strait between Iriomote and Kohama. The water depth between Yubu and Iriomote, at low

The small, oval-shaped islet of Ubanare, off the northeastern corner of Iriomote's coast, is completely covered in thick vegetation.

tide, is shallow, not much deeper than one's ankles. Over the past 20 years, it's become a popular place to visit by means of a cart harnessed to water buffalo. They do the towing, visitors keep their feet dry. The price is fairly steep, about $15 per person, and if you try to walk it on your own the islanders still charge 500 Yen or about $6.00. Yubu Island is open from 9AM to 4PM every day. The carts run about every 15 minutes.

Yubujima is more or less crescent-shaped and about 2,620 feet (800 meters) long from north to south. Its width varies from around

The lobby of the deluxe Nature Hotel Painu Maya Resort, which has a nature and hot spring theme.

820 feet (250 meters) in its southern section to 500 feet (150 meters) in its northern part. The island narrows to as little as 300 feet (90 meters) in between the two sections. Its area has been measured as 0.12 square kilometers. There are dwellings and rudimentary sand roads all over the island, but it's primarily geared to tourism. There are no public schools or ordinary shops. Rather, there are mostly enterprises catering to tourists: souvenir stores and restaurants.

Yubu Island essentially functions as a relaxing vision of times gone by, a chance to see and feel a different sort of life before the fast-paced version we all know from our daily experience. Although Yubu can be criticized as an idealized version of "old" Okinawa—and criticized as an overpriced, romanticized tourist attraction—the fact remains that it is a view into another Okinawa. Merely because times have changed does not mean that there are not those who long for—and reminisce about—such days of old. Yuba offers a little glimpse into a time and place that is mostly gone, but not entirely forgotten.

Returning to the Iriomote mainland, we'll get back onto Route 215 and continue north just about 1.75 miles (3 kilometers)— the road hugs the coast all the way—to the northeasternmost tip of the island, Cape Nobaru (野原崎; Nobaru-zaki) and here, just offshore, we'll find our next little islet neighbor, Solitary U Island.

UBANAREJIMA (ウ離島; U-banaré-jima). At its closest point, this little oval-shaped islet is about 660 feet (200 meters) off the northeastern corner of Iriomote's coast. It's

The Iriomotoe Onsen, the southernmost hot spring resort in Japan, has a beautiful jungle setting.

Ōmija Roadside Park, a seaside observation deck, is reached across walkways through mangroves.

a green place, completely covered in thick vegetation. "Isolated," "Solitary," or "Separated" Ujima, for that's the meaning of its name in English, is long and narrow, 1,310 feet (400 meters) from end to end, north to south, and ranging between 260 and 425 feet (80 and 130 meters) in width from east to west. Its surface area is 0.04 square kilometers. It marks the northern end of Iriomote's section of Manta Way. After the manta rays leave this protected span of waters between Kohama and Iriomote, they cross open water until coming to Ishigaki. Why this sea channel of water is so special, attracting the rays here every year, is not fully understood. Local people may also refer to this islet as Uhanaré or Uritō.

We're now driving due west, then a little north, altogether about 2.5 miles (4 kilometers), a little past the village of Takana (髙那) to our next stop, a very deluxe hotel, the Nature Hotel Painu Maya Resort (ネイチャーホテル パイヌマヤ リゾート; Neichā-hoteru Painu-maya-rizōto). It's situated immediately adjacent to the southernmost hot spring resort in Japan, the Iriomote Onsen (西表島温泉). The hotel is luxurious and incorporates a nature and hot spring theme throughout the property. Room rates start at about $150 per person per night and go up from there. That includes breakfast and dinner.

The next-door *onsen*, which is the only hot spring on Iriomotejima, may be visited without staying at the hotel. It costs 1,500 Yen for the day. There are indoor and outdoor hot soaking pools and steam saunas for both men and women. In the separate men's and women's quarters, people bath without swimsuits. In the common areas, where

both sexes mix, swimsuits are required. There's also a large heated outdoor swimming pool. The *onsen* is open from 10AM to 10PM every day. Overall, this is a lovely public hot spring sited virtually in the jungle. If you enjoy hot springs, the Iriomote Onsen will in all likelihood be a highlight of your stay on Iriomote.

From the hot springs continue west and north about 2.5 miles (4 kilometers) along Iriomote's northern shore to a small unnamed cape. Continue for just over a mile (2 kilometers) across the cape (this is away from the water as it's separated by jungle), then over a couple of small rivers to rejoin the sea along a small open bay. You'll next come to the Ōmija Roadside Park (大見謝 ロードパーク; Ōmija rōdo-pāku). It's a parking lot with a seaside observation deck to the left and a set of stairs leading to a series of wooden walkways through a mangrove forest to the right.

The observatory provides a nice covered shelter in which to enjoy a cool drink or lunch. It has a lovely view of this small bay. If you also descend the steps down to the shore, you'll find several paths through the mangroves. They're elevated above the changing tides and provide a good look at a mangrove tidal swamp without getting your shoes wet and muddy.

From the observation deck or from the road, looking north and east over the water, you can now see the next islet, Akabanare Island. As the crow flies, it's a little more than three-quarters of a mile (1 kilometer) north, a little to the right, east, at the end of the bay, and just offshore, west, of the end of the cape you just came around. After all that, it must be said that it's not much.

AKABANARESHIMA (赤離島; Aka-banaré-shima; also Aka-ritō). This islet, whose name means "Isolated Red Island," is a fairly good-sized rock, mostly covered with vegetation. It's about 820 feet (250 meters) offshore to the north from the end of a small cape on the central northern coast of Iriomote. It's actually a couple of rocks but there is one large one that stands out from its neighbors. It's roughly 500 feet (150 meters) in diameter and has been measured as 1/10th of one square kilometer in area. If you really just have to see it more closely, there is a trail from the road (Route 215) out to the shore. You'll have to back up about three-quarters of a mile (1 kilometer) to where you came around the cape previously.

From this pleasant viewpoint on the bay we'll continue about another 4 miles (6 kilometers) west and north, eventually crossing a long bridge, until we reach Funaura and its small port. It's a pretty drive as this section of the Kaichū dōro follows the shoreline all the way. Funaura used to be the northwestern ferry port from Ishigaki, but it was always troublesome. Essentially, the port's mouth is too narrow and the bay too shallow. When the seas are rough, often in winter, there is not enough room for larger ships to safely maneuver. It was abandoned by the commercial ferry services after the new larger port opened in Uehara several years ago.

There are five *minshuku* in Funaura, but other than that there's not a lot going on. However, it is the jumping-off point for excursions to Pinaisara Falls (ピナイサーラの滝; Pinaisā-ra no taki). The falls are only a few

miles upstream on the Hinai River (ヒナイ川; Hinai-gawa), which empties into Funaura Bay.

Pinaisara Falls have a height of 180 feet (55 meters) and are the tallest in all of Okinawa Prefecture. In Iriomote dialect, *pinai* means "beard" and *sa-ra* means "waterfall." The idea is that the waterfall looks like the long, white beard of an old man from a distance. Since there are no roads to the falls, the only way to reach them is either a rather arduous hike or a kayak trip and then a short hike. Either way, it can be done in about a half a day. It's a very popular excursion and most of the local hotels organize the trips. For an excellent naturalist guide and kayaker, contact Naoya Ojima, who speaks English (090-2497-0463 or www.iriomote-osanpo.com). You can choose whether to climb to the top of the falls or simply enjoy viewing them from below.

A popular activity on Iriomote is a kayak excursion up the Hinai River to the Pinaisara Falls. A small section of the falls can be seen at the top center of this photograph.

Akabanarejima ("Isolated Red Island") comprises one large vegetated rock and one small bare rock.

Picking up again at Funaura, we'll continue northwest another 1.25 miles (2 kilometers) until we reach Uehara. But before reaching there, along the drive, looking north from anywhere on the coast between Funaura and Uehara, there are two more little islands out at sea. Let's have a closer look at them.

HATOBANAREJIMA (鳩離島; Hato-banaré-jima; lit. "Isolated Dove/Pigeon Island"). The nearest place on dry land to this little collection of rocks is a small cape midway between Funaura and Uehara. From there it's slightly less than one mile (1.5 kilometers). From Funaura harbor it's slightly more than 1 mile (1.75 kilometers) almost straight north, and from Uehara's harbor it's 1.25 miles (2 kilometers) due east. Altogether, there are about eight to ten of them, all lined up in a row, measuring 1,400 feet (425 meters) from end to end, roughly east–west. One is much larger than the others, almost 660 feet (200 meters) long and about 250 feet (75 meters) wide. The others are anywhere from 65 to 165 feet (20 to 50 meters) in length or breadth. All are completely covered in vegetation and the largest one has a couple of nice sandy beaches. Essentially, it's one of those places that ships coming and going from either Uehara or Funaura do their best to avoid in order to prevent running aground.

BARASUTŌ (バラス島; Barasu-tō). Coincidentally enough, almost exactly another 1.25 miles (2 kilometers) north of Hatobanare is this next little islet, this one a mere sandbar. Measured from several other points it is 2 miles (3 kilometers) north of Funaura Port and 1.5 miles (2.5 kilometers) northeast of Uehara Port. The islet is about 500 feet (150 meters) long from north to south and ranges from 80 to 130 feet (25 to 40 meters) across

at any given points. It is entirely composed of coarse sand, coral chips and broken shells.

The word *barasu* in Japanese means ballast or the debris from a construction site. The island was formed, and is transformed every year, by typhoons. Until 1990 it was about one-half its present size. Then, after a strong typhoon, a second islet emerged. The two *barasu jima* then remained for eight years. In 1998 the area between them filled up, making it the one larger islet that it is today. Naturally, it is uninhabited, although it's a popular destination for kayak excursions from Iriomote. It is surrounded by coral reef on all sides and is a good place to go snorkeling.

By the standard of Iriomote, Uehara is one of the two big towns, along with Ohara. The village is spread out around the harbor and the surrounding area and includes a couple of nice beaches. In all, there are about 20 *minshuku*, several restaurants and a gas station. Although many of the *minshuku* are perfectly pleasant, one stands out, the Pineapple House (パイン館; Pain-kan; lit. "Pine Hall"). It's a local institution. In the summer months, the owner supplies as much pineapple as you can eat. Tel: 0980-85-6650; web: www.pinekan.com; email: kenbo@pinekan.com.

Many visitors make Uehara their base while on Iriomote because there is a variety of things to do close by. In addition to the kayak trip to Pinaisara Falls south of Uehara Town, 1.25 miles (2 kilometers) northwest, there's one of the nicest beaches on Iriomote, Star Sand Beach (星砂の浜; Hoshizuna-no-hama). It's just east of the very northernmost tip of Iriomote on East Cape (ニシ崎 or 西崎; Nishi-zaki). The beach is yet another one of those rare places in the Ryukyus where the sand is composed of tiny "stars" (see pages 78 and 192).

Hatobanarejima is a collection of eight to ten small rocks strung out along the coast midway between Funaura and Uehara. The largest island has a couple of pleasant beaches.

The Pineapple House stands out among the various minshuku guesthouses in Uehara for two reasons: its pineapple shape and the free, as much as you can eat, pineapple given to guests in summer.

There's something else nice less than 1 mile (1.5 kilometers) down the road, south of Star Sand Beach. Here there's another beautiful beach that many think is the best on the island, Moon Beach (月ヶ浜 or 月が浜; Tsuki-ga-hama). This one gets its name from its perfect crescent shape. It is located on the mouth of the Urauchi River (浦内川; Ura-uchi-gawa) and nestled into a curve immediately below the far northwest end of Iriomote, at Cape Unari (宇奈利崎; Unari-zaki).

Moon Beach has its pluses and minuses. It is a great beach due to its sheltered location. There's no rough surf and it has a long, sloping grade which is calm and peaceful, so it's safe, perfect for young children. But because it's sited at the end of the Urauchi River estuary it's a mixture of fresh and salt water.

Thus, there are no coral reefs here and also it's way too shallow for snorkeling. But there is another plus: the sand is soft and fine, so fine in fact that it's described as "crying" or "screaming" sand. That is, when you walk along the beach or kick your feet, it squeals or squeaks, making a high-pitched noise somewhat like a cry or scream. Try it, it's fun—and kids will love it.

Incidentally, just to keep things a bit confusing—this is Japan, after all—you may well see the name of this beach as Mūn-bīchi (ムーンビーチ), which of course also means Moon Beach. And lastly, if you look at older maps you may see its name as To-udo-umari-no-hama (トゥドゥマリ浜). That was its historic name. Modern times and modern tourism upgraded the name to the more euphonious Moon Beach.

Barasutō is a coral reef-encircled sandbar rather than an islet proper, composed entirely of coarse sand, coral chips and broken shell material. Its shape and size are transformed every year by typhoons.

Moon Beach is considered the best beach on Iriomote, partly for its "crying/screaming" sand.

Nirakanai Sanctuary Resort is located right on the popular crescent-shaped Moon Beach.

Naturally, this gorgeous location has not gone undetected or undiscovered. If you're looking for a very deluxe resort, the best on the island, you'll find it at the Nirakanai Sanctuary Resort (西表 サンクチュアリー リゾート ニラカナイ; Iriomote sanku-chuarī-rizōto nirakanai). It's right on the beach, surrounded by jungle, and has a beautiful outdoor swimming pool. Rates, including meals, start at around $200 per person per night.

We'll leave the Nirakanai Resort and drive 1.5 miles (2.5 kilometers) due south on Route 215 until we come to the only bridge over the Urauchi River. For the most part the road parallels the river's mouth, which here is very wide, shallow and sandy. If coming directly from Uehara, that is, without stopping at Star Sand Beach or the Nirakanai Resort, it's 3.5 miles (5.5 kilometers). On the northern side of the bridge, before crossing it, there is a small parking area, a public bus stop and a small road to the left. This is the entrance for the river cruises and kayak rentals on the

Urauchi River. The dock and ticket office are 500 feet (150 meters) down this little road. The Urauchi Bridge (浦内橋; Urauchi-bashi) is almost 660 feet (200 meters) long, which is just a little longer than the width of the river at this point.

With a length of some 24 miles (38 kilometers), the Urauchi-gawa is not only the longest river on Iriomote, it's the longest river in Okinawa. You'll see and hear countless comparisons—metaphors—to the Urauchi as Japan's "Amazon," but let's get real, 24 miles (38 kilometers)! Come on, the Amazon is the second longest river in the world at 4,225 miles (6,800 kilometers), and for some thousands of kilometers the average width of the Amazon is close to 30 miles (48 kilometers).

Be that as it may, and although there simply is no realistic comparison to Brazil, nevertheless, the Urauchi is a beautiful, tropical jungle river experience, an experience that is for most Japanese tourists truly unique, for Japan is not a country with a great many wild natural places and this is one.

The only bridge over the Urauchi River is 660 feet (200 meters) long.

The dock for Urauchi River cruises and kayak rentals is at the northern side of the bridge.

Cruising up the Urauchi River, the longest in Okinawa, in a wide, comfortable, open-air boat.

The short hiking trail to Mariyudo Falls traverses lush tropical jungle.

A cruise up the Urauchi is without doubt the most popular excursion available on Iriomote. The river's waters are still and the boats are wide and comfortable. They all have sun roofs. The captains give a guided travelogue as the boat motors upstream, stopping here and there to point out the mangrove trees or some bird or fish if sighted. Commentary is in Japanese. The cruises cost 1,800 Yen and depart about every 30 minutes during the busy season. In winter it's less frequent, but there are usually enough people visiting even then that you won't have to wait more than an hour for a departure. For a more physical experience, without any guided commentary, you can rent a kayak and paddle on your own.

The navigable section of the river is a little longer than 4 miles (6 kilometers), so the first part of the tour only takes about 45 minutes. The tour boats and kayaks then tie up at a small upstream dock lashed on to a large rock (軍艦岩; Gunkan-iwa; lit. "Battleship Rock") where the cross-island

trail begins. This first section of the hiking trail is extremely well-trodden. It would be just about impossible to get lost. Depending on your hiking speed, in about 20–30 minutes, a little more than three-quarters of a mile (1 kilometer), you'll come to a viewing platform (マリユドゥ展望台; Mariyudo-tenbōdai) where you'll get your first view of Mariyudo Falls (マリユドゥの滝; Mariyudo-no-taki). Many people will be taking photos here. From the observation deck it will take another 5–10 minutes along the trail to reach the top of the falls.

It's a pretty cascade broken into two halves, tumbling over rock, then emptying into a jungle pond. Mariyudo means "round pool" in local dialect. The falls take their name from the pond. It's quite idyllic and naturally the subject of countless tourists' photos. Although on a hot and steamy summer day you may relish a cool dip, be warned that the fresh waters all over Iriomote are full of leeches. Some people don't care. If you're one of them, bring some

The Mariyudo Falls cascade in two sections over rocks before emptying into a deep pond.

The Kanpire Falls, a 5–10 minute walk from the Mariyudo Falls, is a popular swimming spot.

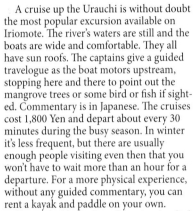

salt or matches to remove them afterwards. They're not poisonous and they really don't do any harm, they're just sort of a nuisance.

From Mariyudo Falls the trail continues and in less than quarter of a mile (half a kilometer), another 5–10 minutes, you'll come to a second waterfall, Kanpire Falls (カンビレーの滝; Kanpirē-no-taki). Kanpire in local dialect translates as "Seat for the God," or more lyrically as "God's Throne." Once again, you'll find lots of tourists by the water, relaxing in the sun, having lunch or taking photographs.

At this point most people will turn around and head back the roughly 1.25 miles (2 kilometers) to the Gunkan-iwa dock. A few hikers, however, will continue on the cross-island hiking trail about 12.5 miles (20 kilometers) to its opposite terminus near the mouth of the Nakama River at Ohara Port. Although it is marked, there are some pretty rough trails, with a lot of ups and downs. For most people the hike will take anywhere

from six to eight hours—and don't forget that you are supposed to register with the police (or at least let someone know) before embarking on the hike.

For those returning to the dock, the boats generally wait until they have a sufficient group of people, so if you miss one you'll catch the next. They then make the return cruise down the Urauchi. The captain will usually have a few more comments and will again point out any sights of interest. Including the cruise up and cruise down and the hike to both the falls, count on at least three to four hours or half a day to make the Urauchi River trip.

After returning to the main dock near the Urauchi Bridge and the mouth of the river, you can visit a little museum they have on the second floor of the ticket building. It has a collection of mounted insects, some so large you might not want to walk in the jungle again. It may be best to check out this museum after your hike to the falls.

The 123456789 Meridian Monument (子午線モニュメント; Shigosen monyumento)

From man's earliest times, cartographers, mathematicians and mariners have been plotting the Earth's distances, reckoning that geographic latitude starts at 0 ° on the Equator and runs horizontally in circles of latitude to the North and South Poles at 90 °N and 90 °S, respectively. It wasn't until the 1884 International Meridian Conference in Washington, DC, however, that most countries agreed that the starting point for longitude—0 ° or the Prime Meridian—would be the Greenwich Royal Observatory near London. From there, geographic coordinates extend vertically around the world until they end at 180 ° East and West. Both latitude and longitude are expressed in degrees, minutes and seconds. Thus, any point on Earth can be expressed in a pair of degrees that uniquely identifies its location. The unique place where the Longitudinal Meridian of 123°45'6,789"E happens to pass through is the western side of Iriomote near the villages of Sonai and Shirahama. The same meridian line continues south through the Philippines, Indonesia and western Australia, and north through China, then Russia. It ends at the two Poles. Each evening, from 7PM to 10PM, each village projects lasers into the sky on the hour to illustrate their special geographic place.

This view of Iriomote's northwest coast shows Uehara and Funaura at upper left, Star Sand Beach at lower left, crescent-shaped Moon Beach at center front, and the Urauchi River and bridge at mid-center.

From the bus stop at the Urauchi Bridge, it is 1.5 miles (2.5 kilometers) south on the Kaichū dōro to the next village, Sonai (祖納). You'll pass the Meridian Monument (子午線 モニュメント; Shigosen monyumento) just before arriving in town. There is a gas station and several *minshuku*. Sonai is an interesting little place in that it's actually two villages in one, separated by three-quarters of a mile (1 kilometer). Both are sited on a small bay. The first Sonai has the gas station, a lovely beach and the *minshuku*, the second Sonai, to the south on Route 215, has the junior high school, the post office and the fishing port. It faces two bays, both with beaches. Each village may have somewhere around 100 residents.

From the fishing port just below Sonai's second village, it's another 1.5 miles (2.5 kilometers), all the while hugging the western shoreline on Route 215 until a large tunnel. The tunnel is 2,300 feet (700 meters) long and empties into the last village reachable by road on Iriomotejima, Shirahama (白浜; "White Beach"). We can go no further, at least by car. If you had clocked the entire route on the Kaichū dōro, starting at the campground at Haemida Beach, all the way around the island to here, on the water at Shirahama Port, you would have measured 34 miles (54 kilometers) on your car's odometer.

That's really not very much, but isn't it strange that such a little distance can take a couple of days of engaging sightseeing? That's the way it is on Iriomote, and that's the way it is on so many of the Ryukyus.

Like a gemstone with many facets, there's so much in a small space that so many overlook.

As for Shirahama, it's a nice enough little place but "little" is the operative word for there are only about 30–40 residences with perhaps 100 persons. There's a fairly good-sized port and dock, a fairly large modern ferry terminal and a school, up to junior high grade. There is another Meridian Monument, for the 123456789 Longitude Line runs through here as well. There is no gas station or any other services of any kind. It would seem that Shirahama is really is the end of the road, literally and figuratively, but in fact there is a bit more.

You will see from the waterfront at Shirahama that there are two rather large islets immediately offshore. Let's first have a look at them.

UCHIBANAREJIMA (内離島; Uchi-banaré-jima). The most immediate islet to Shirahima is Uchibanare. It's about 2,300 feet (70 meters) southwest, in front of the Shirahama dock. Although the islet is uninhabited and mostly covered in jungle, there are several small pastures for the grazing of animals on the northeast side. Compared to some of the really small islands we've seen, Uchibanare is actually pretty large. It's more or less oval-shaped, with the exception of one northern protrusion, and measures 1.75 miles (3 kilometers) long from end to end. Its width varies from 2,130 (650 meters) to just over three-quarters of a mile (1 kilometer) at its widest. Its area has been determined to be

Uninhabited, densely jungled Sotobanare ("Outside Isolated Island") and Uchibanare ("Inside Isolated Island") lie northwest of Shirahama Port.

three-quarters of a square mile (2.10 square kilometers). That's as large as a number of inhabited islands in the Ryukyus. Interestingly, at one time, before World War II, Uchibanare was heavily mined for coal. It had a number of rich seams. These were exhausted and there are none worked today.

Uchibanare's name translates as "Inside Isolated Island." At Uchibanare's northwesternmost tip there is a 1,640-foot (500-meter) strait separating it from its northern neighbor, Sotobaranare. That islet's name translates as "Outside Isolated Island" because it's a little further away. Let's go there.

SOTOBANAREJIMA (外離島; Soto-banaré-jima). This islet lies 1,640 feet (500 meters) north of the top end of Uchibanare or a little less than 1.75 miles (3 kilometers) northwest of Shirahama Port. It is also uninhabited and covered in dense jungle. Sotobanare has a wide crescent shape. It is 1.25 miles (2 kilometers) long at the ends of its crescent and almost three-quarters of a mile (1 kilometer) wide at its midsection. It's surface area is half of a square mile (1.32 square kilometers).

Although our visit to Iriomote is almost over, there is one more place to mention although few people go there. About 2 miles (3.5 kilometers) southwest of Shirahama by water, around and below Uchibanare Island and across Funauki Bay (船浮湾; Funauki-wan; lit. "Floating Boat Bay"), is the truly isolated village of Funauki (船浮; Funauki).

It's the westernmost village of Iriomote and the last survivor of a dying breed of isolated sea villages.

Funauki is located on one of the northern ends of that broken-off southwestern bit of Iriomote that we mentioned at the beginning of this discussion. There are no roads going there, nor any hiking trails. It is only reachable by sea, most usually from Shirahama Port. There's a public ferry service and it

The Funauki passenger ferry from Shirahama Port.

Hateruma, the southernmost island of the Ryukyus.

West Beach (Nishi-no-hama) is Hateruma's largest and most popular beach.

runs three or four times a day depending on the season.

It's as tiny a place as one can imagine, but it is a port town, so it has a dock. There are perhaps 25–30 houses and maybe 50–60 people living there. There is an elementary and junior high school. There are no paved roads and no motor vehicles; after all, there's no place to drive. There is, however, one little grocery store and one *minshuku*. Funauki is truly the destination of choice for those who wish to get away from it all.

There used to be three other villages even further west along the northern coast of this piece of Iriomote, but they all were abandoned over the past 30 years. One in particular, however, Amitori (網取; Ami-tori), a sea village on the next peninsula west of Funauki, was given a new lease on life, albeit in a limited fashion. The government of the Yaeyamas gave the abandoned village to Tokai University to establish their Institute of Oceanic Research and Development. It's a small private operation and not open to the public. Nonetheless, because there are some researchers living there, you'll see Amatori listed on the ferry's route masthead, although they won't take you there. As for the abandoned villages, essentially every year fewer and fewer people are willing to accept the difficult and isolated life that their parents lived only a generation ago. This trend can only continue. Perhaps in the next 10–20 years Funauki will cease to exist.

Our tour of Iriomote is over but our visit to the Yaeyamas is not. There are several more islands to see, however, they are much further away. We'll have to return to Ishigaki and take other ferries to reach them. In one case we'll fly.

10 HATERUMAJIMA 波照間島

We are now sailing to some of the most distant shores in Japan. Haterumajima (波照間島; Hatéruma-jima) is one of the last Yaeyama Islands that we'll discuss, the most southern island of the Ryukyus and the southernmost inhabited island in Japan. As the crow flies, it is 15 miles (24 kilometers) due south of Iriomote Island and 30 miles (48 kilometers) southwest of Ishigaki. The sailing distance from Ishigaki Port, however, is a little longer than the crow flies. It's 35 miles (56 kilometers) and takes almost exactly one hour one way by high-speed passenger ferry. The passenger and vehicle ferry is slower. It takes two hours. The high-speed ferries sail twice daily year round and up to four times a day during the summer months. The passenger and vehicle ferry runs three times a week. Ferries dock at Hateruma Port (波照間港; Hatéruma-kō), located midway along the northwest shore of the island.

Sadly, at the end of 2007, flights to Hateruma were discontinued. The island has a small airport (波照間空港; Hatéruma Kūkō) on its eastern coast. Previously, there were daily flights (several per day during the summer), and although the flying time was only 15 minutes, not enough traffic justified the route. Although for now the airport is closed to commercial service, it is kept in good repair as it may be used for emergency medical evacuations and private aircraft.

Haterumajima is a small island, oblong in shape. Measured along its greatest length, from east to west, it is almost 4 miles (6 kilometers). From north to south, it is 1.75 miles (3 kilometers) at its center, which is its widest. The overall area of Hateruma is 5 square miles (12.77 square kilometers) and its shoreline measures 9 miles (15 kilometers).

The arrival of a ferry at Hateruma Port.

Astronomers have divided the celestial sphere into 88 official constellations, 37 in the northern hemisphere and 51 in the southern. Due to its unique location, 84 out of the 88 constellations can be seen from the Hateruma Astronomical Observatory.

The island is completely flat and almost entirely cultivated, generally with sugar cane.

Although there are a few residences and small farmsteads scattered here and there around the island, most of Hateruma's roughly 550 residents live in the one centrally located village, which is a little more than three-quarters of a mile (1 kilometer) southeast of the harbor. A junior high school, a post office and a gas station are located there. There are car, scooter and bike rental places as well. Because there is good ferry service, it's possible to visit the island on a day trip out of Ishigaki, but if you would like to stay longer there are a half a dozen *minshuku* in town and one on the best beach of the island. There are several restaurants in the village as well. Hateruma is a pleasant and relaxing island on which to stay.

Hateruma's largest and most popular beach is adjacent to the port, to its immediate west, and appropriately named West Beach (西の浜; Nishi-no-hama) It's also spelled ニシ浜 (Nishi-hama). It is 1 mile (1.5 kilometers) northwest from the village. Although perhaps not a great snorkeling site, this beach has really fine clean, white sand, unlike the too often found sand-rock-coral stone mix. Overlooking the beach, maybe 325 feet (100 meters) above it, is one the island's nicest *minshuku*, the aptly named Penshon Sainantan (ペンション最南端; lit. "Pension Southernmost"). It's a little more expensive than those in town, but it's the only one on the beach.

The only other beach on Hateruma is located dead center in the middle of the southern shore. There's no sign, just a little unpaved path leading south from the main circle-island road. Don't worry, the island is so small you really can't miss it. It's called Pemuchi Beach (ペムチ浜; Pemuchi-hama) and although its sand is not quite as fine as that of Nishihama, it's very secluded and you'll probably have it all to yourself. Take note that there are warning signs (in Japanese) about the offshore currents.

About 1.25 miles (2 kilometers) to the east, you'll come to Cape Takana (高那崎; Takana-zaki), which is on the southeast coast of the island. Here you'll find Hateruma's two big "sights," the Astronomical Observatory and the Southernmost Point of Japan Monument.

Looking out over the endless waters of the Pacific Ocean and the East China Sea, for here at this southern place the two bodies no longer have the Ryukyu Islands dividing them, is a small observatory, the Hateruma Astronomical Observatory (星空観測タワー; Hoshizora kansoku tawā), the southernmost in Japan. (Naturally, everything on Haterumajima is the "southernmost in Japan.") It is open every day and there is a small gift shop inside. More interestingly, it is open every evening except Mondays and the planetarium gives a nightly presentation on star gazing. Hateruma is a popular place with tourists because it is one of the rare places in Japan where the Southern Cross constellation may be viewed. It's visible for a few hours each evening from January to June.

About 1,230 feet (375 meters) southwest of the observatory, you'll see the Southernmost Point of Japan Monument (日本最南端の碑;

Japan's Southernmost Point Monument at Cape Takana marking the end of inhabited Japan.

Oceanic Seabirds

Several Ryukyu Islands are home to seabird colonies. One of the most secluded is the marine bird sanctuary on Nakanougan Islet, which holds a rich mix of species. There is no single taxonomic order or class that contains seabirds. They come from a variety of families. But what they have in common is adaptation to life on the open ocean, only returning to shore to breed and raise their young. Oceanic birds are different from most land species in that they feed in saltwater, possess webbed feet, have salt glands that allow them to expel excess salt, have waterproof plumage and have a particular wing structure that either allows them to dive or, in the case of ocean-going pelagic species, glide over great distances. Seabirds also differ dramatically from land birds in that they live much longer but reproduce less frequently. They counter this by investing far more in the care of their young. Ninety-five percent of seabirds form colonies, some of which contain millions of birds and thus constitute some of the largest animal colonies on earth.

Nippon sai nantan no ishibumi, lit. "most southern place in Japan"). As its name proudly states, it marks the most southerly place of the nation of Japan—sort of. To get a little technical about it, the monument marks the southernmost point of inhabited Japan. It is located here, at this place, on this island, at 24°02′ 25′ North latitude; and 123°47′ 16′ East longitude.

However, the real southernmost point of Japan is Okinotorishima (沖ノ鳥島; Okino-tori-shima; lit. "Offshore Remote Bird Island"), which is quite a bit further south at 20°25′ 31′ North latitude; 136°04′ 11′ East longitude. Since each degree of latitude is equal to about 69 miles (111 kilometers), Japan's true southernmost point is really 250 miles (400 kilometers) further south of Hateruma.

Okinotori is an uninhabitable atoll and coral reef consisting of several, mostly submerged, islets. It is approximately 335 miles (535 kilometers) southeast of Oki Daitō, 400 miles (635 kilometers) southwest of Iwo Jima of the Ogasawara Islands, and 1,085 miles (1,750 kilometers) south of Tokyo. From another direction, the atoll is about 530 miles (850 kilometers) northwest above Guam and the Northern Marianas Islands. In English the reef is known as "Parece Vela," its original Spanish name (1565), which means "looks like a sail." The atoll is also known as "Douglas Reef" (1790) after William Douglas, a British sailor who investigated these waters.

Essentially, the Parece Velas are miniscule reef islets held in order to bolster Japan's assertion of fishing rights and seafloor exploration rights to potential oil and gas deposits. Although other nations do not necessarily respect Japan's mineral rights claims, Japanese sovereignty over the reef is not disputed and therefore Okinotori Island is really the southernmost point of Japan.

Disregarding Okinotorishima, Hateruma still has a good claim. After all, it is the southernmost place in Japan where people can live. And it's a pretty place to live. Surrounded by the sea, peaceful and green, it's a nice little island.

11 NAKANOUGANJIMA 仲ノ御神島

Nakanouganjima (仲ノ御神島; Naka-no-ugan-jima). On some charts, an alternative Japanese spelling for this tiny spot in the ocean is 中御神島. It can be pronounced the same way, but it also may be pronounced as Naka-no-kami-shima. Character by character, the Kanji literally translated means "Central Control God Island." It is one of the more remote and least commonly-known islands we'll mention in this book.

On a direct flight path from Ishigaki's airport, it is 40 miles (64 kilometers) to the southwest. You would pass over the southwestern end of Iriomote on your way. The only spot of Japan that is further away is the island of Yonaguni, which is 38 miles (61 kilometers) to the northwest. We'll go there next. Measured from some other

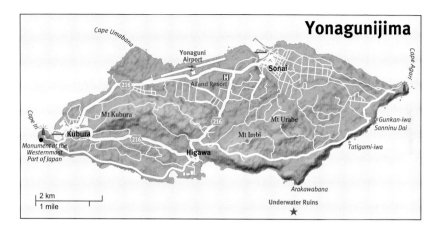

points, Nakanouganjima (仲ノ御神島; Naka-no-ugan-jima) is 9 miles (15 kilometers) from Iriomote's southwestern end and a little more than 15 miles (24 kilometers) northwest of Hateruma's western shoreline. In fact, you can see the island from Hateruma Port and from Nishi-no hama Beach on a clear day.

Nakanougan is a long, thin islet measuring 1 mile (1.5 kilometers) in length from east to west and anywhere from 330 to 660 feet (100 to 200 meters) wide from north to south, depending on where the measurement is taken.

On shipping charts and on particularly detailed Japanese maps, Nakanouganjima is recognized as a seabird breeding ground and sanctuary and is listed as such (海鳥繁殖地; Umi Tori Hanshoku-chi, lit. "seabird breeding site"). There is no commercial ferry service to nor any services of any kind on this islet. It is uninhabited, uninhabitable and protected.

Nakanouganjima is a protected seabird breeding ground and sanctuary.

12 YONAGUNIJIMA 与那国島

This is the end of the line, the final island in the Ryukyu Archipelago and the furthest one can go in Japan and still be in Japan. Yonagunijima (与那国島; Yonaguni-jima) is the southwesternmost island of the nation and Cape Iri (西崎; Iri-zaki) is the island's furthest western point. The island is both Japan's westernmost and southwesternmost place. To reach Japan's opposite extreme end would require traveling some 1,800 miles (2,900 kilometers) by air, all the way to Cape Sōya (宗谷岬; Sōya-misaki), Japan's northernmost place near Wakkanai (稚内市; Wakkanai) on the island of Hokkaidō (北海道; Hokkaidō). Wakkanai, which is the nearest city to Cape Sōya, and Ishigaki, the nearest city to Yonaguni's Cape Iri, are paired as "sister" cities in recognition of their status as Japan's most far-apart towns.

There's a stone marker at the end of Yonaguni's Cape Iri to indicate this final point. It's called Nippon sai seitan no ishibumi

Irizaki—Yonaguni's Westernmost Cape.

The pyramid marker at top marks Japan's northernmost point at Wakkanai on Hokkaidō's Cape Sōya. The stone marker above, at Yonagunijima's Cape Iri, marks Japan's southwesternmost point.

(日本最西端の碑, lit. "most western place in Japan") and it's arguably Yonaguni's most famous sight. Thousands of Japanese tourists come here every year to have their photos taken with this marker. Conversely, there's a northern monument at Wakkanai on Hokkaido's Cape Sōya (Sōya-misaki) to mark Japan's northernmost point.

By air, as the crow flies, Yonaguni lies some 320 miles (515 kilometers) from Naha, 675 (1,090 kilometers) from Kagoshima on the Japanese mainland, 1,260 (2,030 kilometers) from Tokyo and 1,660 (2,667 kilometers) from Sapporo. At its very closest points, Yonaguni Island is only about 70 miles (112 kilometers) from the northeast coast of Taiwan and 65 miles (104 kilometers) due east of Ishigaki. It is a rugged, rocky island, shaped as a long oval, lying on its side. It measures 7 miles (11 kilometers) across from its eastern tip at Cape Agari (東崎; Agarizaki), to its western tip at Cape Iri. From north to south, it measures about 2.5 miles (4 kilometers) for most of its length, but narrowing at both ends. It has a surface area of just under 11 square miles (29 square

kilometers) and a circumference of 17 miles (27 kilometers). Most of the island is surrounded by high cliffs and much of its shoreline is rock, although there are a few beaches sprinkled here and there. Only about one-third of the island is level enough for sugar cane growing or other agriculture. The rest is too mountainous or rocky.

The majority of Yonaguni's population of about 1,615 people reside in three main villages. Yonaguni Town, which is called Sonai (祖内), in the center north, is by far the largest. The town's grown around the fishing port and the airport is immediately to the west. There are about a dozen *minshuku* in Sonai and one small luxury hotel just out of town. It's called the Ailand Resort (アイランドリゾート; Aiundo-rezōto) and it has a fine restaurant, pool and spa facilities.

Kubura (久部良) is the second largest village. It's in the far northwest corner of the island and its port (久部良港; Kubura-kō) is the one used by the twice-weekly ferry service. Although it's a very small village, there are nonetheless about a half dozen *minshuku*.

The Ailand Resort and Spa, Yonaguni's most deluxe hotel, is about 1 mile (1.6 kilometers) east of the airport and west of Sonai Town.

Cape Agari, Yonaguni's easternmost point.

The Yonaguni–Ishigaki passenger and vehicle ferry.

The Hai Donan Minshuku, one of the nicest minshuku on Yonaguni, is right on Kubura Port, 820 feet (250 meters) from the ferry dock.

The smallest village is Higawa (比川), located in the center of the south coast of the island. Although it's really a tiny place, it has two *minshuku*. Perhaps the main attraction for staying there is that Higawa has the longest and most sheltered beach on the island.

Yonaguni is a popular destination for Japanese tourists, especially divers, that's why the island can support about 20 *minshuku*.

Although most people will take their meals at their *minshuku*, and most quoted rates include breakfast and dinner, there are also a couple of restaurants in Sonai and Kubura. There are car, bike and scooter rentals available in Sonai, Kubura and the airport. Most of the *minshuku* will make the arrangements for you.

Ferry service to the island from Ishigaki runs twice a week, on Tuesdays and Fridays, with return trips on Wednesdays and Saturdays. The sailing distance by the ferry from Ishigaki Port to Kubura Port is 83 miles (135 kilometers). It takes from four to five hours one way depending on sea conditions. All ships in both directions depart at 10AM. They are subject to cancellation in case of high seas, which are relatively frequent. The airport (与那国空港; Yonaguni Kūkō), is on the north central coast, near Sonai. The commuter flights from Ishigaki only take about 30 minutes. Depending on the time of year, there can be one or two flights a day. The airport's landing strip was expanded ten years ago to handle larger aircraft and there are several flights a week direct to and from Naha. There has been sporadic air service originating in Taiwan and there seems to always be talk about this becoming a regular route, but to date it has not happened.

Yonaguni is a scenic and hilly island and has several quite impressive cliffs offering sweeping views. On a very clear day Taiwan can be seen from the cliffs at Kuburabari (久部良バリ; Kubura-bari). These cliffs, near the northeastern side of Kubura Port, are also the place to watch the last sunset

Ryukyu Air Commuter (RAC) flights fly into Yonaguni Airport on the north central coast, near Sonai.

Gunkan-iwa ("Battleship Rock") is one of several spectacular rock formations south of Cape Agari.

over Japan. As is the case with many islands of the Ryukyus, the cliff and rock formations host many caves and Yonaguni is no exception, with caves both above and below the waters. Most of them require a guide and there are many dive shops that specialize in this, so that's not a problem.

Nearby, only three-quarters of a mile (1 kilometer) away from the port, is a fairly large conservation zone around Kubura Peak (久部良岳; Kubura-daké), which has an elevation of 617 feet (188 meters). It's a popular hiking area. The island's highest point is Mt Urabe (宇良部岳; Urabé-daké) at 758 feet (231 meters). It's located in the central eastern section of Yonaguni.

Although Yonaguni is not usually known as a prime beach destination, nevertheless, it has several good white sand beaches. The two best, at least for families with children, are in Higawa. Right in town is the largest and most popular, the long, crescent-shaped

Tatigami-iwa ("Standing God Rock"), like Gunkan-wa, lies off Yonaguni's rugged eastern coast.

Higawa-hama (比川浜). A few hundred meters to the west is another, also crescent-shaped beach, Kataburu-hama (カタブル浜). Both of these beaches have long, gentle slopes with easy grades. Higawa-hama may be preferred because its long tsunami seawall and reef protect the beach from breaking waves. Neither is good for snorkeling.

Both of Yonaguni's ports have small, protected beaches. At Sonai it's Nanta-hama (ナンタ浜) and at Kubura it's Naama-hama (ナーマ浜). For a very pleasant little beach

Yonaguni's Atlantis, the Monument

In the 1980s divers in the waters off Yonaguni's southeast shore discovered an enormous and unusual phenomenon now called the Yonaguni "Monument" or the "Underwater Ruins." It's a gigantic rock mass of sandstone formed in a complex series of terraces and steps, with flat parallel faces, sharp edges and mostly right angles. It's rectangular and bounded by near vertical walls. It appears so regular that some scholars have posited that it's man-made, part of the lost continent of Mu, or perhaps built by aliens, although these are minority views. Overall, the formation measures around 130 by 490 feet (40 by 150 meters) and about 90 feet (27

meters) tall. The top is 16 feet (5 meters) below sea level. It's a site for experienced scuba divers. The area is rife with hammerhead sharks and is also subject to exceptionally strong currents.

with a partially rocky shoreline for snorkeling, try Dannu-hama (ダンヌ浜), which is on the northwest coast of Yonaguni, between Kubura and the airport. Finally, although some older brochures list Ubudumai-hama (ウブドゥマイ浜) on the island's northeastern coast near Cape Agari, swimming there has been banned, the result of several drownings due to rip tides and dangerous currents.

The southeast shoreline of Yonaguni, just below Cape Agari, holds several spectacular rock formations. The first is a little less than 1.25 miles (2 kilometers) southwest of Agarizaki. It's called Gunkan-iwa (軍艦岩; lit. "Battleship Rock"), named for its supposed resemblance to a great ship. At this same location are the Sanninudai (サンニヌ台) cliffs and observatory. It's a remarkable vista.

Another kilometer further to the southwest you'll see Tatigami-iwa, also pronounced Tachigami-iwa (立神岩 or タティガミイワ), which translates as "Standing God Rock." Tatigami Rock is one of the most photogenic sea buttes you might find anywhere on Earth.

Yonagunijima's most famous sight, however, is not visible to those above water. For

Yonaguni horses, the island's indigenous small, free-roaming breed.

this one, you have to dive. It's known as the "Monument" or the "Underwater Ruins" (海底遺跡; Kaitei-iseki) and it appears to be a man-made undersea fortress or ruin. It's very popular among divers and one of the main reasons why many tourists come to the island. Although it's only about 330 feet (100 meters) off the southern coast at Cape Arakawabana (新川崎; Arakawabana-zaki), it's fairly deep, so it's really only accessible to scuba divers, not snorkelers. Even then, rough seas can cause cancellations for many

The Pretty but Deadly Coneshell

Conus is a genus of over 600 species of small to large predatory sea snails found mostly in tropical seas around the world. Every member of the group is venomous in varying degrees. Cone snails are carnivorous, and surprisingly aggressive. They have a deadly effective hunting technique that immobilizes their prey using a modified, barbed harpoon (a form of radular tooth) mounted on a long proboscis. The harpoon is a hollow dart loaded from a poison gland of exceptionally powerful neurotoxins. Small species hunt marine worms and mollusks. Larger cones will catch and kill small fish and other cones. They can fire their harpoons in any direction, so handling them, even with gloves on, is dangerous. Their proboscis is long and may reach beyond the gloves and their darts can often penetrate them. The sting of the smallest cone snails is likened to that of a bee or hornet. The sting of a large cone may be fatal. It can cause intense pain, swelling, numbness, tingling, vomiting, muscle paralysis, blurred vision, respiratory failure, even death. Unlike poisonous snake bites, there is no anti-venom for cone shell bites. The "Geographic" cone (*Conus geographicus*) at left, and the "Textile" cone (*Conus textile*) at right, are two of the most dangerous of all cone snails.

Yonaguni Atlas Moth

Moths are closely related to butterflies but are far more prevalent. They are both in the same taxonomic order. Scientists estimate that there may be as many as 200,000 species, ten times the number of butterfly species. Most are nocturnal. Yonaguni's moth, the Atlas (*Attacus atlas*), is one of some 1,500 species of large moths found in the tropics and subtropics of Southeast Asia. The Atlas moth is the largest in the world, with total wing surface areas upwards of 62 square inches (400 square centimeters). Their wing span is also among the largest, some 10–12 inches (25–30 centimeters). Females are considerably larger and heavier than males. Atlas moths do not feed. During their short one to two week adult life, they survive entirely on larval fat reserves built up while they were caterpillars.

dive excursions. Yonaguni's waters are no place for beginners. The island is notorious for its dangerous strong currents. Responsible dive shops only take qualified, certified divers out when conditions are safe. It's also possible to visit the Monument in a glass-bottomed boat, but since the formation's top is about 15 feet (5 meters) deep, you won't see all that much, even in these clear waters.

Even before the discovery of the monument ruins, Yonaguni was a famous dive spot for its collection of hammerhead sharks. It's a seasonal territory for them and every winter, from December to February, they congregate in large numbers. Sighting them and swimming among them, if that appeals to you, can virtually be guaranteed. It is also possible, though not common, to see giant whale sharks. They are also known to frequent these waters.

A maritime warning. If those rip currents don't drown you and the hammerheads don't eat you, there's one more sea creature that may have a shot. It's a little one, the "Geographic" Coneshell, a particularly lethal type of tropical conesnail. Fairly common in Yonaguni's waters, it and its less common friend, the "Textile" Coneshell, are two very attractive cones, temptingly easy to pick up and collect. The geographic cone snail, known locally as Anbonia (アンボイナ), is quite prevalent and very poisonous, even deadly on occasion. They average about 2.5–3 inches (10 centimeters) in length. Though they have no eyes, they have a complex form of chemical "sight" which allows them to aim perfectly. Upon picking one up, it can direct—and will not hesitate to stab— its long, flexible harpoon. The sting can

potentially be fatal. At best, it's terribly painful.

Moving back onto terra firma, Yonaguni has two more unique living creatures. Fortunately, these are far less lethal, they're even benign. First there is the Yonaguni horse (与那国馬 or ヨナグニウマ; Yonaguni-uma), a distinctive, small, free-roaming breed. They've bred in isolation on Yonaguni for generations and are now indigenous to the island. They only stand about 11 hands, that is, about 3.75 feet (1.15 meters) high at the withers. They are almost all wild and graze at will, having free reign of the island. There are two main herds which total about 100 animals. Because they're protected and people are gentle towards them, they're quite tame and can usually be approached and fed or petted. They like what all horses like—sugar cubes, apples and carrots will do.

A second most unusual creature on the island is the Yonaguni Atlas moth (ヨナグニサン; Yonaguni-san, also known as Ayamihabiru). It is the largest species of moth in the world. Although they also can be found in Taiwan, China, India, Malaysia and other parts of Southeast Asia, they were first collected and identified on Yonaguni Island. They are a protected species.

The Atlas Moth Museum (アヤミハビル館; Ayamihabiru-kan) is about 1.25 miles (2 kilometers) southeast of Sonai and breeds live caterpillars. In the proper season, they return the cocoons to the forests to hatch and start the cycle all over again.

That wraps up our coverage of Yonaguni and all the other Yaeyama Islands. From here, we'll visit two far more isolated groups: the Senkaku and Daitō Island chains.

Chapter 13

THE DAITŌ ISLANDS 大東諸島
Precipitous cliffs, sugary sights

1 **Kita Daitōjima** 北大東島
2 **Minami Daitōjima** 南大東島
3 **Oki Daitōjima** 沖大東島

The Daitō Islands (大東諸島; Daitō-shotō), a part of Okinawa Prefecture, lie in the Pacific Ocean almost 250 miles (400 kilometers) due east of Naha, Okinawa, on the other side of the great Ryukyu Trench. From the late 1500s, and for the next 200 years, one or more of the islands was occasionally spotted by a passing ship, charted (sometimes erro-

neously), then forgotten and lost again. On almost each of their sightings, their "discoverer" rechristened them. Hence, they have carried many names, among others "Islas sin Probecho," "Amsterdam Island," "Breskens-Eylant," "Malabriga," "Dolores," the "Grampus Isles," "Kendrick Island," the "Bishop Rocks" and "Île de la Canonnière."

The accepted Western names for the Daitōs for close to 100 years arose in the early 1800s. In 1815, what is now called Oki Daitōjima was resighted by a Spanish galleon

The Daitō Islands are separated from Okinawa and the Ryukyu Archipelago by the Ryukyu Trench (Ryūkyū kaikō), a 1,398-mile (2,250-kilometer)-long great oceanic rift that parallels the southeastern edge of the Ryukyus along their entire length from southern Kyushyu Island to northeastern Taiwan. The trench has a maximum depth of 17,100 feet (5,212 meters).

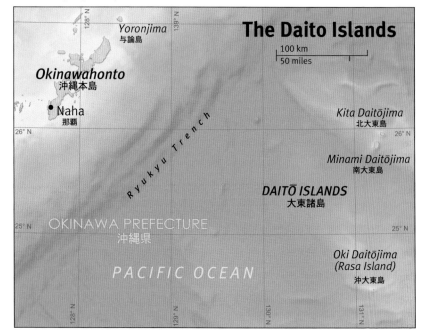

The weekly ferry from Naha to Kita and Minami Daito.

out of Manila, the frigate *San Fernando de Magallanes*. The island was called "Isla Rasa," that is, "Flat island." Five years later, in 1820, Minami Daitōjima and Kita Daitōjima were resighted by a Russian Naval officer sailing on a ship of the Russian-American Company, the *Borodino*. He called them "Ostrova Borodino" (Russian: Острова Бородино; English: Borodino Islands) after his ship, named for the Russian battle against Napoleon in the War of 1812. Thus, these three tiny islands became known in the West and on shipping charts as the Borodino Islands and Rasa Island. They are still sometimes called by these names.

The islands remained uninhabited until the Meiji period (1868–1912) when people from other parts of Japan settled on them, starting around 1900. They were renamed by the Japanese at this time. Collectively, the group was called the Daitō Islands (大東), which means "Great East." Individually, they were named Kita (北), Minami (南) and Oki (沖), which mean "North," "South" and "Offshore," respectively.

Oki Daitō lies about 95 miles (152 kilometers) south of North and South Daitō Islands and is uninhabited. It is not served by a ferry or air service.

The two larger islands, Kita Daitō and Minami Daitō, are only 5 miles (8 kilometers) apart at their closest points and are serviced by a scheduled ferry once a week from Naha's Tomari Port (泊港; Tomari-kō). The trip takes 12–16 hours each way depending on the weather. The ferry *Daitō* (フェリー だいとう; Ferrie Daitō) stops at one island, then the other, then returns to Naha. If you are moving cargo or transporting a vehicle, you must take the ferry. However, most tourists won't need their car for a couple of days and, besides, rental cars are available on either island although they are expensive. The islands are small enough that most people can get by walking around. Alternatively, motor scooters and bicycles are available on both the islands for rent. Both Kita and Minami are relatively flat, so biking and hiking are not difficult. Island residents naturally have cars and scooters, and there is one gas station on each island for fuel. Other than a car, scooter or bike rental, there are, in fact, very few services on either island. There are no beaches, few restaurants or bars and no stores for shopping.

The ferry service is unique in one particular way. It is often cancelled. It's a long passage to the Daitōs and when the shipping line or captain has a three- or four-day forecast that includes any poor weather or rough seas, they cancel. Although, ultimately, this is due to bad weather, it's more complicated than that. The problem is greatly exacerbated by the lack of a safe harbor on either island. Both Kita and Minami are completely encircled by high walls of jagged rock coral and neither has an adequate port. Rather, on both islands there are several unsheltered concrete piers that simply front the open ocean. Ships can only anchor and offload by means of a cargo crane. The sea's waters rise and fall too greatly for the use of a gangplank. Even passengers must ride in a crane box to board and disembark the ship.

Depending on wave conditions, the prevailing winds and currents, any given landing may be on one or another of each of the island's several piers. Or a landing may be cancelled altogether, and thus a round-trip voyage will have been made for nothing. Because there is no shelter on either island—and there is no stopping place along the

Due to the lack of a good harbor, passengers and cargo arriving at Kita and Minami Daito Islands must be unloaded and loaded by crane.

Ryukyu Air Commuter (RAC) turboprops fly three to four times a week to Kita and Minami Daito from Naha.

way—when the ferry departs Naha, the captain must be reasonably certain that the weather is presently good, and will remain good, for the duration of the round trip journey to the Daitō Islands.

Alternatively, and perhaps because of this, there is fairly decent air service to both islands out of Naha Airport (那覇空港; Naha-kūkō). Although not daily to either, both islands are served about three or four times a week by twin-prop RAC commuter turboplanes. They hold about 45 persons and only take 60 minutes one way. Flights return to Naha the same day. Additionally, several of the flights each week fly from one island to the other before returning to Naha. This is particularly important because without this connection one would have to wait a week for the ferry to return or fly back to Naha in order to reach the other island. The inter-island flight takes six minutes and is known as the "shortest flight in Japan."

Although with less than 6 miles (10 kilometers) separating the two islands one might think that there would be some local ferry service or perhaps even an enterprising fisherman, there is not. The Daitōs are not fishing islands, again due to poor anchorage, and so there are very few boats of any kind. For the few fishing boats that are based on the islands, there is a small harbor on each island carved out of rock, but they are completely inadequate for a ship the size of the Naha–Daitō ferry.

In the Daitōs, and unlike almost every other Ryukyu Island, there is not the usual collection of available *minshuku* inns. Surprisingly, there are very few. However, each island has one hotel and both are quite nice. As for dining, both islands' hotels include meals in their daily rates. Your hotel

will pick you up and return you at the ferry or airport on arrival and departure. On Minami there is a small village with a couple of nightclubs/bars and *minshuku*. On Kita there is a tiny village that does not appear to have any drinking establishments, although there is one *minshuku*. Don't worry, both of the islands' hotels have more than adequate supplies of *saké*, *awamori* and beer.

As mentioned, both Kita and Minami Daitō have rocky, inaccessible coastlines, and therefore neither island has any beaches. People do swim, however. In the warmer summer months there are naturally formed swimming holes carved out of the coral rocks on several places along the shore. Although you can't swim laps, and there is no diving or snorkeling, you can get your feet wet and cool off.

Both the Daitōs are first and foremost sugar cane growing islands and almost all the islands' inhabitants are sugar cane farmers. There is very little tourism, although there are a few things to see on each island. Minami is about twice the size of Kita and, accordingly, there is somewhat more available on that island. Although not too many tourists visit the Daitōs, those who take the trouble and come out always find that the people are friendly and that the islands are an interesting, if seldom visited, corner of Japan.

1 KITA DAITŌJIMA 北大東島

Kita Daitōjima (北大東島; Kita Daitō-jima), or "North" Daitō Island, is shaped somewhat like the lower portion of an oval that's been cut in half, that is, straight across at the top and 180 degrees round the bottom. It's a coral island, the smaller of the two inhabited Daitōs, about 3 miles (5 kilometers) from east to west at its northern end and around

Aerial view of Kita Daitōjima from the south.

Kita Daitōjima Airport.

1.75 miles (3 kilometers) long from north to south. Its total area is approximately 4.6 square miles (12 square kilometers) and its circumference is a little over 11 miles (18 kilometers). The island is mostly flat. Its highest point is on the northwest side, only 243 feet (74 meters) and capped with an automated lighthouse. Most of Kita is covered in sugar cane fields. There is a very

The Hamayū-so Ufu Agari Shima on Kita Daitō offers both Western- and Japanese-style rooms.

The rugged coast of the Kita Daitō ferry landing dock is visible at right rear.

small village, which includes the island's only primary and middle school, in the central plain. The sugar cane mill is there as well. The airport's runway parallels almost the full length of the island's eastern side.

Kita Daitō has a population of a little more than 600. Food and most other cargo are brought in by ship. Islanders order their supplies, nowadays primarily online, and these are delivered by the ferry service. Some goods, including daily mail, arrive by the RAC commuter flights. Because of the extra transportation, everything is a little more expensive than in Naha. Unless you have family or friends on Kita, most visitors will stay in the island's one hotel, the Hamayū-so (ハマユウ荘; Hamayū-so Ufu Agari Shima; tel. 09802-3-4880). It's a fairly large, modern, concrete structure with about 25 rooms. All have private baths, air-conditioning and high-speed internet cable access. About half the accommodations are set up Western style, the other half feature tatami mats and traditional Japanese futon mattresses. The hotel has a large dining room and serves good food at set hours every day. Breakfast and dinner are included in the room rates and, very simply, there is no other place to go. The hotel staff can also rent you a bike, scooter or car. The rental prices for cars and scooters are high.

There's not all that much to see on Kita but the island is ringed by service roads and you can hike or drive from one end to the other and all around. The seashore is nearly always dramatic, though almost always inaccessible. If you should be traveling with children, near the island's northwest corner, a little more than half a mile (1 kilometer) from the hotel, there is a small children's park and playground. Nearby this park there are the ruins

Aerial view of Minami Daitōjima.

Aerial view of Minami Daitōjima Airport.

of a phosphorus ore processing plant (燐鉱石貯蔵庫跡; Rinkō seki chozō koato) and a great mechanical winch for hauling ships out of the sea. Phosphate used to be mined on Kita Daitō before the World War II. The winch cables were used to pull ships up a great steep ramp carved into the coral rock, another sign of the efforts made because of the lack of a harbor. The winch mechanism was abandoned years ago and is now just rusting away. Evidently, it's more practical to use cranes to move cargo.

② MINAMI DAITŌJIMA 南大東島

Minami Daitōjima (南大東島; Minami Daitō-jima), or "South" Daitō Island, only 5 miles (8 kilometers) south of Kita Daitō, is the largest of the three Daitōs both in terms of area and population. It's a fairly well-rounded oval, mostly level, about 3 miles (5 kilometers) across from east to west and about 4 miles (6 kilometers) north to south.

Minami occupies a total land area of 12 square miles (30.5 square kilometers) and has a shoreline of 13 miles (21 kilometers). Its highest point is 246 feet (75 meters) above sea level. It presently has about 1,500 residents. In 1975, it had approximately 2,000, in 1965 it had 3,000.

Like Kita Daitō, Minami Daitō has no harbor large enough to accommodate the Naha ferry. Rather, as at Kita, there are several locations around the island's shore where there are massive concrete piers running parallel to and fronting the open sea. Depending on wave, wind and current conditions, the ferry moors alongside one or another and loads and offloads its passengers and freight by crane. On the northwest corner of the island, there is a fishing port blasted out of the rock, but it is not large

Minami Daitōjima Airport and its runway are located along the eastern side of the island.

The entrance to Daitō jinja Shinto shrine.

Minami Daitōjima's only hotel, the Yoshizato.

enough to handle boats above 50–60 feet (15– 20 meters).

Due to the vagaries of the sea, it should be no surprise that most visitors today come to the island by plane. There are several round trip flights per week out of Naha on RAC commuter airlines. The airport and its runway are located along the eastern side of the island and, of course it's only a couple of miles/kilometers from the airport to anywhere on Minami. The island has one village of several hundred people located in the southwest central plain. The post office, gas station, lower and middle schools, town hall, sugar cane factory (製糖工場; Seitō kōjō), one hotel, three *minshuku* and several bars/ nightclubs and restaurants are located there. The town's big "sight" other than the sugar mill is the sugar cane train, preserved and on display under a shed near the city hall.

Just outside town there is a fairly grand Shinto shrine (大東神社; Daitō jinja) and not far from there a series of ponds which make for an excellent canoe excursion. A little further afield, but not much, is an outstanding cave, one of the best in the Ryukyu

Islands. On the top north side of Minami there's an interesting coral wall which forms a long narrow cleft you can enter. In the south there's an observation deck which affords a view over most of the island. There's also a rudimentary golf course on the island and visitors are welcome.

There are three small *minshuku* in town, but many visitors stay in Minami Daitō's sole hotel, the Yoshizato (ホテルよしざと; Hoteru Yoshizato; tel. 09802-2-2511). It's a family-run place and the husband-wife owner-operators couldn't be nicer or more accommodating. They both speak good English—maybe the only people on Minami Daitō who do! The Yoshizato has over 30 rooms and they're all clean, modern and spacious. All rooms have a private bath, air conditioning and cable TV. Internet, however, is only available in the lobby. Meals are included in the room rates, and the food is excellent. You'll look forward to dining here. If, by chance, you are looking for a change of venue for a meal, there are several small restaurants in town, all within one or two blocks from the hotel. Finally, the hotel's owners can arrange a car, scooter or bike rental for you if you ask. Naturally, they'll pick you up and return you to the ferry dock or airport on arrival and departure.

There are several things to see and do on Minami. Like its smaller sister island to the north, Minami Daitō is almost completely devoted to sugar cane farming. For its own

Minami Daitō Sugar Train

For the greater part of a century, from 1917 until 1984, the sugar train ran a grand circuit, with a half a dozen spur lines, around the island. The railroad's narrow gauge tracks are still visible in a few places. Its mission was to transport the vast quantities of cut sugar cane to the processing factory.

Ō Pond is part of a network of interconnected freshwater ponds just north of Minami Daitō.

little claim to uniqueness, the island bears the distinction of once having held the only functioning railroad in the Ryukyus. It was a narrow gauge train line used for hauling cut sugar cane from the fields to the sugar mill. It's just a block from the town hall and there are two trains on display. You still can find traces of the narrow gauge tracks on a few places on the island (レール跡; Rēru ato). It was abandoned in the mid-1980s when large truck transport proved more flexible and economical.

One of the more popular attractions on Minami Daitō is the set of ponds located just to the north of town. The central section of the island was formerly swampy. By dredging and enlarging a number of small canals and streams, these former marsh areas have been transformed to a series of interconnected ponds. None are deep, but they are no longer mere swamps. They all have names, but the largest and the one furthest north, is Ō Pond (大池; Ō-iké; lit. "Big Pond"). The pond network provides freshwater shelter for migrating birds and a natural habitat for frogs and fish. It's possible to rent a canoe and paddle through these ponds from end to end. Check with your hotel or *minshuku*.

Perhaps Minami Daitō's best-known attraction is Hoshino Cave (星野洞 or 星の洞; Hoshino-dō). It's near the northwest end of the island and has visiting hours in the morning and afternoon. It's privately owned, so there's an admission charge (800 Yen), but it's worth it. It's one of the most spectacular caves in the Ryukyus. It's large and fairly deep. It's been completely upgraded with steel staircases and adequate lighting so you can find your way around. The cave's collection of stalactites and stalagmites is quite

spectacular. Evidently, since the time it was discovered, it's never been looted by souvenir collectors. It's been preserved as it was found.

For real spelunkers there is a second cave on Minami Daitō, Chiteiko Cave (地底湖洞; Chitei mizūmi hora). It's located in the southeast of the island, just below the airport. It's open by appointment only and is undeveloped. You'll need rubber boots, a hard hat and lanterns, but these will be supplied by the cave operator. Scuba diving is also possible on Minami. There is a dive shop in town, Borodino Dive. Check with your hotel for caving or diving expeditions. Everyone knows everyone on Minami. The dive shop can also arrange fishing trips.

For a swim, not a dive, there's a group of saltwater pools along the island's southwest shore. Called Shioyakaigan (塩屋海岸; Shioya-kaigan), it's a natural shelf extending from the mainland. Depending on the surf, the Shioya Pools (塩屋プール; Shioya pūru) can be a peaceful, relaxing dip or a torrential, dangerous and foolhardy place to bathe. There are similar pools, though not as dramatic, at Kaigunbō (海軍棒プール; Kaigunbō pūru) on Minami's southeastern coast.

In the south central part of the island, midway between these two oceanic swimming pools, is the Hinomaruyama Tenbodai (日の丸山展望台; Hino maru yama Tenbo dai), a small observatory. From this little point, one of the highest spots on Minami Daitō, you can see about 70 percent of the whole island. A bit further north you'll find the Minami golf course in the central part of the island. Rental equipment is available.

At the center top north of the island you'll come to the last attraction we'll mention, the Baribariiwa (バリバリ岩; Bari bari iwa). It's

Hoshino Cave's stalactites and stalagmites are among the most spectacular in the Ryukyus.

Shioyakaigan, a natural shelf extending from the mainland, holds pools for bathing in good weather.

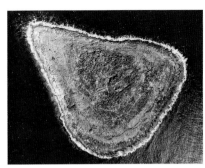

Oki Daitōjima is used as a shooting and bombing range by the US military and is thus off-limits.

a large coral stone formation that has some-how, geologically, split in half. Whether from an earthquake or a shift in the earth on the rising of the seas—the lifting of this island above sea level—it's impossible to say, but what stands today is a several hundred meter-long narrow canyon. Both sides are sheer coral rock. It terminates with an above ground cave that leads down to the Pacific Ocean. The pathway down through the Baribariiwa ("Crunchy Rock") is not for the claustrophobic.

Baribariiwa, a long narrow canyon formed of two large coral stone formations split in half.

3 OKI DAITŌJIMA 沖大東島

The small Oki Daitōjima (沖大東島; Oki Daitō-jima) was historically known as Rasa Island (ラサ島; Rasa-shima; lit. "Flat Island"). Now called Oki, which means "offshore," Daitōjima is the smallest of the three Daitōs. It's no longer or wider than a little more than a kilometer in any given direction and its total area is only 0.444 square miles (1.15 square kilometers). Its shape is almost the same as Kita Daitōjima, the bottom portion of an oval cut in half. The island is uninhabited and there is no commercial service to it.

Japan has exercised sovereignty over Oki Daitō since the end of the 19th century. The island was commercially mined for phosphate ore deposits, and thereby popu-lated, during the first half of the 20th century, up until World War II. Under American control in the postwar years, it's been used as a shooting and bombing range by the US military. For this reason, the island has no trees and travel to it is prohibited. There is much possible unexploded ordnance on the island.

That completes our look at the Daitō Islands, and our look at the whole of the Ryukyu Island Archipelago. As we've seen in our coverage of these several hundred islands, there are many beautiful places in this part of southern Japan. To see these islands all it takes is time and, since this is Japan, some money. It also takes the desire to see this interesting part of the world and a way of life that is rapidly disappearing. I hope that you have enjoyed this more than 685-mile (1,100-kilometer) tour and I hope to see you soon on one of these wonderful places surrounded by the sea.

Index

The Tuttle Story: "Books to Span the East and West"

Many people are surprised to learn that the world's largest publisher of books on Asia had its humble beginnings in the tiny American state of Vermont. The company's founder, Charles Tuttle, came from a New England family steeped in publishing.

Tuttle's father was a noted antiquarian dealer in Rutland, Vermont. Young Charles honed his knowledge of the trade working in the family bookstore, and later in the rare books section of Columbia University Library. His passion for beautiful books—old and new—never wavered throughout his long career as a bookseller and publisher.

After graduating from Harvard, Tuttle enlisted in the military and in 1945 was sent to Tokyo to work on General Douglas MacArthur's staff. He was tasked with helping to revive the Japanese publishing industry, which had been utterly devastated by the war. When his tour of duty was completed, he left the military, married a talented and beautiful singer, Reiko Chiba, and in 1948 began several successful business ventures.

To his astonishment, Tuttle discovered that postwar Tokyo was actually a book-lover's paradise. He befriended dealers in the Kanda district and began supplying rare Japanese editions to American libraries. He also imported American books to sell to the thousands of GIs stationed in Japan. By 1949, Tuttle's business was thriving, and he opened Tokyo's very first English-language bookstore in the Takashimaya Department Store in Ginza, to great success. Two years later, he began publishing books to fulfill the growing interest of foreigners in all things Asian.

Though a westerner, Tuttle was hugely instrumental in bringing a knowledge of Japan and Asia to a world hungry for information about the East. By the time of his death in 1993, he had published over 6,000 books on Asian culture, history and art—a legacy honored by Emperor Hirohito in 1983 with the "Order of the Sacred Treasure," the highest honor Japan bestows upon a non-Japanese.

The Tuttle company today maintains an active backlist of some 1,500 titles, many of which have been continuously in print since the 1950s and 1960s—a great testament to Charles Tuttle's skill as a publisher. More than 60 years after its founding, Tuttle Publishing is more active today than at any time in its history, still inspired by Charles Tuttle's core mission—to publish fine books to span the East and West and provide a greater understanding of each.